TIGER GIRL
AND THE
CANDY KID

TIGER GIRL

AND THE

CANDY KID

America's Original

Gangster Couple

GLENN STOUT

HOUGHTON MIFFLIN HARCOURT

BOSTON • NEW YORK • 2021

Library of Congress Cataloging-in-Publication Data
Names: Stout, Glenn, 1958– author.
Title: Tiger Girl and the Candy Kid : America's original gangster couple / Glenn Stout.
Description: Boston : Houghton Mifflin Harcourt, 2021. |
Includes bibliographical references and index.
Identifiers: LCCN 2020033857 (print) | LCCN 2020033858 (ebook) |
ISBN 9780358067771 (hardcover) | ISBN 9780358067252 (ebook)
Subjects: LCSH: Whittemore, Richard, 1901–1926. | Whittemore, Margaret, 1903–1993. |
Criminal couples — United States — Biography.
Classification: LCC HV6785 .S86 2021 (print) | LCC HV6785 (ebook) |
DDC 364.15/52092273 — dc23
LC record available at https://lccn.loc.gaov/2020033857
LC ebook record available at https://lccn.loc.gov/2020033858

Book design by Lucia Bernard

Printed in the United States of America
DOC 10 9 8 7 6 5 4 3 2 1

To all the reporters, correspondents, columnists, sob sisters, ink-stained wretches, and journalists of the era, the thousands of men and women whose reporting and dedication to the craft contributed not only to this story but to so many others, and to all the many newspapers that supported their work. Their cumulative efforts are the only reason it is possible to begin to know the past and re-create long-forgotten stories of an era that still resonates with readers today.

Even when your friend, the radio, is still; even when her
   dream, the magazine, is finished; even when his life, the
   ticker, is silent; even when their destiny, the boulevard,
   is bare;
And after that paradise, the dancehall, is closed; after that
   theater, the clinic, is dark,

Still there will be your desire, and hers, and his hopes
   and theirs,
Your laughter, their laughter,
Your curse and his curse, her reward and their reward, their
   dismay and his dismay and her dismay and yours—

— FROM "X MINUS X" BY KENNETH FEARING

CONTENTS

TIGER GIRL
AND THE
CANDY KID

THE ROBBERS OF THY PEOPLE SHALL EXALT THEMSELVES TO ESTABLISH THE VISION; BUT THEY SHALL FAIL.

— DANIEL 11:14

Prologue

—————

PARTICULAR PEOPLE

ach member of the gang had a job. Margaret Whittemore, soon to be known all over America as "Tiger Girl," knew exactly what to do. And she played her role to the hilt.

Early on the morning of January 11, 1926, Margaret Whittemore, not quite twenty-two years old, rose just before dawn. Daylight would reveal a sky as dull as a mollusk and gray as concrete on this early winter day, but at this hour, as the sky slowly brightened, the lights of the streets of Manhattan still twinkled outside the window. Most days Margaret and her husband, Richard Whittemore, rarely opened the curtains before noon, if at all. They stayed out late and awoke even later, often stumbling home at four or five or six in the morning, after spending the early morning hours at the Club Chantee, where over the sound of a jazz band Richard laughed and held court long into the night.

But this day was different. In fact, for the last several days they had stayed at home and turned in early to make sure that on this day they would awake clearheaded and alert.

It was a big apartment—two bedrooms, two baths, with a nine-foot beamed ceiling, formal dining room, eat-in kitchen, and large entry foyer, one of half a dozen or so apartments on the twelfth floor of Chester Court, a fancy, brand-new fourteen-story building at 201 West Eighty-Ninth Street on Manhattan's Upper West Side.

Margaret liked nice places, and so did Richard. They'd never had much growing up in Baltimore and were making up for it now. There had been nothing wrong with their previous place, a fine town house on West Eightieth Street, but this place was nicer, newer, bigger, and had more room, more class, more everything. Advertised as "High Class Apartments for Particular People," Chester Court was a full-service building, with staff available to fulfill every whim. It was almost like a hotel, the housekeeping apartments already partially furnished, with electric refrigerators, stoves, and ranges. Even the closets had their own electric lights. The lobby was appointed in gleaming pink marble trimmed in gold gilt, and a doorman out front held the door for Margaret every time she entered and exited the building. Whenever she needed a taxi, he would stand on the curb, blow a whistle, and wave, then open the door and help her in.

He treated her with respect, and the way the building's staff spoke to her, saying things like, "Yes, Mrs. Vaughn. Of course, Mrs. Vaughn. Right away, Mrs. Vaughn," must have made her feel good—classy. She was younger than most of the other women in the building, who were wives of serious people, attorneys and architects and stockbrokers, and they jealously might have wondered how someone so young seemed to have so much.

Chances are the apartment was cluttered after a rare stretch of nights in, stacks of magazines spilling over the side tables. Richard favored adventure stories in pulps like *Argosy* and *Dime Detective*. Margaret liked the movies and, like other young women at the time, probably favored popular magazines that catered to her generation, glossy titles like *Photoplay, Motion Picture Classic,* and *Vogue* and pulps such as *Dream World, True Confessions,* and *Flapper Experiences,* all of which presented fantasies now close enough to touch. The ashtrays were full of cigarette butts—Richard was a chain-smoker—and a radio sat on the table. Their little dog, a brown and white spitz mix named Bades, a gift from Richard to Margaret, bounced back and forth. The dog was important to her. She'd had one before, a poodle, but after the couple were arrested in Philadelphia, police had taken the dog away. Margaret's clothes were still packed and hanging in oversized trunks, as if the Whittemores had either just arrived or were preparing to leave. In fact, their life at Chester Court was the first time, really, the pair had stayed in a place of their own, by themselves, for long enough to live together like a regular couple.

That was what made their little dog so important. When Richard had bought it for her shortly after they moved in, it was a sign that maybe their life on the run was coming to an end, that they could in some way settle down.

Margaret and her husband still kept nearly all their belongings in several wardrobe trunks, clothes as well as jewelry, some cash, and a gun, just in case. Even that was a risk, but it was easier to dump one gun in a hurry than a whole stash. At any moment, the whole gang might have to bolt.

Margaret was a flapper, a modern young woman. Her short blond hair was cut in a smart and daring version of the "Eton Crop," a hairstyle enhanced by a finger wave that curled just over the ears, like the models in the magazines, exposing the porcelain skin of her bare neck and leading the eye to the perfect boyish silhouette created by her nearly flat chest and slender figure.

Because it was a cold winter day and she had a job to do, she would have passed over the smart and sexier outfits that she wore at night, dresses made of crepe de Chine or taffeta and trimmed in silk or satin. For daywear, she usually selected something more conservative, like a ready-to-wear ensemble suit, sophisticated but sharp, and a pair of stockings. She didn't wear the cheap rayons that were often so shiny that they had to be dulled with skin powder. She could afford real silk now. Her dress lingered just below the knee.

She applied her makeup carefully, her nails perfectly manicured.

Her jewelry box, now sitting open, was like a small treasure chest from a children's book, all gold and diamonds and platinum and pearls. And there would soon be more, she knew. In the past few months, Richard had given her almost everything she wanted, and if everything went well, there would be even more coming. This was nothing like the way she had lived before, when he was in prison and she worked for the phone company or as an artist's model and had to wear the same outfit nearly every day, or when they were on the run and Richard had to dye his hair to avoid being identified.

While she dressed, Richard also prepared for the day. He splashed his face with water and then drew a straight razor over his neck and cheeks, where a handful of scars hid beneath the stubble of a face both hard and soft. He had a job too, and it was important to look the part, to blend in among the people on the street in New York's Diamond District.

You couldn't be too careful.

Women were marching on Washington, DC, demanding equal rights, and Fall River High School in Massachusetts had just outlawed jazz, calling it a "travesty of music." Richard mostly read the papers for the baseball and boxing news. But he also paid attention to the automobile advertisements, in particular one for the car he would soon buy, the 1926 Cadillac Imperial Suburban Sedan, series 314, with a list price of $3,435, capable of seating seven, and with a ninety-degree V-8, one of the most powerful engines available. It was a fast car, much faster than the four-cylinder Fords and Chevys used by the police and even faster than the car he already owned, a pricey Locomobile that now sat in a nearby garage. Truth be told, given his line of work, in some ways the armored edition of the Cadillac made more sense. It was the perfect car for "commercial" purposes like bank transfers, but everybody also knew it was bought only by top-of-the-line rumrunners. For a guy on the lam, the Suburban model attracted less unwanted attention.

In a few days he would have one, after paying for it with cash.

Richard Whittemore—Margaret usually either called him Dick or referred to him by his middle name, Reese, or sometimes, when they were out, by John or whatever other alias he was using at the time—was of average height, five-foot-seven, but "strongly built." His face was wide, with sleepy gray eyes, heavy lips, and a slightly flattened nose that said he could take a punch and hinted at a life that might have had a rough beginning. But dressed in his tailored and sharply creased pinstriped pants, with a crisp silk shirt over his T-shirt, suspenders, a tie and matching jacket, topped off by a "smartly cut" overcoat, he did not look like someone who had already killed at least three men and maybe four or five more. Or like someone who in another day would spend hours in an opium den on Mott Street, or who later that morning would smash a gun against the skull of a man and then rob him of hundreds of thousands of dollars' worth of uncut diamonds in the middle of the street in broad daylight.

That crime would make the front pages and eventually put both his picture and Margaret's in newspapers from Long Island to Los Angeles.

The tabloids would call Margaret "Tiger Girl," and Richard "the Candy Kid." Together they would become real-life celebrities, almost movie stars, as familiar to readers as the smart young couple Boots and Rod Ruggles in the popular comic strip *Boots and Her Buddies*.

He looked like a businessman, a professional. And that was precisely the way Richard Whittemore liked to think of himself now, as a man with a profession, a somebody who had places to go and people to see. To the building's rental office he was Horace Waters, but when he met a stranger, he was someone else —Johnny Gario or John Vaughn—and Margaret was the missus. When anyone asked what he did, his face lit up, he smiled and flashed his teeth, and then he simply said, "Sales." Never mentioning what he sold or for how much, he let his gold cufflinks, diamond stickpin, and tailored suit do the talking for him.

That was enough for most people—it was not a time to ask too many questions. Some probably figured he was a bootlegger; in 1926 bootlegging was considered hardly a crime, certainly not a rarity, and it barely raised an eyebrow, even on the Upper West Side. Nearly every day, even in his own building, he saw someone who gave him the same impression. Everybody, it seemed, was either a bootlegger or working for someone who was, making deliveries or working in a speakeasy or selling illegal liquor from under the counter at the butcher shop. Even the other "businessmen" who lived in the building were in on the game in one way or another—a lot of attorneys and accountants got rich keeping bootleggers out of jail. So did a lot of cops.

Bootlegging was what Richard Whittemore had thought he would probably end up doing too, until a few years before, when everything had seemed to fall in place. After spending many of the past fifteen years in reform schools, jails, and penitentiaries, he'd met Jacob Kraemer during his last stint, in the Maryland State Penitentiary. Jake, as he called himself, was different from the other prisoners, who were mostly dope fiends and stickup artists almost begging to be arrested. Kraemer was older and smart, spoke a bunch of languages, and seemed to have everything figured out. Along with his brother Leon, the Kraemers had lived a life of crime on two continents, cracking safes. They had already stolen and then squandered several fortunes. But now, nearing middle age, they were tired of getting caught and wasting time in prison.

Together, the two brothers had figured out a new way to steal diamonds and other jewels, get rich, and, they believed, not get caught. But they needed help from someone young and hungry. Then they met Richard. Everyone knew him in the pen and saw him beat men down with his fists in the prison boxing ring. The Kraemers had the brains, but they admired and needed Whittemore's brawn and brazen ambition—he was sick of being a small-time hood and wanted more of everything.

Whittemore and the Kraemers had schemed and plotted together, and when they all got out of prison, they put those plans in place. They worked just as smoothly as the "can opener" the Kraemers had perfected and once used to crack safes. The brothers did most of the planning; the execution was Whittemore's responsibility.

He was good at it, and he knew it. When things got hot, he stayed cool. Gunfire did not scare him. He threw a punch with the best of them, and he kept the other guys in line and got rid of them when they strayed. What he said was the law.

It was working so far. In a little over six months, the gang had pulled a half-dozen big jobs and a like number of small ones, making off with more than half a million dollars' worth of cash and jewelry. No one had gotten caught, and no one had gotten badly hurt . . . no one in the gang anyway. Even better, not only did the police have no idea who was committing the crimes, but they did not even know that one gang was responsible; that was how good they were, and how good their plans were. After each job, they didn't really need to hide or run. Instead, under assumed names, they stayed in plain sight, sometimes in Cleveland but more recently in New York. Then they went out and spent money like they, well, had just robbed somebody.

Today was a big day. It was time for the gang to *really* show what it could do. They were all getting used to the life, to having what they wanted when they wanted it, and as much as they wanted for as long as they wanted. Richard liked to walk into a nightclub, snap his fingers, and get the best table. He liked to tip cigarette girls a week's wage, drop the equivalent of a month's rent on a bottle of wine, order suits like calling a cab, and lose track of the days in a dope den with his friends or at the craps table. He liked sharp suits and fast cars and had his eye on that Cadillac.

Over the past few weeks the Kraemers and the rest of the gang had plotted and watched and waited, and now was the time to act. Later that morning two jewelers would pick up a shipment of uncut, untraceable diamonds from a bank vault and walk down West Forty-Eighth Street toward their office in the most heavily policed area of New York, only a few blocks away from a busy police precinct, with a traffic cop on every corner.

So what? When the time was right, Richard Whittemore and his gang planned to smash the men to the ground in the middle of a busy street, take the diamonds, and disappear in less than a minute. By nightfall, the entire lot would be sold and everyone would receive their portion of the take. No one would go to bed early.

Each one had a job. They had gone over it a million times, diagramming and plotting every move. In a few minutes Margaret would head downtown to Pennsylvania Station and Richard would meet everyone in Midtown. When Margaret got to the train station, she would take a ticket for a locker from her clutch and remove a valise full of guns, including one in particular that her husband wanted on this day, an oversized .38 pistol along with the usual assortment of .45s. Then she would meet Richard in Midtown, give him the guns, and return home. It was safer that way. She did not yet have a record, and if the men, most convicted felons, were caught with the guns, that meant an automatic jail term. For Richard, it might mean a death sentence.

Then the plan would unfold. The gang would split up, travel to the scene, and take their places. When Jake gave the signal, the whole gang would spring into action, make a violent lightning strike, and then scatter.

Margaret put on her coat and finished her look by pulling a cloche hat down low over her forehead, so low that she had to tilt her head back to peer out from beneath it to know where she was going. She looked smart and sharp.

She'd been looking at the ads, too, and had her eye on a new $800 squirrel coat. In a few days, it would be hers.

Together, the Whittemores would have almost everything they had ever dreamed of.

One

―――――――――

TILL DEATH

O n a cool, gray morning in October 1921, Richard Reese Whittemore stood in front of West Baltimore's Caernarvon Methodist Episcopal Church South, flanked by a motley collection of his pals, smoking and spitting on the sidewalk. More at home in a poolroom than a church pew, they sported off-the-rack "jazz suits." Only weeks past his twentieth birthday, Whittemore was already beginning to spin out a new life from an old one, reaching toward a vision of himself only he could see.

Some of the girlfriends of the bride-to-be were already seated inside, quietly chatting away, awaiting the arrival of Margaret Messler for what was supposed to be the happiest day of the young couple's lives.

In many ways that would prove to be true. The next five years would be marked with enough tragedy to last several lifetimes and end with the Whittemores on the front page of virtually every newspaper in the country, their tabloid love story more improbable than any motion picture. It would also leave at least a half-dozen men buried in the ground, a half-dozen more hanging from the bars of a jail cell, and the whereabouts of several hundred thousand dollars in cash and gems an enduring mystery.

• • •

T iger Girl and the Candy Kid are not important because of the crimes they committed, the lives they took, or even, really, their relationship. Their story is no simple romantic coupling; it is the torrid romance of an entire era, one that only matters for the glimpse it offers into a time and place, America in transition at the end of the Progressive Era, hurtling headlong and head-down into the Jazz Age, a time when everything was changing so fast and revealing so many obvious contradictions and inequalities that what made sense yesterday did not make sense today and no one quite knew what tomorrow might bring. Just as the lives and crimes of Bonnie and Clyde Parker provide admittance into the Depression Era, when desperate times drove people to ever more desperate measures, Tiger Girl and the Candy Kid punch a ticket into the Roaring Twenties.

Yet their world was not the same as that chronicled by F. Scott Fitzgerald, where money and status and privilege turned hedonistic self-destruction into a kind of new aesthetic. For Richard and Margaret, the Jazz Age wasn't about raccoon coats and cocktails, sis-boom-bah and profligate excess, but how those romanticized mythologies of the era provided an irresistible fantasy, and how trying to live that fantasy played out, life and death in real time.

As America remade itself in the 1920s, becoming recognizable as the place we still inhabit today, it took kids like Richard and Margaret and created the Candy Kid and Tiger Girl. They came of age just as a twisted pathway to a new warped version of the American Dream first came into focus, one built not on morality but on money, not on personal freedom but on personal indulgence, not on the promise of a better future but on a mouthwatering appetite for the present.

As Richard and Margaret became Tiger Girl and the Candy Kid, they went together down a dark back alley, taking a shortcut toward the kind of instant gratification the era worshiped. "Everywhere," as Malcolm Cowley wrote in *Exile's Return*, "was the atmosphere of a long debauch that had to end; the orchestras played too fast, the stakes were too high at the gambling tables, the players were so empty, so tired, secretly hoping to vanish together into sleep and . . . maybe wake on a very distant morning and hear nothing, whatever, no shouting or crooning, find all things changed."

All of a sudden, it seemed, you could just flip a switch and have the lights come on, hear music blaring on the radio and an automobile roaring to life and offering a thousand destinations. Richard and Margaret and others of their generation careened down one crooked street after another to grab those few morsels of the Dream that seemed within reach, then reached for the next, and then the next, until they finally landed in a place where the errors and extremes of the age were exposed in bloodstained relief. Theirs is a story of what can happen when the American Dream is exposed as folly and about the nightmares—personal, private, and public—it can inspire.

As Richard and Margaret became Tiger Girl and the Candy Kid, real blood was spilled and real people died, real kids were left orphans, and real women became widows. Lives were destroyed and erased, fortunes acquired and squandered, careers both made and ruined. Tiger Girl and the Candy Kid were among the first to drive a stiletto into the swollen balloon of the era. Before them, there had been no such figures as the romanticized gangster and his femme fatale gun moll—real-life antiheroes the public would find both repulsive and irresistible, a coupling impossible to embrace but also impossible to ignore, one the culture has both celebrated and exploited ever since.

What a time to be alive. And what a time to die.

O n the day of the wedding, amid the flowers and too-sweet cake, the Candy Kid and Tiger Girl did not exist. There was nothing special about either Richard or Margaret, apart from the fact that their stories were so common, as well as a little sad and tawdry. Like so many others their age, all they wanted to be was something other than what they were.

A spiffy-looking couple, they were just beginning to look the parts they yearned to play. Margaret, with her wide blue eyes framed by blond hair cut into a fashionable bob parted on the side, certainly turned a few heads. Although she would later describe herself as "a good girl" at the time of her marriage, she was anything but demure.

"Brassy" was more like it. A year before, a new film had debuted at Baltimore's Parkway Theater on nearby North Avenue. A romantic comedy, *The Flapper* was written by a thirty-two-year-old woman named Frances Marion and starred Olive Thomas in the title role of Ginger. It was the first American film to exploit the flapper lifestyle, an entirely new kind of young American woman who didn't adhere to the social norms of her parents but thought for herself. As one observer described them, flappers were "frivolous, scantily-clad, jazzing . . . [and] irresponsible and undisciplined, to whom a dance, a new hat, or a man with a car, were of more importance than the fate of nation." The film introduced the term, whose origins are still murky, into common speech. More than that, it helped create an archetype for young women, a way of life and of living that appeared to be of their own making, one that was exciting, beguiling, intoxicating, and utterly befuddling to people like Richard's and Margaret's parents.

Newspaper ads for the film teased, "You've met her often, she's the little girl who's always misunderstood, whose 'love affairs' are never taken seriously. In her efforts to grow up, everything she touches goes wrong." The film's innocent title character, Ginger, meets a man described as "delightfully wild and dangerous" and declares, "A woman dares anything for the man she loves." Ginger falls in with the wrong kind of people, becomes tangled up in a scheme to rob a safe and ends up dazzled by the allure of flapper fashions and stolen jewelry. She travels "alone to the wicked city," New York, where she presents herself as a "woman of experience," smoking cigarettes, wearing lipstick, draping herself in gems, showing her ankles, and even going to a nightclub.

At the end of the film, the title character realizes the error of her ways and reforms. But for young women like Margaret, the moral lesson of the last reel and the spate of wildly popular *Flapper*-inspired films that followed didn't stick. What remained with them was Ginger's freedom—to smoke, dance, drink gin, flirt, wear makeup and gaudy jewelry, go to wild parties, and use their bodies in any way they wanted, to get what they wanted.

Like Ginger, young women were dazzled by the clothing and ornaments and the exhilaration of discovering who they could be. They now wanted to shed their innocence, control their own destiny, and play a starring role in imitation of the movies. And it all seemed so easy to achieve. There was even a popular "recipe" to become this new woman: "Two bare knees, two thinner stockings, one shorter skirt, two lipsticks, three powder puffs, 132 cigarettes, and three boyfriends, with eight flasks between them."

Margaret and other young women like her would have been wise to pay attention to the fate of actress Olive Thomas. The end of her story had already been splashed across the headlines. A small-town girl who moved to New York City at age nineteen after winning a "Most Beautiful Girl in New York City" contest, Thomas was swept up and away. She became a Ziegfeld Girl, posed nude for a pinup painter, and then began making films. Shortly after *The Flapper* debuted, she traveled to Paris for a second honeymoon with her husband, actor Jack Pickford, the brother of film star Mary Pickford. By then, her story was fueling similar dreams in young women all over America.

Together, as Frances Marion later described them, the couple soon became "much more interested in playing the roulette of life than in concentrating on their careers." Early on the morning of September 5, 1920, in their hotel room after a night of drinking, Thomas, drunk, downed the contents of a flask. It was not full of gin, but a solution of mercury bichloride used by her husband to treat the sores caused by his chronic syphilis.

The tabloid press exploded with news of her death, a story that hit every sweet spot: sex, scandal, celebrity, and tragedy. Although eventually ruled an accident, there was rampant speculation, and some evidence, that she either killed herself intentionally or had been murdered by her husband. Rumor also had it that Thomas may have been a heroin addict caught in the criminal underworld, and that she and her husband had recently indulged in a cocaine-fueled orgy that lasted days. Poisoned, she died five days later, only twenty-five years old.

Hearing of Olive and Jack's fate, Margaret and Richard and scores of young people like them in the generation that came to define the Jazz Age mostly appreciated the story for its titillating thrills—not as one that would foreshadow their own destiny.

L ike her husband-to-be, Margaret, only eighteen when she married, dressed in the style of the day. She had abandoned the confines of the Gibson Girl corset and looked to the styles popularized in magazines and currently in vogue in France that were now beginning to make their way across the Atlantic—dresses made of loose fabric that draped around slender, ever more boyish figures. Although wedding dresses remained conservative and hid more than they revealed, in other settings women like Margaret now wore their stockings rolled down and allowed their skirt lengths to creep up, showing men a tempting calf.

Richard cut a pretty keen figure in his wedding suit as well. Slim yet muscular, he had dark brown hair that framed a face sporting a slow rakish smile that could turn to a sneer in an instant. The newspapers would later note that his heavy-lidded chestnut eyes hinted of a vaguely "mixed strain, perhaps that of some Oriental race," as if, according to the prejudices of the era, that somehow explained how he had turned out. Almost from birth, Richard rebelled against anything or anyone who sought to pin him down and hold him back. Nobody had ever been able to tell him what to do or how to behave.

Yet people liked him. It was hard not to. He was the kind of guy who instantly knew how to tell people what they wanted to hear, whether it was true or not, and who could spit out a bald-faced lie without breaking a sweat. To the girls, he was something of a sweet talker, aka a "candy kid," in the slang of the day, but when the sweet talk didn't work, he wasn't averse to using a strong arm to get what he wanted. He was ruled by impulse. His friends knew better than to cross him.

Richard's mother, Edna, hadn't lived long enough to see her son take a bride and maybe that was for the best. She had suffered from tuberculosis and become an invalid before passing away in 1916. Her friends blamed her oldest son and whispered that she'd really died of "a broken heart."

Richard had given both of his parents plenty of reason to worry, to stay up nights wondering what he was up to and where he was. His father, Rawlings Whittemore, must have hoped that married life would inspire Richard to settle down, get a steady job, or, at the very least, stay out of jail.

Nothing had tamed Richard so far, not the Coast Guard, not reform schools, not even a stint in Baltimore's St. Mary's Industrial School for Boys. That institution had worked wonders for another lost Baltimore boy, George Ruth, who had turned his life around and become "the Babe," the best ballplayer in the country.

Even as they were buoyed by the wedding, it was hard for the couple to feel optimistic about the future, given the state of the world they had grown up in. Like almost everything else Whittemore did, the wedding was a rush job, an impulsive act that showed he didn't think too far beyond the next day, or the previous evening. Most nights he was out all hours, sometimes with Margaret and sometimes not. He'd tried working and going straight—clerking in a cigar store, selling fruit and other goods on the street—but late nights simply did not agree with early mornings.

So Richard was usually a dollar or ten behind. His father would always bail him out, thinking maybe this time would be the last time, but it never was.

Rawlings felt bad for his son. When Richard was only two, he'd fallen out a window, only a four-foot drop, but had been knocked unconscious and experienced seizures. After that, as his father later remembered, "I'm wondering if maybe that had something to do with" his pattern of antisocial behavior. His parents blamed themselves and always found excuses for their son's conduct. Since then, it had been one thing after another. A few weeks before the wedding, Richard had lifted some stock certificates from his father and cashed them in, money he quickly lost in the dance halls and while gambling with his pals. Rawlings looked the other way. It was easier to believe the lie that his son would turn his life around than face the truth.

The truth was that, so far, Richard had proven utterly incapable of taking care of himself, much less a young wife.

Whittemore and his fiancée seemed to view the wedding ceremony like a big night out. Without a great deal of thought to what would come after, they had made the decision to marry showing little more foresight than they'd have brought to picking out a motion picture show at the Hippodrome. Weddings held at the Caernarvon Methodist Episcopal Church South didn't make the society pages, and no wedding announcement made its way into the *Sun*. Margaret was Catholic, but Whittemore had laughed at the notion that he would go through the time-consuming process of converting, as her mother wanted. Religion wasn't going to stop the young couple, even if Whittemore's family was embarrassed that he was marrying a Papist and Margaret's mother was appalled that she was marrying outside the church.

For two bucks, they'd picked up a wedding license only a few days before, the church was available and affordable, and for another small fee the minister agreed to perform the service. Whittemore had probably borrowed the money for these meager expenses, or maybe a horse had come through at the nearby

Pimlico racetrack. They had few other options besides marrying in the church, as the state of Maryland did not allow civil wedding ceremonies and landlords didn't rent to unmarried couples.

Until recently, Whittemore had lived rent-free with his father and younger brother in a row house on Bentalou Street, just west of Sandtown. But Whittemore promised his wife they'd have a place of their own. He managed to get a room nearby above a tire shop at 1200 West Fayette Street, in a building later revealed to be a drug den. If Margaret did all the housework, it was rent-free.

That was just like Richard, always depending on someone else. Margaret was the one with a steady job. She'd signed on with the phone company as an operator at a time when many calls still had to be put through manually. But she made only about $20 a week, far less than the average annual wage of $3,000 earned by men, and hardly enough to buy a thin winter coat. For now, the young couple would start their life together as boarders, living on the cheap but in a hurry to grow up.

Maybe married life, and the specter of a future and maybe a family to support, would rein Richard Whittemore in. That happened to a lot of boys.

Maybe it would happen to him.

As Margaret and Richard said their vows, the modern world was rushing in. Rawlings had grown up in a Baltimore where the horizon stretched only a few blocks, a place that all but shut down after sunset. His children were coming of age in a place that, thanks to electricity, never went dark, where poolrooms and saloons and nickelodeons did a booming business, automobiles choked the streets, planes were beginning to crisscross the sky, and a better life seemed just around the corner.

The streets of Baltimore revealed a different reality. Nothing, it seemed, ever came easy there, and right around the corner was just another dead end, the apparently limitless future more stick than carrot. By the fall of 1921, for Richard Whittemore, his wife, and so many others their age, the past didn't seem to matter. And the future didn't seem like anything you could count on. The city had been electrified, cars had replaced horse-drawn carts, and trams and streetcars ran everywhere, but as one young man wrote in the *Atlantic*

Monthly, despite these advances, their parents' generation had already "pretty well ruined this world before passing it on," leaving behind "this thing knocked to pieces, leaky, red hot, threatening to blow up."

The twentieth century had opened with a series of tragedies in the burgeoning city of Baltimore: fire, war, and flu, followed by a quick and brutal economic depression. By the time Richard and Margaret entered their teen years, they were keen to say goodbye to what was left of their hometown.

Steady, if dreary and monotonous, work had once been easy to come by in Baltimore, particularly after the Civil War, when the combination of the Baltimore and Ohio Railroad and the Calvert Company's development of ten thousand acres along the harbor and in southeast Baltimore created one of the greatest industrial waterfronts in the world, one that featured all manner of industry—shipbuilding, lumber, iron, coal, canneries, distilleries, breweries, and, in 1916, Bethlehem Steel, then the largest steel plant in the world.

For years, workers had streamed into Baltimore from all directions—freed southern Blacks included—and the immigration pier at Locust Point rivaled that of Ellis Island as more than 1.2 million immigrants, first from Ireland and then from Germany and central and eastern Europe, started their American journey in Baltimore. Nearly 20 percent of these immigrants found work and decided to make Baltimore home.

Then, on February 7 and 8, 1904, the center of the city of Baltimore was consumed by fire. In thirty hours, more than 1,500 buildings and an area spanning some seventy city blocks—140 acres—were completely destroyed.

Although one man was killed in the blaze, the *Baltimore Sun* called it "a blessing," for the fire marked the beginning of the end of old Baltimore. As the sixth-largest city in the country rebuilt and expanded, Baltimore pitched forward into the twentieth century with astonishing speed. Before then, the city had remained something of a relic from another time, its colonial past still on view. Baltimore was staid, conservative, and hardworking, but a little sleepy and utterly segregated. Even after the fire, the city still clung so tightly to the Victorian Era for a while that in 1908, when Mademoiselle de Joire, a Parisian model, displayed an Edwardian Directoire gown from Paris that dared to reveal the slenderest portion of her lower leg, Police Deputy Marshal Manning declared the sight "only fit for private circulation." If the lady appeared on the street in the dress again, he threatened, she would "be subject to arrest for disorderly conduct."

Then came the Great War, a conflict the United States entered in the spring of 1917 with the full expectation that in a few short months American troops would return home wrapped in glory. But an initial burst of public patriotism was followed by absolute lethargy at recruiting offices. The War Department instituted a "work or fight" order and a draft to round up the slackers. Eventually the United States shipped more than a million young men into the most brutal and deadly conflict the world had ever seen. The American military ballooned from a force of only 127,500 in 1917 to more than three million active members by war's end. Of those sent overseas, 53,000 were killed in combat and another 63,000 died from the horrific conditions in the trenches. Nearly all the fallen were under the age of thirty. For them, Armistice Day, November 11, 1918, came too late.

And then, just as the war began winding down and returning soldiers were already regaling their civilian friends with stories of both battlefront bravery and life in Gay Paree, the Spanish influenza reached the epidemic stage. It spread across the nation with the speed of a telegram, and unlike other strains, which preyed upon the elderly and infirm, this flu primarily infected the young and previously healthy. By the time it played out, another 675,000 Americans were dead. Baltimore buried more than 4,000.

Those who survived these tragedies just wanted to get a job, forget all that had happened, and blow off some steam. That didn't seem like too much to ask.

At first, the war offered a promise of prosperity and fueled a booming local economy. Work was plentiful, and working-class boys and girls growing up in Baltimore looked to an optimistic future when a job wouldn't necessarily mean toiling twelve hours a day for the rest of their lives down at the docks or in the rail yard or a factory. Women entered the workforce in numbers never seen before, taking over for men who were off in combat and working at new military bases and in factories making war goods. In taking on responsibilities the old world had never allowed women to shoulder, they left the drudgery of housework behind. The combination of electricity, canned goods, home appliances, and prophylactics gave these women something they'd never had before—free time. And now many had money of their own to spend, creating something brand-new, the independent woman. Instead of diving into marriage straightaway, women could afford to wait to get married and experience the world on their own terms. The Nineteenth Amendment, giving women the right to vote, passed in 1920, and seemed to promise women even more freedom to control their own futures.

Swept up in these changes, Margaret Messler quit school shy of a high school degree and got that job with the phone company. Her family needed the money, but they had also lost control of their daughter. Her parents, August and Theresa, had emigrated from Germany in 1882, two of several hundred thousand German immigrants to call Baltimore home. August worked as a tailor. The couple had five children, one who died in infancy, followed by William, Philip, Margaret, born on March 2, 1903, and Paul. After August Messler passed away while Margaret was still in grammar school, money became tight. Theresa was forced to take a job working as a cleaning lady, known as a charwoman, in a factory.

Soon after the war ended, the booming economy sank like a U-boat hitting a mine in the English Channel. As veterans returned to the workforce in droves, the US government, overreacting to concerns over the federal debt and wartime inflation, slashed the federal budget by nearly two-thirds. The result was one of the most dramatic economic downturns in history, one far more abrupt than the later stock market crash of 1929. The industrial engine fueled by the war sputtered. Unemployment of non-agricultural workers went from almost zero to more than 15 percent, the stock market lost half its value, business sector profits dropped 75 percent, and wholesale prices fell by nearly 50 percent. Baltimore's economy couldn't take the hit. Industrial unemployment skyrocketed past 20 percent, and the jobs lost by Baltimoreans never really came back as manufacturing in the Midwest and Great Lakes took up the slack and most of the work. Women were booted out of the workforce en masse, and soldiers who'd fought for their country scrounged to get by. Job prospects were even worse for younger men. Optimism for a postwar future marked by peace and prosperity rapidly became mired in another miasma, a trench of despair and the widening gap between reality and desire. Fractures in society that had always been present were now made obvious. A comfortable middle-class life seemed about as real as a silent film.

And what made it even worse for kids and young adults like Richard and Margaret was that there were just so damn many of them. Fueled by the children of immigrants, between 1900 and 1930 enrollment in American high schools increased 650 percent while colleges and university attendance more than tripled. For this new generation, the old ethics and mores that had bound most Americans to a life of labor suddenly vanished. Without a future, they looked toward the present, trading the hope of long-term security for more immediate pleasures.

So far, Richard and Margaret had enjoyed few of the material benefits of the Jazz Age. While F. Scott Fitzgerald's monied, upper-crust characters celebrated the ennui of their privileged status through conspicuous consumption and the accompanying emotional wasteland, kids like Richard and Margaret didn't have that luxury. If you were born rich, it was a great time to be alive. But the gulf between the haves and have-nots had rarely been greater, or more obvious. The good life was on exhibit every day in the movies and in the magazines, and young people hungered for the swanky promise of a world where men swaggered through the night in shiny new cars, squiring women draped in furs and diamonds, cocktails in hand, the sound of a jazz band blaring in the background. Every night an endless party called out to them, one that seemed both tantalizingly close and simultaneously unreachable, for there was one reality that could not be ignored. The high life required cold hard cash.

That was what mattered now. That was what they wanted. That was what they *all* wanted. And that was something Richard Whittemore had grown up believing he deserved.

The Whittemores, well known and respected, if not particularly prosperous, had been in Baltimore for generations and were also known for being hardworking, honest, and caring, a reputation they had earned through service to others.

Rawlings's mother, Hannah Hoffman, described as being of "splendid character," had dedicated much of her life to public service, which had brought her into contact with Baltimore's wealthiest families. When she was widowed in 1882 and left with three children to support, a local philanthropist arranged for her to be named the first superintendent of the Colored Girls' House of Refuge on Courtland Street, one of four houses of refuge created by the state, each segregated by race and gender. Such institutions were inspired by reform efforts that swept the country in the middle of the nineteenth century—reforms that would shape Richard's life.

Soon enough, houses of refuge were being run like prisons for minors, more akin to "houses of refuse" for the way they treated the throwaway children in their care. During Hannah's tenure, though, the Courtland Street house of refuge continued to aspire to its original lofty purpose. Later, Rawlings and Edna Whittemore and their growing family would even live in the same building that housed the Society for the Protection of Children from Cruelty on Franklin Street.

This heritage eventually made Richard Whittemore even more of an embarrassment to his family, because he had become precisely the kind of kid such institutions were designed for—utterly incorrigible, someone adults didn't understand and feared. A later observer even traced the young Whittemore's downfall to the family's time living at the Society, where he had grown up as an entitled boy who was constantly told he was better than the unfortunates who were temporarily housed in the same building.

Richard's mother, Edna Grady, had also grown up in the world of reform schools. Her father, Bernie, had taught at the House of Refuge for Boys, where he organized the boys' band. The Gradys enjoyed a fine reputation. One uncle served as a dentist at the US Naval Academy, and another helped start the Baltimore Polytechnic Institute, whose graduates would include both the author Dashiell Hammett and the legendary Baltimore journalist H. L. Mencken.

Class mattered to the Whittemores, although Rawlings hadn't been nearly as successful as his forebears. He worked as a stationary engineer at the Calvert Machine Company down by the harbor, a fancy title for a kind of big engine and boiler mechanic. It was a dirty job, and he earned barely enough to raise a family. Meta was born in 1900, Richard on September 8, 1901, and a third son, Rawlings, in 1905. After Hannah's death in 1903, Rawlings bought a house and the family settled in Baltimore's old Fifteenth Ward, a multiethnic, working-class neighborhood.

It wasn't a place where respectable people wanted to live, at least not for very long. Restrictive covenants had already crammed most of ethnic and Black Baltimore into only a few neighborhoods, making Baltimore perhaps the most segregated city in America. In 1910, the city even passed segregation laws that made it illegal for Blacks or Whites to move onto a block where either would be the minority. Although the law was eventually struck down, by 1920 half of all Blacks in the city had already been herded into Sandtown, just south of the Fifteenth Ward. Most nearby White residents, a mixture of Germans (like the Messlers), Jews, eastern Europeans, and poor Whites, either newcomers to the city from the rural South or more established families who had lost status (like the Whittemores), were all looking to leave. Maybe that's why it was known locally as "Fearsville."

It was no romantic melting pot. Lawrence Adler, who later found fame in Hollywood, on the stage, and in the recording industry as the world's foremost harmonica player, grew up in the neighborhood and described Baltimore during this era as "a town from which I spent the first fourteen years of my life plotting my escape . . . nobody seemed to like anybody. Catholics, Protestants, Poles, Negroes, Jews cordially feared or detested one another, and there was hardly any contact between groups. I was called 'Jew bastard' my first day of school but was also cautioned by my parents not to play with 'the little nigger boys.'"

By 1920, most adults in the Fifteenth Ward were intimidated not just by their Black neighbors but by the hordes of children roaming the streets who survived by forming youthful gangs to prey on and do battle with a never-ending onslaught of "others"—kids from the next block and the next neighborhood—in a sidewalk version of social Darwinism.

All the Whittemores had, really, was their good name, which the family pronounced "WHIT-a-more." Fortunately for Richard's older sister Meta, that still mattered. Only a few months before her brother's wedding, Meta, now twenty-one, had parlayed her family name into a fine marriage to a young doctor, the son of a Maine legislator.

Now *that* had been a wedding, taking place in the prestigious and now historic St. Paul's Church Rectory on Cathedral Hill, one of Baltimore's oldest buildings. You had to be somebody to marry there. The *Baltimore Sun* covered the event in a small but detailed story that even made special mention of Meta's bridal gown and wedding bouquet and reported that after the ceremony the couple embarked on an "extended wedding trip North." The Whittemores' oldest son had apparently cleaned up and behaved at that affair, and now Rawlings could only hope that would hold true at Richard's own wedding. "Hooch" had been Richard Whittemore's near-constant companion since grammar school, and Prohibition hadn't changed that. If anything, Richard had become even more besotted with rearranging his senses at the altar of alcohol.

He wasn't the only one. Prohibition provided the final spark that lit Richard and Margaret's world. At a time when the possibilities seemed almost endless and opportunity seemed to be shrinking just as fast, breaking the law emerged as the fastest and easiest way to get ahead.

Ever since the Eighteenth Amendment prohibiting the sale and distribution of alcohol had been ratified on January 16, 1919, and gone into effect a year later, there had been increasingly little respect for the law of any kind. Among the young, lawlessness acquired a certain thrilling appeal.

Even the state of Maryland got into the action. Despite the Volstead Act, which empowered the federal enforcement of Prohibition, Maryland was the only state in the union that didn't bother to pass a similar state law to help the feds enforce the statute. By 1921, with the local economy in collapse, breaking the law was Baltimore's only growth industry.

Guys from the neighborhood like Richard Whittemore—poor and uneducated in little more than the ways of the street corner—cashed in legitimately, illegitimately, and every way in between in the kind of action that flourished in Prohibition's wake and generated enormous amounts of cash. There was money to be made running liquor, working in speakeasies, serving as gofers for gangsters, smuggling, heisting trucks, rolling drunks, skimming cash, or just plain robbery, preying on anybody or anything floating on the same boozy tide. "Whatever it took" was a way of life, and the cops and politicians often let it happen with a nod and a wink. Many were on the take themselves, and not shy about it. Baltimore's democratic boss Sonny Mahon was so bold as to brag that "politics is my business and I make it pay." Almost every person of power, in one way or another, was presumed to be working some kind of racket. Bad was good, the cops were crooks, and the crooks were the heroes.

It was the kind of thing that made Rawlings Whittemore shake his head and wonder what had happened to the world, and what had happened to his son. All over America a lot of other parents of Rawlings's generation felt the same about their own children. As Warner Fabian noted in his scandalous popular period novel *Flaming Youth,* "They're all desperadoes, these kids, all of them with any life in their veins; the girls as well as the boys; maybe more than the boys." They were all out of control, thinking only of the next fifteen minutes.

And all over America young guys like Richard Whittemore, who had little more than wit and nerve, looked up to so-called butter-and-egg men, the big spenders, guys who never seemed to work and never seemed to be without a bankroll. And young women like Margaret Messler, who with the turn of an ankle could make a man swoon and peel a few dollars off his bankroll, wanted to be with someone just like that, a man who didn't expect her to sit at home and be good.

She didn't much seem to care how he got the bankroll. And neither did he.

Richard and Margaret each repeated the standard wedding vows, committing to each other "for better, for worse, for richer, for poorer, in sickness and health, to love and to cherish, until we are parted by death." Neither realized how soon these vows would loom over their union. They then dashed from the church, presumably under a few handfuls of rice, and headed into the rest of their lives with no known destination other than a rented room. There seemed no obvious way out of the Fifteenth Ward.

The newspapers carried no mention of their wedding, no description of Margaret's dress or her bouquet or the feathers in her hat or a honeymoon. They apparently had no real plans for anything beyond the next few days . . . except for each other.

For that, they would do anything.

It was love, or at least lust for something more than what they had. Dizzy over each other and drunk on the era, they dove together headlong into the sordid depths of this new world. Maybe Margaret thought she could save her husband, maybe Richard thought he could take her away to a better place, maybe together they could both be more than what they were alone. She was impressionable and eager, and as she later said, trying to explain all that happened next, "I wanted a good time. He has given me one, and all these lovely clothes."

But eventually, hidden in her desire for "a good time" and nice things, was something more. Maybe the two of them, *together,* each driving the other, could have more than that. Maybe together they could make a life just like the ones they saw in the movies and read about in the magazines. Maybe he could find a way to give her all the good times she dreamed of, and maybe she could help make that happen. There was no family money to fall back on, no career or particular skill available to either of them to make a decent wage, much less to become prosperous. All they had was each other, Margaret's devotion and material desires paired with Richard's criminal guile and greed.

Eight days after their wedding, as the joy of holy matrimony faded and the flowers from Margaret's modest wedding bouquet turned brown and began to drop, Richard Reese Whittemore was arrested and charged with burglary.

They were on their way.

Two

A VERY ACCURATE PREDICTION

They couldn't afford it, but the couple decided to go on a honeymoon anyway. Richard had been to "the wicked city," New York, when he was in the service, and like Ginger in *The Flapper,* that's where he and Margaret wanted to go. Whittemore scraped a few dollars together, they took a train to New York, and there they spent a few days in a hotel in the bliss of matrimony and the boozy haze that came from a few nights on the town.

By then, after seeing how the other half lived in Manhattan, Richard had made a decision. He'd had it trying to live the straight and narrow life and blamed the cops for telling people in the neighborhood he couldn't be trusted. A few years later, in a fifteen-thousand-word autobiography, he wrote that soon after he married he became "disgusted with everything, as there was no pleasure in anything I did." He grew to hate "every copper I saw" and decided "to cause the coppers all the trouble I could."

So much for his father's dream that he would settle down.

Eight days after the wedding, Whittemore and a street-corner acquaintance, Joe Eskowitz, walked up to a home on North Bentalou Street, only two hundred yards south of where Whittemore had lived with his father. The classic Baltimore two-story row house was nearly identical to every other home Whittemore had ever lived in with his family, with a brick facade, a small porch, a painted white stoop that stretched to the sidewalk, and an interior layout as familiar as an old hat. The sidewalls were shared with the houses on either side. A small backyard fronted a narrow alley, separated from the next by a low fence, a place that offered space to hang the wash but little privacy. At night, it was easy to walk up to the front or back door, fumble with a lock, and then realize you were at the wrong house. The only differences were the wallpaper and cheap furniture inside.

The owners of the home, shoemaker Harry Rosenberg and his wife, were away, but Whittemore and Eskowitz already knew that. It was the Sabbath, after all. Over the last few months, Whittemore had been a familiar face in the neighborhood, either kibitzing on the corner or selling fruit and vegetables and other goods from his cart. Little that went on there was a secret to him.

Whittemore and his partner sidled down the back alley and then, waiting until there were no prying eyes glancing their way, quickly made their way to the rear of the house, jimmied open a window with a pry bar, and climbed inside. It took only a few seconds—burglary was something Whittemore had learned instead of geometry. Robbery was becoming commonplace throughout much of Baltimore, and not just in tough neighborhoods like the Fifteenth Ward; people who had very little were trying to take what they could get from somebody else who had very little. Since the war ended, it had only gotten worse.

Once inside, Whittemore and Eskowitz took their time pulling open drawers and rifling through closets. They found a suitcase and filled it with everything that caught their eye and fit inside, clothing and jewelry, stuff they could sell quickly. Then they walked to the front door, glanced around until the sidewalk was clear, and skipped down the steps with the suitcase of stolen goods.

Two doors down, Rosenberg's neighbor, Ida Shipley, saw two young men who didn't belong emerge from the house and walk nonchalantly away. Only amateurs ran. The men didn't rush, didn't look her way, didn't pay her any attention at all.

Shipley called the police. Within minutes, three sergeants came to her house and she described the two men she'd seen.

The police weren't surprised. Every cop in the neighborhood recognized one of the men she was describing. In the Fifteenth Ward, Richard Whittemore was already something of a legend, the kind of guy parents would warn their kids about: *Don't be like him.*

Within a few years, a ghostwritten autobiography about that other Baltimore boy, Babe Ruth, would begin with the words, "I was a bad kid." The same could have been written about Richard Whittemore. He might not have been bad from birth, but before he was out of short pants he was well on his way.

When Richard was a young boy, he attended an oyster supper with his family at the Methodist church where his mother sang in the choir. He came home with his belly full and his pockets bulging with eight silver spoons and three delicate glass cups, which he probably hoped to sell on the street for a few coins. His parents discovered the items in his room and returned them, apologizing for their son and explaining it away as a prank, but the pattern of his life was set: he took what he wanted.

At school in West Baltimore, Richard was an indifferent student, later writing that he excelled only at arithmetic. "In the other studies I was only fair," he said. "So I can say I was not a dummy or a brilliant scholar." Otherwise, he claimed, he "only did what was expected from a boy in this age . . . hook school and fight and annoy the neighbors and storekeepers," the kid you didn't want living next door. Margaret attended the same school.

She was a few years younger, but the two were smitten with each other from the start, grammar school sweethearts playing at puppy love. Her parents worried every time they saw them together.

The two families never lived more than a few blocks apart. They both moved from one row house to another as family fortunes ebbed and flowed. The Messlers lived on Presbury Street, North Gilmor, and West Mount, and the Whittemores on North Monroe and North Fulton, each family apparently keeping a buffer between themselves and Sandtown.

At least once, Margaret's family moved simply to put a precious few more yards between her and Richard, but it was pointless, particularly when her father died before Margaret was out of grammar school. After that, she followed Richard around like a puppy as he hung out in poolrooms where no respectable girl was supposed to go and no young boy should have.

Richard was about ten when he was first brought before a judge, charged with firing a gun within the city limits. He received a warning and was told to pay a $2 fine and court costs. Rawlings felt that his son shouldn't have been hauled before a judge at all—the Whittemores simply weren't that kind of people. But the judge didn't like Richard's looks, or his attitude. Before sending him on his way, he tried to scare the boy, delivering a stern warning that if he didn't change his ways he'd end up in reform school or jail, or perhaps even pay with his life. It was, Whittemore later admitted wryly, "a very accurate prediction."

Over the next five or six years, he would bounce around the Baltimore juvenile justice system like a rubber ball. He started out as a truant. By the time the system was done with him, he was a criminal.

School could not contain Richard Whittemore. He would skip, get caught, then skip again, regardless of what anyone said or did. Exasperated school officials sent him to Baltimore's Parental School to live full-time in a dormitory in a converted mansion. Of the eighty thousand students enrolled in Baltimore's public schools, only twenty-five were deemed trouble enough to live there. He was warned that if he ran away, his next stop would likely be reform school, the Maryland School for Boys. He bolted, was charged with truancy, and was given parole.

Whittemore never reported to his parole officer, and when his father tried to excuse him again—saying, "What! A boy his age report to you? I will not allow it!" as if his son were immune to the law—the court disagreed. The next time Richard Whittemore was brought before the judge, he was sentenced to the Maryland School for Boys.

The facility opened as the House of Refuge in 1850, the first state facility built in Maryland for the sole purpose of housing juvenile offenders. It was inspired by the same reform spirit that resulted in the Colored Girls' House of Refuge once overseen by Whittemore's grandmother, and the very institution where Whittemore's grandfather had once taught music and directed the band.

It was a tough place. Reform may have been the school's original charge, but over time it became ever more punitive, more jail than school, a dumping ground for boys no one else could straighten out. The rules were beyond strict: playing hooky, breaking curfew, or simply acting out could get a boy labeled as incorrigible and out of control. Many hadn't even misbehaved at all but were originally put away for being a "minor without proper care and guardianship," either remanded by the courts or given up by their own families. Others were the victims of abuse at home, mentally ill or deficient, boys considered too stupid to learn or too crazy to manage, or boys who were simply too bored.

It didn't matter. State law said children had to attend school till age sixteen, so the miscreants were all warehoused together at the School for Boys, out of sight and out of mind, tossed in with those who had committed more serious infractions, such as burglary, assault, and robbery. Once inside, they were subjected to much the same treatment and restraints as adult criminal offenders, under the misguided belief that they could be force-fed discipline. That was a recipe for failure.

The results were predictable—most kids came out worse than when they went in. After a 1908 riot during which the superintendent of the school was knocked to the ground and kicked half senseless, the House of Refuge had been renamed the Maryland School for Boys and moved from Frederick Street to more spacious quarters on a hilltop about ten miles north of downtown Baltimore in Loch Raven.

It was an idyllic location for what was, for many, the beginning of a horrific experience. New buildings and a new name changed nothing for the two hundred boys between the ages of five and twenty confined there. The methods of control remained the same, but now there were no passersby to notice.

From the outside, though, everything looked swell. The boys lived in what the school called "cottages," multistory buildings with a dormitory and classrooms. The boys earned their keep laboring in the machine shop, woodworking, printing, tailoring, or on the 360-acre farm. Their days were broken up only by the school band, sports teams, and a handful of other activities. Boys were supposed to reflect on their behavior through enforced discipline. The "silent system" made even whispering to another kid forbidden. The staff doled out corporal punishment like porridge, delivered by paddle. Problem boys were handcuffed and sent to solitary confinement.

In theory, if a student maintained his grades and didn't act up, he earned special privileges, got his sentence reduced, or was released. The odds were against that, though, and it didn't happen very often. The only other options were suffering or escape. Differences in age and criminality led to abuse. Older, more violent students preyed on the young and weak. If a boy ratted out his tormenter, he was certain to face retribution. Most took it in silence.

Only fear kept them there. Although the doors were locked and guards constantly stood watch, no fence surrounded the property, and most windows lacked bars.

Institutional violations often trumped the circumstances that had led to their incarceration. Boys could be sentenced for six months for a minor offense and end up serving years. Even those committed by their parents owing to some unfortunate family circumstance would not be released when their parents requested it if they had broken the rules. Escapees were beaten upon their return, followed by weeks of solitary confinement.

It was a great place to turn adolescent Richard Whittemore into a real crook. During his first month, he escaped with another boy one evening after attending chapel. They wandered all night through the dark woods surrounding Loch Raven before coming upon a set of railroad tracks. They hopped a freight train, then jumped off the next day in Georgetown, Delaware, too hungry to go on. There they broke into a store, swapped their school uniforms for plain clothes, and lifted several hundred dollars from the till, Whittemore's first serious crime. They walked all night, trying to get as far away as possible, only to be captured the next day by a posse of local farmers. Arrested and sent back to Loch Raven, Whittemore was kept in a cell by himself for the next month, and Superintendent Alfred Upham beat his backside raw with a leather paddle.

Whittemore never spoke in much detail about the School for Boys except to declare his time there left him "brutalized, criminalized and hardened," words learned not from a book but from experience. He remembered it as "my first meeting with a large crowd of boys of the underworld . . . where I learned to break locks and other petty larceny things." Had they passed out grades for these skills, Whittemore would have been a straight-A student.

Between bouts of confinement at Lock Raven, Whittemore also spent time, like that other bad boy Babe Ruth, at Baltimore's St. Mary's Industrial School for Boys, the Catholic institution operated by the Xaverian Brothers. Ruth's scant recollections of the details of his stay at St. Mary's lack the treacly nostalgia his biographers have draped over his experiences there. "I was always hungry," he remembered. Whittemore's own memories of his time there were likely no better. He never mentioned his time at St. Mary's, and any records of his time there were destroyed by a fire in 1919 that raced through the institution.

No wonder that after being beaten by Upham, Whittemore and his pal escaped from Loch Raven once again, this time making it back to Baltimore. Whittemore showed his father his bruises and welts and begged him not to be sent back.

Henry Raynor, a newspaper reporter convicted of larceny, later served time with Whittemore. After Raynor's release, he wrote several stories about his fellow inmate. Loch Raven, he claimed, turned Whittemore into "a wild, uncontrollable hot-tempered young whelp, as much of a crook as he was known to be later." When he snuck back home, Whittemore treated his parents with utter disdain—except when he needed something. Once, in a fit of rage, he grabbed a butcher knife and took a swipe at his mother's hand "with such force that had she not snatched it away the blow would have cut it off."

After his son's latest escape, Rawlings Whittemore knew that if Richard was caught, he'd be shipped back to Loch Raven. But he didn't want him at home either. He peeled a few dollars from his wallet and sent Richard and his young friend away. They rented a room in Wilmington, Delaware, where they worked for a few months in a silk mill. When a former classmate, out on parole, recognized them and squealed, the two were returned to Loch Raven and received the accustomed punishment.

Without Whittemore around, or at least not around very often, Margaret appears to have behaved herself. Unlike Richard, she apparently had no run-ins with juvenile or school authorities, although at one point her family reportedly enrolled her in Catholic school to give the nuns a crack at her. Her family was relieved when Richard was sent to Loch Raven, but worried that Whittemore would return and never knew from one day to the next if he'd show up in the neighborhood and let Margaret tag along. Every time Whittemore returned to the neighborhood she found him a little more attractive. And each time he came back he was a little older, a little better-looking, a little tougher, and a little harder—the classic bad boy.

Whittemore's father contacted the school in October 1916 and told them Richard's mother was on her deathbed. Richard was allowed to visit her for an hour, under guard, wearing handcuffs. Afterwards, Edna begged her husband to "help him to get released from that place."

She died the next day from tuberculosis. Whittemore attended her funeral under escort.

Edna's uncle, Richard Grady, the Navy dentist, tried to intercede. Mortified that Richard was sullying the family name, he offered to pay his tuition at a prep school and told Richard that if he kept his nose clean, he could have him appointed to the Naval Academy in Annapolis.

But Whittemore was no longer under his parents' control. After his many escapes and the robbery, the state of Maryland had taken over guardianship. Unless the state released him or he was sentenced to the Maryland State Penitentiary or the Maryland House of Correction for a more serious crime, he was theirs until age twenty-one.

At this point, Richard Whittemore was no criminal, not really. But after years of incarceration and cruel and sometimes barbaric treatment, while under the care of the state, Richard had gradually hardened.

Only for someone like him could a world war be counted as a lucky break.

W hen the United States entered the Great War on April 6, 1917, its military was still a horse-and-buggy operation, using weapons that dated back to the Spanish-American War. Upon the declaration of war, when fewer than 100,000 men enlisted, a draft was instituted for recruits between the ages of twenty-one and thirty-one. Enlistees, however, only needed to be eighteen years old.

The Maryland School for Boys began allowing boys who were old enough to join up. But all over America, some younger, underage boys with an enlarged sense of adventure or patriotism often found a way to join up too, either by forgery, by having a parent vouch for their age, or by simply lying to recruiters who were eager to meet a quota and look the other way. Although he was only sixteen years old, Whittemore begged to be allowed to enlist. With Rawlings's consent, he went to a recruiting station shortly after the start of the war and tried to join the Navy. But when the military doctor learned that Whittemore's mother had died of tuberculosis, he rejected the potential recruit, citing "palpitation of the heart." Whittemore thought the school had tipped off the doctor and sabotaged him. Undeterred, a week later Whittemore ran away and went straight back to the recruiting station. The doctor, recognizing Richard, left the examination room to turn him in, but Whittemore jumped out the window and ran down the street, free again.

He'd never return to the Maryland School for Boys.

While on the run, he found a more cooperative doctor and, in March 1918, enlisted in the Coast Guard.

Military service seemed to agree with Whittemore—at first. After reform school, he was used to people telling him what to do. As an ordinary seaman (OS), Whittemore was stuck with scaling, sweeping, and buffing the deck, loading and securing cargo, and other mind-numbing labor. He would soon demonstrate that he wasn't satisfied being a swab and taking orders.

Assigned to an ammunition barge, he was accused of larceny when some cash and liberty bonds came up missing. Sent to New York to await a general court-martial, he talked a guard into letting him out of the brig. He planned on visiting his uncle in Annapolis, hoping he'd pull some strings, but was arrested for desertion. Although he was eventually acquitted on the larceny charge, desertion earned him two years at the Navy prison in Portsmouth, New Hampshire, a term later reduced to only eight months.

Whittemore's spiral didn't end there. Soon after his release, he fought with an officer. Facing another court-martial, Whittemore once again used his powers of persuasion and talked a guard at the brig into deserting with him. They went AWOL, landing in Yonkers, New York. Along with another man, they stole a car and broke into a house. One of Whittemore's two companions was picked up on suspicion and squealed. Arrested at a boardinghouse in possession of a suitcase full of stolen goods, Whittemore was tried and convicted for burglary. Now he faced one to ten years at New York's Elmira Reformatory and the end of his military service with a dishonorable discharge. His criminal résumé was growing longer, and his criminal mindset solidifying.

Despite its name, by the time Whittemore entered Elmira, little of the reform spirit remained. This was no school for boys, but a place where already
hardened criminals became even harder.

From the start, the American penal system has been driven by the contradictory impulses of punishment and reform. The so-called Pennsylvania System emphasized solitary confinement under the belief that reformation could
only be achieved through penitence, a long period of enforced self-reflection.
Prisoners were confined alone under harsh conditions, given little to do, and
expected to realize the errors of their ways. Apart from prison staff and the
rare visitor, prisoners were allowed neither to speak nor to interact with one
another, as it was widely believed that criminal behavior was learned from interaction with other criminals.

In practice, this led to barbaric treatment, both physically and psycholog-
ically. The Elmira System, when it was first established with the opening of
the Elmira Reformatory for young felons in 1876, had represented a break with
tradition. The facility's goal was not punishment through enforced silence, the
lash, and labor, but reform through psychology, rewards, and military discipline. Considered salvageable, Elmira inmates were supposed to receive in-
dividualized treatment that emphasized vocational training and moral and
spiritual guidance. Prisoners were classified according to their behavior, and
with all sentences of five years or less considered indeterminate, the inmates
could earn parole through good behavior and demonstrations of progress in
their personal development. Conceptually, the Elmira System appeared to be
a significant step forward.

Yet, as in many other penal systems, reality was something else entirely.
Only a few years after the reformatory opened, prisoners were routinely
abused. They were shackled to walls as punishment, made to work obscene
hours, kept in solitary confinement, fed only bread and water, and subjected
to all manner of cruelty by guards and other inmates alike. These included, as
the *New York Sun* reported in 1894, "the vilest forms of sexual perversions, the
extent of which was appalling." An 1893 investigation found inmates beaten
into unconsciousness, emerging with blackened eyes, broken teeth, and broken
noses. They were strung up by the arms and lifted off the floor, even paddled

to death. The director himself was charged with punching prisoners in the face and kicking them in the stomach.

By the time Richard Whittemore entered Elmira, conditions had barely improved. Whittemore called Elmira a "school of crime" where he learned "how to beat the law ... a very strict place and they did not care if they killed you or not when you broke any of their rules." He worked in the blacksmith shop, learning a trade that was rapidly becoming obsolete, and earned an additional six-month sentence when a shipment of hacksaw blades turned up missing.

Elmira exposed Whittemore to older career criminals, hard guys schooled in New York City street gangs who knew how to break every law there was and were adept at using muscle and guns to get what they wanted. By the time he finally earned his release, with contacts throughout the criminal underworld, he was better connected in that realm than an Ivy League graduate in finance and politics.

Foremost among these contacts was Anthony Paladino. A tough-talking Italian thug, Paladino immigrated to New York with his parents in 1897 when he was only sixteen months old. He started stealing and robbing while working the docks in New York as a longshoreman and shipping clerk, then dabbled in opium before being arrested for burglary and grand larceny and being sent to Elmira.

Paladino called himself "Tony Palace," a name that said it all. He was slick, wise to the ways of the street, and, like Richard Whittemore, eager to leave the world of dead-end jobs behind. They would meet again on the outside.

After Whittemore's release from Elmira in 1921, he found himself back in Baltimore, running down the same empty alleys he had roamed as a young boy. Under the terms of his New York parole, he needed to get a job and stay employed for two years before being fully free. But in 1921 in Baltimore, getting any job, much less staying employed for two years, was almost impossible.

He'd been gone a long time. Soon after his release, he later claimed, he met a far more grown-up Margaret in a cabaret. Their youthful infatuation became a full-blown love affair. She promised to love him forever.

For richer or poorer, for better or for worse. Until death—or prison— pulled them apart.

. . .

After the Rosenbergs returned home and discovered the break-in, they noticed that a ring was missing. The police fanned out over the neighborhood. They knew the thieves could turn it into cash quickly.

Following the crime, Whittemore and Eskowitz walked a few blocks to a saloon owned by Thomas McGuigan, who operated more or less openly on North Calhoun Street, selling liquor both by the glass and, if you knew how to ask, in bulk. Earlier that year, in fact, a man had called the police after he felt he'd been overcharged for a case of whiskey. In Baltimore, Prohibition hardly prohibited anything; if you'd been cheated trying to buy liquor, you felt like it was okay to complain to the cops.

When the two regulars asked McGuigan if they could stash a suitcase in a back room, he had to figure they weren't waiting for a train.

The cops canvassed pawn shops and secondhand stores in the neighborhood. They learned that only a few hours after the burglary Whittemore and Eskowitz had tried to pawn the ring. Now the cops were certain of their suspects.

A little more asking around led them to the rooming house on West Fayette Street where Whittemore lived with Margaret. They knocked on the door, and he answered. Just over a week after the wedding, the honeymoon was officially over.

Hauled to the station house, Whittemore copped, likely hoping the judge would go easy on him. After all, he was already on parole from Elmira. He told them about the suitcase at the saloon and said that Eskowitz had the rest of the jewelry. The police rounded up Eskowitz at his home on Baker Street, then found the suitcase in the saloon. It had barely taken twenty-four hours to crack the case.

Both men were tossed in the city jail.

Neither had money for bail. Charged with burglary, they were quickly arraigned and sent before a judge. Eskowitz got off easy. He had been in trouble before, but this was his first adult arrest. The judge sentenced him to a one-year term in the city jail.

Whittemore wasn't as lucky. His court-martial didn't help, and being busted also violated his New York parole. If Maryland chose to let him go, New York wanted him back to finish his term there. But he'd first have to serve a sentence of one to ten years in the Maryland State Penitentiary. For a young man who had already made the decision "to cause the coppers all the trouble I could," the Maryland State Penitentiary would prove to be the best place in the world to add to his growing ability to do exactly that.

One week into married life with Richard, Margaret moved back home with her mother. For the new bride, that was its own kind of sentence.

Three

EASY MEAT

I t was a short trip from the courthouse to the Maryland State Penitentiary, a gaggle of buildings on Forrest Street scattered over the fifteen-acre site like dice thrown up against a wall. The inner grounds were confined by two cellblocks and granite walls several feet thick and twenty-five feet high, topped by guard towers and a catwalk and patrolled by sentries carrying machine guns.

The wall served two purposes. It kept the men inside from getting out, but just as importantly, it kept people outside the prison from seeing what went on inside. The flower beds fronting the street were purely decorative.

Opened in 1811, the penitentiary was what the state called "a monument to its humanity and wisdom." No one who ever entered it, as either an inmate or employee, would have agreed, and no amount of improvements over the years had made much of a material difference. Many buildings dated back nearly one hundred years and had been repurposed into prison work factories and for other uses. A new Romanesque Revival central administration building, on the corner of Eager and Forrest Streets, fronted by the warden's house, served as the fulcrum for the two huge cellblocks that extended in both directions. Guards could see all five tiers at once from a central location.

Located just east of the new Jones Fallsway, the highway built atop the Jones

Falls waterway, and adjacent to the Baltimore City Jail, the Maryland State Penitentiary that Richard Whittemore entered in 1921 was a human stockyard. Nearly eight hundred men, almost 60 percent Black, were herded into crude dormitories and cells segregated by race, worked nearly to death, and spit out at the end of their sentences like offal from a slaughterhouse . . . if they survived.

Upon his arrival and after being checked in, Whittemore was sent for a haircut and shave before being issued his prison clothes. Like Whittemore, the prison barber, Harry Howard, was a graduate of the school of crime that was the Maryland School for Boys. They had done time together, both had been beaten, and both had begged to be returned home after escaping.

To the older prisoners, the so-called oldheads, Whittemore was a "hopper," a fresh young guy, but he didn't stay that way. From his earlier incarcerations, he knew what awaited him inside, and he was familiar with standard jailhouse procedures and prison lingo, a mishmash of slang that allowed the inmates to speak to each other without the guards always knowing exactly what they were saying or what they meant. He fit right in.

Before stripping down and being issued standard prison garb, a gray shirt and a pair of thin, greasy trousers, a guard, with some contempt, told him, "Keep your underwear and shoes."

That was something new, one of the many reforms instituted over the last few years by the warden, Colonel Thomas Sweezey, a West Point grad and veteran of both the Spanish-American War and the Great War. His celebrated appointment had come on the heels of a near-riot and the revelation that a "blackjack squad" of guards took systematic, sadistic pleasure in beating inmates. The State Board of Prison Control, following calls for reform, introduced a new set of rules that promised more humane treatment of prisoners. It was left up to Sweezey, who believed, as the *Sun* noted, that prisons should "not be a place of punishment but a place to make over a criminal and turn him back as a man fit to take his place in the outside world," to put those reforms in place.

Sweezey took charge of the facility in 1920, promising to put his military experience into practice, by "dealing" with the men, rather than "handling them." In a speech to inmates after his appointment, he said, "I'm going to give you fellows a 'square deal' and I expect every one of you to give me a square deal." The cheers of the inmates nearly tore the roof off the place. On his first day,

Sweezey announced that, taking a page from the Reformatory philosophy, he intended to classify prisoners according to behavior. The most compliant and best behaved would be allowed to attend what he called the "Sweezey Club," a sort of group rec room for those who followed the rules. There, for a few hours after dinner and before lights out, inmates would be allowed to gather together, play checkers and cards, talk, even watch movies and listen to music on a gramophone. He also started a prison baseball team and held weekly boxing matches between inmates. Prisoners were assessed a charge of twenty-five cents a week for the privilege of joining the club and were even issued special Sweezey Club pins, as if they were being rushed into a fraternity. Sweezey allowed prisoners to wear regular working clothes rather than striped shirts, citing its impact on morale, and he opposed the death penalty.

The reforms were popular with inmates, but rankled most of the older guards. As Raynor reported, they were "imbued with the belief that a convict must be despised and nagged and humiliated," and they considered the reforms "mushy sentimentality."

So did many outside the prison. The acerbic H. L. Mencken of the *Baltimore Sun,* one of the most influential journalists in America, derided the club, writing: "To elect a man to the Sweezey Club for robbery and murder is fundamentally as idiotic as to elect him to the Maryland Club for piracy on the high seas." Mencken preferred the English notion of penology. In England, he noted, "they never elect a man to a club for robbery or murder. They hang him."

Sweezey soon realized that the guards, barely better behaved than the prisoners themselves, were the greatest impediment to his reforms. It was a job no one wanted, with a salary of only $1,500 a year (minimum wage today), and far less than most factory workers earned. But as civil service workers, once hired, guards were almost impossible to fire. As a result, many guards still did things the old way, with brute force.

Whittemore was assigned to a cell about the size of a closet, lit by a bare electric light, and containing a toilet, sink, and metal bed frame covered by a thin mattress, a sheet, and a blanket. It was freezing in winter and sweltering in the summer, as guards used ventilation and heat as yet another way to wield their power over the men. Neither the blanket on Whittemore's bed nor the mattress was likely to have been changed or even cleaned for years. In fact, the bedding was so poor that prisoners fought over the old straw mattresses still in use that dated back to 1811. They were a little thicker. Bedbugs ruled the night and left most prisoners covered with welts.

Most imprisoned men worked under what was known as the contract system, whereby either the state or private contractors employed inmates in prison shops, coughing up a dollar or so a day per man to the prison. Generally less than one-quarter of that amount went into the inmate's personal account, which they could save, squander at the prison commissary, send to their families, or pay out in tribute to guards or in protection money to other convicts. In theory, an inmate could earn as much as a couple hundred dollars a year and at the end of their sentence have enough to support themselves for a few months —or to go on a bender. The state depended on the system to underwrite all operating costs apart from capital improvements. Otherwise, the penitentiary was entirely self-supporting and cost taxpayers nothing.

In many ways the contract system was little better than slave labor, as foremen, guards, and trusties had almost free rein to overwork or abuse the prisoners. Foundry workers, for example, weren't given gloves for protection as they forged cast-iron and enamel cookware, and they often suffered burns and wounds that reached to the bone.

On Whittemore's second day, Deputy Warden Patrick Brady sized him up and sent him to the pants shop. He'd start at the bottom, unloading and sorting bundles of cloth to be sewn into clothing by more experienced workers.

Whittemore started out with a swagger, yelling out to the others in the shipping room, "Where's the guy who handles the piece goods? I want three bales of this number," as he handed the order slip to another prisoner. When the man hesitated, Whittemore jumped down his throat, barking, "I want it right now —I'm not going to hang around here!"

He was serving notice: Richard Reese Whittemore wasn't a guy to be messed with.

That got the attention of the prisoner trusties who ran the shop—surly, wizened Jacob Kraemer, thirty-eight, and his brother (although the two denied it), jowl-faced Leon, twenty-nine, who at the time was going by the name of Leon Miller and was only slightly less surly than his older brother.

Older, wiser, harder, and sharper, Jake was the dominant brother, and Leon his toady; the lisping younger brother did as he was told, when he was told, almost acting as his older brother's enforcer. Jake had the brains and the experience, while Leon supplied the blind devotion his brother craved. Whatever Jake said went; Leon confirmed and agreed with every word he uttered. Together, the brothers were a formidable pair in the Darwinian nightmare of penitentiary life, where an innocent slight or a raised eyebrow could get you killed.

Nearly one hundred years later, the Kraemer brothers' full story remains murky, as do their true identities and the full details of their life before coming to the United States. At various times in various places, they chose to be whoever they wanted to be, chameleons able to adapt to almost any situation, blend in with the crowd, and seamlessly move between several different ethnic groups and social strata.

Depending on the circumstances, they used the surnames Kraemer, Kramer, Borg, Kalleheztein, Miller, Lis, Liss, and List. But their motivations never varied. They acted as one and kept each other company their entire adult lives, thieving and robbing together, sharing the proceeds, even living in the same apartments, hotels . . . and prisons. The Kraemers were dedicated only to each other and to their own collective enrichment. They were utterly unconcerned about anyone else, apart from the degree to which a relationship might benefit them. Had it not been for the Kraemers, Richard Reese Whittemore might have remained as obscure as any of the other inmates, and Tiger Girl and the Candy Kid might never have captured the imagination of a nation. Then again, if not for the Whittemores, the Kraemers too might have remained obscure.

They were different from the other inmates, smarter and more cunning. Jake in particular stood out. Henry Raynor described him as "bull-headed, self-opinionated, domineering . . . convinced that he was superior to the rest of the inmates in all respects . . . the meanest and slickest crook that ever served time in that place." But the brothers were smart enough either to follow the rules or, when they didn't, to make sure that they paid someone to look the other way. After first entering the prison in 1916, they had worked their way up in the system and were now entrusted with running the pants shop, a task that rewarded them for their organizational acumen.

Sometime during his various incarcerations, Whittemore had become a pretty good baseball player and amateur boxer. Shortly after he started his sentence, he made the baseball team and took turns in the boxing ring at the Sweezey Club. He got tight with two other prisoners in the pants shop, Joe Dietz and Julius Schaefer, common thugs who also boxed and played a little ball.

The Kraemers soon took notice of the three but were particularly taken with Whittemore. He seemed to take the same disdainful attitude toward most other prisoners as the Kraemers did. He still saw himself as a Whittemore, as not like everybody else. Raynor later noted, "He was easy meat for the older crook. Just what Jake needed and ready for the picking."

The more the Kraemers saw of Whittemore, the more they liked him, or at least liked what they thought he could do for them. As Raynor noted, "Whittemore was just the man for Kraemer's plans. For Kraemer, though crafty, selfish, greedy, was a coward. Whittemore though, was a fighter, utterly cruel, utterly fearless, without mercy or honor."

It was the beginning of what would be a cruelly beautiful relationship.

B efore the Kraemer brothers came to Baltimore and eventually found themselves imprisoned in the Maryland State Penitentiary, they were already legends. Natives of Kielce, in what was then known as the Kingdom of Poland or Russian Poland, Jacob was born in 1883 and Leon in 1892. As young men, the Jewish brothers—or half-brothers, according to some accounts— first made their way to Germany and then Belgium before landing in England in 1915. Along the way, they became familiar with the Jewish-dominated gem and jewelry trade and learned several languages in addition to their native Polish, including Yiddish, German, Russian, English, and French. They learned to fit in without standing out, leaving little tangible trace of their presence in the world and using their Jewish identity to gain trust in a community suspicious of outsiders.

In London, they posed as antique dealers and opened a small business, peddling old furniture, statuary, and the odd piece of jewelry. Using the shop as a front, they haunted Hatton Garden, London's diamond district. As they cased the neighborhood and everyone in it, getting to know who was whom among jewelry dealers and, most importantly, who had what kind of merchandise, they were laying the groundwork for their real goal: burglary.

Their approach was simple. Upon entering a shop, one brother, usually Jake, would engage the shopkeeper while Leon took note of the interior layout, the number of employees, the security measures, and potential entry points. They'd sometimes make several trips to gain more information on inventory, delivery times, and, most importantly, the location of the safe.

That's what they were after, the safe. Sometime before reaching England, the Kraemers had figured out a new way to crack a safe. Most safes were sheathed with heavy cast-iron over a layer of cement, for fireproofing and the bulk and strength it provided. An inner steel chamber, accessed by the safe door, held the valuables.

Before the Kraemers, safecrackers used two methods. The lock could be either picked or laboriously drilled out, a task that took a great deal of expertise and practice. Most thieves weren't so skilled, or patient. The second approach used brute force to blow the safe open with either nitroglycerin or its more stable cousin, dynamite. That was effective but also dangerous. Explosions drew unwanted attention and, as often as not, destroyed or damaged the contents.

The Kraemers devised their own method. They applied Archimedes's law of the lever to invent what became known as "the can opener," a tool similar to a long iron crowbar with one significant difference: one end featured a sharpened forked tip of hardened tempered steel. The Kraemers used a brace to drill a hole just large enough to insert the tip of the tool in the back of the safe. Then, using the leverage provided by its length, the can opener "peeled" open the safe, cutting through cast-iron like a tin can, hence the name.

They then simply broke up the brittle cement with a hammer and cut through the thinner interior walls. That still took some time, but the method was relatively quiet, quick, effective, and wholly original. That would prove to be their downfall, as for a time the brothers may have been the only safecrackers in the world using the method. They might as well have signed their names to each job.

After a series of robberies soon after their arrival in London, all bearing the same unmistakable signature, Scotland Yard came to realize that master criminals were at work. Basic gumshoe detective work eventually led them to the Kraemers' little shop on Tottenham Court Road.

When confronted by police, getting either brother to talk was harder than cracking a safe. They even refused to provide their real names or admit to being related. The brothers didn't keep their safecracking tools on hand and often abandoned the easily replaced tools on site. Meanwhile, the stolen gems were long since gone. Unable to make a case against them, Scotland Yard rid themselves of a nuisance by having the Kraemers deported as "undesirables."

En route to Russia, they escaped custody in Sweden and went from there to America, likely arriving in late 1915, not as poor immigrants hoping to build new lives, but as master criminals virtually unknown to law enforcement. America was as unprepared for them as it would later be for the Spanish flu.

They settled in New York and used the city as home base, committing crimes elsewhere. They operated with impunity at first, peeling safe after safe. They accumulated wads of untraceable cash and stashed their gains in safety deposit boxes or invested in real estate while living in what the press later described as a "fashionable residence district" in New York. The Kraemers were professionals. Their only vices were fine clothing, which enabled them to blend in at the better hotels and neighborhoods, high-stakes gambling, which they were skilled at, and women.

But in Detroit in February 1916, after relieving a safe of jewelry worth $15,000, police finally caught up with the Kraemers.

Once again, there was no hard evidence, and the Kraemers said nothing. A receipt to a safety deposit box at a New York bank led police to a stash of cash and bonds, but no gems, and in the brothers' New York apartment they found only "dozens of suits of every description, from riding and hunting outfits to immaculate evening and dinner dress." One Detroit detective reported that the Kraemers were "craftier and more polished than any other men I have dealt with."

The Kraemers hired a high-priced local attorney and beat the case owing to lack of evidence. Then it was back to business as usual.

Almost. While in custody, they were photographed and forced to submit to the Bertillon system of identification.

Although fingerprinting was just coming into use, first as a means of identification post-arrest rather than an investigative tool, in 1916 the standard method to identify criminals was the Bertillon system. Developed in 1879 by Alphonse Bertillon, the system consisted of a series of five measurements of the body — head length, head breadth, length of middle finger, length of the left foot, and forearm length — that, in combination, were theoretically unique. Paired with a standard mug shot, another Bertillon innovation, the system allowed police to identify individuals in custody and share that information with Bertillon Bureaus in other jurisdictions, each creating a "Rogues' Gal lery" criminal index. Although the system wasn't entirely accurate, it was close enough, and once in the book, crooks were no longer anonymous. Now the Kraemers, or whoever they really were, were in the book.

That didn't slow them. They relocated to Philadelphia, used their stash to open another shop as a front, and got back to work.

In the fall of 1916, they came to Baltimore. On the evening of Saturday, September 23, the last clerk working at the jewelry firm of Steman & Norwig on North Howard Street locked the front door and went home. Visible through the front window, inset in a wall, was the firm's enormous, three-thousand-pound safe. A gas jet flickered overhead so when a night policeman sauntered by every hour, he could peer in and see if anything was amiss. Over the course of the night, he noticed nothing.

Two days before, the Kraemers had cased the shop. Jake had asked to see a lady's wristwatch and other pricey pieces of jewelry while Leon wandered about acting disinterested. Over the next two days, they did the same in the surrounding neighborhood, timing out the policeman's rounds. They discovered an attorney's office that, although accessed through the adjacent building, was situated directly above the jewelry store's safe. Now they had a plan.

At about midnight on Saturday, the brothers slipped into the building next door carrying a satchel heavy with tools, illuminating their way with electric "flashlamps" — flashlights — a relatively new invention. They then jimmied the door to the attorney's office, pulled a heavy rug off the floor, and tacked it over the window so that no light could escape. Pulling out their tools, they cut an opening in the floor and lowered their tools, then themselves, by rope into the shop, directly behind the safe.

By then, they could taste it. The safe was old, the back encased in only a thin layer of steel. A chisel and a hammer, its head wrapped in leather to deaden the noise, was enough to break through, exposing a plate of cast-iron half an inch thick. A steel bit and brace gave them purchase, and the can opener did the rest.

Next they used the hammer and chisel to dig out the cement, creating an enormous pile of fine dust in the process, before reaching the inner compartment. They then cut two rectangular openings into the chamber, just big enough to extract the trays.

Even in the dim light of the flashlamps, the haul sparkled and glimmered: diamond rings, lavalieres, bracelets, watches, brooches, bejeweled Masonic charms, and other items, many set in platinum, featuring rubies, sapphires, and even a number of loose "first water" diamonds of the highest quality. They dropped anything that looked to them to be worth less than $150 or so in the cement dust as worthless.

Every contingency was covered. After dropping three newspapers on the floor, one from New York and two in Italian, so that police would assume the job had been pulled by Italian gangsters from New York, the Kraemers left the same way they entered.

It had taken several days of planning and several hours of work, but they stepped back out onto the darkened street with at least $15,000 worth of gems and jewels, worth about $350,000 today.

When Harry Norwig discovered the theft the next morning, the *Sun* reported, he found "the back of the safe a big wreck," the floor covered in cement dust, littered with price tags and twenty-five empty wooden trays.

The cops were as stunned as Norwig. They'd seen break-ins before, but nothing like this: a hole cut through the ceiling and the safe slit open like a knife through a bag of flour, and all of it done while a cop peered in the window every hour. One muttered to a reporter that it was one of the best-planned "jobs" he'd seen.

Norwig soon gathered himself and recalled the two men who had been in the store on Thursday. Now, he realized, the one pacing the floor had been eyeing the safe. From their accents, he surmised they were Jewish and foreign-born. He gave police a basic description.

The Bertillon system brought them down, as the two men were identified through photographs. A Baltimore grand jury rendered an indictment, and a judge issued an arrest warrant. Now police had to find them.

A piece of jewelry in a pawn shop in Philadelphia led Baltimore detectives to the Kraemers' home on Ridge Avenue, where they learned that the two brothers were having their baggage shipped to New York. The detectives followed them to the train station, then to New York, and watched them check into the Aberdeen Hotel on West Thirty-Second Street.

After several days of observation, detectives burst into their room, finding the brothers with two women. When the women tried to run, the detectives leveled their pistols as the Kraemers stoically looked on. They arrested all four, charging the brothers with the burglary and the two women with conspiracy.

They were just in time. Inside the trunks, along with clothing, was a can opener, dynamite, and tickets for a steamship bound for Cuba the next morning. Apparently, there were safes in Havana too. One of the women wore two rings from Norwig's.

The four were returned to Baltimore, and the two brothers, as was their custom, clammed up, except to exonerate their companions, who they claimed knew nothing. The cops tried to squeeze the two women, but they mostly kept their mouths closed too. They didn't realize that the cops had already traced the rings to Steman & Norwig.

That was all the prosecution needed. One month later, the brothers went on trial, represented by defense attorney Eugene O'Dunne, one of Baltimore's best, most expensive, and most flamboyant attorneys.

As the *Baltimore Sun* once said of O'Dunne, "When he is good he is very, very good, but when he is bad he is awful." He'd eventually earn a reputation as an attorney who was obsessed with social justice but was equally capable of flaunting the law and running roughshod over the rights of the accused. His intersections with the Kraemers and, eventually, Richard Whittemore would give him the chance to demonstrate all those qualities.

A former state's attorney and husband of the great-grandniece of John Quincy Adams, the well-connected O'Dunne knew the ins and outs of Baltimore's byzantine judicial system well. By hiring him, the Kraemers bet that his knowledge and his connections would set them free. This time, however, after a bitter two-day trial, O'Dunne failed. It was hard to argue against Norwig's identification of the two rings. After they were found guilty, the judge upbraided the brothers for the cost of the investigation, which had tied up detectives for weeks, and sentenced each to ten years in the penitentiary. A few days later, the Pennsylvania Board of Censors banned the showing of any motion pictures that depicted safecrackers at work.

The brothers received the sentence with the same stoicism they had shown since their arrest. Once inside the Maryland State Penitentiary, the brothers acted with the same care they brought to casing a job. They didn't plan to escape, as O'Dunne promised a quick parole, but supported by their intellects and their bank accounts, they made their time there as easy as possible. Incarceration also gave them plenty of time to plan their next move. After a 1920 petition for a pardon from Maryland governor Albert Ritchie was shot down by Baltimore detectives, those plans began to come into focus.

Richard Whittemore would prove to be precisely the hardened steel tip their next move required.

Four

UNUSUAL SACRIFICES

By 1921, the Kraemers had had five years in the can to think about what they'd done wrong and figure out how to get a lot better at being crooked.

They knew they were too well known to continue cracking safes, but had no intention of going straight. So how could they still use their knowledge of the gem trade and the meticulous organizational skills that set them apart and gave them an edge without shouldering all the risks? In order to thrive as criminals on the outside, what they needed were some heavies to help out with the dirty work.

Richard Whittemore was just the kind of impressionable young heavy they needed, someone unafraid of violence. And the Kraemers were just what Whittemore needed—crooks with brains and big ambitions who needed what he could provide.

After getting to know Whittemore, Dietz, and Schaffer in the pants shop, the Kraemers started cultivating the three men. They gave them easy assignments and allowed them to throw their weight around among prisoners who were older and more established. Among the inmates, the brothers were the most Machiavellian, buying small favors with bribes and goods from the commissary that others couldn't afford. It made sense to stay on their good side, otherwise you might be assigned to the foundry or find yourself crushed under a big bolt of cloth in some "accident." When pants went missing and were discovered for sale on the outside, a disappearance undoubtedly organized by the Kraemers, they knew nothing and let other prisoners take the blame, as well as the punishment. No one said anything.

Every night the Kraemers kibitzed in the Sweezey Club with the three young men, all of whom were young, rugged, and eager to make a name for themselves in the criminal underworld. They fell for the "sly whispered accounts," the stories the brothers told of busting into safes full of diamonds and the life that safecracking had allowed them to lead on the outside. Crimes, the Kraemers taught, had to be planned. You had to cover all the angles ahead of time and leave no loose ends. And, oh yeah, they told them, "let the skirts alone." If they hadn't given one of the girls stolen rings from Norwig's, the Kraemers were convinced that O'Dunne could have gotten them off.

Whittemore lapped it up. According to Raynor, Jake showed the younger men that "they were pikers; that with no more risk they could pull jobs which would yield real money." Whittemore began to realize he had been going about a life of crime in all the wrong ways. There was no sense in risking arrest for pennies. The idea was to score and score big, to get in and then get out. The Kraemers knew how to do that.

At the same time, the brothers came under Whittemore's spell too, charmed by the American tough guy from a good family who could talk both tough and sweet, shoot pool and use the right fork, yet knew the ways of the criminal underworld.

To that end, Whittemore, for the very first time in his life of incarceration, behaved. If he kept his nose clean, he'd probably serve only two or three years, and the Kraemers figured they'd get out by then as well.

Whittemore did as he was told, giving the two brothers the fealty he'd never shown his own father, earning their trust. He played what one prisoner described as a "snappy" third base on the baseball team, boxed in the weekly matches held in the Sweezey Club, and earned a reputation as one of the best boxers in the joint—one who, according to Raynor, was "utterly cruel, utterly fearless, without mercy or honor," yet also "prone to hitting below the belt."

Margaret came to visit most weeks, and the two wrote letters back and forth. She was working for the phone company, trying to save some money. She promised that when he got out, she'd be waiting.

Another reason to behave was that his Maryland arrest violated his New York parole and if Richard was released in Maryland, New York expected him to complete his earlier sentence. But if he stayed out of trouble, a letter of recommendation from Warden Sweezey might set him free.

Although conditions inside the jail remained horrific in many ways, his day-to-day life fell into a predictable pattern—work in the shop, eat a few crummy meals, play a ball game every week, spend a couple of hours every night whiling away time and bullshitting in the Sweezey Club, scratch at bedbugs all night, then rinse and repeat. Living each day under the protection of the Kraemers made prison a little more tolerable, and as the pages on the calendar flipped over from 1921 to 1922, then to 1923 and into 1924, he had even more to look forward to as the Kraemers' plans came into sharper focus.

The oldheads could see it coming. As they watched the group huddled together in the Sweezey Club each night, Jake and Leon holding court while Whittemore hung on their every word, one commented to another, "That Polack will make a real crook out of that kid. He's just the sort for a gunman, and Jake'll clean up."

It was time for the Kraemers to pair their greed and brains with Whittemore and his crew's ambition, muscle, and fearlessness.

Easy money. That was the pitch.

As the days passed, what the Kraemers learned of the world outside made that prospect ever more enticing. The brothers had missed the war, Prohibition, the flu epidemic, and the 1920–1921 depression. Not only were Whittemore and an influx of younger prisoners describing the new world outside, but hell, they saw it every week in the movies they showed at the Sweezey Club. There was a lot of money floating around and suckers everywhere. Prohibition was turning a lot of poor guys into rich guys.

The Roaring Twenties had taken off. Those who had money flaunted it, spending big on cars, girls, jewelry and diamonds and furs, and booze and drugs and the nightlife. Bank vaults were full and brimming over, and all the businesses that catered to this newfound wealth—the jewelers and furriers and nightclubs and jazz joints and new car lots—were raking it in by the fistful, especially in Maryland and in Baltimore, where Prohibition was treated as a minor nuisance.

It was an extraordinarily easy time to be a crook. Almost every transaction was made in cash, and there was little coordination between police in different jurisdictions. The reach of the only national police agency, the Bureau of Investigation (today's FBI), founded in 1908, was still limited to the investigation of federal crimes, which didn't even include Prohibition violations; that fell under the jurisdiction of the Department of the Treasury. It wasn't until after J. Edgar Hoover took over as director in 1924 that the Bureau really became an effective investigative body, though it would take several more years before his reforms had a significant impact.

Despite the Bertillon system, determining the true identities of suspects was still a challenge. Fingerprints were only just beginning to be used as an investigative tool. If a criminal wasn't caught committing a crime, or if someone didn't squeal, they were hard to catch. And even when they were caught, the cops and judges and politicians found it easy to accept an envelope or a girl or a case of liquor and look the other way.

Stupid guys, penny ante crooks—those were the ones getting caught and thrown into the pen for robbing a store or jacking a car or smashing a storefront window. The bigger operators, it seemed, never got caught. Organized crime on a large scale was just gaining a foothold in the United States, primarily involved in gambling and vice. Most law enforcement efforts were kept occupied by bootlegging and other crimes directly fed by the liquor trade. That left a lot of opportunity.

It was also an easy time to be a cop and a prosecutor. Suspects didn't have to be informed of their rights, and even if they were aware that they had the right to an attorney, if they didn't have the money to pay for one, tough luck —the main job of public defenders, where available, was to expedite guilty pleas. Confessions were routinely gained by beatings or other acts of coercion, eyewitness identification was still the best evidence, and plenty of guys were willing, especially because of Prohibition, to trade testimony for time off, a bottle of booze, or a fin in their palm. Other evidence was easy to manufacture and just as easy to make disappear, if you knew who to pay. Unless a criminal had plenty of money, it was almost impossible to fight a serious charge. Justice was something bought and paid for.

Whittemore knew more about the changing conditions outside the prison walls than the Kraemers, and the Kraemers knew how to best extract wealth from those who had it. Since peeling safes was out, they came up with another way: using the same kind of meticulous planning, not to crack safes, but to steal cash and jewelry and gems by force. They wouldn't bother much with banks—they were too heavily fortified. As before, the Kraemers planned to use their knowledge of the jewelry and gem business to identify targets. Then they'd spend days, if not weeks, casing each job and plotting the crime with the same care that a novelist brings to outlining a story, or a choreographer choreographing a Broadway dance musical, accounting for every contingency so there would be no surprises.

They needed a gang in which everyone would play a role culminating in a flawless performance. Eventually, the gang was "organized along the lines of a huge corporation . . . the traits which have since appeared in the crimes which startled the country clearly were manifest." Using false identities and stolen cars with swapped plates, they would pretend to be people they were not, spinning wheels of deception and misinformation. The police couldn't catch someone if they didn't know who they were looking for. And when the time came to act, everyone would know exactly what to do and what everyone else was doing —who would drive, who would carry a gun, who would pull the trigger, and who stood on watch.

The Kraemers would run the puppet show while Whittemore and his pals did the heavy work of carrying out the brothers' plans. This time, instead of burglarizing safes with $5,000 or $10,000 worth of gems, they'd only go for big scores worth five or ten times as much, maybe more.

They'd case their targets just as they'd cased jewelry stores—at length and in advance—and identify a trusted fence for the goods even before the crime took place. They'd come together for a job, make a lightning strike, fence the take, then share the proceeds and scatter until the next job. If everyone did exactly as they were told, if the Kraemers picked the right targets, the approach was nearly foolproof, and no one would be the wiser. This time around, the

Kraemers' brains would be the can opener, and Richard Whittemore would brazenly wield the lever by the force of his personality, his easy embrace of violence, and his insatiable appetite for cash.

That was all Whittemore needed to hear. Money meant access to this new world, not just for him, but for Margaret.

Then they could be the people their generation read about and watched in the movies, the swanky swells who waltzed through life and saw the world spread out before them like some fancy banquet. For now, all Richard Whittemore and the Kraemers had to do was keep their noses clean, get out of prison, and then strike.

For the first time in his life, Whittemore's life had a plan, and a purpose.

While her husband scratched the days off the calendar, Margaret Whittemore didn't stay inside and do tatting with her mother. She wasn't a girl anymore, but a young woman, a married woman at that, even if her husband was imprisoned. While Richard and the Kraemers were hearing about what was going on in the world outside the prison walls, Margaret was living it.

Margaret, wrote one observer, had been attracted to Whittemore and men like him "because she liked lively companions" and enjoyed evenings out at the cabarets. Unlike Ginger in *The Flapper*, she didn't have to pretend to be a woman of experience. She already was.

Margaret might have been lonely without her husband, but she was rarely alone and there was plenty for a young woman like her to do. Nightlife beckoned.

Jazz music first began to filter out into the streets of Baltimore around 1917, first by way of player piano rolls and 78 rpm recordings. But with a player piano costing nearly $500 and a Victrola almost $100, the new music was out of reach for most Baltimoreans—except for those who lived in Sandtown, where the new music percolated and would later prove formative in the development of jazz icons such as Cab Calloway, Eubie Blake, and Billie Holiday. Soon enough, though, young Baltimoreans were flocking to places popping up all over town that featured the hot new sound, the new dances, and the freewheeling behavior the music celebrated.

The jazz cabarets inspired an inevitable backlash as the new music and lifestyle were blamed for the rapid erosion of moral values. In 1918, Baltimore's Board of Liquor License Commissioners, having decided that such venues were sources of crime and wrongdoing and that "wine, women and song are to be separated," threatened to ban either the sale of liquor or the attendance of women at any establishment featuring jazz or dancing. Those efforts would prove to be even less effective than stopping liquor poured from bottles or beer drawn from taps.

By the time of Whittemore's imprisonment, diatribes against jazz and the resulting moral decay that the older generation claimed it spawned were nearly a daily staple in Baltimore's newspapers. So too, of course, were ads for flapper outfits (a decent dress cost anywhere from $25 to $100), jazz records, and nightclubs.

Young women like Margaret couldn't afford this lifestyle on their own, but there were plenty of men who could, in exchange for either a dance partner or the chance at another kind of companionship. A more or less straight exchange of sex for a night out was a practice widely known as "treating."

Carlin's Pavilion at Park Circle, a short jaunt from the Fifteenth Ward, was the place where, for a few hours every night, the Jazz Age came to life in Baltimore, where young women could don the clothes of their dreams and adopt the personas of the people they wanted to be. Promotor John Carlin bragged that as many as eight hundred couples could dance to a jazz band on the nearly twelve-thousand-square-foot dance floor every evening but Sunday. Without saying so, he was also offering the chance to neck and pet and load up on liquor in cars on the surrounding streets or under the trees in nearby Druid Hill Park. For a few hours, and for an admission fee of as little as five cents for women and twenty-five cents for men, they could be just who they imagined themselves to be.

For a woman like Margaret, there was another attraction. She didn't necessarily have to keep quiet and act demure and wait for some man to tell her what to do.

Margaret wasn't the only young woman dipping her toes into the nightlife, as underscored one night in the spring of 1923. Mineralava Beauty Clay, one of hundreds and hundreds of beauty products to come on the market to entice the new American woman to spend even more money on her appearance, sponsored a nationwide beauty contest judged by film star Rudolph Valentino. On May 16, the contest came to Baltimore to select a representative of the city to compete in the finale in New York, where the grand prize would be a chance to appear in a Hollywood film.

Valentino, an Italian immigrant who started his career in entertainment as a dancer before turning to films in 1919, was the biggest celebrity in America. Even the mighty Babe Ruth was no match for the screen heartthrob.

Valentino had appeared in *The Four Horsemen of the Apocalypse* in 1921, the first American film to gross $1 million. His smoldering good looks reeked of sex and made women swoon. His big feature, *The Sheik*, solidified his position as the nation's top film star, and with it, "sheik" became part of the Jazz Age lexicon, slang for a man whose appeal was defined by his raw masculine appeal, not his virtue. By the time the contest started that night and Valentino finally appeared, the pavilion was packed, the thousands of flappers in attendance "keyed up like a lot of tightened 'E' strings," squealing and screaming.

Thirty-six flappers decked out in their finest flirty outfits took the stage, selected beforehand by local judges. One of them "competing in the contest" was Margaret.

She tried her best to stand out. One of the few blondes paraded onstage, she wore a beaded Egyptian revival dress that sparkled in the stage lights and caused one onlooker to yell out, "There's King Tut!—that blonde with the bobbed hair!" The contestants were then ushered into Valentino's dressing room, where, after ogling each one, he selected Mildred Adam as Baltimore's most beautiful girl. After making a brief appearance on stage, Valentino scurried off, and "his caravan left Carlin's Park dancing pavilion by a back door, pursued by 5,000 wild women who chased him clear down to his eight-cylinder camel, begging to be kidnapped."

Margaret, only twenty years old, had rolled the dice to take control of her life and reach for what she wanted, grasping at the slenderest of straws, only to fall short. But the moment, and the aspiration, stuck with her. She later would imply that her interaction with Valentino had been something more than a quick meet-and-greet, that she had in fact "helped show him about Baltimore," leaving exactly what she meant by that mostly to the imagination.

Like her husband, as well as many other young women, Margaret was be-

ginning to figure out there were other ways to live outside the home or factory. There was a lot of loose money floating around for the taking by those
who had given up on straight life to cash in on Prohibition, and a lot of men
with money to spend were looking for women like Margaret for a few nights
of fun. In fact, there were suddenly a lot of willing young women everywhere
in America eager to flaunt their newfound sexual freedom and use it to their
advantage. The availability of birth control allowed young people to engage in
sex outside of marriage and also to marry for reasons that didn't lead to diapers
and motherhood. For the first time, women could pursue their desires just as
so many men did. Yet at the same time, their male paramours' expectation of
sex, and the inherent power imbalance, made for some enormous disparities in
relationships. As more and more men were expecting to have sex, more young
women were finding that the price of being allowed to say "yes" also made it
harder to say "no."

For younger, working-class women like Margaret, that freedom went both
ways, and liaisons didn't always mean relationships anymore. The Zelda Fitz-
geralds and Olive Thomases may have been better equipped to make decisions
about their own bodies with less consideration about the consequences than
common flappers like Margaret, but they were all swimming in the same pool,
the men and the women. In the end, everybody involved got a little of what
they wanted: a thrill, a moment of passion and intimacy, a dance partner, a
dinner, a suit of clothes, a night on the town, a gaudy bauble, help with the rent,
or extra money to place in a husband's prison account.

While Richard was imprisoned, Margaret scrambled to survive in this new
world. She made what the Baltimore police euphemistically referred to as "unusual sacrifices in order to keep Whittemore supplied with money in prison"
and to "buy her Dick little luxuries to brighten his prison life." She became an
"artist's model," a term that often had very little to do with art. It was work for
women who were willing to pose nude, or nearly so, and often to do a little
more than that, and sometimes a lot more. While a handful of artist's models
did pose for genuine artists, most were essentially prostitutes. It was a quick
way for a girl to make money and to meet men of means searching for women
of easy virtue under a thin veneer of respectability and in relative safety.

Margaret was looking out for herself, in her own way, as best she could. Both

Whittemores, Margaret no less than Richard, had come to the same conclusion and decided to do whatever they felt was necessary. As one reporter would later note, "The Man she loved was a crook, but 'what of it,' she loves him, is her reason." You had to survive, and it didn't make much sense, for either of them, to ask too many questions about how they went about doing that.

It was probably better not to know the details.

Apart from the occasional scuffle with guards or other prisoners, Whittemore and the Kraemers stayed out of trouble, although the Kraemers, after being turned down for parole time and time again, became ever more frustrated. O'Dunne had taken a lot of their money and made a lot of promises but hadn't come through. Working overtime to ingratiate himself with the powers that be while angling for a judicial appointment, he had abandoned the brothers.

As Whittemore's sentence wound down, he was transferred from the pants shop, probably through the Kraemers' machinations. Thinking ahead, they may well have thought it best to put some distance between themselves and Whittemore. After all, it was looking like he'd leave prison before they did. That was fine. He'd have time to put together a trusted crew and lay the groundwork for their plans.

Whittemore "Yes sir'd" and "No sir'd" his way to a job in the hospital ward, where he worked as an orderly, soft duty given only to the most trustworthy prisoners. He spent most days shuttling prisoners back and forth between the cellblock or prison shops and the hospital, usually unsupervised, having gained the trust of the warden and guards. He'd earned good time and by the spring of 1924 seemed likely to be paroled on the Rosenberg burglary.

There was still the matter, however, of his New York parole violation. Shortly before his parole hearing, Rawlings Whittemore requested a meeting with Sweezey in the warden's office. Sweezey was accustomed to hearing sob stories, and Rawlings Whittemore gave him one, explaining away his son's long record as a combination of bad luck, bad choices, and bad influences. He argued that his boy didn't deserve more time and begged Sweezey to write to

New York and request that they release Whittemore from the remainder of his sentence. Rawlings believed his son deserved a fresh start.

Sweezey pondered the request for a moment. The Whittemore name still meant something, and he had been getting a lot of grief in the newspapers lately owing to a few recent escapes that his own disgruntled staff blamed on the warden's reforms. Six prisoners had recently slipped away from the Sweezey Club through an unguarded door, broken a padlock on a barred window, and made their way to the roof of the administration building and then to freedom through the warden's house. Sweezey was in Washington at the time, helping in the search for his trusty chauffeur, who had simply walked away after driving the warden to an appointment outside the prison. Then, early in 1924, the notorious bandit Jack Hart, who killed a man during a payroll robbery, and another prisoner had escaped after prying the bars apart on a window, a task undertaken while cooperative guards looked the other way and supplied him with a key to the gate.

Sweezey needed all the success stories he could muster, and he couldn't help liking Richard, who, for all his faults, could still pull off what one called a "suave, courteous manner." The warden hoped to count him as one of the triumphs of his tenure, a tough kid who'd played by the rules and now looked to make good. With his background, and his name, that would make a story.

Sweezey wrote the letter, and New York agreed to release its claim on Whittemore. They had their hands full with the fallout from Prohibition and needed room in New York prisons for the growing number of bootleggers and gangsters now shooting it out on the streets. Maryland could have Whittemore. He was their problem now, not New York's.

In April 1924, Richard Whittemore shook Sweezey's hand and walked out of the Maryland State Penitentiary after thirty months of imprisonment and breathed the sweet air of the outside world.

Margaret was waiting on the steps outside the main gate. He fell into her arms. Unless she chose to, she'd never have to kiss another man again.

Five

———————

TIGER GIRL

here was a new dance craze.

First featured in the musical *Liza* in the spring of 1923, the Charleston gained its name from a song of the same name in another musical production, *Runnin' Wild,* which debuted later that fall. The dance, which made the hips sway, the knees separate, and the breasts heave, swept the country and before long was blamed not only for its corrosive effect on morals but even as a physical danger. When Evelyn Turner, a dancer at a downtown Baltimore hotel roof garden, died after a night of frantic dancing, her demise was blamed on nervous and physical exhaustion brought on by the frenzied dance. Such sensationalized stories soon became a staple of Baltimore's daily press.

The excesses of the era were made for the tabloids, which provided news for the masses and found a steady readership reporting on fads like flagpole sitting, dance marathons, the swallowing of goldfish, and other attention-grabbing feats. And that was the point. If you couldn't be a movie star and gain fame that way, well, you might make the newspapers and bump the president or the latest strike from the front page by doing something crazy. That was almost as good.

Featuring oversized photographs, cartoon serials, and other graphics, the papers were meant to be picked up for a penny or two, read during the morning commute or during lunch at the plant, then brought home to wrap fish or used to light the stove. Utterly disposable, the tabloids provided little more than a quick thrill.

The first American tabloid, the *Illustrated Daily News,* debuted in New York in 1919. Renamed the *New York Daily News,* it soon spawned a host of competitors. One, the *Mirror,* bragged that it intended to provide "90 percent entertainment and 10 percent information," its news philosophy summed up in the motto "short, quick, and make it snappy." Another New York tabloid, the *Evening Graphic News,* pioneered the use of "composographs": photographic montages that proved to be so salacious and over the top that they earned the paper the nickname "*Porno-Graphic.*"

The tabloids' basic news philosophy was best explained in a ditty that later appeared in the *New York World:*

Oh, print us views without much news,
Of nudes and sheiks and racing horses,
Knife-battles, mobs, kidnapping clues,
Fire-setting fiends, love-theft divorces.
Let's have some war ships, railroad wrecks,
A riot caused by racial trouble,
True stories, contests and some sex—
Why, in a week your sales will double!

In Baltimore, tabloid journalism began to thrive with the debut of the *Baltimore Post* in 1922. Within a year, circulation had soared to more than 100,000, and the *Baltimore News* soon followed suit. The competition forced the venerable *Sun,* Baltimore's long-established paper of record, to publish somewhat milder versions of the same kinds of stories.

Nothing quite sold like crime. Stories of bandits and bootleggers created true-life dramas far more compelling than the fictional tripe about housewives on the women's page. The *Sun's* H. L. Mencken referred to the flaunting of the law as "a national sport" that was bigger than baseball.

Dubbed "jazz journalism," such reportage exploited the lingo and lifestyles of the criminal underworld, lifting the veil on a subculture just beginning to thrive. Reporters portrayed its major characters as if they were members of the cast in a gangster film. This hard-edged street literature created a new style of reporting, one both more cynical toward institutions and more sympathetic to those on the margins of society. A number of writers who covered Richard Whittemore would take what they learned from either reading or writing for the tabloids and create a new style of clear-eyed, hard-boiled crime fiction, while others would relocate to Hollywood to crank out screenplays using the rough language of the street that helped usher in a new genre in American film.

But when Richard and Margaret walked away together from the pen, there were no gangster films, not really. Hollywood hadn't quite discovered the criminal underworld, at least not as a lucrative subject for exploitation. Not yet. During the silent era, there really were no tough-talking, gun-wielding thugs and their dames to emulate.

That's where Richard, Margaret, and other gangsters of the era would soon come in. Their stories were tailor-made for the times. In many ways Richard Whittemore would become the prototypical tough-talking gangster and Margaret one of the first gun molls, both of them iconic stereotypes that in a few short years would be as familiar to Americans as the cowboy or the cad. The way they looked, dressed, acted, talked, and behaved echoes through American popular culture to this day.

Yet unlike so many of the gangsters and criminals who would follow in another decade and who took their cues from the gangsters they saw in the movies and in newsreel reports, Tiger Girl and the Candy Kid weren't play-acting or imitating anyone. They were the real thing, utterly original.

Readers would soon hang on every lurid word.

W hen Richard and Margaret Whittemore left the Maryland State Penitentiary together in the spring of 1924, Baltimore was a different place. Richard had heard about all the changes that had taken place from inside the penitentiary walls, but now, with Margaret by his side, he could see it and experience it all for himself. The underground scene of jazz clubs and cabarets had gone mainstream. The best hotels now advertised jazz bands in their ballrooms. Radios blared from every window, providing a whole new soundtrack to city living. They were even in cars now. There was a frenzy to life that hadn't been visible before, a fever pitch underlying everything as both yesterday and tomorrow became blotted out by today. The only time that mattered was now, *Now, NOW!*

Any thought Margaret may have ever entertained about living a quiet life was gone. She threw herself into the frenzy with her husband, fully and completely, jumping on a merry-go-round that was already spinning faster and faster. Any ideas that Whittemore ever held about escaping his past had long since evaporated in glistening dreams of diamonds and reflected glory.

At first Richard moved in with Margaret and her mother, Theresa, in her dumpy row house on North Gilmor Street. It wasn't the life they wanted. As the rest of the world lurched forward, they were still stuck in the Fifteenth Ward.

Richard rested a week, visiting family and getting to know his wife again, then hit the sidewalks. He was supposed to look for work.

That was the plan anyway. He needed to stay out of jail so that when the Kraemers got out they could go into business together. He wasn't supposed to hang out with other ex-cons or criminals, which would violate parole, but those were the only people he knew. Even his little brother could mean trouble. Rawlings Jr. was on the same path as Richard, just not quite as far along it. He'd earned a stint of his own at St. Mary's when he was busted as a teenager for shooting a deaf-mute with a .22 for kicks.

Almost everybody the Whittemores knew was bootlegging, breaking the law with as much concern as spitting on the sidewalk. While the national economic outlook had improved, Baltimore was lagging behind. Baltimore's Family Welfare Association warned in 1924 that "demand on our association has been quite as heavy this year as it was during the first few months of 1922," during the peak of the earlier depression. The plants and factories that had boosted the city's economy in decades past were still cutting back.

Richard didn't need any convincing that times were bad. "Work," he wrote, "was harder for me to get than money." Everywhere he applied he was met with either a line of unemployed men who had gotten there first or a stack of applications already submitted. A temporary job at the Pimlico racetrack lasted only a couple of weeks, and a handful of other jobs proved to be just as fleeting. Apart from checking in once a week with his parole officer, his choice was either to stay home all day, stuck with Margaret's mother while his wife plugged away again at the phone company, or try to make some money in a way that didn't mean clocking in.

Despite the Kraemers' admonition to keep away from "the skirts," Whittemore had no intention of leaving Margaret behind. He planned on making her part of the gang.

She was game too. A few years before, she might have dreamed of the bungalow and the picket fence, a husband who worked dawn to dusk and then came home to wife and baby, but the past few years had changed everything.

With Richard out of prison, she wouldn't have to live week to week anymore watching other people have all the fun while men leered at her and she put up with saps just to have enough money to buy a hat. Early that spring the papers had breathlessly reported on the so-called "Bob-Haired Bandit," a gun-wielding young woman who, with her male companion, had pulled off a string of robberies in Brooklyn, leaving police mystified. Well, the Whittemores needed a stake to see them through until the Kraemers were free. Maybe it was time for a Bob-Haired Bandit to make an appearance in Baltimore.

Richard Whittemore never copped to the crime, and with the precise date of his parole uncertain, it's even possible that he was still in the penitentiary when the caper took place, which, tellingly, was just a few days before or after his release. Clearly, his release factored into the timing of the execution of the crime. What is more certain is that Margaret was involved in the crime, which displayed all the earmarks of Whittemore spending three years hanging on the Kraemer brothers' every word and soaking up information.

Over the course of a few days in early April, Margaret and either Richard or other members of the nascent gang staked out Ortman's Confectionery on North Howard Street in downtown Baltimore. The combination bakery, candy store, and restaurant was a popular place where ladies could grab a nice lunch, top it off with some ice cream or a tart with coffee, and maybe bring home a box of bon-bons.

It was easy for the crew to spend a few hours giving Ortman's the once-over —wandering through the shop, eyes wide open, and figuring out when it was busy and when it wasn't, how many people worked there, and where they were as the workday unfolded. You could grab a cup of coffee, sit in the second-floor restaurant like a deer hunter in a tree stand, and watch the restaurant fill up and then empty after lunch. During the post-lunch lull, the only employee left working on the ground floor was the sales girl operating the cash register near the entrance. That was exactly the kind of useful observation the Kraemers had been preaching.

The day of the crime was selected carefully: Friday, April 11. It was a payday, just over a week before Easter, a busy time for Ortman's. The cash register was certain to be full. The shop didn't seem too concerned about being robbed. There were no guards, and the girl at the counter didn't look a day over twenty.

That morning Margaret got up early, applied her makeup carefully, and dressed for the part in what the papers later described as "excellent taste," wearing a dark coat trimmed in gray, her blond bobbed hair topped by a small blue straw hat. Getting ready to play a part in a crime was almost like being in the movies, and a lot more exciting than putting through phone calls or rolling down a stocking.

She entered the confectionery about 1 p.m., just as lunch was beginning to wind down. She looked about the shop and then, according to plan, made her way to the lunchroom on the second floor, where she took a table that faced the large plate-glass window and allowed a view of the street. She was one of only about a dozen lunchtime patrons still in the dining room. Margaret ordered lunch from the waitress, a big meal that would allow her to linger—a bowl of soup, a small steak, rolls, and coffee. The steak was an extravagance, but then she didn't plan on paying for it anyway.

She took her time, enjoying the fiction that she was a lady of leisure. After almost an hour, her plate was empty. Waitress Helen McCulloh delivered her check. Margaret started to walk away before pausing at the top of the stairs and sitting in a chair intended for those who had to wait for a table, rummaging through her purse and fixing her face as if preparing for an afternoon of shopping.

At first, the waitress thought she might have neglected to leave the check, then saw it in Margaret's hand and thought nothing of it. But McCulloh got a good look at the young woman and later said that she would "know her again if she ever saw her." It was now 2 p.m. The lunch rush was over. Only a couple and their young boy remained in the restaurant.

Margaret rose and strolled down the stairs to where the cashier stood behind a counter. A couple of dozen patrons milled around the store, looking at baked goods and sweets on display, glibly chatting away, their backs toward the register. At the bottom of the stairs Margaret glanced toward the door. A man she knew would be waiting was just outside, maybe her husband, maybe one of his pals recruited to help out.

Everything was in place.

Behind the cash register, twenty-one-year-old clerk Alice Hahn looked up and smiled as Margaret smiled back, handed her the bill, and then reached in her purse. Hahn rang up the sale, and the cash register popped open.

As Hahn took the check, Margaret dropped the smile, stepped around the counter, leaned in close, and fixed the girl with her gaze. Instead of producing a wallet from her clutch, Margaret pulled out a small handgun and aimed it at the girl's side.

Hahn started to snicker. She thought the gun was a fake and that the other employees were all having a good laugh at her expense. Then Margaret pressed the weapon hard against her ribs and hissed, "Not a word out of you. I'll shoot and I'll shoot to kill. I'm not joking."

Hahn froze, her eyes darting around in a panic. All the other employees were either in the back or busy filling orders, and no customers looked her way. She was too afraid to shout.

Margaret reached into the open drawer and, as Hahn later noted, took "everything in sight." Leaving behind only small change, she grabbed thick wads of cash, ones and fives, tens and twenties. Then, with what one paper described as "pronounced suavity," Margaret stepped back into character, put the gun in the pocket of her coat, and walked out the front door, a busy woman with things to do and places to go, stuffing the bills "down the bosom of her dress." As she passed through the door, the man waiting outside wheeled around and snapped a padlock over the door latch, locking everyone inside. The two then walked off down the street, a couple on an afternoon errand, and disappeared in the preholiday crowd.

Everything had gone as planned.

Hahn started screaming. The owner, Charles Ortman, rushed from the back. Hahn sputtered that she'd been robbed, and Ortman ran to the door to give chase, but couldn't force it open. By the time he raced out the back door and came around to the front and broke open the latch, Margaret, her companion, and $350 in cash were long gone.

The crime, the gang's first, had gone down perfectly. When Hahn told the police she'd been held up, not by a man, but by a fashionably dressed young woman with bobbed hair, the police suspected that Brooklyn's mysterious "Bob-Haired Bandit" and her companion had come to Baltimore. She was a brunette, not a blonde, like Margaret, but that could have come out of a bottle of peroxide. Within a few hours, police had canvassed area roadhouses, hotels, and train stations, but the search was fruitless. There were a thousand young blond women in Baltimore of medium height, and on a Friday night nearly all of them were escorted by young men. A number of suspects were questioned, only to be released when the waitress and Hahn said they had the wrong girl.

The police may have been baffled, but Margaret had to be pleased with the outcome, for afterwards there is no evidence that her allegiance to the gang and to her husband's way of life ever wavered. This was *easy*. She'd managed to stay calm and proven she could handle a gun, and now she had more money than she'd ever seen in her life, equal to three months of her salary. She'd gotten a free lunch too.

Although Richard later claimed to have turned back to crime months after his release, having decided "that I was not going to be broke any longer," in reality he'd made that decision before he even walked out of the penitentiary. According to one inmate, as soon as Whittemore was free, he "frequented tough cabarets and wild dives, particularly a notorious rathskeller in the heart of the downtown section . . . a hangout for dope fiends and crooks and the low type of chorus girls," sometimes with his wife and sometimes not. Also known as the "Bad Lands of Baltimore," the short stretch of East Baltimore Street around the corner from Holliday and Gay Streets was one of the most sordid vice districts on the Eastern Seaboard, home to notorious cabarets like the Argonne, the Folly, and the Gayety Theater, which featured a not-so-secret basement bar where dancers entertained men after the show.

At joints like these, hard drinks cost nearly a dollar, and even a beer usually cost a quarter. A decent bottle of wine could set you back four or five bucks. Richard and Margaret started burning through whatever stash they had. He liked sampling the drugs too: cocaine to stay up all night; opium, usually in the form of heroin or morphine, and usually either smoked or taken in tablet form, to take the edge off the next day; and marijuana, which was hardly unknown in cabaret circles. US Commissioner of Narcotics H. J. Anslinger would later note that the Whittemore gang "all used drugs." If not yet a full-blown habit for each of them, it was a common pastime, part of their scene.

Soon after his release, Richard was working nights with Joe Dietz and a few others, often Al Lott and Tommy Philips, but Whittemore's circle was expanding, and he soon fell in with other hoods, guys he knew from the cabarets or the Fifteenth Ward, like Milton "Shuffles" Goldberg, Willie Unkelbach, and others from his time in the Maryland School for Boys and the Elmira Reformatory. They were all older now, jaded, street-wise, and increasingly ruthless. Julius Schaefer, after being freed, had been arrested on a small charge and found himself in the Maryland House of Correction in Jessup, but soon sawed through the bars and joined the party.

Someone in the group came up with some false Federal Revenue agent IDs and badges, and they started rousting bootleggers and saloonkeepers. Again, that took planning, and at first they were careful, doing their homework and not taking many chances, only going after sure things. They kept their ears open, Margaret too, and after learning of a stash of liquor, they'd flash their badges, take everybody's guns, load the booze into a stolen car, and take off. The cops couldn't keep up.

There was a lot of money in booze. A case of whiskey — three gallons — was worth at least ten bucks, more if it was bonded, government-certified hooch still allowed to be produced for "medicinal purposes," a widely abused loophole. A car could hold as much as $500 worth of booze, and a truckload could easily be worth ten or twenty times that much.

Just as the Kraemers did with diamonds, making arrangements with a fence before committing the crime, the gang probably did the same with booze and knew who they were going to sell the stuff to before stealing it. They wouldn't get the full value of course, but it was still easy money. Even then, after splitting the take and celebrating afterwards, the money didn't always last long. It wasn't like they were putting it in the bank to save for a rainy day. Stormy weather was a thing of the past.

But they weren't always so cautious. By the fall, when the Kraemers had been denied parole yet again, some gang members were growing anxious and developing drug habits that made them increasingly careless and prone to pulling jobs without their usual foresight. Sometimes they ran low on cash and, under the haze of booze and dope, didn't always think straight. What they lacked in brains they made up for in firepower.

Guns were as easy to get as a shot of rye. In Maryland, you were supposed to show identification and gun sales were supposed to be registered, but in the days before photo IDs, false papers were easy to come by. There were also plenty of guns on the street, and nearly every time they hijacked a shipment of booze, they walked off with a gun or two. Those were worth money too.

Margaret usually stayed behind while Whittemore worked. She'd established herself as trustworthy, and her mother's place served as a sort of safe house.

But the women were still useful. After the Ortman robbery, Margaret and the other wives and girlfriends were occasionally called in to do reconnaissance. The gang would send them out to case a potential target, telling them what to look for, and then report back. Nobody got suspicious when a woman lingered around a store. Step by step, Margaret became an ever more valuable and integral part of the gang.

One evening a week before Thanksgiving, Richard and a companion, likely Dietz or Schaefer, robbed two gas station attendants on Cathedral Street at gunpoint. That cash didn't last long, and a week later, on the evening of November 22, the gang pulled two more robberies an hour apart. The first, in West Baltimore, netted only $20 from a tea shop when the clerk tossed another $200 out a window as the bandits were forcing him into a back room. The gunmen had been looking the other way and didn't notice. Disappointed, an hour later in East Baltimore they held up a grocery store and made off with $165. All the cops knew was that the jobs usually involved two or three young men of average height, all about twenty-five years old. They pulled pistols and worked fast, and their pictures didn't appear in the Rogues' Gallery.

These rush jobs were risky and didn't always pay off. A garage robbery netted all of three bucks. Another time they carried a cash register out of a tea shop and found only $3.65 inside.

Even so, Whittemore was becoming ever more daring, and ever more willing to take risks. On the night of December 5, he was out at a cabaret on Franklin Street with Shuffles Goldberg and Willie Unkelbach and met an attractive young woman there, twenty-one-year-old Mrs. Leola Kassel. Richard noticed that she had two diamond rings on her hand, but wasn't with her husband. She might have been a widow. Or she might not have cared.

Richard turned on the Candy Kid act. Kassel swooned. She thought him to be "quiet, well-mannered, and somewhat reserved," not like the toughs she usually met. Over the course of the evening, and presumably a few drinks and a few dances, Whittemore's silver tongue got to work. At the end of the night he left the boys and the two piled into a taxi together, headed to her apartment on Eutaw Place.

At the curb, he threw the driver a big bill. Kassel was impressed. Whittemore then took her by the arm and walked her into the vestibule of her building. He smiled, held her in his arms, and leaned over. She closed her eyes and puckered up, trying to decide whether to ask him in.

Instead of a kiss on the lips she got a punch in the face, then another and another. As she bent over from the pummeling, Whittemore grabbed her hand and, as her screams echoed through the streets, violently wrenched the rings from her fingers.

A patrolman only a block away heard the commotion and rushed toward the sound. He saw a man running away and a woman crying and screaming, holding her hands to her face. The rings, she said between sobs, were worth $100 each. Taken to the hospital, Mrs. Kassel was treated for contusions and a broken nose.

All that ring time at the Sweezey Club had paid off. It may have been Whittemore's first violent crime. Either way, busting Leola Kassel's nose didn't seem to bother him at all. She had something he wanted. And now he had it.

A week later, Whittemore got a tip about a railroad car full of beer in the B&O railyard in Mount Clare. He and a few others were off-loading the beer into a truck when a railroad cop, Luther Welch, discovered the theft.

The thieves saw Welch first, got the jump, and beat him nearly unconscious. They left him on the ground, but not before taking his gun and badge. Both could come in handy.

The gang had more beer than they knew what to do with, and they each took a few cases for personal use. Christmas was coming, and when one of Margaret's older brothers stopped by the house to visit, Richard gave him a case.

What Whittemore didn't know was that Messler was pals with a police detective. A few days later, Messler had the guy over for a few, unconcerned about sharing booze with a cop. The detective was impressed: this wasn't the usual swill, or low-alcohol "near beer." He asked Margaret's brother where he got such "good stuff." He said his sister's husband was a bootlegger.

The detective had heard about a recent hijacking of quality beer and put two and two together. Bootlegging was one thing, but stealing from another bootlegger, well, people paid good money to keep that kind of thing from happening. It would look good if he cracked the case.

A few days later, a couple of policemen came around to Margaret's house. Richard answered the door. They told him to come to the station—they wanted to ask him a few questions about that beer. Richard played it cool, knowing that if they pinned the heist on him, he could end up back in the penitentiary. Only half-dressed, he told the cops he'd finish dressing and meet them outside.

While the cops cooled it on the stoop, Whittemore dressed, stuffed an armful of clothes in a bag, and headed out the back door.

It was the dead of winter, but suddenly too hot to stay in Baltimore. Taking another lesson from the Kraemers, the gang decided to relocate to Philadelphia, where the Kraemers, conveniently enough, still had some contacts. For the time being, the gang would use Philadelphia as their base of operations, only going into Baltimore or some other place, like Atlantic City, to pull a job, then returning to Philly and living quietly until they found a target too tempting to ignore.

The skirts, including Margaret, would come along. It was time to start collecting nice things and good times. The Kraemers would be up for parole again in April and were optimistic that this time they'd get out.

Before bolting, the gang pulled one last job in Baltimore. On the night of January 5, 1925, Whittemore, Dietz, Schaefer, Tommy Philips, and another man, likely Lott or Goldberg, dropped into Gaffney's, a saloon on Park Heights Avenue, near Pimlico. Whittemore knew the area well.

The five made no attempt at disguise. In fact, they ordered drinks for the handful of customers already bellied up to the bar, ensuring that everyone dropped their guard and made themselves comfortable.

They shot the breeze for a while. The bartender, John Gaffney, thought one of the men looked familiar. Then, without a word, the group split up. One man walked to each end of the bar, blocking Gaffney's way out, and each pulled a gun.

Whittemore backed up, keeping everyone in sight, and leveled a pistol before barking, "Line up there; stick 'em high, and if you move, you'll get drilled."

Hands overhead, the men lined up and then were ushered into a back room. One of the robbers produced some rope, tied everyone's hands behind their back, and then rifled their pockets. The customers didn't have much, but Gaffney held over $2,000 in cash plus a check for $75. When they were finished, Whittemore sneered, "Stay right there, and make no outcry if you want to continue living." With that, the men backed out of the room, the last one wedging a chair under the doorknob. Then Whittemore cackled and called out, loud enough to be heard through the door, "Good-*bye!*"

By the time Gaffney and the others were free, the gang was on their way to Philadelphia. The Whittemores, Lott, Schaefer, Dietz, Philips and his wife Flo, and another woman they knew as Mary Krieg, aka Marion Davis or Mary or Chickie Gray, moved into an apartment on Green Street. Flush with cash, Whittemore admitted they spent the next week or so "having a good time and not worrying about a thing in the world."

Every night was a party.

That still left the daytime, and they still had those revenue IDs and badges. They found out about a gas station in Atlantic City that was selling a lot of liquor and decided to take advantage of both.

Dietz and Whittemore burst in, showed their badges, and threatened the owner with arrest unless he handed over $2,000. The proprietor wasn't surprised by the request—a lot of revenue agents were crooked. The man didn't have the money on him but offered to go to the bank and get it. Dietz and Whittemore took him to the bank, he withdrew the funds, and they all returned to the gas station. A cop came in, and the station owner thought fast and had the cop check their government IDs.

The cop took a close look and said they checked out. He wasn't about to interfere. Besides, he was there to buy booze.

Dietz and Whittemore waltzed out $2,000 in the black, and it wasn't until the gas station owner complained to city authorities that he learned he'd been scammed.

Not everyone in the gang stayed happy. Philips thought he was being shorted, and his wife worried that her husband would be sent back to prison. They returned to Baltimore, where Philips went to the police. He told them he knew who had pulled the Gaffney robbery and quite a few others. He could clear a lot of cases if they'd cut him a break.

Police interrogated Philips for several days, and he pinned job after job on what the cops were starting to call the "Whittemore-Schaefer gang." In truth, they weren't an organized gang yet, but a looser aggregation of like-minded, opportunistic crooks. In addition to the Gaffney robbery, Philips surprised the cops by eventually implicating the crew in some crimes they hadn't connected to them, including a home invasion on Belair Road where they terrorized two sisters and one of their husbands before taking off with $45 worth of liquor, some cash, and a sealskin coat valued at $150 that would later help send them all to prison. Philips also claimed that the gang was in the midst of planning a heist of the payroll for the Bagby Furniture Company in Baltimore and expected to come away with at least $25,000 in cash.

Philips told the cops that the gang all lived together in a second-floor apartment on Green Street in Philadelphia. The Baltimore police shared the information with their counterparts in Philly. Authorities quickly tied them to the Atlantic City scam and suspected that they might be responsible for several other jobs, in particular a theft of $50,000 in gems from a prominent Philadelphia jewelry dealer the previous fall.

The gang's tastes were getting richer by the day.

Samuel Dickson supplied precious stones to jewelers to turn into rings and bracelets. The morning of October 24, 1924, he and a messenger boy had gone to meet with a jeweler, taking along three satchels containing $50,000 in gems. But the meeting fell through, and on his way back to his office at the corner of Master and Thirteenth Streets, Dickson pulled over to the curb and decided to stretch his legs and take a look at a construction site. He parked the car and stepped out, leaving the gems in the car with the boy.

He'd probably been tailed, because a minute or two after he left the car, two men hopped in, pulled a gun on the kid, and sped away with the gems. A few blocks away, they threw the sixteen-year-old out of the car and took off.

Dickson's wife recalled that two suspicious women had visited their shop a few days before. As Dickson himself said, "I believe I was the victim of a gang that specialized in jewel thefts and they have been spotting me for some time." That sure smelled like something inspired by the Kraemers.

In mid-January, two Baltimore detectives who had traced a car abandoned after the Atlantic City robbery to Dietz traveled to Philadelphia. Accompanied by two Philadelphia detectives who had confirmed the presence of the gang, on the afternoon of January 14 they made their move. The Baltimore detectives guarded the front door as the two Philadelphia cops made their way upstairs. From the street, the apartment looked quiet. The drapes and shades were closed.

Inside, Dietz, the Whittemores, Schaefer, Al Lott, and Marion Davis were all sitting around a table, eating a late lunch. Margaret's new puppy, a poodle, paced the floor. They may have been discussing a letter they had just received that was later found in the pocket of Margaret's dress. If they weren't, they should have been. It read:

Tom [Philips] is in jail and the bulls are in Philadelphia.
For God's sake leave there and go to some other town.
Stay under cover.
—Kate

The door suddenly flew open, and the two detectives burst in, guns drawn, and announced that everyone was under arrest. An instant later, the apartment was plunged into darkness. Someone had hit the lights.

The next few seconds were utter confusion. The gang tried to scatter, ducking under tables and turning over chairs. The women started passing out guns, one after another, and the gang fired blind into the darkness. The detectives returned fire as everyone ducked and scrambled.

Joined by their Baltimore counterparts, one of the detectives managed to flick the switch back on. Everyone held still as they disarmed the thugs with the guns. But one of the women was gone.

Hearing a noise behind the door in an adjacent room, a detective pulled open the door and saw a woman, skirt hiked up to her hip, climbing out a window onto a fire escape. She stopped, wheeled around, reached into a bureau drawer, and pulled out a gun.

The detective acted fast. Before she could lift it to shoot, he hit her with a roundhouse. The gun fell from her hand and spun beneath a bed.

Now the detectives had the upper hand. The six suspects were placed in handcuffs and arrested, and a quick search of the apartment turned up six high-caliber pistols—probably .38s or .45s—more than $2,000 in cash, and trunks of fancy clothes. One of the cops grabbed the puppy and everyone was brought into custody. Margaret's Bertillon card later noted she was five-foot-three and 109 pounds.

Margaret pleaded to be allowed to keep the dog in her cell. The request was refused. She stamped her feet and cried, "I think it's terrible to take away my dog!" She would never get it back.

Until the arrest, the police didn't know exactly who they had. Dietz and the Whittemores gave their real names, but it took another day to confirm the identities of Lott, Schaefer, and Davis.

The fact that there'd been a shoot-out got the attention of all the papers, but each one told a slightly different story. Although authorities initially believed that Davis had tried to make the break and gone for the gun, other reports claimed it was Margaret, and that Margaret had been the one who passed weapons to the men before the lights came back on. In fact, the press had a hard time keeping the two women straight. The *Baltimore News* even misidentified the photos of the two in the paper.

That's who the papers were really interested in, the women. Male bandits were as common as sawdust on a barroom floor, but the two bobbed-hair babes, particularly two so photogenic, were the real story. The public ate up stories about fallen flappers, good girls gone bad.

In the *News* the next day, photos of Margaret and Davis dwarfed the pictures of the four men, with Margaret, albeit misidentified as Davis, earning a place above the fold. She looked a little scared, and a little startled, and her hair wasn't quite in a full bob, but that mattered little to the *News*. More importantly, her teary doe eyes stared straight into the hearts of readers, dramatic as those of any screen queen.

Most of the accompanying story, however, focused on Davis, known as "Chickie Gray" in Baltimore. She looked a little older than Margaret, a little harder, and a lot haughtier, staring down the police photographer as if he were beneath her, chin up, jaw clenched, cloche hat pulled down tight. The accompanying story played her up as a cautionary tale of the modern age. She said she had skipped out on her husband, a Chesapeake Bay boat captain, because "married life was too monotonous . . . my husband was good to me but he was too slow. Why lots of time we were in bed before midnight! There were no parties, no music, no bright lights." According to the *News*, she preferred the company of "the 'live ones' of the night life."

The men were thrown in jail, while the women remained overnight at the Northeastern Police Station, where, the *News* reported, apart from their concern over the puppy, they seemed "cheerful and unconcerned about their fate" and spent their time doing puzzles. Davis, the police claimed, had often served as the gang's driver, while both women were thought to serve as what the *Philadelphia Inquirer* called "pathfinders . . . looking over the ground and familiarizing themselves with various obstacles to be overcome in arranging for the theft." And Margaret earned a nickname. According to the *Sun*, in the Baltimore criminal underworld, she was known as "Tiger Lil." (The *News*, in its confusion, first hung the name on Davis.)

The nickname was not completely unknown, but until recently had been rather benign, inferring a woman who was soft and pretty but could turn sultry and sexy, both a delicate virginal flower and an aggressive sexual tiger. It likely derived from the 1915 film directed by D. W. Griffith starring Lillian Gish entitled *The Lily and the Rose*. Gish played a temperamental but flirtatious character who entertains multiple suitors.

Over time, however, the moniker "Tiger Lil" attached to Margaret evolved into "Tiger Girl," a name also used in the title of a popular song, "My Beautiful

Tiger Girl," written by Alfred Bryan and Jean Schwartz for the Broadway show *Schubert Gaieties 1919*. In the show, the song was performed as a coterie of caged women in tiger-striped dresses wriggled and writhed. *Variety* called it "the best novelty song number Broadway has seen in a decade." Baltimore jazz legend Eubie Blake brought the tune to the masses when it appeared in a medley from the show he recorded on a player piano roll later that year.

In 1922, the moniker became notorious after a young Los Angeles woman, Clara Phillips, beat a female rival to death with a hammer. A newspaperman called her a "tiger girl" and splashed the name like blood in a headline. After that, just about any young flapper who committed a particularly heinous crime got hung with the sobriquet. For example, another California girl, sixteen-year-old Dorothy Ellington, described as "jazz mad," earned the name when she shot her mother to death after being scolded for going out and dancing with men.

Attached to Margaret Whittemore, "Tiger Girl" would become even more notorious, ripe with meaning. It fit her like a tight silk stocking.

No one was calling Richard "the Candy Kid," not yet, at least not in the newspapers. But that's what he was, a sweet talker when he chose to be, a man who could whisper words in a girl's ear that would make her blush and consider doing things she maybe hadn't thought of doing before, or at least not so quickly.

Richard's tabloid nickname also evoked a popular song, dating back to 1910, "Oh, You Candy Kid," the phrase a term of endearment ("sweet as honey, manly and sincere"). But "candy" was also a slang word for jewelry, while in the jazz joints "candy" meant drugs—specifically cocaine, a drug that made you laugh and talk and dance and laugh and talk and dance some more. A cokehead was a "candy kid" too. And on those long nights out in the cabarets, that also described Richard. For every imaginable use of the phrase, Richard Whittemore fit the definition.

All six appeared before a Philadelphia judge the next day at a preliminary hearing. During the proceeding, Samuel Dickson's wife was asked if she recognized anyone in the courtroom. She spoke of seeing two women in her husband's office building only a few days before the October robbery and then dramatically pointed to Margaret and Davis.

As if rehearsed, the two women jumped out of their seats, each shouting, "That's a lie!" and sending the courtroom into an uproar.

Philadelphia authorities didn't yet have enough evidence to charge any of the six with anything. Pennsylvania didn't have a law like New York's Sullivan Act, which criminalized simple gun possession; had the crime taken place there, it could have resulted in charges for the whole crew. Still, the judge ordered them all to remain in custody while the investigation continued. The next day in Baltimore, a grand jury indicted Richard Whittemore and the other men in the Gaffney robbery while the cops there tried to build more cases against them.

It wasn't very hard. Margaret had been arrested wearing the sealskin coat stolen in the home invasion. Whittemore, Lott, Schaefer, Dietz, and Philips, the rat, were all indicted, the police taking care to keep Philips away from his former companions, whose only interest in rats was in their extermination.

Margaret and Davis, after the initial splurge of publicity, remained locked up in Philadelphia while police tried to tie them to the gem theft. Then, as now, the Sixth Amendment right to a speedy trial for the accused was often ignored by the police and the courts. A couple of weeks behind bars sometimes inspired confessions.

It may have been easy to be a criminal in Baltimore, but it was a bad time to be charged with a crime there. Justice moved fast.

In November 1923, Herbert O'Conor, an ambitious twenty-six-year-old attorney who had worked as a reporter for the *Baltimore Sun* while attending the University of Maryland Law School, was elected state's attorney in Baltimore after serving for several years as an assistant.

A Baltimore native, O'Conor was the young man Richard Whittemore might have been had he been born just a few years before, and a few blocks to the east, in different circumstances. In fact, when O'Conor was ten years old, the same age as Whittemore when he'd harmlessly shot a gun into the air, O'Conor had tied a lit firecracker to the tail of a horse. Whittemore had been hauled before a judge and threatened with reform school for firing the gun. In contrast, O'Conor's uncle had only laughed and patted the little scamp on the head.

O'Conor grew up with a reputation for unquestioned moral integrity and a pronounced commitment to law and order, a shining example of a young man unaffected by the temptations of the Jazz Age, someone who still carried the values of the Victorian era. In 1922, the dashing young attorney had become a darling of the press and the public when he essentially abducted a man from a New York courtroom and returned him to Maryland to stand trial.

Nineteen-year-old Walter Socolow was one of five suspects in the shooting of local contractor William Norris, who was killed in broad daylight during a payroll robbery on August 18, 1922. The crew was headed up by Jack Hart, a well-known Baltimore gangster who would later stage a brazen escape from the penitentiary. Socolow fled Maryland for New York, where he was arrested. Before he could be extradited, his attorney filed a writ of habeas corpus.

O'Conor raced to New York with several detectives, awaiting an extradition order that had yet to arrive, afraid that New York might set Socolow free during the court hearing. That's exactly what happened.

But O'Conor seized the moment. He pushed his men forward and shouted, "Take him, boys!" Without any legal authority, they kidnapped Socolow and dragged him back to Baltimore. O'Conor was heralded as a heroic defender of justice. A year later, in his first try in the race for state's attorney, O'Conor won elected office as a crusading maverick promising to prosecute criminals with zeal.

Baltimoreans were beginning to fear going out on the streets, partly because of crime inspired by Prohibition, but also because of the growing impact of the tabloid daily press, represented by the *Baltimore Daily Post* and the *Baltimore Evening News*. Their sensationalized, photo-heavy coverage of crime scared Baltimore half to death. In truth, crime really wasn't increasing that much in the city, although its tenor was becoming more violent. After the Great War, gun use had become far more prevalent, and the number of automobiles in the city exploded: with the number of registered cars in Maryland rising from nearly 18,000 in 1913 to more than 217,000 ten years later, crooks had far more mobility than ever before.

The real problem with crime in Baltimore was the criminal judicial process. The system had bogged down. If you had any money, bail was easy to come by, as were an endless series of postponements and delays engineered by a cottage industry of lawyers who lurked in the courthouse. They had learned that the best way to gain freedom for their client was to simply wait out the courts until they either forgot about the case or kicked it down the road by "stetting" it—a procedure for indefinitely postponing a case that judges and prosecutors had abused for years.

In theory, stetting a case allowed the charge to be prosecuted later if the offender committed another crime or additional evidence was developed. In practice, however, it was used to clear the docket, allowing thousands of cases to linger unresolved and leaving criminals on the street. O'Conor took issue with that practice.

The indefatigable young attorney applied his work ethic to attacking the problem, regularly putting in sixteen- to eighteen-hour days and working weekends and holidays. He extended court hours from dawn to late at night and prosecuted cases with speed and aggression that appear shocking today. He took the admonition in the Sixth Amendment to the US Constitution to heart, ensuring that, in Baltimore, it would be far easier for the "accused [to] enjoy the right to a speedy and public trial." State law allowed defendants to choose to be tried before a judge rather than a jury, and 96 percent of them chose to do so, freeing the court from the laborious process of selecting a jury.

In 1924 alone, O'Conor's office, with only six attorneys, disposed of a remarkable 5,000 cases, bringing 4,499 to trial and gaining a conviction rate of 86 percent. On average that year, criminals in Baltimore were tried and either convicted or acquitted within *eight days* of arrest, and often much more quickly than that. In one instance, a man was arrested for larceny at 7:45 a.m., arraigned and indicted by a grand jury before lunch, then put on trial and convicted by 1:30 p.m.

There wasn't much real justice in the process, particularly for those who were Black, poor, or both, as it was virtually impossible to mount a defense in such shotgun proceedings. Many innocent defendants were railroaded into convictions, and guilty parties were sentenced to terms far out of proportion to their crimes. In such a rigged system, it made sense for many defendants simply to plead guilty and hope for a light sentence. But O'Conor was undeterred. He stood behind the shield of the greater good and enjoyed the support of both the Baltimore press and the city's political establishment.

Only two weeks after their arrest, Schaefer, Lott, Dietz, and Whittemore were scheduled for trial. According to Whittemore, if they pleaded guilty, O'Conor's office promised them each a sentence of only five years. But after Dietz balked and pleaded not guilty, O'Conor reneged and the deal fell apart.

Whittemore, Schaefer, and Lott received fifteen-year terms, and Dietz was sentenced to sixteen years for failing to cooperate. Tommy Philips, referred to as "Mr. Squealer" by Whittemore, received a sentence of only four years, was promised an early parole, and for his own safety was sent not to the penitentiary but to the Maryland House of Correction. The charges against Whittemore for beating and robbing Leola Kassel were stetted after O'Conor concluded that the other sentences served "the ends of the State." That decision also saved her the embarrassment of testifying.

O'Conor's office chose not to charge Margaret Whittemore and Marion Davis at all. They had certainly benefited from the crimes, and they may have known more than they let on, but the other defendants refused to implicate them. Also, Margaret had yet to be linked to the "Bob-Haired Bandit" robbery. They likely also benefited from their gender. In a world where women were only beginning to shake off Victorian confines, female criminals, particularly White women, were often viewed almost as victims themselves, good girls led astray, rather than as equal co-conspirators. They were released from custody on February 9, 1925. By then, the Candy Kid was already doing time. Margaret didn't even have a chance to say goodbye.

Whittemore had been free less than a year before he entered the penitentiary for the second time, on January 29, 1925. He was not eager to stay. In fact, upon sentencing, Whittemore told a guard, "You may send me over there, but I won't be there long." Since first being sent to the Parental School, apart from his brief tenure in the Coast Guard before being court-martialed, Whittemore had spent only about a year and a half living outside an institution.

After processing, the men were escorted in pairs to the warden's office to meet with Sweezey. He wanted to know each prisoner, not as a number but as a name and a face.

Whittemore and Schaefer went together and stood before the warden, who sat at his desk as a guard looked on. "Well, Whittemore," he said, "I see you are back again. This time you will not leave so soon as you did on your first stay."

Whittemore stared him down. Then Sweezey addressed Schaefer. "It will be a little harder to get out of here than it was to get out of the House of Correction," he said, referencing Schaefer's escape a few months before.

Some would have taken issue with that. Since Sweezey took over as warden in 1920, ten separate successful escapes had taken place, and they were becoming more frequent. In 1923 alone, the prison reported four escapes, and three more took place in 1924, including that by Jack Hart. After each one, Sweezey again blamed his staff and deflected responsibility for what some viewed as his lax coddling of inmates. In recent months, both Governor Albert Ritchie and the director of the Board of Public Welfare, who oversaw prison policy, had bowed to public pressure and convened an investigation.

Sweezey wasn't too worried about the probe and had publicly argued that the penitentiary was far more secure than similar institutions in other states. The Sweezey Club, he maintained, made all the inmates easier to control. But he still wanted the right to hire and fire guards, unencumbered by civil service rules.

Now, with two repeat offenders before him, Sweezey motioned to the guard to take them away, saying, "You boys, I suppose, know your way around here."

As the guard led Whittemore away, he called out over his shoulder, "I certainly do know how to get around in here," then added, "I know *everything* about this place."

His words should have given Sweezey pause.

The Kraemers welcomed him back as well. They all had a lot of catching up to do, and after spending the last nine months free, Whittemore had a far better handle on conditions outside than before. He assured the brothers that he'd only been caught because of "Mr. Squealer," Tommy Philips. If it hadn't been for him, Whittemore and the others would all still be living the high life. They didn't need to wait on Dietz or Schaefer to go free either. Whittemore had met other guys on the outside, like Shuffles Goldberg, who could be just as useful, maybe even more so, guys without long records who were better connected.

Now that he knew the value of planning, Whittemore was already mulling over a few ideas on how to escape. He even bragged to Dietz that all he needed was a couple of hundred dollars to throw around to get a little help. There were always some guards ready to take a payout to look the other way or even, as had happened in Jack Hart's escape, provide a key.

Word of Whittemore's intention filtered back to Sweezey, who warned Deputy Warden Patrick Brady to have guards "watch Whittemore and never let him out of their sight." Whittemore had been a model prisoner when he was last there, but when Sweezey learned what Whittemore had done while on the outside, "I wanted to take no chances with him." When Margaret finally called to pick up Whittemore's civilian clothes and other personal belongings, Sweezey kept the visit short. Husband and wife were barely able to exchange more than a few words.

Margaret had moved back in with her mother, far better dressed this time. The cops confiscated $2,000 during the Philadelphia arrest, but they hadn't been able to touch much else. She no longer had the sealskin coat, but during the short time her husband was free, as Whittemore later indicated, he had started to fulfill his promise of good times. She'd likely indulged in a few new stylish dresses and genuine diamonds to replace her costume jewelry. For the time being at least, she would have had more than enough money to get by. "Tiger Girl" didn't need to work as an artist's model or at the phone company anymore.

Sweezey realized that Whittemore had become more hardened and dangerous, and the warden knew from his record that he had no compulsion against wielding a gun or using violence. Slugging a woman in the face and tearing the rings off her fingers was evidence enough of that. When Whittemore asked to go back to his old job at the hospital, he was turned down. Instead, he was assigned to the shoe shop, tasked with correcting imperfections in shoe leather with an electric iron.

A short time after he began his sentence, a fuse blew in the iron, according to Whittemore, shorting it out and giving him a nasty burn on his arm. But authorities believed that he had burned himself on purpose.

The burn required daily treatment in the prison hospital. Almost every afternoon a trusty would come for Whittemore at the shoe shop and escort him past four guarded checkpoints in the prison yard before they reached the hospital just inside the southern edge of the facility. More guards were stationed inside, one on each floor and another who was responsible for locking and unlocking the doors and gates that led in and out. On the north side, a door opened onto the prison yard, and down a short flight of steps was a locked gate. On the building's south side, another locked door led to a flight of steps and then a passageway that cut through the prison wall to the Madison Street gate, which was generally kept open so that hospital staff could come and go and accept deliveries.

Whittemore knew his way around the hospital, where he had served as an orderly, as well as he knew his way around the Fifteenth Ward.

For sixty-year-old Robert H. Holtman, a guard in his nineteenth year at the pen, it was easy duty. Stationed on the first floor, all he had to do was lock and unlock the doors leading into and out of the hospital; he spent most of his shift just killing time. Holtman had taken a particular shine to Whittemore during his earlier incarceration, when he had worked in the hospital and would share food and conversation with the prisoner. Like many of the other guards, despite the warning from Sweezey, Holtman didn't look at Whittemore as a threat.

On February 19, the Board of Public Welfare released its report on prison conditions, which the *Baltimore News* would soon call a "whitewashing." The report concluded that, while "we find the system in vogue unusually mild . . . we do not believe it causal to escape or attempted escape." It noted a need for more guards and cleaner facilities, but praised the quality of the prison food. Security presented an issue, and the "matter of locks and other mechanical appliances has been allowed to fall below normal."

Newspaper coverage of the report made for some close reading in the Sweezey Club. If you were a prisoner intending to escape, the words were significant: even small changes to established routine could affect escape plans. But if you were Richard Whittemore, one of the report's recommendations may have been particularly alarming: "The methods of handling scrap material in the metal shops and yards increase very greatly the danger from prisoner assaults. We believe that by a few changes this danger can be removed."

Those two sentences may well have inspired Whittemore to make his move.

On February 20, having defended the prison in the report's wake the day before and brushed off any concern for drastic changes, Sweezey was away on administrative business. He had left Assistant Warden Patrick Brady in charge. Earlier that day, Brady had approved the prison physician's list of prisoners scheduled for treatment that day.

At about 2:10 p.m., trusty Willie Greene went to the shoe shop to get Whittemore for his daily round of medical treatment.

Robert Holtman unlocked the door. Greene stepped into the yard, and Holtman locked the door behind him. Greene walked briskly through the cold to the shop, passing four checkpoints, each manned by a guard. They all knew the routine and waved him past. He asked the foreman for Whittemore.

Whittemore stopped working, put down his iron, and went with Greene. As the two men walked past each checkpoint, a guard called ahead to the next, "Coming down," the standard notice that a prisoner was on his way.

Along the way, Whittemore and Greene came upon a pile of debris left behind after a plumbing project. As they passed, Whittemore spied a length of what was later described as a lead pipe or iron bar. In another day, if the yard had been cleaned up, it might not have been there. He had to figure this was his chance.

The guard ahead was looking the other way. Whittemore, a step or two behind Greene, glanced over his shoulder. The guard at the last checkpoint wasn't paying him any attention. With the practiced move of a boy stealing a banana from a street vendor, Whittemore, not breaking stride, swiped a short piece of pipe from the pile and stuffed it down the pant leg of his coveralls.

No one saw him.

When they arrived at the hospital, Holtman unlocked the gate leading to the yard and let Whittemore in, locking it again after he passed, just as he had done every day for the past few weeks. Greene lingered outside, waiting for the return trip.

Whittemore climbed the stairs to the third floor for treatment, a guard on each floor calling to the next as he climbed the steps.

Whittemore removed his shirt to give the nurse access to his burn wound. Chatting idly, he quipped, "It's the last time I'm going to have it dressed," adding, "I'm going to give it the open air treatment," a comment that was either entirely innocent or brazenly premeditated. When the nurse finished, Whittemore put his shirt back on and walked down the stairs. Guards on each floor yelled out, "Coming down," alerting Holtman that the prisoner was returning to the first floor.

According to Whittemore, Holtman, generally described as kindly by others, hadn't been quite as friendly toward Whittemore since he had returned to prison. In fact, Whittemore later claimed that on his first day back he'd gotten "a sneer from him about coming back" and that Holtman had teased him about his sentence. Although Holtman was sixty, he wasn't infirm. A few years earlier, while guarding a road crew, he had chased an escapee for several miles and then shot the man in the chest.

John Bowie, a Black prisoner and a trusty working as a janitor, was down a hallway when Whittemore came down the stairs. In a nearby office, a dentist sat at his desk, doing paperwork. As Whittemore approached, Holtman, keys in hand, turned his back, unlocked the door, walked down the steps, and placed his keys in the lock on the gate.

Whittemore reached inside his clothing and pulled out the pipe from his coveralls. He raised it high over his head.

Without a word, Whittemore brought it down, striking the guard on the right side of the back of his head. Holtman crumpled to the floor. The only sound was that of metal striking bone and flesh and a limp body hitting the ground.

Blood poured from the wound, pooling on the floor.

Bowie froze, suddenly in fear for his life, afraid he might be next. Whittemore kneeled over the fallen man, grabbed the keys clutched in the guard's hand, then reached into his holster and removed his pistol. Keeping Bowie in sight, Whittemore reached into Holtman's back pocket, removed his wallet, and stuffed the contents inside his pocket.

Finally, Whittemore stood, pointed the gun at Bowie, and hissed, "You had better keep your mouth shut." Without being told, Bowie lifted his hands in the air.

Whittemore motioned the trusty to walk ahead of him to the locked door on the south side of the hospital that led down the steps and then through the wall, then pressed the gun against his back. When they reached the door, Whittemore unlocked it. Then, leaving the keys in the door and with the gun still pressed to Bowie's ribs, the two men walked down the stairs and through the open gate that led to freedom.

Only three weeks after entering the penitentiary for the second time, Richard Reese Whittemore was a free man. This time he left with blood on his hands. In a few days, Richard Reese Whittemore would be a murderer.

Leaving Bowie standing at the gate, Whittemore ran south down the Madison Street sidewalk, hugging the prison wall.

—◆—

Six

BEFORE HEAVEN

Bowie screamed, "Holtman's dead, Holtman's dead!"

He could have followed Whittemore to freedom, but Bowie was more concerned about the guard. Still screaming, he ran back into the hospital, where his calls got the attention of the prison doctor. The doctor found Bowie bent over Holtman. The trusty sputtered out an explanation—Whittemore had escaped. The doctor took one quick look at Holtman, raced back to his office, and called the prison surgeon.

Atop the Madison Street wall, a guard heard yelling but couldn't tell if the voice came from inside the prison or from the street. In the distance he saw a man wearing a cap and overalls and gray sweater walking fast down Madison Street. The man let out a whoop and then crossed the street to Constitution Avenue, but the guard thought nothing of it. A lot of men in the industrial area wore work clothes, and under Sweezey prisoners still wore clothing that did not identify them as such. They looked like everyone else.

Now the other two guards stationed in the hospital appeared before the stricken guard and sounded an alarm. They helped Bowie carry Holtman back inside the hospital. By then, nearly five minutes had passed and Whittemore was out of sight. The unconscious Holtman soon followed him out the same gate, strapped to a stretcher, on his way to University Hospital.

All over the prison, guards sprang into action. They herded prisoners back to their cells for a head count and locked the facility down, but it was too late. Sweezey rushed back to the prison as Brady contacted the police. Patrol boxes all over Baltimore flashed, calling police to their posts as Detective Captain Charles Burns gave the order that Whittemore was to be shot on sight. The police soon fanned out, trying to lock down the city, guarding all railroad stations, wharves, and roads leading out of Baltimore. Police distributed a bulletin with Whittemore's description, noting that he was wearing—"a blue cap, gray coat sweater, blue work overalls and low black shoes."

It would take a day or two to distribute a photo. For now, he looked a lot like every other man scrambling to make a living.

Inside the prison, Whittemore's cronies were pulled in and interrogated. No one admitted to knowing anything except for Dietz. Trying to curry favor, Dietz said that Whittemore had bragged that he intended to escape and had figured out how he would do it, but hadn't shared any of the details.

Outside the penitentiary walls, there was one person authorities wanted to speak to as soon as possible: Margaret. If anyone knew anything, it would be her.

The police arrived at the home she shared with her mother on South Gilmor Street just an hour or two after the escape, knocked roughly on the door, and demanded entry. Her mother answered. Margaret wasn't in, and Theresa Messler knew nothing about the escape. A couple of officers stayed behind to await her daughter's return—if she returned. For all they knew, she and Richard were already on the run.

It was no surprise that Margaret wasn't home. In the days since her husband was returned to prison, she hadn't exactly been a wallflower. On this afternoon, she and a girlfriend had gone to a movie. A new picture, *Flames of Desire,* had just opened at the Parkway, the story of "a wrecker of men's hearts and happiness . . . the drama of a girl who knew beauty's power." One in a spate of films Hollywood was churning out to appeal precisely to young women like Margaret, it described her to a tee.

After the movie, Margaret and her friend went shopping. At about 6 p.m., Margaret was on her way home and stopped at a drugstore on the corner of Baltimore and Gilmor Streets.

She walked inside and saw a patrolman standing in front of the newsstand reading an evening newspaper. A photograph of her husband emblazoned across the top of the front page snatched her attention. In huge type, she saw her husband's name paired with the word "escapes."

Margaret screamed and turned rigid, falling to the floor in a dead faint. The police officer carried her to a chair and a drugstore clerk waved smelling salts under her nose and gave her a glass of Vichy mineral water until she stirred and regained consciousness.

Margaret sputtered an apology—she didn't know what had come over her. At the same time her mind was racing. *Where was Richard? What had happened? What was she to do?* Of course she knew he wanted out, but she hadn't been privy to the details. She had to get home. *What if he was waiting there?*

With no idea who she was, the cop offered to drive Margaret home. When they pulled up to her house, a handful of detectives were waiting in a knot outside.

The jig was up. Playing dumb and thinking fast, Margaret told the cop that the detectives were there because she was Dick Whittemore's wife, but she didn't know anything. The detectives pulled her inside, filled her in on the rough details, and started grilling her.

Blinking away tears and sputtering, makeup streaking down her face, Margaret swore that she didn't know anything about anything. "Before Heaven, I know absolutely nothing about my husband's escape," she said, laying it on thick. "Oh why did he hit that poor man? I was over to see him a few days ago and he said 'Margie, you are my wife . . . time will go fast, I have made up my mind to go behave myself, serve five years and then try for a pardon. I know you'll be true to me. All that you can do is wait for me.'"

She sounded like she was reading some passage torn from the pages of *Dream World,* and she recited her lines to perfection, adding, "I haven't the faintest idea where Reese is . . . he told me he was going to go straight, live the right sort of life and be the right sort of husband to me."

Her words played well in the papers the next day—the devoted wife shocked by the actions of her husband. After the detectives left, they assigned two patrolmen to keep watch on the house. They walked back and forth, up and down the block, eyeballing everyone who walked past on the sidewalk and scrutinizing every car. If Whittemore tried to reach Margaret, he wouldn't make it to her alive.

Now it was Margaret who was under guard. Pacing the house, trying to think along with her husband and figure out where he might be and what he expected her to do, she made her way to a rear window, flung open the curtain, and looked outside. Another patrolman, Jerry O'Brien, stood in the dim light, watching the house from the back alley. Their eyes met.

Pure rage welled up inside her. Everything she had gained, everything she had, was now at risk. She couldn't take it for one more second. Standing before the window, the woman the papers called "Tiger Girl" made her first public appearance.

She threw open the sash, leaned out, and started screaming and cursing at the officer and, as the *News* described it, "told all within hearing of her shrill voice what she thought of policemen in general and of O'Brien in particular." O'Brien never moved, just stared back until her rage flamed out. He later quipped that the worst part was not being able to yell back.

Police also visited both Rawlings Whittemore and Richard's brother, Rawlings Jr. Richard's father also knew nothing. After they left, Rawlings stayed inside, curtains drawn, once again ashamed of his son.

Rawlings Jr. wasn't home. He was working as a blacksmith, but he was also bootlegging and stealing, already well along on the path his brother was already traveling. When he learned of Richard's escape, he celebrated, going on an all-night bender with his pals, bragging to everybody about their relationship as if Richard had just scored the winning touchdown in the big game, buying drinks, and talking big as if he himself had escaped the pen.

At 5 a.m., he reeled and staggered down the sidewalk toward his house, sloppy drunk. Spotting a cop, he couldn't help himself. Whittemore whooped it up, waking the neighborhood with his hollers and cheers and taunts.

The cop slapped him in handcuffs, charged him with disorderly conduct, threw him in a police vehicle, and hauled him away. Rawlings Jr. didn't know anything about the escape, he leered. He only knew that he was happy that his brother was free. On the street, being a Whittemore now had the same cachet the name once had in more polite society.

Making a very brief and very hungover court appearance the next day, Rawlings Jr., his head pounding, was much more subdued. After sobering up and paying a fine of $6.45, he was released.

R obert Holtman lay in a hospital bed, unable to speak. His wife Marie, his two brothers and a sister, and his four adult children held a vigil at his bedside.

Holtman was dying. Shards of bone had penetrated his brain, causing a massive hematoma.

A surgeon did the only thing he could, the only thing he knew how to do. Using a hand drill, he penetrated the skull to relieve pressure, removed shards of bone and any loose fragments caused by the initial fracture, cleaned and debrided the wound to try to thwart infection, and washed his hands. There was little hope. Although Holtman's vital signs stabilized soon after the surgery, his chances of recovery were virtually nonexistent. He had lost too much blood and had clearly suffered brain damage.

Herbert O'Conor sat at his bedside and gently asked a few questions, attempting to take a dying statement. Holtman sometimes gave a small nod or subtly squeezed the attorney's hand in response, but he did not speak or open his eyes. O'Conor left him to his family, later saying that seeing Holtman in his bed was one of the "most pathetic" sights he had ever witnessed, one that he believed would have served as a good "cure" for anyone opposed to the death penalty.

No sympathetic portraits of the guard appeared in Baltimore newspapers over the next few days, no heartrending photographs of his wife and children or grandchildren, no interviews with neighbors or coworkers attesting to his character or fleshing out his biography. He was just a name.

There was nothing strange about that. Stories about victims didn't sell newspapers; stories about criminals and crime did. Besides, one way or another, almost every working stiff was a victim in some way and that wasn't news to anyone. Victims were simply a necessary part of the plot, collateral damage. Neither the press nor the public saw much of interest in their stories.

And that wasn't all that surprising. As far as the public was concerned, prison guards were on par with the police: they were guys who simply got paid to do a lot of the same things that landed everybody else in jail. It wouldn't be until well into J. Edgar Hoover's tenure as director of the Bureau of Investigation before those attitudes began to turn. Hoover needed money to run the Bureau the way he wanted to, and that meant petitioning Congress for more funds. That required the support of voters. By cultivating the press, trading access for favorable coverage, and feeding stories to the mass media that framed law enforcement in a heroic light, Hoover was able to gradually shift public opinion. By the 1930s, as tales of "G-Men" provided fodder for radio dramas and motion pictures, the public would slowly begin to perceive law enforcement officers in a new light, as some kind of American hero.

O ver the next day or two, the police chased rumors as Whittemore remained a phantom. Several female acquaintances of the Whittemores' suddenly became scarce, and police speculated that they might be harboring the fugitive. Their alternative theory was that he had made it out of Baltimore or was hunkered down somewhere else in town.

Baltimore authorities must have sensed that public sentiment lay not so much with Holtman as with Whittemore, and they provided the press with information they hoped would persuade readers to turn him in. Captain Burns stated that in Baltimore, Whittemore had "no friends" and had a reputation as a "rat" and a "squealer," though he provided little evidence of either claim. Police released a statement from someone they described as a "Baltimore crook" who had recently been sprung from the pen: he described Whittemore as "no good" and said, "He'd 'queer' his best friend to get himself off and he'll kill anyone who gets in his way. I'd turn him up if I knew where he was and tell the world I did it." That would prove to be wishful thinking.

Circulars containing Bertillon records, mug shots, and Whittemore's physical description were distributed to more than five hundred cities across the nation by every possible method, including mail and telegraph, and wire reports in newspapers spread word of his escape almost everywhere else. Soon, Whittemore sightings flooded in from everywhere. People claimed to have spotted him in Baltimore, Washington, New York, Philadelphia, Canada, and a dozen places in between. They said they'd seen him in a car, on a train, walking the tracks, panhandling, drinking in a bar. Baltimore police and Maryland State Police hauled in dozens of suspicious characters, but none proved to be Whittemore. They kept watch at newsstands all over the country, scrutinizing anyone asking for a Baltimore newspaper, certain that the fugitive wouldn't be able to resist reading about the hunt. Law enforcement had recently caught another recent escapee, Daniel Bender, that way. At Maryland's behest, San Francisco police had staked out an out-of-town newsstand and nabbed Bender buying a Baltimore paper.

At 5 p.m. on February 21, Robert Holtman died without ever regaining full consciousness, the cause of death a fractured skull. At that moment, Richard Reese Whittemore became a murderer, and one of the most sought-after criminals in Maryland history. As soon as O'Conor learned of Holtman's passing, he began to prepare a grand jury indictment for murder. The Bureau of Public Welfare offered a $500 reward for information leading to Whittemore's arrest.

Richard Whittemore wasn't in New York or Washington or anywhere else. He was still in Baltimore.

After braining Holtman and racing down Madison Street to Constitution, Whittemore had quickly disappeared, blending in with the crowd of working men on the street. Only a few blocks from the prison, Whittemore managed to hop on a public bus, just another workman on his way home from a job. He got off and then, figuring that the cops would be everywhere, hid out in the woods surrounding the Bayview Asylum in southeast Baltimore, emerging only at night to raid their garbage pails for discarded food. On his third night free, he decided he'd better leave town. He made his way to Route 7, the Philadelphia Road, stuck out his thumb, and received a ride to nearby Bel Air, some twenty miles northeast of Baltimore. He continued walking and encountered "a fellow fixing a flat tire . . . one of my former friends."

At least that's what Whittemore always claimed. Miraculously enough, his savior just so happened to be another denizen of the underworld, Tommy Langrella, aka "Chicago Tommy." *Imagine that.* He ran a restaurant on East Baltimore Street that fronted a speakeasy featuring a still on the premises.

Whittemore said that Langrella told him Holtman was dead and he was now wanted for murder. Then, depending on when Whittemore was asked, he claimed either that Langrella handed him $100 and drove him to Philadelphia, or that they both went to Chicago and lay low there. Either way, by the time O'Conor presented evidence before a grand jury on Monday, February 23, indicting Whittemore for murder, he probably wasn't in Baltimore. The police dragnet had come up empty, and Captain Burns admitted that the police were now playing a game of "watchful waiting," hoping that Whittemore would make a mistake.

One day later, Holtman was buried in the Baltimore Cemetery on East North Avenue. Penitentiary guards served as pallbearers.

The press and the public had already begun to cast about for someone to call to account for the escape. The blame fell on Thomas Sweezey.

The warden tried to blame the escape and murder on his assistant Brady, for failing to have Whittemore escorted to and from the hospital by guards; on the guards themselves, for being overly friendly; on the board, for not hiring an adequate number of guards; and on the civil service system, for leaving too many guards on the payroll who either wouldn't or couldn't do their job. Sweezey released a statement that concluded, "I have been doing all I could possibly do to prevent escapes." But that didn't satisfy either the state or the public. Someone had died, and now someone had to pay.

Democratic governor Albert Ritchie, the former state's attorney general and a man with presidential aspirations, began a personal investigation of the circumstances surrounding the escape, saying that "the time has come for me to see the conditions myself and see for myself whether any additional safeguards or changes should be taken or made to keep the convicts inside the prison walls," but he had already concluded that the guards were not to blame. Stuart Janney, the director of public welfare, announced that he too would undertake an investigation.

The newspapers unloaded on Sweezey, publishing cartoons that showed the prisoners lolling about in the Sweezey Club and guards passing out keys upon request. In one, the penitentiary was renamed "Hotel de Sweezey" and the warden himself was stationed at the front desk, wondering why "I can't keep all my guests" as prisoners filed out the door.

The investigations, which all took place in only a matter of days, concluded that Sweezey should roll back most of the reforms he had incorporated. They recommended that prisoners be given standard-issue clothing identifying them as inmates, that the warden institute stricter discipline, and, most of all, that he abolish the Sweezey Club. Sweezey balked; rather than institute changes, he tendered his resignation on March 9. Patrick Brady was named the new warden and agreed to all of the recommended changes. The Sweezey Club closed. From then on, if the men weren't working or eating, they were locked in their cells.

The brief era of penal reform at the penitentiary under Sweezey ended. Over the next few years, often citing the Maryland experience, prisons in many other states also rolled back reforms they had put in place. Sweezey's lofty ideal that prisons were a place not of punishment but of preparation for a productive life outside the prison walls was dead. Whittemore's freedom had cost not only Holtman's life but the small measure of freedom Sweezey had allowed every other inmate at the Maryland State Penitentiary.

Richard Whittemore could not have cared less.

And now Margaret was in prison, or at least it had to feel that way. She couldn't go anywhere or do anything without people knowing who she was. And every time she did leave the house and a stranger looked her way, she figured it was a cop tailing her, watching to see if she was meeting up with Richard, or meeting up with someone who had met up with Richard.

She couldn't trust anyone now.

Seven

A MOVIE THRILLER

Whittemore was white-hot. Being wanted for murder gave him status in the underworld far above that of other two-bit stickup artists, bootleggers, and hijackers. He was a somebody now, his picture in all the papers and his name on everyone's lips.

Margaret was white-hot too, and almost as well known as her husband. But notoriety didn't pay the bills or fuel Whittemore's efforts to avoid arrest. They both needed money.

For a few weeks, Richard stayed underground and out of sight, steering clear of known haunts and away from old acquaintances, at least those being watched by the police. Now his only potential companions were criminal outcasts like himself and a few trusted friends from the Fifteenth Ward, guys who suddenly found it useful for others to know they were close to Whittemore. If you were known to hang with a stone-cold killer, the crowds parted when you entered the cabarets. Whittemore was now a killer, and everyone knew there was little difference between one murder charge and two.

Baltimore police kept the pressure on him, and not just by keeping an eye on his family. They inferred that he was somehow involved in just about every crime that went down in Baltimore more serious than swiping an apple from the corner grocer. Nearly every arrest they made came with an interrogation or even a jailhouse beating for information on his whereabouts. They learned nothing useful.

Richard was still waiting for the Kraemers to go free. In the meantime, he found a ripe target, an opportunity too good to ignore. It was time to put his newfound expertise to work.

A middle-aged messenger for the American Bank, J. Wahl Holtzman, picked up deposits each day from small businesses in northeast Baltimore. On some days he carried up to $10,000 in cash before depositing it in the bank.

Armored vehicles were just coming into use, but they were expensive. It was cheaper for banks to employ a couple of armed guards to move large amounts of cash in private cars, and cheaper still to use non-uniformed personnel like Holtzman, working alone and only carrying a gun for their own protection.

Whittemore tabbed Shuffles Goldberg to help out, and Langrella steered him to some other local thugs eager to help: Spike Kenney, age twenty-four, was a well-known Baltimore heavy connected to Jack Hart. Twenty-one-year-old Leapold "Simon" Gilden dabbled in bootlegging and would do anything for a dollar. Both men were well known in the cabarets and gin joints throughout Baltimore. Charles Gross, a former Baltimore cop, had gone over to the other side. Familiar with police patrols and procedures, he was a valuable guy to have on your side.

With Goldberg doing the stakeout and tail, Whittemore learned Holtzman's routine, what kind of car he drove, and where he lived, and confirmed that he always went home for lunch. He'd be easy to find. Then, taking a page from the Kraemers, Whittemore outlined a plan and made arrangements to meet the gang in Baltimore. He dyed his hair blond, grew a mustache, which he also dyed blond, and added a pair of glasses. Early in the morning on Monday, March 16, looking like a bank clerk himself now, he then took an early train from Baltimore to Philadelphia.

He arrived shortly after dawn and met up with Gilden, Kenney, and Gross. A few days before, at Whittemore's instructions, they'd stolen a stylish four-door maroon touring car, with a rigid "California Top" that featured sliding windows.

Late that morning, they drove to Holtzman's home, a tidy semi-detached brick bungalow at 1714 Thirty-Third Street, and pulled over to the curb. As expected, Holtzman's car was parked outside, and the four men patiently waited for him to emerge after lunch. He came out right on cue at 11:40 a.m., carrying two satchels containing around $9,000, almost all cash. He waved to his wife and mother-in-law watching from a window and then climbed into his car.

As soon as he did, Whittemore and Gilden climbed out of the maroon touring car and jumped into Holtzman's vehicle, Whittemore in front and Gilden in back. Gilden put Holtzman in a stranglehold while Whittemore, his face covered with what was reported to be either a bandage or a handkerchief, laughed and, showing a gun, told Holtzman to do as he said, "or you'll be a dead guy." The clerk never had a chance to reach for his own weapon, later saying, "I didn't want to be killed, so I did as they told me to." Whittemore told Holtzman to drive.

Holtzman's wife and mother-in-law witnessed the hijacking and raced to the phone to call the police. Holtzman, quaking with fear, drove to Fenwick Avenue, nearly striking a bus on the way. The stolen touring car then pulled alongside, and Whittemore and Gilden forced Holtzman to stop. Gilden climbed out, calmly walked to the front of the car, popped the hood, and pulled the wires to the ignition. The two men in the touring car climbed out, entered Holtzman's car, and grabbed the two bags of money. Then Whittemore got out, keeping his gun trained on Holtzman, and all four jumped into the touring car and drove off fast, leaving Holtzman happy to be alive.

They abandoned the car on Twentieth Street, where Gilden had stashed another car. The four quickly divided up the money. Gilden, according to plan, then drove Whittemore to the train station and bought him a ticket to Philadelphia. Whittemore jumped on the train just as it was pulling away, $3,000 richer. It seemed the heist had gone off without a hitch.

There was just one problem, at least for Whittemore's companions. Both a passing cabbie and a bus driver recognized Kenney and Gilden from local cabarets. When questioned, police showed Holtzman and the two drivers an array of Bertillon records and each of the men identified the two suspects.

Both were known to the police, who had little trouble tracking them down at their homes. Before it was even dark, Gilden and Kenney had been arrested. Gross, learning that he was also under suspicion, turned himself in on the advice of his attorney a few days later. All three men refused to talk, and none of the money was found, but Herbert O'Conor had little trouble securing an indictment. They all paid bail and were released, their trial scheduled to begin on April 22.

Whittemore returned to Philadelphia. The first thing he did was treat himself to a new wardrobe.

He had reason to look his best. On April 15, 1925, after serving a little more than nine years of their ten-year sentence, the Kraemer brothers were finally paroled. For that, they may have had Whittemore to thank. The new security measures at the penitentiary put in place after his escape had left cell space at a premium.

But the Kraemers were not exactly free. As the two men walked out of the main gate into fresh air for the first time in almost a decade, two Baltimore detectives stopped them before they reached the sidewalk, placed them in handcuffs, and brought them to headquarters. After their 1916 arrest in New York, authorities there had filed a charge, still outstanding, for possession of burglary tools.

Baltimore police held the two men for several hours until New York authorities finally decided not to pursue the charges.

Even so, Detective Charles Burns, still ticked off about all the time they'd spent catching the brothers in the first place, made it clear that the Kraemers' days in Baltimore were over. He drove the two men to the train station, put them on board the next train to New York, and watched until their car pulled away, hoping never to see or hear of the two men again.

As soon as the brothers arrived in New York, they collected money they had stashed away, slipped into their old skin, and wormed their way back into the jewelry trade, posing as wealthy dealers.

Now it was only a matter of time.

G ilden went on trial a week later, O'Conor hoping to get a conviction on him first. But Whittemore threw a little sand in the prosecutor's face. He mailed a letter that, upon receipt, was certain to draw some attention.

On the first day of Gilden's trial, after the selection of a jury, assistant state's attorney Bernard Wells delivered the opening statement. Gilden's attorney, Harry Nice, then stood and, with a flourish, waved Whittemore's letter in the air, calling attention to its Baltimore postmark. Nice, who had narrowly been defeated by Ritchie in a run for the governor's office in 1919, had a great deal of credibility.

He used it all. The letter's author, he claimed, masterminded the job and fully exonerated Gilden, Kenney, and Gross, providing details of the crime that could only have been known by the perpetrator. Then Nice, his voice rising with indignity, claimed that police had confirmed not only the veracity of the author's signature but also his identity by fingerprints lifted from the stationery. The letter, he concluded dramatically, was signed "Reese Whittemore." Nice demanded that the charges against Gilden be dismissed.

O'Conor and Wells jumped from their seats. The letter was hearsay, they said, and Gilden and the rest could easily have fed Whittemore the information, even if the letter was actually from Whittemore. The letter, O'Conor exclaimed, amounted to pure "propaganda." Judge Arthur Stamp banged his gavel to restore order and suspended the trial to consider the motion.

The following day he ruled in the state's favor and ordered the jury to ignore the letter, but it called into question the testimony of witnesses. Gilden, who was a bootlegger as well as a robber, had plenty of dough for Nice to mount a vigorous defense. Even though the judge didn't allow the letter into evidence, it had still planted a seed of doubt, or perhaps even fear, in the jury. It was all over the papers the next day.

When the defense took over, Nice stoked that doubt and fear by producing more than a dozen witnesses of his own, all of whom claimed Gilden was at home and could not have committed the crime.

Then came the kicker. Nice called *a cop* to the stand. Motorcycle patrolman William Childress testified that, at precisely 11:40 a.m., the exact moment the hijacking took place, he had spoken to Gilden near the bandit's home on Reisterstown Road, several miles away, something Childress had previously neglected to mention. Perhaps his memory had been jogged by a little cash, or a lot of intimidation.

O'Conor was livid, but Childress's testimony, combined with the letter, had queered the jury. They acquitted Gilden, delivering O'Conor's office a rare defeat. He had little choice but to stet the case against the others.

For the time being, Gilden and Kenney resumed their lives of crime. Gilden's defense had cost a small fortune, but his lifestyle showed that crime still paid.

Meanwhile, Margaret had to continue to watch her back. Although the police surveillance of her home soon ended, both she and her husband had to suspect the police were still keeping close tabs. It made sense for her to maintain a low profile, and for the next six months she stayed in Baltimore and did just that.

O ther than his wife, Whittemore's only friends now, the only people he could trust, were the Kraemers and other criminals. Over the next few months he kept their company, traveling to Philadelphia, New York, Cleveland, and perhaps as far west as Chicago. He used this time to put the gang together and likely pulled off a few more robberies large and small, maybe to buy a new suit or two, or to send a bit of cash back to Baltimore.

One day Rawlings Whittemore opened his mail and found, in an otherwise empty envelope, two crisp $100 bills. His son also wanted to put some money in Margaret's hands, but instead of using the mail, which might give away his travels, he asked Si Gilden to serve as a go-between. After all, Gilden had earned Whittemore's trust by not squealing on him. Gilden agreed to serve as Whittemore's bag man. That would prove to be a costly decision.

Meanwhile, Whittemore put the gang together. Milton Goldberg, William Unkelbach, and Anthony Paladino became his most trusted allies. If he ever needed a few more men, Kenney and Gilden were eager to help.

Whittemore and twenty-five-year-old Goldberg, whose father emigrated from Russia in 1891 and was a kosher butcher, had known each other since they were kids. This mousey childhood acquaintance from the Fifteenth Ward had ears that stuck out like two open car doors, and his distinctive shuffling gait had earned him the nickname "Shuffles." Although Goldberg briefly attended the Baltimore Polytechnic Institute, he had fallen hard, like Whittemore, for the nightlife, and he had started using morphine. To feed his habit, he drifted into Baltimore's crime underworld, where he was known as a guy who could be trusted to wield a gun, ride along on a holdup, and keep his mouth shut. It was that simple, a transactional bargain he'd accepted long before. Goldberg had been implicated but not charged in the Norris killing that had sent Jack Hart and Walter Socolow to jail. A sickly man, his slight stature and odd appearance masked a cold, black heart that made him both easy to underestimate and the ideal toady.

To all outward appearances, Willie Unkelbach, aged twenty-nine, shared little with guys like Goldberg. Tall and angular, hard cases referred to men like Unkelbach as "cake eaters"—guys who wanted to have their cake and eat it too, to reap the benefits of crime while living a soft, middle-class life. Like Goldberg, he had fallen for the nightlife and worked the fringes of the Prohibition trade. Married, Unkelbach told people he was a salesman to explain away his occasional disappearances. Known to be a ladies' man, a swain, he wasn't as hard as the others and, in his desperation to earn their approval and respect as a tough guy, was easy to manipulate. He kept his ear to the ground in Baltimore, letting Whittemore know what was going on, currying favor.

In New York, Whittemore reconnected with his old pal from the Elmira Reformatory, Anthony Paladino. "Tony Palace" lived with a girlfriend in his old Brooklyn neighborhood.

Paladino knew his way around New York—all the best places, all the crooked cops, and all the lawbreakers. The Mafia was beginning to emerge as a real force in New York, slowly taking over bootlegging and other vices. While Whittemore and the Kraemers were independent operators, Paladino was connected. He dabbled in morphine too, had drug connections on Mott Street on the border of Chinatown and Little Italy, and introduced the gang around so they could score. When Whittemore told him what he and the Kraemers had planned, Paladino signed on.

What all these men had in common, apart from their growing appetite for opiates and cash, was their utter submission to Whittemore. After all, the next best thing to being the guy everyone else feared was to be friends with the guy everyone feared. Richard's friends were completely in thrall to him. He was a

leading man, the kind of guy Goldberg and Unkelbach and Paladino all wanted
to be, but they lacked his force of personality and cunning.

They were only bit actors. Richard Reese Whittemore was the star.

A fter only a month in New York, the Kraemers pulled the trigger on a
yearlong crime spree by what would one day be called "the Whittemore
gang," whose heists would leave the New York Police Department befuddled.
Nearly all followed a familiar pattern as distinctive as the Kraemers' use of the
"can opener": each was meticulously planned and rehearsed, pulled off with
clocklike precision and an overwhelming show of force, took only a few minutes, and left behind little evidence.

Whittemore and the gang began by setting up shop, taking rooms under assumed names in a series of New York apartments and residential hotels. They
blended in as young men of indeterminate but substantial means. Periodically
they gathered and were given the script by the Kraemers detailing the next
heist. Their target would be diamonds. Other gems were nice, but diamonds
were the goal.

The Kraemers first scoped out a jewelry store at 390 Grand Street on the
Lower East Side, in New York's traditional Diamond District, centered near
Canal Street, Maiden Lane and the Bowery, and Nassau Street and Fulton.
Some dealers were beginning to migrate to the district's current location on
Forty-Seventh and Forty-Eighth Streets between Fifth and Sixth Avenues, and
for a time both districts flourished.

The setup on Grand Street almost screamed for a robbery. Each day, as
Jacques Ross's store was opening, the manager and three clerks left the safe
wide open as they went back and forth placing stock in the window and display
cases. You could see the open safe from the front counter. After a few days stak-
ing out the place and making a few excursions inside, the gang was ready to go.

New Yorkers who flaunted their wealth in the city's better restaurants and
nightclubs, where old and new money intermingled and a woman's jewelry
could set her apart, were under siege. Nearly every day the tabloids—the *Daily
News,* the *Mirror,* and the *Evening Graphic*—reported on the latest apartment
break-in, store robbery, or mugging that added to the hundreds of thousands of

dollars of stolen gems and jewelry showing up on the street. New York newspapers even regularly compiled lists of lost jewelry that ran in columns the full length of a page. An entire cottage industry popped up, supported by the insurance industry, to recover merchandise the police seemed powerless to locate as private detectives negotiated payouts to thieves to return stolen jewelry.

Many thieves, if not tripped up during the execution of the crime, failed afterward in trying to dispose of stolen goods without knowing who to go to and who to trust. But the Kraemers had that figured out too. They cultivated a relationship with Joseph Tropp, a well-known and flamboyant New Yorker the papers described as a "gem speculator."

Tropp, a Warsaw-born Polish-Russian Jew, later claimed to have known the Kraemers in Poland. While the Kraemers were developing the can opener in Europe, Tropp, after serving time in jail in Boston for pickpocketing, went to New York and learned the jewelry trade.

By 1925, Tropp worked as a middle man between wholesalers and importers and the retail trade. It was both a legitimate business and a front, for his primary income came from fencing stolen gems and jewelry. Tropp, a large, balding, gregarious man, belonged to more than fifty fraternal organizations and was friends with New York politicians and police. He could get you a good deal on that little special something and was known as a soft touch when approached to donate to charity. In exchange, that earned Tropp a measure of protection from the authorities, and he operated more or less openly, sometimes in possession of millions of dollars of gems and jewels. He made it his business to know who wanted what and who had what.

Unlike many of the other thieves Tropp dealt with, the savvy Kraemers already knew the value of what they were stealing. They had even worked out a system with Tropp to ensure that neither was being set up. The Kraemers would go to Tropp a few days before each robbery and tear a dollar bill in half, each party taking one half. After each crime, the Kraemers would call on Tropp and slip their half-bill under the door. Tropp would match it up with his, and then slip both halves back out. The Kraemers would make sure of the match before entering. In this way, both parties were relatively sure who was on the other side.

"Disposing of stolen jewelry," Whittemore later wrote, "is as easy as stealing it." Within only a day or two after Tropp had the merchandise in his posses-sion, jewelers in his employ or who bought from him had removed the gems, melted down the metal, and either created new pieces or added the gems to their collection of loose stones, making them all but untraceable. Since the Kraemers already knew what the stolen gems were worth, Tropp gave them a better deal than many other thieves, who generally received only ten cents on the dollar. The Kraemers still didn't receive full value from the fence, as Tropp had to account for the resale cost: the difference between retail and whole-sale pricing and his risk. Finished pieces stolen by the gang that needed to be broken down and their metal and gems reset might return only 20 percent of full value, whereas loose stones and raw metal could be worth as much as 50 percent, particularly if they were diamonds. The latter were the items of real interest to the Kraemers. That's where the money was.

Tropp didn't take everything the gang stole—he wasn't interested in cheap stuff—but he was their main market, and he also had a reservoir of invaluable knowledge about which dealers and shops favored which jewels, useful infor-mation to know. The Kraemers' leftovers usually went to Benny Levy, Paladi-no's pal, who owned a hotel in Coney Island.

On the morning of May 9, the gang pulled up near Ross's shop on Grand Street in a stolen touring car with stolen plates, just as the store opened. Leav-ing a driver in the car, three men, all well dressed and looking for all the world as if they belonged there, entered the shop. As they expected, the store was empty of customers as three clerks set up merchandise in the front window and another worked behind the counter.

The three gang members all produced guns and handcuffs, and one barked out the orders. In a matter of seconds, all four employees were cuffed, herded to the back, and locked together in the washroom. One of the robbers produced a satchel, dumped in the contents of the display cases in the front window as pedestrians passed by, unaware, and another did the same with the remaining stock from the open safe. Then the three men rushed out to the car, and all four sped away with nearly $100,000 worth of gems. Within a day or two after the gems were fenced, everybody met, Whittemore made the cut, and everyone scattered. Whittemore later indicated that the gang walked away with $30,000 in cash from the Grand Street heist.

In this instance, precisely who in the gang did what is uncertain. In future jobs, Whittemore and one or both of the brothers would enter the store, and initially either Goldberg or Paladino would drive, help out inside, or keep watch outside. That's how it went every month or two into the fall of 1925, the Kraemers in New York and Whittemore and the rest of the gang traveling back and forth between New York and Cleveland.

In all the wide-open towns in between, where crooked cops and corrupt politicians reigned, it was easy to find drugs, booze, and women, especially when you were flush. They stayed in nice hotels and went to the best clubs. They traveled by car, since detectives, with well-known faces from the Rogues' Gallery committed to memory, lurked around train stations. The gang soon added another man to the squad, a driver, who added another layer of protection in transit.

Nate Weinzimmer, twenty-five, came from a well-to-do Cleveland family, but like Whittemore, he found the street far more exciting than anything else. Arrested for the first time at the age of eleven, he'd already been arrested nearly two dozen times by the time he met Whittemore, most of those offenses related to smuggling liquor. A big burly man with a broad face, in the right clothes Weinzimmer could pass for a member of the Chamber of Commerce. He was married and lived in a posh apartment with his wife and two children.

After meeting Whittemore, Weinzimmer fell under his spell and soon became the gang's gofer and chauffeur. He was responsible for stealing vehicles and, when they were in Cleveland, helping the gang dispose of some of the proceeds. Weinzimmer helped them buy cars and make other expensive purchases, much of it hot, like fine clothes and furs for their girlfriends. Except for the Kraemers and Paladino, the gang eventually settled in Cleveland between jobs, keeping at least two apartments.

Whittemore liked Cleveland. With no fewer than three thousand speakeasies and another thirty thousand home sellers and "blind pigs"—joints that just sold booze, often through a drawer so the buyer and seller never even saw each other—the city was the perfect place to set up shop and hide out. It was far enough from Baltimore that there were few prying eyes. One day, Richard thought, "we would go into a business" in Cleveland, maybe open his own speakeasy, and settle down there with Margaret.

He used a variety of aliases when he went out. Only the rest of the gang knew him by his true name. Goldberg also had an alias, Joseph "Joe" Langdon, and the gang knew Unkelbach as Willie Rogers or "Baltimore Willie." With no standard form of ID yet in use, it was easy to be whoever you wanted to be. Driver's licenses were just coming into use, but they were just paper cards, without photos, that usually were kept in the car.

The gang struck in New York again on July 16. This time they targeted Stanleys, a jewelry store at 269 West 125th Street in Harlem. The job showed the same meticulous planning, an identifiable modus operandi.

Once again they struck in the morning, just as the store opened, when the safe was wide open and the clerks were ferrying merchandise to the display cases. They also chose a day when a downpour had cleared the usually crowded streets of pedestrians.

After Weinzimmer collected the gang in a stolen Packard, he drove to the location and pulled up just down the street from the store. First Whittemore and Paladino got out, followed by the Kraemers and Goldberg. This time Paladino and Whittemore entered the unlocked door and immediately pulled guns on the two clerks inside. Whittemore delivered the order: "Stick 'em up. Get into the rear room."

Then Leon Kraemer and Goldberg entered, pulling out guns and handcuffs, as Jake Kraemer waited outside. A third employee, a porter, entered the store, but the gang had accounted for this contingency. Before he could run back out and sound an alarm, Jake blocked his way and shoved him back inside. Cowering, the porter joined the other employees, their arms in the air. The bandits herded everyone into a back room, where they were all cuffed and held at gunpoint. Then, as the *Daily News* reported, "each of the two bandits who entered the shop drew a pillow case from his shirtfront and the pair went to the open vault. Carefully and methodically, they looted the contents," wearing silk gloves to make certain they left no fingerprints behind. Meanwhile, the others, ungloved, wiped every surface they touched with a cloth. When they discovered a separate, locked compartment inside the main chamber of the safe, they threatened a clerk with a pistol whipping until he produced a key. Loose diamonds glittered inside.

It all took just a few minutes. Warning the employees to stay where they were or be shot, the gang walked out, jumped into their waiting car, and roared off with $125,000 in jewelry and loose gems. By the time the clerks, hobbled by handcuffs, mustered the courage to start yelling for help, the bandits were gone. In another day, the gems had been fenced, and the gang had made the split and quickly scattered.

By now Whittemore, alone, was sitting on more than $15,000. He pondered getting away for a while and taking off for Europe, but he couldn't secure a passport, later reporting that he "gave it up when I nearly got caught." Instead, he traded in his old car and bought a new one. It wasn't just any car, but a Locomobile 48, the Tourer edition, touted by the manufacturer as "an exclusive car for exclusive people," like the Vanderbilts and Mellons and movie stars, the kind of car that turned heads as it passed by.

But Whittemore missed Margaret. It was still too dangerous for him in Baltimore, and he fretted over trying to contact her directly, or going to her home. So he planned a heist—of her. One night after dark he and Goldberg drove into the city, and Goldberg asked around until he learned that Margaret was at the movies. While she watched a film flickering on the screen, oblivious, the two men staked out the theater, cooling in their car parked along the curb. When Margaret walked out, they waited till she was alongside the shiny new Locomobile, then jumped out, grabbed her by the arms, and shoved her into the car.

Richard didn't have to use much force. She must have been thrilled to realize her husband was her captor, and doubly so when she found out where they were headed. Whittemore had a reservation at a pricey resort in Long Beach, Long Island, and had already sent his belongings and a few things for her ahead in a trunk. It was time to live like the other half did for a while.

For a few short weeks, they rubbed elbows with other moneyed gangsters, celebrities, and the well-to-do, got sunburned, and splashed in the shallows along the white sand beach that served as a playground for the wealthy far more exclusive than garish Coney Island. They dressed up for dinner at night, and afterwards they would have stepped out at places like Castles by the Sea, a dance hall on the boardwalk, dancing the Charleston and the foxtrot and whatever other new dance was all the rage—the Chicken Scratch, the Turkey Trot, the Castle Walk.

Now that the heat was off, or at least down to a simmer, Richard had plans to bring Margaret along and make her a valued member of the gang.

She could be useful — as her holdup of Ortman's Confectionery had demonstrated — and she herself wanted to be useful. The gang also needed someone like her they could trust to handle the guns.

That was an important job. In 1911, corrupt New York state senator Timothy "Big Tim" Sullivan, a member of New York's Tammany Hall political machine, rammed through the toughest gun control law in the nation, requiring a license for any weapon small enough to be concealed. The Sullivan Act made unlicensed possession of guns and weapons like brass knuckles and blackjacks a felony. Although Sullivan argued that the law would deter crime, some historians believe his real goal was to give the cops an excuse to arrest his rivals. If you could plant a gun on a guy, you could send him to jail.

For a gang living under assumed names and carrying guns around, a Sullivan violation was a concern. Getting caught with a gun, even by accident, would lead to an arrest and now, through fingerprints and the Bertillon Bureau, almost certain identification. And for Whittemore, capture now meant a murder charge. The gang remained cautious and rarely carried any guns other than small pistols that could easily be hidden or discarded except when needed. They stashed everything else in a locker at Penn Station.

But it was different for a dame. Cops usually went easy on them and often fell for sob stories. If Margaret handled the guns, running them back and forth between the locker and a heist, not only was she less likely to get caught in the first place, but if she was, she might even be able to squeeze out some tears, play dumb, and talk her way out of it. She'd already proven she could be trusted. Although she'd been arrested, she'd never been charged. That meant she wasn't in any Rogues' Gallery of known crooks. The cops probably wouldn't even be able to learn her real name.

After a few weeks working on his tan, Richard had burned through the bulk of his bankroll and it was time for the gang to get back to work. For now, Margaret returned to Baltimore and waited for Whittemore to either call for her or swoop in and snatch her again. She went by train, to be safe, and her husband promised he'd call for her soon.

By September, the gang was back at work, robbing jeweler David Peck on September 14 of $45,000 in gems, a crime Peck managed to keep out of the papers.

On October 5, the mob targeted diamond dealer John Linherr's shop at 193 Sixth Avenue. A few days before, Jake Kraemer had taken Paladino along as he cased the place, sending him in to buy a signet ring and leaving a $5 deposit under an assumed name. This time they varied their pattern and pulled what the Kraemers called a "closing-time" job: they struck as the clerks were returning merchandise to the wide-open safe.

Weinzimmer again drove. The five gunmen entered, forced three clerks and two female customers into the back, then trussed the men with wire, gagged them, and forced them to the floor. They let the ladies stand. When a porter entered unexpectedly, Paladino walloped him with the butt of his gun, the man fell bleeding to the floor, one of the ladies cried out, and then they were tied and gagged as well. As the five thieves left with the goods in a canvas bag after cleaning out the safe, Whittemore called out, "Life is short! Be good!" This time their haul was around $100,000.

Two weeks later, the Kraemers learned that John Sanford, a jewelry salesman for Larter & Sons, a Maiden Lane wholesale jewelry firm, planned to call on retailers with samples for the Christmas trade. Like most big-name jewelers, he kept his goods in a safety deposit box in the vault of the Harriman National Bank on Fifth Avenue in Midtown. Jake Kraemer and Paladino tailed Sanford, identified his automobile and driver, staked out the location, and struck on the morning of October 19.

That morning Sanford, driven by his armed chauffeur in a Ford sedan with a special compartment to hold the samples, pulled up at the bank, and Sanford went inside to retrieve his merchandise. Jake waited outside as Paladino watched from across the street and Whittemore walked back and forth in front of the bank. When Sanford emerged, Jake Kraemer gave a signal, and they all piled into Weinzimmer's Cadillac. They were moving up in the world. Instead of stealing cars, the gang had collectively purchased the car specifically to use in the city, stealing new plates as needed.

As the Ford pulled onto Fifth Avenue, neither Sanford nor his driver noticed that the Cadillac had pulled in close behind. They drove through Central Park before heading uptown and stopping outside Henry Nockin's jewelry store at the corner of Broadway and Eighty-Fourth Street.

Sanford went inside Nockin's, one of the most secure jewelry stores in the city. An alarm box was mounted on the outside of the building, and a mechanical system inside it allowed employees to press a button and release tear gas in the event of a robbery.

But the gang had done their homework and already knew that. They had no intention of going inside.

As soon as Sanford entered the building, a car described by the *Times* as "a big sedan of an expensive make" pulled up just ahead of Sanford's more modest Ford. Jake said, "Let's walk over now." Paladino, Whittemore, and Goldberg got out, walked back toward the Ford, and then, in a flash, opened the driver's door and grabbed the chauffeur. They dragged him from his seat and rammed a gun into his side, promising to "shoot him full of holes" before they stripped him of his gun. Jake and Leon waited on the sidewalk as Paladino, gun pressed to the driver's ribs, walked him to the sidewalk and told him to keep walking. With a Kraemer brother on each side, they escorted the chauffeur down the street, where they made him stand directly under the alarm box and the sign that read "HOLD-UP ALARM." The press got a kick out of that.

Meanwhile, the others calmly and efficiently transferred the jewelry cases to their own car. When they finished, after warning the driver to stay put and stay quiet, the gangsters climbed into the Cadillac and the car sped off. The *Times* later reported that despite "scores of persons" passing by on the street, "only a few realized what was going on." All the petrified chauffeur could say afterwards was that all six were young and well dressed, "like college boys." The gang made off with $50,000 worth of jewelry, including an undetermined number of loose diamonds.

In just five months, the gang had scooped up more than half a million dollars' worth of jewelry, which they had likely turned into somewhere between $100,000 and $250,000 in cash. They may have stolen even more than that. These crimes were only the ones police later definitively pinned on the gang.

They had it down and were becoming ever bolder. They could have gone on forever, but success led to both overconfidence and greed.

Whittemore and the Kraemers always took the lion's share and divided the rest between the others. They were still getting a lot of money, but it wasn't quite like stealing cash. The rest of the gang wondered if they were being lowballed, as sometimes the amount reported stolen in the papers didn't quite match the amount the Kraemers said the jewels were worth. After the Sanford robbery, for instance, although the papers claimed the haul was worth $50,000, the Kraemers claimed that Sanford transferred only "watches, cufflinks, and penknives," worth just a few thousand dollars, from the bank. That didn't pass the sniff test.

The gang's tastes were also becoming ever more extravagant. In the days following a robbery, Goldberg and Whittemore, and sometimes Unkelbach, liked to linger in New York and enjoy themselves. They'd first spend a few days in the opium dens on Mott Street before following up with some expensive nights on the town. The Kraemers were more conservative. They invested most of their money; apart from taking weekend jaunts to Philadelphia to meet up with some longtime girlfriends, they generally left it to the others to act like playboys.

Whittemore in particular was always game to go after some cash. He was still sending money to Si Gilden to ferry to his father and Margaret. But he sensed that Margaret was becoming impatient and that maybe somebody was getting a little too familiar with her. He suspected Spike Kenney, who, despite being married, was known to have a wandering eye. To keep Margaret close, he bought her a Cadillac and gave it to Si Gilden to give to her.

They were all just getting started, and in another year's time, if they could just stick together, everyone would have enough to last the rest of their lives. In the meantime, a cash job promised to make everyone happy. Cash didn't need to be fenced, and in one fell swoop the boys would more than double what they'd each taken in so far.

During their drives through Buffalo back and forth from Cleveland to New York, the gang stumbled upon an opportunity they couldn't ignore.

Buffalo, a city of 700,000 and, at the time, the eighth-largest manufacturing city and the second-biggest railroad center in the country, with the world's second-largest inland port, was awash with money. All those workers needed to be paid, and the Federal Reserve Bank of New York had a branch in Buffalo.

Most manufacturers and private businesses still paid employees in paper money, and the transfer of piles of bags of currency from the Fed to area banks, and from there to area businesses, created a security nightmare. Although bank robberies themselves were not uncommon, robberies of these cash transfers from the Fed were almost unheard of. The money moved in trucks retrofitted with light armor and manned by armed guards, and most banks also employed armed guards on their end to help with the transfers. Anyone thinking of hijacking a truck from the Fed had to think of that. Still, in early October the People's Bank of Buffalo was concerned enough to become the first bank in the city to purchase a fully armored car, the Reo-National, a six-cylinder car that featured bulletproof glass and armored steel plating.

The bank had some cause to be alarmed. Some believed that the city's flamboyant mayor, Frank Schwab, encouraged crime and had created "a city where thieves can colonize and operate with reasonable security from police molestation." Armed robberies were becoming ever more common. Earlier that summer, local thug Harry Harris had commandeered a $6,000 payroll heist. Arrested for the crime in Detroit on October 7, he easily made $50,000 bail but failed to show up for his arraignment a week later. Harris immediately became a suspect in any large robbery from Detroit to Niagara Falls and Pittsburgh.

Harris's mug shot appeared in all the Buffalo papers. And he happened to look *a lot* like Richard Whittemore: same size, same build, and same hair and eyes and nose. That coincidence may well have sparked an idea among the gang. If the police already believed that Harris was on a robbery spree, why not give them one more? Although the Whittemore gang never took public credit for the subsequent crime—and given the result, for good reason—it had all the earmarks of a Whittemore gang heist. It featured the painstaking choreography of their jewelry store heists combined with the boldness displayed in the Holtzman robbery—the Kraemers' brains paired with Whittemore's growing ruthlessness.

This time cash would be the target.

Every Thursday, like clockwork, a truck from the Federal Reserve delivered cash for Friday payrolls to the Bank of Buffalo branch of the Marine Trust

Company on North Division Street between Main Street and Washington Street. As the *Buffalo Times* later reported, as "has been the custom," the same two armed guards drove the exact same short, circuitous route through the city every week, ending their trip by turning west onto North Division, a one-way street, and arriving about 9:15 a.m., fifteen minutes before the bank opened. Each time the armored truck would pull up in front of the bank and an armed bank messenger would come out the front door, lock the door behind him, approach the car, and remove satchels of currency. As the guards in the truck watched, the messenger would return to the bank, unlock the door, then reenter the building, locking the door behind him. The guards would then drive off and return to the Reserve to make their next pickup.

The routine never varied. You could set your watch by it, and that's precisely what the gang did. They decided to strike on October 29, a Thursday, one day before payday.

The gang spent weeks planning the heist. They didn't want to risk using their own car to pull an out-of-town job. On September 30, they stole a Buick sedan in New York and added stolen plates. The gang then drove to Buffalo in the Buick and the Cadillac, which they planned to use to get out of town after the robbery. On the evening of October 28, after the gang checked into downtown Buffalo hotels under assumed names, Richard Whittemore parked the Buick overnight in a garage at 908 Ellicott Street. Early the next morning, one of the men retrieved the car from the garage and staged the Cadillac. The gang all checked out of their hotels, reunited, and went over their plans.

At about 9:10 a.m., the Buick, now bearing at least four men and a driver, turned onto North Division Street, drove just past the bank, did a U-turn, and pulled over to the curb in front of a shoeshine stand, facing the wrong way on the one-way street. That was no accident.

Whittemore, wearing a gray overcoat and cap, climbed out and walked a few yards up the street to the locked bank door and stood outside, huddled against the limestone facade, as if waiting for the bank to open. Within a few moments, another customer, Alfred Guggisberg, walked up — as he later claimed — carrying $10 in his pocket to deposit at the bank. They chatted for a moment about the weather, and then Guggisberg, realizing the bank would not open until 9:30, walked down the sidewalk to the Noah-Foster cigar store to kill time.

It was a quiet, gray morning. Most office workers were at their desks, and only about two dozen pedestrians sauntered down the block on errands. At the same time the Buick was parked, the bank truck left the Federal Reserve, only a few blocks away on Main Street, to drive the usual route and reach the bank at 9:15 a.m. When it arrived, it pulled in at an angle directly across from the impressive arched main entrance. Behind the wheel was Charles Clifford, age forty-one, a Rochester native in his seventh year driving for the bank. Riding shotgun was fifty-year-old Louis Yarrington, working his third year as a guard after leaving the railroad. Both men carried pistols. Half a block away, police officer John Bunce stood in the street, directing traffic.

Inside the bank, John Meyer, the bank messenger, peered out the window, waiting for the delivery. Seeing the truck arrive, Meyer came out of the bank, locking the door behind him. As he did, Yarrington left the truck and unlocked the door, just as he did every week. He greeted Meyer and removed two large bags of cash, one containing $93,000 in $5, $10, and $20 bills, the other $24,000 in $1 and $2 bills, and handed them to Meyer.

Nothing seemed amiss. Neither the Buick nor the man in the gray overcoat lingering outside the bank caused any suspicion; it was a day like any other. Yarrington walked with Meyer to the sidewalk and waited for him to reenter the bank, the two bags under his left arm. Although guards in cities like New York and Chicago often wore bulletproof vests and used satchels that released tear gas if dropped, such precautions were not taken in Buffalo. Meyer paused to unlock the bank door, pulling the key out of his pocket with his right hand.

As he did, Richard Whittemore stepped toward him and smiled. Several of Whittemore's companions, also wearing overcoats and caps, nonchalantly climbed out of the Buick. Meyer looked up as Whittemore approached, thinking he might know the man, and said, "Good morning."

It wasn't. Whittemore's smile turned hard, and he pulled a revolver from his pocket and spat out, "Stick 'em up!"

With his gun holstered at his hip, one arm wrapped around the money bags, and his keys in the other, Meyer hesitated.

Whittemore did not. He aimed and pulled the trigger.

The bullet shattered Meyer's elbow, and he dropped the two bags of cash, yelling, "My God I've been shot!" Startled onlookers stopped in their tracks.

As Whittemore swept over to pick up the cash, the Buick pulled out headed the wrong way on the one-way street, away from the traffic cop on the corner, and slowly accelerated down North Division Street, in what one witness later described as "in second gear." Whittemore's companions pulled out revolvers and started firing. Pedestrians began to run, ducking into offices and shops for cover, as shots echoed down the street. Meyer staggered through a nearby doorway, calling out, "We're being held up!"

From inside the armored truck, Clifford watched the scene unfold through the windshield. Before he could move, one of the gunmen, from point-blank range, shot him in the side of the head. Clifford never even saw him.

Bunce, the patrolman, heard gunfire and started running down the street toward the fire, pulling his revolver from his holster. Whittemore, bags in his left hand and his gun in his right, ran down the street toward the corner of North Division and Washington Street.

Yarrington began firing at Whittemore. One of the gunmen fired at Yarrington, who spun around when the bullet hit his body, staggered, and dropped to his knees as another gunman opened fire from inside the car.

Bullets from every direction rained down. Whittemore grabbed his wrist, stumbled, dropped one of the bags, then kept running. As Yarrington fell to the ground, Bunce chased after the car, shooting as he ran, shattering a side window and striking a tire. Two gunmen and then Whittemore all jumped onto the running board of the moving car, some diving in through the windows as someone still kept shooting from inside the car. Both Bunce and the gunmen kept firing as the car pulled away. Bullets slapped off the bank's stone facade, shattering the window of a cigar store across the street, clipping a young woman's ear, and whistling over heads. A shoeshine boy raced to Yarrington and started dragging him away. Bunce commandeered a car and ordered the driver to give chase, but a passing streetcar at Washington Street blocked the way. The bandits turned onto Ellicott Street and were gone.

At least, that's probably what happened. In the confusion, more than twenty witnesses saw *something,* yet not a single person saw the entire event, and as everyone ducked and ran, no two people saw the scene exactly the same way. One man told the *Morning Express* that it was like a "movie thriller." There were four robbers, or five, or six, two cars or one. Joe Schabo, an employee of the *Buffalo*

Courier, swore that he saw another gunman, a lookout, run down the street the opposite way. He might have been right.

There was no question, however, about what was left behind; a bag with $24,000 in cash laying abandoned in the middle of the street, clouds of gun smoke still hanging in the air, John Meyer clutching his shattered arm in a doorway, Louis Yarrington gasping for breath on the ground, and Charles Clifford slumped in his seat, deathly still, blood oozing from a hole in the side of his head.

From the first shot to the last, it hadn't taken more than fifteen seconds.

Their car riddled with bullets, the right rear tire flat, the gang drove away according to plan. Perhaps five minutes later, just as police alarms were going off all over the city, they pulled over about a mile and a half away in a quiet residential neighborhood on Dodge Street, just off Main, where they had stashed the Cadillac. The gang piled out of the Buick and into the other car. They dumped the two big guns they'd carried in case their plan fell apart, a sawed-off 12-gauge shotgun and a short stock the cops called a "freak" gun, a Marbles Game Getter, featuring two triggers and two barrels, one for a .22 and the other for a .44. They wouldn't need them now. They got on the road, $93,000 richer, Whittemore sporting a flesh wound just above his wrist and cackling, and everyone's pockets about to bulge with cash.

The police, the press, and the public flooded the area around the bank, taking statements, interviewing witnesses, and gawking at the blood on the pavement. Clifford was dead on the scene. Meyer and Yarrington were rushed to the hospital by good Samaritans, Meyer with a broken left arm, Yarrington with a bullet wound through both lungs.

Reporters called in frantic accounts to the papers, copy boys raced through the offices, and linotype operators got to work. The presses whizzed with a new front page, "EXTRA" emblazoned across the top, as they raced to get out word of the biggest bank robbery in Buffalo history. Police took statements, gathered the best witnesses, and brought them to headquarters to view Bertillon records and mug shots. About half were too confused or too excited or too frightened to identify anyone, but the rest, one right after the other, were certain they recognized the man who had shot Meyer and run down the street with the money.

It was that rat bastard Harry Harris.

Based on more eyewitness accounts, police soon believed that a couple of other local toughs, Mike Sperrazzo and Joseph Kobierney aka "Polack" Joe Edwards, had joined Harris. One witness swore he'd seen Dutch Anderson, partner of Gerald Chapman, who until his recent capture had been the most notorious gangster in the country, famous for robbing a New York mail truck of $2.4 million in cash, bonds, and jewelry. Anderson's presumed involvement was big news, a sign that Harris had made contact with the larger criminal underworld.

As police tried to lock down the city, Chief of Police Charles Zimmerman ordered policemen to "shoot to kill." Even without any evidence, cops blamed supposed "guerilla gunmen" Harris brought in from New York, the kind one policeman described as the type that "never gives his victims a chance . . . absolutely the worst kind of criminal in the world." The *Courier* later called it "the most intensive manhunt in the history of the city." The cops found the Buick and the guns before lunch. A witness saw everyone drive off in a Cadillac. But when Bertillon expert Joseph Whitwell arrived to check the car for fingerprints, the cops had already crawled all over it, destroying any possible evidence. They'd passed the guns around like souvenirs. Hanging from the dash was a driver's license with a New York City address in a name the cops were certain would be fake. In the backseat was an empty bag from the bank. There wasn't any blood in the Buick.

Louis Yarrington died at 10 p.m. From his hospital bed, Meyer said of the robbers: "They're dogs, those fellows, shooting us down the way they did, in cold blood." Each dead man left behind a widow the papers didn't bother to name.

By the time one murder had become two, the Whittemore gang was miles away, maybe in Cleveland, maybe on their way to New York, or maybe in some other burg in between, probably celebrating after a fine meal.

All night long Buffalo police were besieged with phone calls. A man came into a hotel bleeding. A Cadillac was seen speeding through the streets at night. Supposed suspects lurked behind every car window and in every hotel. The next day the Buffalo newspapers had all but convicted Harry Harris of the crime, their lurid headlines enticing readers who'd missed the show. One from the *Courier* read "Eye-Witnesses Drink Deep of Thrills as Bullets Graze Heads; Screams of Women Mingle with Barks of Pistols." They couldn't get enough.

That two men were dead was almost ignored in favor of the chase. Like the money, Clifford's and Yarrington's lives were insured, and the bank announced that it intended to turn the proceeds over to their families. The two bank employees joined Robert Holtman as little more than names in the paper. Some of the papers didn't even get Clifford's age right, and the funeral report in his hometown paper, the *Rochester Democrat and Chronicle*, was buried on page 22. The victims were just statistics, their deaths simply detritus of the times.

For the next few weeks, Buffalo police chased after their own tails, flooded with leads that went nowhere. Dutch Anderson was killed in a police shoot-out in Muskegon, Michigan, on October 31, and police discounted his involvement in the robbery. Still, they distributed circulars nationwide that identified Harris as their suspect, though within a few days admitted they had no leads. The police department took out an ad in one of the Buffalo papers claiming crime was down.

Some weeks later, the police admitted, with some chagrin and without explanation, that Harry Harris wasn't their man after all.

By then, the Erie County court had authorized twelve indictments, six charges each for the first-degree murders of Charles W. Clifford and Louis Yarrington.

The defendants named on the indictments were telling: James Doe, James Roe, Richard Doe, Richard Roe, John Roe, and John Doe.

For almost a month, Buffalo police had been looking for the wrong guy. Two men were dead, two women widowed, and another man crippled, and the police had no idea whatsoever who they were even looking for, no idea at all that Whittemore and the Kraemers and the others were laughing all the way to the bank and would soon be spending blood money like water.

Eight

A GREAT MANY GOOD TIMES

Back in Baltimore, Si Gilden never gave Margaret the Cadillac.

He never gave Rawlings Whittemore any of the money his son had sent for him either, keeping both the car and the cash. And Spike Kenney had been shooting off his mouth and making moves on Margaret. That's what Margaret said anyway, although Kenney's wife later showed her claws over that charge, saying she herself rarely let her husband out of her sight and besides, he didn't like "bleach-bottle blondes." Gilden and Kenney would soon regret getting on the wrong side of Richard Whittemore.

After the Buffalo bank heist, something in Richard Whittemore came unglued. Killing the bank employees wasn't like killing the prison guard Holtman, which he would later excuse as simple self-defense. Now that he'd taken a bullet himself and witnessed just how easy it was to kill from the end of a gun, and how a flood of money seemed to justify the flow of blood, killing didn't seem to bother Whittemore at all. Whenever trouble showed its face, he began to view it as his first option.

He first targeted Spike Kenney. After joining forces in the Holtzman hijacking, relations between the two men had soured, maybe over Margaret, maybe over something else. All Richard Whittemore would say was that Kenney had been shooting his mouth off.

Kenney may have just been talking big after drinking too much gin, but Whittemore didn't like it. "The news came back to me that Spike cracked he was going to get me," said Whittemore. "I don't like those sort of wise cracks."

After the bank robbery, Whittemore and the rest of the gang swept back toward New York City. Winter was coming, and they couldn't afford to waste time pushing through snowdrifts once the Kraemers lined up another target. During the worst of the winter season, they all planned to remain in New York.

But first, Whittemore made a detour into Baltimore. He took Paladino along for the ride, just in case he needed help.

On Halloween weekend, the night of Sunday, November 1, Whittemore learned that Kenney and his wife were at the Old Taylor Roadhouse in Middle River. He waited outside, lurking in the shadows as the crowd began to disperse.

At 4 a.m., Kenney called a cab. It pulled up just as he and his wife were standing at the door, putting on their coats. As Kenney stepped onto the porch, Whittemore called out his former partner's name. He wanted him to know who shot him.

Kenney looked up, and Whittemore, silhouetted before the glare of the cab's headlights, fired what the *Sun* described as a "volley of shots" that left Kenney's overcoat "riddled." Only two bullets struck flesh, one in the arm and the other through his abdomen. As Kenney collapsed and his wife screamed, all the cab driver saw, or at least admitted to seeing, was a gunman disappear into the night. Kenney was rushed to Baltimore City Hospital. Whittemore and Paladino were probably back in New York before doctors stopped the bleeding.

For the next few days, Kenney lingered near death. Although the bullet in his side didn't strike a major organ, Kenney lost so much blood that a transfusion (which would be provided by his wife) was needed to save his life. When he regained consciousness, he refused to tell police who shot him, even though the cops knew full well who did it: everyone on the street was naming Whittemore. All Kenney would say was, "They ain't got me yet . . . I'll settle this in my way when I get out." His condition stabilized, and doctors said that he'd likely live, though he would need weeks of near-constant care.

Kenney's wife hired two private nurses to look after him. Four days after the shooting, at 3:30 p.m., the phone rang in Kenney's hospital room. Kittie Tims, the day nurse, answered.

The woman caller delivered a warning: "You had better get off that case. They're after Kenney, and they intend to get him if they have to shoot their way into the hospital and kill doctors and attendants." Then she added, "I am warning you because I don't want to see a woman get hurt."

It may have been Margaret, or it may have been someone else, but the timing was suspicious. What other woman in Baltimore would Whittemore trust to make such a call? Or maybe Margaret had a soft spot for Kenney, or at least for a couple of innocent nurses.

Tims called the police. Kenney was immediately placed under police guard at the hospital, and the two women nurses were replaced by men. But the warning had its desired effect: Kenney kept his mouth shut. He finally left the hospital on November 25.

By then, Whittemore was staying warm back in New York, satisfied that now Kenney would keep quiet and leave Margaret alone. Although most of the rest of the gang stayed in hotels for the winter, Whittemore felt safer in an apartment. Hotels had cops hanging around the lobby and hotel dicks poking their noses into everybody's business. In an apartment, he could come and go as he pleased and have visitors without arousing much suspicion.

Under an assumed name, he first rented an apartment at 110 West Eightieth Street. It was no third-floor, cold-water, walk-up flat either, but an apartment in a five-floor Renaissance Revival–style brownstone, only a block and a half from Central Park and half a block from the American Museum of Natural History.

Even then, you had to be somebody to rent a place like that—until recently, George S. Kaufman, the playwright, had lived just a few doors down. And that's exactly the way Whittemore saw himself now: a real somebody, with a fancy car, fancy clothes, and soon, a fancy girl on his arm. It was time for Margaret to join him and to take a more active role in the gang. From this moment on, she'd serve as the classic gun moll, actively playing a key supporting role, ready to carry the guns, scope out a store, or do just about anything else required short of pulling a job herself.

But the place on West Eightieth wasn't the right kind of place for the two of them to live as husband and wife, at least not for long. He needed that place for the gang business of making plans and divvying up the goods and for entertaining when, well, he didn't feel like going home. Margaret would only be in the way there. For the two of them he soon rented another apartment, in Chester Court at 201 West Eighty-Ninth Street, a newer building that provided what the realtors called "day and night" service, doormen and elevator operators, guys who wore uniforms, ran small errands, and called residents "sir" and "ma'am." Margaret would swoon when she saw that. There, at last, they would live as man and wife.

To the real estate agent he presented himself as Horace Q. Waters, likely after the manufacturer of popular organs and player pianos whose son, Horace Waters Jr., was a well-known figure in Maryland. It didn't hurt for the realtor to think he was renting to a somebody, for a whiff of older money and the privacy that came with it. Once established, they'd go by yet another alias, Mr. and Mrs. John Vaughn.

If the cops ever came knocking, let them try to figure that one out.

F lush with cash, Whittemore made one more trip to Baltimore, his last as a free man. Once more he surprised Margaret, "taking her away just as she was getting dressed in the morning" and sweeping her into a car bound for New York. She had to leave all her clothes behind again, but that just meant she'd have an excuse to do more shopping.

They weren't even out of Baltimore before Whittemore was ready to turn back. He'd asked Margaret about the Cadillac. She didn't know what he was talking about. *Cadillac? What Cadillac?* Margaret told her husband Si Gilden hadn't given her any Cadillac, but she'd seen him driving one around. Richard asked more questions, and Margaret told him his father was barely scraping by. While Gilden had given Margaret a little money, none had made its way into Rawlings's pocket.

Whittemore was steamed. He wanted revenge, and now that he had killed at least once and attempted another, he knew killing solved problems.

He began plotting a possible return trip to Baltimore. Gilden's time would soon come.

Richard Whittemore didn't know it, but Baltimore police were beginning to get wind of his activities. Someone, maybe Kenney, now out for revenge himself, was talking.

T he gang's next two jobs hardly met their usual standard. On December 2, they robbed jewelry dealer R. M. Ernest on Columbus Avenue. One of the gang asked for a cigarette case he previously ordered that was stored in the safe, and the rest pulled their guns once the safe was opened. But they made off with only $25,000 worth of merchandise, far less than they'd been led to believe. After being fenced, the haul brought in only a few thousand dollars.

Although the big jewelry firms were beginning to move uptown, where the big money was, Danish-born Folmer Prip still ran a small jewelry manufacturing business on the eighth floor of the Armeny Building at 90 Nassau Street on the corner of Fulton. He kept a half-dozen craftsmen busy in a top-floor loft making high-end bracelets, necklaces, rings, and miscellaneous baubles for other jewelers and the occasional private commission for some swell who wanted to keep a woman happy.

Prip kept a lot of stock on hand stored in two safes, one for gems and finished pieces, and the other for raw materials. They were generally left open all day so his craftsmen could take what they needed.

In addition to precious gems, Prip kept a large supply of platinum on hand. Among the flapper set, platinum was the new gold, and on the side of the building Prip's firm touted "FLEXIBLE PLATINUM BRACELETS" in big block letters.

Around December 15, the Kraemers began to case the job, first wandering the block and checking out the surroundings, taking special notice of a patrolman stationed on the corner.

Prip shared the building with other offices and businesses, and the brothers paid particular attention to when employees and other tenants arrived and left. In 1924, another manufacturer in the same building, Charles Kresney, had been robbed of $125,000. Prip was certain to be cautious.

The building was accessed by two separate entrances. The craftsmen used a service entrance on the Nassau Street side, but that door was usually locked on the inside. Public access was by way of the Fulton Street address. Most businesses shut down at 5 p.m., when workers would stream out from both exits, but Prip and his employees didn't leave until a little later. It was almost Christmas, after all, their busiest season.

On their next visit late one afternoon, the Kraemers went inside. Entering on Fulton Street, they checked the building directory and noted that the elevator only went to the sixth floor, the top floor of the original building; what were now its top two floors had been added later. To access Prip's they would have to either walk up two additional flights or take the stairs the whole way.

The elevator operator delivered them to the sixth floor—they could check out the staircase on the way down—and then the two men walked up two more flights. To the left were two doors, the first to the workshop, and the other to Prip's office. The workshop door was unlocked. They watched men exit and enter without pause as they worked at a series of long tables with bright, incandescent lights hanging low overhead.

Leon Kraemer opened the office door. A bell rang, designed to alert Prip to visitors. He walked into a small outer office, separated from Prip's inner office by a small swinging gate. Prip came out and greeted him. His secretary, who kept a desk in the vestibule, was out. Jake lingered in the doorway.

Leon told Prip that he was from Philadelphia, and that a "Mr. Siegel" had recommended him. He told Prip he wanted "a good bracelet, a platinum bracelet," and asked to see some stock.

Prip returned to his office and brought out a few trays from the open safe. Leon squinted at piece after piece, holding them up to the light to get a better look, then asked to see "something fancy."

Prip told him his salesman was "out with the stock" and would be back about 5 p.m. Feigning impatience, Leon told him that he wanted a bracelet made for twenty-two diamonds and already had the stones.

That got Prip's attention. *Who has twenty-two diamonds and just walks in off the street?*

As Leon sniffed and snorted at the mountings and the watch Prip offered, Prip noticed Jake glancing around, peering over Leon's shoulder into the office, which contained the safes, the largest of which was eight feet high and five feet wide, and had a door that led out to the main workshop. While he browsed, the craftsmen kept going back and forth from the workshop to the safe in the office.

After a bit, Leon told Prip that he would "come back later." With that, he left and met Jake in the hall, where he'd also spent his time scoping out the workroom. The brothers left, this time taking the stairs all the way down. They'd seen enough.

So had Prip. He said later that "I felt there was something coming off." Returning to his office, he reached into his desk and grabbed a gun he kept for protection. He took a small hammer from his workbench "and put a nail right inside the door to my office," where he hung the gun "to have it handy."

Over the next few days, the Kraemers put together a blueprint. Weinzimmer would drive the two brothers, Whittemore, Paladino, and Goldberg. Unkelbach was either away or not needed. Their guns, as usual, would all be stashed at the train station, in a small bag. The afternoon of the crime Margaret would head to Penn Station, pick up the bag with the guns, then go back uptown, probably by cab. At about 4 p.m., the gang would meet up at Whittemore's apartment on West Eightieth Street, get the guns, and drive together downtown to Nassau Street. Margaret would hang behind—if anything went haywire, they needed someone on call to drive, hire a car, or ring up a doctor or an attorney.

Just after 5 p.m., when the building had mostly emptied, Whittemore and Leon Kraemer would take the elevator up to the top floor while the others took the stairs. The elevator boy would have no idea the men were all together. Whittemore would lead the way. Leon would walk up two flights, followed in a moment by Goldberg, Paladino, and Jake Kraemer. After Leon and Whittemore entered Prip's office, the others would wait precisely one minute and, as Whittemore and Kraemer held up Prip, they would enter the workshop, pull their guns, and tie up the workers. The gang would then empty the safes and take whatever else might be lying around.

Whittemore and Kraemer would exit through the stairway, get in the car with the haul, and drive off. The others would emerge a few minutes later, split up, and walk away. The Kraemers would soon deliver everything to Tropp. In another day or two, they would all meet up again on West Eightieth Street, divide the proceeds, and go their separate ways until the Kraemers set up another job.

The gang struck on December 19. Everything went according to plan until they gathered at the sixth floor and Whittemore started up the stairs. To his surprise, he heard a commotion up ahead, loud voices and the sound of people just leaving work and starting to clomp toward the stairs. Another jewelry manufacturer, Andrew Mander & Son on the seventh floor, must have decided to work late too.

That meant too many witnesses and too much uncertainty. Whittemore turned on his heel, skipped back downstairs, and called the job off, saying, "There ain't no use going on this robbery." Jake Kraemer agreed, saying, "It's the wrong time." The gang left according to plan and decided to try again a few days later.

That was fine with Whittemore. He had some other business to take care of: Si Gilden. And he wouldn't even have to go back to Baltimore.

Gilden had been skittish ever since the Kenney shooting, and for good reason. He'd been involved in more gunplay, some beef over liquor, and now, even though Kenney survived and kept quiet, Gilden was left looking over his shoulder. He likely also knew that Margaret had skipped town. After taking her Cadillac for himself, Gilden had to suspect that Whittemore had him in the crosshairs.

Gilden was in hiding, staying with his father, too afraid to go home to his wife and their two young children. Ida hadn't even seen him in several weeks. She'd received a death threat too, warning her that she'd better "shut up" or she'd be killed. But the holidays were approaching. Gilden needed money, and people needed booze.

Shuffles Goldberg did Whittemore's bidding. Gilden apparently didn't know the bat-eared gangster was still working with Whittemore, and when Goldberg told him he could get a good deal on champagne in New York, Gilden listened.

Somebody had been talking. A few weeks before, Baltimore detectives had received a tip that Whittemore was in New York with the Kraemers. They were even provided an address, 81 Mott Street, the dive in Chinatown near Little Italy where the gang hung out. Baltimore police sent a letter to that effect to their New York counterparts, and a few days later Baltimore detective

Cornelius Roche and a subordinate went to New York to stake out the location and see who turned up.

After arriving in New York, the two detectives blended into the neighborhood. They scanned faces on the street and pretended to be Italian, muttering a few Italian phrases they had memorized when anyone came within earshot. At night they even cruised the cabarets to see if they spotted Whittemore. But after a week they had nothing. They shared what little they knew with New York police and returned to Baltimore. New York police were intrigued, but they had yet to connect Whittemore to the string of jewel robberies. He was Baltimore's problem, not theirs.

Then the Baltimore police received an anonymous telegraph reporting that Whittemore had been spending time in Cleveland with Weinzimmer. Cleveland police staked out the Thornhill Drive address and determined that Weinzimmer lived there, but they didn't spot Whittemore.

Meanwhile, Goldberg helped set up Gilden. On Monday, December 21, with $2,000 in his pocket, Gilden drove to New York, not in the Cadillac, but in a car registered in his wife's name. He stopped in Paterson, New Jersey, where he made a phone call to learn the precise wheres and whens from Goldberg. He planned to grab the champagne and get out of New York before anyone, particularly Whittemore, was the wiser.

Gilden was next seen two days later, early on the morning of December 22, dumped amid the tombstones in the graveyard of Trinity Church at 25 Rector Street in Lower Manhattan, his face kicked in, five slugs in his body, his bullet-riddled car parked a short distance away, and, apart from a few dollars, his wallet empty. Whittemore hadn't gotten the Cadillac, but he did get revenge.

The killing sent a chilling message to the other gang members. After Whittemore shot Kenney and now had killed Gilden, Goldberg, Unkelbach, Paladino, and even the Kraemers all knew what would happen if they ever squealed on him. A threat of assassination bought a lot of silence and enforced a lot of discipline.

Baltimore detective James Manning went to New York and started poking around again. And now that Whittemore was dumping bodies in one of their churchyards, New York police were a little more interested.

The gang was already back at work. Only one day after the killing, it was business as usual, and time to try Prip's again. It began just as their previous attempt had. When they arrived at Nassau Street, Milton Goldberg begged off, claiming he was ill. He was—a short time later, he'd learn he had tuberculosis.

Whittemore ordered him to stay in the car with Weinzimmer. Again the men all met outside the elevator on the sixth floor. This time they didn't hear anyone in the stairwell or the hallway upstairs as they walked up the two flights. Whittemore and Leon Kraemer entered the office while Jake Kraemer and Paladino lingered outside the workshop door.

The bell rang as Kraemer and Whittemore entered. This time Prip's secretary, Rosa Pollack, was in. She was putting on her hat, preparing to leave for the day, when the two men entered. Prip, hearing the bell, put down his jeweler's tools and stepped into the front room, where another customer was waiting to pick up an order.

Holding a small suitcase, Leon Kraemer thrust out his hand and gave Prip a hearty handshake, again referencing Siegel and saying, "How are you, Mr. Prip? I want to see that diamond-studded wrist watch you showed me last week. Do you remember me?"

"No, I don't," answered Prip.

But he did. Prip turned around and went back toward his office. Kraemer started to follow, and Pollack said, "Wait out here please," as Prip, ignoring his revolver hanging on a nail next to the door, stepped quickly to the large safe. Instead of reaching inside, he slammed the door shut and spun the dial.

Then he heard the words "stick 'em up." His secretary and the unfortunate customer reached for the ceiling as Whittemore and Kraemer motioned them at gunpoint into the office, warning them both not to look at their faces.

In the workshop next door, one of the craftsmen, Andrew Sarinsky, started to leave and opened the door leading to the hallway. He was met by Jake Kraemer and Paladino. Kraemer barked out, "Hands up!" and shoved the man back inside. At the same time, another employee, Jacques Japka, heard the commotion in Prip's office and went in, only to be met by Leon Kraemer and Richard Whittemore and their guns.

Terrified, Sarinsky slid back into the shop. Kraemer ordered him to lie face down on the ground. He did as he was told. The other workers didn't wait for orders.

Prip, seeing the gun in Richard Whittemore's hand aimed at his gut, realized that perhaps closing the safe hadn't been the smart thing to do. Expecting
to be shot, he clutched his stomach, sickened by fear. Whittemore raised his
gun in anger and brought it down hard on Prip's head, saying, "Take that for
closing that safe." He probably intended to pistol-whip Prip until he opened the
safe, but hit him too hard—Prip fell unconscious. Japka then made a move to
close the other safe but received the butt of Kraemer's gun instead.

Working quickly, Paladino tied up each of the employees by the ankles and
wrists, dragging one out of a washroom where he tried to hide. They draped
Pollack over Prip, still unconscious, on the floor. The gang then emptied the
small open safe, which contained mostly platinum and gold. They found little
else of value apart from $250 in the pocket of the quivering customer. The real
goods, upwards of $50,000 worth of gems, remained out of reach, locked inside
the big safe. There was nothing to do about that now.

They all left according to plan, Whittemore turning as he closed the door to
tell everyone they'd wait outside for ten minutes and if anyone made any noise,
they'd all be killed. A few minutes later, as Prip groaned back into consciousness, everyone banged their feet on the floor and yelled out the windows until
workers on the floor below heard and came to their rescue. By the time the
police arrived, the gang was long gone.

The take was disappointing. The Kraemers got a decent price for the platinum, but after the split each member of the gang received only about $300,
hardly worth the trouble. They needed to do better than that.

Even so, it was a happy holiday for the Whittemores. Richard had an extra
couple thousand dollars courtesy of Si Gilden. There was perhaps no better
time to be young and rich and ready for fun, an era when New York City first
gained its reputation as the city that never sleeps. For the next few months, the
Whittemores cut familiar figures in New York's nightlife as they started going
on the kind of spree kids dream about growing up, living the way they imagined others did, indulging every fantasy with no thought of tomorrow and no
plans for the future to slow them down. They behaved as if there would always
be another big score and the money would last forever.

Most days didn't start until afternoon or even later, and most evenings they
didn't even bother going out to the clubs until almost midnight, when the ama-

teurs headed home and the after-theater crowd and the hoofers and musicians and hangers-on all went out and stayed out, every night unfolding as if it were a Saturday night. That Richard and Margaret were new and unknown in New York didn't matter—everyone was new and unknown, pretending to be more than they were. It didn't matter who you really were anyway, as long as you had the money and could look the part, and they did. She was slim and sleek and blond, and Richard sharp and snazzy. He wasn't buying off the rack anymore either. He had his suits made to order.

There were a hundred clubs and cabarets to choose from, most in Midtown off the Theater District, the best ones anyway, generally between Forty-Sixth and Fifty-Fourth, just out of the glare of Times Square—the Blue Hour, the Furnace Club, the Jungle Club, the Beaux Arts, La Frera, the Knight, the Silver Slipper, the Merry-Go Round. The menus were peppered with French phrases, and the floor shows featured jazz bands and chorus lines of enticing ingenues. In the audience, butter-and-egg men with fat wallets flirted with dancers draped in diamonds and pearls or at least imitations of the real thing. They were places where rumrunners acted respectably and respectable people acted shamelessly, where everyone laughed over loud music, dribbled gin down their chins, and left big tips.

Most clubs skirted New York's laws governing cabarets by claiming to be private clubs and charging a membership fee—a cover charge—at the entrance. It often cost $5, $10, $15, even as much as $25 just to get in the door. That was enough to keep the gawkers and riffraff out, and even then you sometimes had to tip the toughs working the door to squeeze past. It cost even more inside—$5 and $10 entrées, $20 or $25 for a fifth of real scotch or bottle of champagne. At a time when the average workingman was lucky to make $3,000 annually, a night out at a nice place cost more than most guys made in a month, while a big spender might drop more than a regular fellow earned in a year.

Richard and Margaret could hardly believe the people they saw, the people they met and brushed up against. Names in the paper made flesh—film stars like Gloria Swanson, Broadway stars like Marilyn Miller, and other well-known New Yorkers from the worlds of entertainment, business, society, and politics—were regulars at their favorite haunts.

Richard later called them "very fine people," and noted that "none of them suspected us," proud that the same hand that wielded a gun or a lead pipe could rub elbows with New York's slumming upper crust with no one the wiser. He later claimed to have met New York mayor Jimmy Walker's brother while being fitted for a custom suit and to have attended parties with police captains and detectives where he pretended to be a bootlegger, even palming them $50s and $100s to sell the lie. He would later realize that some of the cops and attorneys who would one day try to put him away were often the same people he saw drinking themselves under the table and cheating on their wives.

Richard and Margaret soon settled on several favorite clubs where everybody recognized them, places that took most of their time and a lot of their money. They usually started out at Guinan's 300 Club at 151 West Fifty-Fourth Street, where Marie Louise Cecilia Guinan, its brassy, blond, and blowsy owner and impresario, whom everyone knew as "Tex," welcomed customers with her signature greeting: "Hello, Sucker."

Their next stop was usually either the Twin Oaks at 163 West Forty-Sixth Street, a place the *New York Daily News* called "as beautiful a night club as can be found in this city of cabarets," or the more up-tempo and salaciously risqué Club Richman, owned by entertainer and band leader Harry Richman and located at West Fifty-Sixth Street, near Carnegie Hall. Seating 240 people, the interior of Richman's nightclub resembled an outdoor patio and featured false windows that looked out onto painted pastoral scenes, giving the eyes a place to rest in between entertainments by "nearly naked cuties" whose entire costume sometimes consisted of a single flower.

Only a few years before, Richman had hired a young Joan Crawford as a club dancer before Hollywood discovered her. Richman himself would even have a brief movie career in which he was best known for performing the Irving Berlin classic "Puttin' on the Ritz" in the movie of the same name. The song could have been the soundtrack for the entire era, a time when even people like Richard and Margaret could "mix where the Rockefellers walk with sticks."

If that wasn't enough, they wrapped things up at their favorite place of all — the favorite place of everyone who knew about it — the super-exclusive Club Chantee. During its brief life in 1925 and 1926, the Chantee was known as a place that, well, if you had to ask where it was, you had no business going.

The club's name was derived from a French slang word that initially referred to singing but came to mean a particularly attractive and enticing woman men found irresistible. At the Chantee, located on the second floor of a building at 132 West Fifty-Second Street, the site of a former food and grain mill, the Whittemores lived like spoiled kids with a bottomless trust fund. The club even earned write-ups in *The New Yorker,* which was rapidly becoming the magazine of the moment for New York's expansive nightlife.

Writing under the pseudonym "Lipstick," twenty-five-year-old Lois Long was the magazine's resident flapper correspondent, the embodiment of the women who came of age during the Roaring Twenties and were obsessed with everything new and hot and stylish. Provided with an expense account so she could write all about it, Long described the two-hundred-seat Chantee as "grand ... nicely decorated and softly lit," the kind of place where "everybody from [Broadway actress] Marilyn Miller to your favorite society benedict might be ... it has that indefinable quality known as pep." It was, she wrote, a place that had been "beating off hopeful aspirants with a stick" and was "very hard to get into."

Hard to get into, that is, if you weren't Richard Whittemore or, like Margaret, someone with him. Most patrons had to know somebody to gain entry, and Whittemore did. He knew the head waiter and resident heavy, Pasquale Chicarelli, who had done time for robbery and whose brother Frank was part owner. Whittemore also was tight with the club's manager, Joseph "Barney" Mortillaro.

As he presided over the best table at the Chantee, Whittemore was known to most as John Gario. Playing the role of a wealthy bootlegger to the hilt, he was familiar enough with the chorus girls that they knew enough to act one way around him when he was out with the boys, another when he was squiring Margaret.

Beyond the crowd, which usually included the celebrities of the moment, the draw at the Chantee was the house band, George Olsen and his orchestra. Featuring vocalist Fran Frey, Olsen's orchestra was the most popular club band of the era. While at the Chantee, the band was riding the wave of its greatest hit, the song "Who," which in 1926 sold a million copies and was later recorded by everyone from Judy Garland to Frank Sinatra.

The song was a house favorite. When it asked the question, "Who means my happiness, who would I answer to?" couples must have liked to believe that the answer, "You ought to guess who, no one but you," referred to each other.

Margaret and Richard were in their glory, a young couple on an endless date, living out the fantasy lives expressed in all those flapper films. Richard later remarked, "We lived very nicely and had a great many good times." That was like saying he liked to collect costume jewelry. Richard acted as if utterly unconcerned that anyone might ever identify him as a convict on the lam and a fugitive wanted for murder. When they married, the Whittemores had been a couple of nobodies, but in New York the opposite was true—they were somebodies so important that they could live by rules they made up as they went along. The Club Chantee provided proof of that almost every night of the week. Then, as the sun rose over Manhattan and the working stiffs marched to the subway, they'd lurch out of a car at Chester Court and collapse into bed, only to lift the needle from the phonograph record later that afternoon and start the whole song over again.

The gang had a similar routine. When Richard decided to go out with some of the boys, their escapades started with a late lunch and drinks with Shuffles Goldberg, and sometimes the Kraemers, at their favorite lunch spot, the Hotel Astor. They'd then proceed to somewhat sleazier or more dangerous clubs in Greenwich Village or Harlem, often leaving the Kraemers behind. Some nights —and some mornings—Goldberg and Unkelbach and Paladino liked to swing by Mott Street to score drugs or shoot dice and maybe make a quick trip into a nearby opium den, and then either crash at the apartment on West Eightieth or at Bennie's, a small nondescript hotel in Coney Island owned by Paladino's pal Bennie Levy. There the gang could go on a bender or sleep it off, and prying eyes didn't question the addition of a dancer or two or three out for a fling.

If they could have had more than two candle ends to burn, the Whittemores and the rest of the gang would have lit them all with a torch. The holidays raced past in a woozy blur, but soon it would be time to get back to work.

During 1925, the gang had perfected their method. Now, as the amateurs at Times Square rang in the New Year and the calendar turned from 1925 to 1926, they had big plans.

Nine

———

THE USUAL ROUTE

J oseph Tropp saw it all. From his domain at 152 Second Avenue, he could see the entire New York diamond and jewelry industry splayed out before him. He was a man everybody had to know and a man who knew everybody in the trade, a guy who knew what everyone had to sell and what they wanted to buy — not bad for someone who had started out as a pickpocket. By 1926, Tropp was one of the best-known fences in New York, topped only by gangster and crime boss Arnold Rothstein, who remains notorious for fixing the 1919 World Series and is familiar to modern audiences through the video series *Boardwalk Empire*.

Even though everybody knew Tropp was a fence, he was almost untouchable. In the course of doing business, well, Tropp learned things, and information was as valuable as gold — or better yet, untraceable, high-quality loose diamonds.

In late December 1925, Tropp learned that Goudvis Brothers of Amsterdam, one of the world's best-known diamond importers with offices at 22–26 West Forty-Eighth Street in the heart of New York's rapidly growing new Diamond District, would soon receive an allotment of several hundred diamonds.

Goudvis Brothers specialized in high-quality stones gleaned from other dealers in Europe and suppliers in Africa. A year later, the firm would acquire and cut a 5.05 carat red diamond known today as the Kazanjian Red Diamond, the second-largest diamond of that type in the world; one of the rarest and most valuable gems on the planet, it is valued today at approximately $50 million. Goudvis Brothers had an impeccable reputation, and their diamonds were held in high esteem.

Tropp learned that the diamonds would arrive on Saturday, January 9, and would first be deposited at the Harriman National Bank on Forty-Fourth Street and Fifth Avenue, where Goudvis Brothers regularly kept inventory. They would be carried by Emmanuel Veerman, brother-in-law of Albert Goudvis, who managed the New York office. Veerman would arrive from Amsterdam by boat for his annual trip to look over the firm's books and deliver stock for the upcoming year.

Albert Goudvis was a creature of habit. Trusting no one else, each day he personally picked up stock from the secure vault at the bank and carried it the four short blocks to his office, a trip of only five or six minutes. The Monday after Veerman's arrival, Goudvis was certain to take possession of the shipment and begin to let others in the district know what he now had for sale.

There was nothing strange about a diamond dealer carrying diamonds on his person. Many firms in the area did the same thing. The area was heavily policed by the New York Police Department's elite Fifth Avenue Squad, a special unit of plainclothes detectives. Initially created to combat confidence men and pickpockets working the streets around Times Square, in recent years the squad had evolved to become, in effect, almost a private security force policing the growing Diamond District. The police knew it was wise to keep the rich safe and happy; they had a lot of political pull.

As a result, most dealers in the district felt secure enough that they didn't bother to use armed cars or guards when transferring their valuable merchandise. To do so would only call attention. Although jewel thefts, per se, were not unusual in New York, the intense police presence kept robberies in the Diamond District rare. It was far too risky, like trying to steal an elephant from the circus.

Tropp surmised that the shipment had to be worth in excess of $100,000 at wholesale prices, maybe more, and maybe even a lot more.

Upon arrival, Veerman was certain to bring the stones directly to the bank for the weekend. It was the Sabbath, and the firm's office would be closed.

Then, on Monday, Goudvis and Veerman would pick up the stones and bring them to the office.

After the Prip debacle, the Kraemers were eager for a big score to make up for all the time they'd wasted at 90 Nassau Street. Tropp was also keen. The holidays had left him short too. He had customers who wanted diamonds at a good price, and his stock had dwindled.

Tropp told the Kraemers about Veerman and Goudvis and the new shipment. That was all the brothers needed to know.

Robbing Veerman of the stones after he arrived in New York on his way to the bank was out; they didn't know if he'd made special security arrangements from the pier, not to mention that they didn't know what he looked like. And of course, their days of cracking bank safes were over. Besides, the eleven-story Harriman Bank at 527 Fifth Avenue, on the corner of Forty-Fourth, was a fortress, as were the Goudvis Brothers offices on the eleventh floor at Forty-Eighth Street. That left the street. If Tropp's information was correct, the diamonds would be carried by hand, unguarded, for four short blocks down the sidewalks of Midtown. Yes, they were certain to be teeming with people, and yes, there would be police and private guards all over the place. But all that had been true in Buffalo too, and the gang had still walked away with $93,000, shooting when they had to. This time there would be no armored car or armed guards to worry about.

The Kraemers decided to see if an opportunity might reveal itself.

For several days in early January, they "tailed it up"—in other words, they staked out the four-block path that Albert Goudvis walked every day from the bank to his office. Although he kept a low profile, he wasn't exactly anonymous. Unlike his brother-in-law, the Kraemers knew what Goudvis looked like— they'd been frequenting the district for the last year. A few days of observation confirmed that every day, just before 10 a.m., Goudvis walked the same route from the bank to the office. On most days it was impossible for the Kraemers to tell whether or not he was carrying gems, although he almost certainly was. Dealers usually carried diamonds and other gems in a zipped gemstone wallet, divided and wrapped in paper according to size and grade. Even a small wallet could hold hundreds of stones and be tucked inside a coat pocket.

When Goudvis walked his usual route, four blocks north up Fifth Avenue, then turned left onto Forty-Eighth, he remained aware of his surroundings. He stayed in the flow of pedestrians, using them as a sort of shield. Police were everywhere. The commercial district had a cop on almost every corner directing traffic, and the Fifth Avenue Squad of detectives constantly patrolled the area. With so many cops around, they couldn't just pull out guns, as they'd done in Buffalo.

Still, the Kraemers concluded that robbing Goudvis and Veerman, while difficult, would not be impossible. The challenge would be to quickly disable the men, grab the goods, and get away before anyone raised an alarm or, ideally, before anyone even noticed.

That would require a precise level of criminal choreography beyond any previous job the gang had contemplated, one that would draw on the collective experience of both the Kraemers and Whittemore—brains and brawn in combination—to pull off. For this crime they would eventually draw on elements of half a dozen of their previous jobs, such as the Holtzman hijacking, the Stanley robbery, and even the safe robbery in Baltimore back in 1916. To succeed the gang would need to rely on every ounce of experience they had. Everything they had all learned from a lifetime in crime would be put to use.

Observation was everything. After tailing Goudvis on his journey several times and getting a feel for his routines, they noticed something. As he turned left and walked west onto Forty-Eighth Street, nearing his office, he passed the entrance to another, smaller building at 14 West Forty-Eighth Street. The entryway was set into the structure a bit, providing a protected space, a vestibule outside a doorway where visitors might close an umbrella or stomp snow off their shoes before entering.

The vestibule was narrow, only ten or fifteen feet across, and almost out of view of pedestrians, apart from those who walked past in only a few quick steps. Even better, the building was temporarily vacant. There was no doorman poised on the street, no window displays tempting passersby to browse or linger, and no chance that someone might exit unexpectedly or try the door.

That was the place. All the gang needed to do was to get Goudvis and Veerman off the sidewalk and into the vestibule. Then it would be almost like dropping in from the ceiling to the back side of that safe in Baltimore. The small vestibule would serve the same purpose as the safe and create a screen for the actual act of robbery. Of course, no one would be carrying a can opener to crack a safe. Gun butts used as blackjacks would be the can opener; all they'd need to do was crack a few heads and grab the diamonds.

Now that the Kraemers had a plan, they began to loop in the others, bringing them down in ones and twos to walk the blocks between the bank and the building at West Forty-Eighth, learning a little more each time, determining everyone's precise role.

If—and that was an important word—if the gang did everything right, then the robbery would go down like the cautious opening of a combination lock. At one precise moment, the tumblers would all fall, an untold number of diamonds would drop into the gang's hands, and *poof!*—everyone would disappear, leaving no sign that anything had happened. On a street teeming with people, no evidence would remain apart from two men slumped on the ground, the pedestrians oblivious as to what had just taken place.

In the days before the robbery, the gang, save for Margaret, met up several times in the apartment on Eightieth Street. Each member was given his task, and all were drilled until each man knew exactly what was expected of him. There would be no messing around, no late nights, and no hangovers.

On the weekend before the robbery, Richard and Margaret, for once, stayed in. They rose early, ate their meals, and went to bed. Anthony Paladino stayed home in Brooklyn. Unkelbach and Goldberg, who shared a place on Eighty-Third Street, made sure they had enough morphine to feed their habit and stay calm. The Kraemers, living at the Hotel Alamac, met up with Joseph Tropp, tore a dollar bill in half, and handed one half to him. Jake stuffed the other half in his wallet and set up a time to meet at the Hotel St. George afterwards. Tropp promised to have cash on hand, and a lot of it.

On Sunday, the gang met one last time. Nate Weinzimmer, driving the Cadillac, took Whittemore, Paladino, and Goldberg to Brooklyn, where Goldberg and Whittemore stripped license plates from a car and placed them on the Cadillac. Paladino then went home to Brooklyn, the Kraemers returned to their hotel, and everyone spent a quiet night in anticipation of the next morning's activities. There would be no backing out. They knew that if someone failed to show, Richard Whittemore would likely come looking for them. No one wanted to end up like Si Gilden.

Early the next morning, after leaving Richard, Margaret traveled to Penn
Station, like any other lady on the way to meet a friend. There she retrieved a
bag from a locker. Inside was a robbery kit of items none of the men risked carrying in bulk themselves—revolvers (Richard's big .38 and .45s), ammunition,
silk masks, gloves, handcuffs, and blackjacks.

The kit was particularly important on this job. Richard wasn't about to take
a chance trying to knock out the jeweler with some small snub-nosed revolver
tucked into his waistband. Measuring more than a foot long from barrel to grip,
his weapon was almost as big as a sawed-off shotgun. He planned to swing it
like a club, using the grip as a hammer head, pulling the trigger only if needed.

While Margaret went downtown, Richard left to rendezvous with the gang
in Midtown. Dressed in a tailored suit and charcoal overcoat and cap, he was in
work mode, hard and focused.

After picking up the guns, Margaret likely met up with her husband in Midtown, where he stuffed the needed weaponry and ammunition into his overcoat. There was no time for small talk. They both knew that each time he went
on a job like this, they might never see each other again.

Margaret knew her role. She would return to Chester Court and wait for
Richard's return—if he returned. If he was arrested, or shot, everything was
certain to end. She had to stay off the phone in case something went wrong.
And there was no surefire way for her to know if it had. She simply had to wait.

About 9 a.m., the gang converged in Midtown. Paladino, like most of them,
took the subway. He carried his own weapon, and his task would be to
watch the traffic cop on the corner and gun him down in the event he opened
fire.

They dressed like businessmen, like they belonged on the street. Whittemore
distributed the remaining weapons, probably under the cover of Weinzimmer's
Cadillac, and then the group scattered. Each would walk a different route to
a specified location on West Forty-Eighth Street, save for Weinzimmer, who
would drive.

Paladino arrived first. As he took his place, one after the other, he spotted
the others, except for Jake, who headed to the bank.

Weinzimmer parked the Cadillac on the south side of the street directly in front of 14 West Forty-Eighth Street, screening the vestibule from anyone on the opposite side of the street. He sat inside, maybe browsing a newspaper, the engine idling, not an uncommon sight on a cool weekday morning. With a cap perched on his head, he looked for all the world like a chauffeur waiting for a client.

Paladino stood leaning against a building on the north side of Forty-Eighth with a clear view of the cop directing traffic on the corner. Goldberg took up his place on the opposite corner, in front of Black, Starr and Frost's jewelry store. Given his small stature, he was easy to overlook, completely nonthreatening. From a distance, he might have even looked like a boy, his fedora looking too big for his head. Leon Kraemer stood farther up West Forty-Eighth, and a few steps beyond him, lingering by the Cadillac, were Willie Unkelbach and Richard Whittemore.

All six men carried guns buried in their overcoat pockets, but if everything went according to plan, they wouldn't have to fire a shot.

As they waited, alert, but pretending not to be, Whittemore noticed someone walking back and forth in front of a jewelry store at 8 West Forty-Eighth, a smaller, older man in a green coat. He didn't like his look. He gave Unkelbach a nudge and told him he thought the guy was "a bull," underworld slang for an undercover cop.

Whittemore's instinct was spot on. Henry Helwig had retired a month before after twenty-eight years on the force, where he specialized in missing persons. He had taken a job as a private detective for a consortium of Diamond District jewelers and spent his day walking the block, popping in and out of the shops, and keeping his eyes open. Whittemore sniffed him out. On the fly he told Unkelbach, who was supposed to be part of the actual attack, that there was a change of plans. He told him to keep a close eye on Helwig instead and to kill the former cop if he made a move and drew a gun.

Several blocks away, Albert Goudvis and Emmanuel Veerman, after taking the diamonds from the vault, left the Harriman National Bank and walked toward West Forty-Eighth Street. Both men wore overcoats. Goudvis carried the wallet containing the diamonds tucked into his coat pocket, holding it tight.

Jake Kraemer spotted the two and followed them, trailing eight or ten yards behind, not close enough to raise suspicion but not so far away that he couldn't cross the street whenever they did. The two diamond dealers chatted, catching up, probably sharing family and business news. Veerman was undoubtedly anxious to see the firm's new offices, which he'd never visited since the firm moved there in 1925.

Kraemer kept pace, but as they walked the final block from Forty-Seventh to Forty-Eighth Street, his stride increased and he drew closer.

At the intersection of Fifth and Forty-Eighth, as Paladino and Goldberg watched from opposite corners, Goudvis and Veerman turned left onto Forty-Eighth. Jake Kraemer, now on their heels, increased his pace a bit and slipped ahead of the two men. As the group passed Goldberg, the little man fell in a few yards behind, sandwiching Goudvis and Veerman in between the two gang members.

Paladino saw them make the turn and fixed his gaze on the traffic cop in the middle of the intersection. His reactions would tell Paladino everything he needed to know. If there was any kind of commotion and the cop reacted, well, that's what his gun was for.

Leon Kraemer spotted his brother and started walking east down Forty-Eighth toward him. Richard Whittemore fell in behind, the two diamond dealers and the four robbers all converging on the few square yards of sidewalk opposite the vestibule in front of the vacant building. Unkelbach, a bit farther down the street, watched Helwig as he sauntered toward the corner, oblivious to the men walking past.

As the Kraemer brothers neared each other, coming closer with each step, Jake tipped his hat, as if in greeting. That was the signal, the sign to the others that their targets, Veerman and Goudvis, were right behind him.

With the exactness of a fine watch, they all sprang into action at once, all the dominoes falling. As Leon and Richard passed on either side of Jake, opposite the vestibule, they spun and overwhelmed the two oblivious diamond dealers, Goldberg closing in from behind and Jake Kraemer spinning on his heel, the two diamond dealers suddenly surrounded on all sides. The gang half lifted and half shoved the two men into the vestibule, pinning their arms against their coats. As the group disappeared from the view of passersby, Whittemore and Goldberg and the Kraemers pulled guns from their pockets and, without a word, smashed the weapons onto the heads of the two shocked jewelers.

Goudvis collapsed immediately into the vestibule, unconscious. Veerman lurched against the wall, where one of the men rammed him up against the bricks before he crouched, holding his head and slumping to his knees, blood pouring out of a deep wound atop his head as Whittemore swung again and again. Unkelbach kept walking, keeping his eyes on Helwig, a couple dozen yards up the street. A few pedestrians, witnessing the commotion ahead of them, stopped in their tracks, trying to process what looked like some kind of scuffle, as others turned and just kept going, steering clear of trouble. Everyone else on the street was unaware of the attack, their view blocked by the vestibule and, from across the street, by the Cadillac on the curb. Of the scores of pedestrians on the block, only a handful witnessed the attack. Most noticed nothing at all.

Whittemore grabbed the wallet from Goudvis's coat pocket. Weinzimmer, watching from the Cadillac, dropped the car into gear. The four bandits left their victims bleeding, turned from the vestibule, and walked swiftly to the car, busy men with places to be and people to see. They flung open the doors and climbed in. The Caddy seated seven, plenty of room for everyone. Helwig had yet to react, and now Unkelbach turned on his heel and jumped in alongside the driver. Weinzimmer floored it, and the car lurched away from the curb as a few shocked pedestrians, now realizing that there were two men bleeding in the vestibule, started shouting.

Startled, Paladino took his eyes off the cop, turned to look, and saw the Cadillac roaring up the street. When he looked back at the cop, he was gone. But he wasn't giving chase. He was all the way across Fifth Avenue, bawling out a taxi driver over some minor infraction.

Helwig finally realized something was up. After first following the shouts and running down the sidewalk, he noticed the speeding car, turned around, and began chasing after it. The auto careened down Forty-Eighth and onto Fifth Avenue against the light as oncoming traffic screeched to a halt and horns blared. Helwig emptied his revolver at the receding Cadillac, which had rapidly accelerated to more than fifty miles an hour.

This was why Nate Weinzimmer was part of the gang. He knew how to handle an automobile, and just in case anyone commandeered a car to give chase, or a police vehicle on patrol happened to be nearby, the escape route had already been determined. He pushed the V-8 engine to the limit.

At Forty-Seventh Street, Weinzimmer turned left and headed east against the one-way traffic, driving onto the sidewalk to make the getaway as pedestrians jumped and leaped out of the way. A sergeant in the Fifth Avenue Squad spotted the car going the wrong way and opened fire, joined by a traffic cop on that corner, but in the confusion none of the bullets found a human target.

Approaching Madison Avenue, Weinzimmer lurched the Cadillac off the sidewalk, careened between cars, turned north, accelerated, and disappeared. In another block or two, it became just another car maneuvering through Manhattan's midmorning traffic.

His work over, Paladino simply walked away. According to the plan, he grabbed a cab a few blocks away and headed uptown to Eighty-Third Street, hoping to meet Unkelbach and Goldberg at their apartment. He rang the bell, but they weren't back yet. Unconcerned, he decided to have lunch. It had been a tense morning.

Weinzimmer wound his way through traffic and soon dropped everyone off separately. Later that afternoon they rendezvoused again at the gang's apartment on West Eightieth Street. Once inside, it was time to find out if Tropp's information had been accurate.

They unzipped the wallet and found it full of a number of folded packets of paper. Unfolding the first one and then the others, no one needed to tell them Tropp had been correct. Dozens of diamonds spilled out of each one, sparkling like so many stars and leaving wide smiles on the faces of the bandits. All told, the wallet contained over two hundred top-quality loose diamonds, big ones. And in the wake of the war, fueled by the flow of money and liquor, prices were high. Perhaps the Kraemers had seen diamonds like this before, but no one else had, not this many, not all at once.

Giddy, the Kraemers and Whittemore put them back in the wallet, placed the wallet in a bag, and left to meet Tropp at the Hotel St. George in Brooklyn Heights. Paladino finished lunch and then went again to meet Unkelbach and Goldberg, who told him what they'd seen. The men sat around for a few hours, winding down and playing pinochle, before Paladino went back to Brooklyn. After the goods were fenced, they'd all be contacted to pick up their share.

Albert Goudvis and Emmanuel Veerman, meanwhile, were in Bellevue Hospital. Goudvis needed eight stitches to close the wound on his head and Veerman needed six, although his wound was much deeper. Neither had a fractured skull or any other serious lasting injury.

At Chester Court, Margaret began to relax. News bulletins were making mention of a big robbery in the Diamond District, but reported that the unknown crooks had gotten away.

Richard was safe.

Ten

⎯⎯⎯⎯⎯⎯

KING OF THIS
EMPTY DOMAIN

The *Brooklyn Times Union* called it "an ambush," the *Daily News* a "crime of great proportion," the *Philadelphia Inquirer* "the boldest in local crime annals." Even the *New York Times* called the robbery "extraordinary." The heist was a page 1 story from New York to California and a lot of places in between.

The robbery had been all those things and more, and the gang didn't even know for sure yet how much it had been worth, only that they had scored packets and packets of diamonds, first-rate stuff. And everything had gone just swell, as well as it could have. Nobody had been nabbed, and no one, apart from the two jewelers, had been hurt. Also, with the payout they'd get for the diamonds, there was no chance that anyone would squeal, and from the look of it, there was no chance to tie the robbery to any of them.

But to the New York Police Department and other authorities, it was something else:

Embarrassing.

Although robberies in New York City were hardly a rarity, one like this —in daylight, under the nose of the police, in the most secure area of the city—sent ripples through not only the jewelry industry but the police department and the political machine that ran New York. Crimes like this could cost powerful people their jobs and change elections. This wasn't a crime that would fade away in only a few days and be forgotten. Oh, maybe the newspapers would forget, but the well-heeled denizens of the Diamond District were sure to call for someone's head.

In the minutes after the robbery, police had pored over the area, questioning everyone, and they came up with . . . almost nothing. Not a pedestrian on the sidewalk saw a damn thing beyond a bunch of well-dressed men in overcoats getting into a Cadillac, and although someone did memorize the plate number, the cops already assumed the plate was stolen. And trying to identify one Cadillac from another in New York in 1926 was like trying to identify a chorus girl from a description of her haircut.

Police Commissioner George McLaughlin did his best to stay ahead of the story. Having taken over the force only two weeks prior, it was the first great test of his new regime.

Only thirty-nine years old, McLaughlin was a money guy with no law enforcement background, a CPA and bank examiner who had once been the state superintendent of banks. Being named police commissioner was a big deal. From 1895 to 1897, Theodore Roosevelt had served in a similar position, as president of the police board of commissioners; there he earned a reputation as a nationally prominent reformer that he would eventually parlay into the presidency. Roosevelt, in fact, created the role of commissioner after he became governor of New York, empowering the position with singular authority that could either make or break a career. McLaughlin had been appointed with the expectation that an outsider might be able to stamp out the criminal enterprise that the New York Police Department had become since.

A few hours after the robbery, he wisely held a press conference at police headquarters at Centre and Grand Streets. Before speaking, McLaughlin conferred with his top aides, Inspectors John Coughlin and William Lahey. He put the focus directly on the department, saying, "We want to know where the police were and what they were doing at the time of the escape . . . Somebody must have known that the men were in the habit of carrying diamonds daily through the streets and informing the thieves about it."

No kidding. Inspector Lahey hardly sounded confident when he described the crime, after noting the presence of so many police officers in the area, as "just one of those things."

The next morning, before meeting at the apartment on West Eightieth to wait for Whittemore and the Kraemers, the gang read all the morning papers and learned a few things. One was that, after leaving the hospital, Goudvis and Veerman had gone to the Criminal Bureau of Identification to look at mug shots, but neither identified anyone. The second thing they learned was that the take was worth at least $100,000, but as a spokesman for Goudvis Brothers said, "The estimate of $100,000 is a conservative one." They also learned the identity of the private detective patrolling the Diamond District; Henry Helwig was a potential loose end, but now a loose end with a name and a target on his back.

In fact, the haul was far more than $100,000, and even more than the $180,000 value Goudvis admitted to a short time later. Eventually, the value of the heist would be estimated to be as much as $500,000.

It was so lucrative that Joseph Tropp couldn't afford to pay the gang off, at least not all at once. They received their cut in increments over the next week—a first payment of $1,500 apiece, then another few thousand, until each man's take came to $11,000. At least, that's how much Paladino eventually received. Not bad pay for standing in the cold on a street corner for a few minutes. Weinzimmer, Goldberg, and Unkelbach also likely received that amount, enough that no one complained about it.

Of course, the only guys who really knew how much Tropp really paid out were the Kraemers and Whittemore. Even after the split, it was enough for them to pay off the gang's car in full, drop $30,000 in cash into a safety deposit box for attorneys and payoffs in the event of capture and for whatever it cost for some auto body man to keep his mouth shut and patch the bullet holes in the Cadillac and give it a new paint job.

If the way Richard Whittemore lived for the next few months is any indication, he and the Kraemers received far, far more than $11,000. In fact, the payout seems to have been so high that people would still be killed over the remaining balance for almost another decade.

When Richard finally returned to Margaret at Chester Court after going on a bender of dope and dice that cost him several thousand dollars, there was enough left over for the couple to go out and pick up a few nice things. Richard got his new Cadillac, paying $3,500 in cash, and when "Madame asked for a fur coat," as a Buffalo paper put it, Margaret got the $800 squirrel coat she'd had her eye on. The couple visited "an exclusive store" where Richard picked out a top-of-the-line suit; he took Margaret out for a night on the town that cost $1,800 and also loaned $800 to "a young woman," squandered another $300 on opium, and dropped $1,700 in an hour in a gambling den.

At a time when a can of tuna cost fifteen cents, silk stockings went for ninety-nine cents a pair, and a couple bucks got you a good seat at a Broadway show, every member of the gang now had enough money to live as they pleased for years ... if they could hold on to any of it. But who wanted to do that? It was more fun to drop thousands of dollars all over the city satisfying every whim and acting like big shots. Although they weren't quite making Babe Ruth money—$52,000 a year in 1926—at a time when the average working stiff still struggled to make more than $100 a month, they were doing better than okay. In the past year they'd all pulled in at least $30,000 each—not quite as much as F. Scott Fitzgerald bragged about squandering in his legendary essay "How to Live on $36,000 a Year," but still a handsome sum. And if they ever got desperate, there were always a few baubles to pawn. For the time being, with no need to do another job, they apparently took the next couple months off.

Weinzimmer headed back to Cleveland to spend some time with his family, and Goldberg, Unkelbach, and the Whittemores tagged along. Whittemore and Goldberg were still kicking around the idea of opening their own cabaret to fuel their lifestyle in their second home. There was a lot of cash floating around in Cleveland cocktail glasses. The Chantee was pulling in $7,000 in profit every week. If they did even half as well in Cleveland, that would be a lot of money. And factoring in the chorus girls and the ready-made nightlife, well, it wasn't so much a plan for the future as a way to extend and expand the present.

Maybe they were also starting to worry a little about the police and realizing it might be a good idea to leave New York for a while, let the gang's apartment go and keep their heads down. They weren't quite sure about that private detective, Helwig. Since Whittemore had recognized Helwig as a cop, there was some chance that Helwig had recognized him too.

Whittemore had already had a couple of close calls in New York. Once, a detective thought Whittemore looked familiar while he was lunching with Margaret and some friends at a high-end restaurant. The detective later approached one of Whittemore's companions and started asking questions, but was put off when Whittemore's pal told the cop the guy he'd lunched with was just an old friend who owned a shirt factory in Brooklyn.

Paladino went back to Brooklyn, but the Kraemers stayed in New York, knowing that if anything big came up, they could get everyone back in a couple of days. There was no pressure to bother with small jobs now.

Once he arrived in Cleveland, however, Richard Whittemore got antsy. There was a loose end back in New York that concerned him a little more each day.

T he gang was wise to lay low. The cops had finally realized that at least some of the robberies were connected and that, if they wanted to keep their jobs, they had to find out who was responsible.

The gang didn't know it yet, but they did have a nemesis, someone just a little smarter than they were and even more determined. He was fifty-two-year-old John D. Coughlin, the austere, barrel-chested chief inspector for the New York City Police Department. He was thought to be free of corruption, a rarity for the department at the time, even if the 1,200 New York City detectives he supervised were not.

Coughlin, a brooding black Irishman whose narrow, untrusting eyes looked out at the world from beneath a pair of dark, bushy eyebrows that matched his mustache, was a cop's cop. He had joined the force under Roosevelt and worked his way up through the ranks when promotions had as much to do with connections as with talent. There were two ways to go for young Irishmen in New York—into the political machine or onto the streets. Coughlin chose the former, and as he rose he encountered many childhood friends who had chosen the streets. He cut his teeth chasing down "scuttle thieves"—break-in artists who specialized in rooftop burglaries—then took over the pickpocket squad that worked New York's racetracks. There he became familiar with the yegg-men (safecrackers), touts, sportsmen, and rogues who worked at the fringes of the law. He learned their language and gained a reputation among them as a straight shooter. As he rose in the ranks he spent time working the Tenderloin, Manhattan's infamous red light district, commanded detectives in both Brooklyn and Queens, and even worked Chinatown during the Tong Wars. As *The New Yorker* put it, he was equally comfortable at the "race track or watering resorts." Coughlin knew the city better than anyone and moved smoothly between the criminal world and that of the law.

As Coughlin listened to the stories the crooks spun, he learned how the criminal mind worked. His creed was simple: "Crooks are caught by information." Coughlin learned that once you got suspects talking, you often couldn't get them to shut up. He became particularly adept at using what others thought were useless bits of conversation and random information to crack a case. Coughlin taught the men under his command to work the streets, memorize faces, keep their ears open, and report what they heard back to him. Then his viselike memory processed everything and made connections no one else could.

After the Goudvis Brothers robbery, Coughlin focused on finding the perpetrators. He needed to prove himself to McLaughlin, and McLaughlin needed to prove himself to the mayor. The two men needed each other.

Coughlin already had a hunch. He was beginning to realize that among the thousands of robberies in New York each year, the hundreds that involved jewelry and gems, and the dozens that took place during the daytime involving groups of well-dressed young men who got in and out quickly, a cohesive, disciplined gang of thieves had been at work. And it was a gang growing in confidence, greed, and capacity for violence.

I n early February, after only a few weeks in Cleveland, Richard Whittemore was the first of the group to return to New York. Margaret, who'd become friendly with Weinzimmer's wife, stayed behind. Richard had a few things to attend to.

On February 11, a month to the day after the Goudvis robbery, Henry Helwig disappeared.

Not only had Helwig been named in the papers, but they'd printed his address—he lived with his sister at 509 East 150th Street. Or he *had* lived with his sister. No one knew where he was now, except perhaps Richard Whittemore.

Flush with cash and unencumbered by his wife, and with that nasty bit of business out of the way, Richard Whittemore now *really* cut loose. He went out on the town nearly every night, leaving an impression on everyone who saw him, including Mark Hellinger. The journalist served the same role for readers of the *Daily News* that Lois Long did for *New Yorker* readers with his Sunday column "About Town," which detailed everything that happened on Broadway and in the cabarets after the curtain went down and after hours.

Hellinger, who in another decade would become not only a syndicated columnist but also an author, playwright, and film producer (his productions included the 1939 classic *The Roaring Twenties* starring James Cagney and Humphrey Bogart), got familiar with Whittemore at the Chantee during this time. As he later wrote, "Dick was always welcomed there with open arms. He threw money away with a lavish hand. A hundred. Two hundred. Three hundred. A thousand. Money, seemingly, meant nothing to him.

"The girls of the club smiled prettily at him. The waiters bowed before him. The band played furiously at his command. The show became a show just as frequently as he requested . . . for Dick was a spender. And a spender in night life is king . . . There was none in that club who knew Dick's business. Some said he was a millionaire bootlegger. Others claimed he owned a string of horses in the west. Still others insisted that millions had been willed to him. But who really cared? He had the money. That's all they ever have to know on Broadway . . . Thus, four nights of the week, each and every week, Dick was the king of this empty domain. The best was his. But always his eyes were hard and cold."

Well, his eyes weren't always quite so hard and cold. Sometimes they wandered. In late February, while Margaret was lunching in Cleveland with Weinzimmer's wife and her friends, Richard Whittemore's eyes landed on a sixteen-year-old dancer and singer from Brooklyn at the Club Chantee named Laura Lee.

Despite her age, Lee knew her way around. She had started dancing at age seven in a vaudeville act with her three sisters. The past few years she had been singing on the radio and was chaperoned to chorus jobs by her stage manager mother. The job at the Chantee was her first working alone, and the Chantee more than made it worth her while. Chorus girls could earn $75 a week in the cabarets, with the added benefit of meeting plenty of wealthy men with money to spend.

Lee was already being pursued by fifty-six-year-old Harry K. Thaw, a millionaire heir to a railroad and mining fortune who had a thing for chorus girls. Twenty years earlier, on June 25, 1906, Thaw had become notorious for killing renowned architect Stanford White at Madison Square Garden before hundreds of witnesses after learning that White, a longtime nemesis, had made a play for chorus girl Evelyn Nesbit. In the resulting trial—still often referred to as the "trial of the century"—Thaw had been found not guilty by reason of insanity. He'd been in and mostly out of asylums ever since, but being a millionaire covered for a lot of sins. He was still rich and was beginning to make inroads in Hollywood when he met Lee. Whittemore may have just been lonely and looking for a fling, but it seems he was also starting to believe he really was that guy Hellinger saw at the Chantee, a nightlife king for whom none of the rules or norms applied.

Blond, vivacious, outgoing, and quick-witted, Lee looked a bit like Margaret, only younger and more dazzling. She'd worked at the Chantee for only a few nights when Whittemore asked Pasquale Chicarelli to introduce him.

Telling her his name was John Gario, he took possession of the girl from the start, magnanimously offering to protect her from other men at the club. He explained that yes, he was married, and that, though recently separated, he was back with his wife, feeding Lee the sob story that his marital issues came about after his wife allowed their five-year-old son to wander into the street, where he was struck and killed by a truck. "Imagine," she said later, "me taking that down whole."

It was easy to be impressed. "He spent money like a millionaire," she said, flashed a big three-carat diamond ring, and showered her with small but pricey gifts, such as a gold pencil case. Lee did wonder, though, why the initials on the case didn't match either of their names.

He called her "Miss Lee" and tried to act and talk suave. She just assumed he was a bootlegger. Most nights Whittemore waited for her after the club closed. He'd drive her back to Brooklyn and take a room at the Hotel St. George, where his money made the house detective look the other way, before Lee went home to her mother.

On one rare night off, Whittemore even took her out on a date, having scored tickets to Charles MacArthur's *Lulu Belle,* Broadway's hottest play.

The serious dramatic musical aimed to provide theatergoers with a taste of Harlem's Jazz Age nightlife without having to go uptown and mix. The play followed the salacious life of a blues singer and prostitute, Lulu Belle, who was loosely modeled after Josephine Baker. She seduces a married man and lures him away from his family and into her more decadent lifestyle, before eventually jilting him for a slumming French vicomte. Along with its depiction of Harlem life, featuring a notably realistic set punctuated by references to all manner of vice, the cast of more than one hundred actors was integrated, a rarity at the time, although the two main parts were played by White actors in blackface. The play, which opened on February 11 at the famed Belasco Theater, was a huge hit and eventually ran for nearly five hundred performances.

Whittemore had to see a bit of his own story in the plot, which pivoted around a married man having an affair, ruining his life, and ending up in prison. Not only did the title character end up murdered, but she stole diamonds.

Lee later recalled, aware of the irony, that as they watched Lulu steal the diamonds onstage, her companion "was thrilled." Whittemore also "sat on the edge of his seat" during Lulu's murder and "wallowed in the excitement."

It wasn't quite the kind of play meant to woo a teenager, no matter how experienced she was. He was clearly trying too hard, as if he somehow knew he had only a short time left and decided, with Margaret away in Cleveland, to take one big roll of the dice to prove he was who he imagined himself to now be.

Seducing Lee was evidence of that. Now considering himself untouchable, he felt that every desire and every fleeting whim could be his. He would also still have Margaret whenever he wanted. That was how all the swells worked it, a wife at home and a girl on the side.

He could have whatever he wanted, whenever he wanted it.

T he Kraemers, meanwhile, had identified a few more lucrative targets and were beginning to time out what they hoped would be the gang's biggest robbery yet. By early March, everyone was back in New York. Margaret fell back into her luxurious life in Chester Court, sometimes accompanying her husband around town at night and sometimes not. Laura Lee was smart enough to know that when the missus was in town, she needed another ride back to Brooklyn.

The gang's behavior over the next few weeks made them appear increasingly suspicious. The whole gang, often sans Margaret but, unlike in the past, now sometimes including the Kraemers, went out on the town, mostly at the Club Chantee, celebrating in an intensifying orgy of spending.

The mob would have done well to temper the festivities. Over the previous few weeks, the cops had been putting two and two together. Now the gang was being watched.

Back in Cleveland, Shuffles Goldberg, operating under the name Joseph Langdon, had run afoul of local authorities, perhaps in connection with his and Whittemore's plans to open their own place. At any rate, in late February or early March Cleveland authorities learned that "Joe Langdon" had bolted Cleveland for New York. They sent what was known as a "fly tip" to New York police, telling detectives there that he was likely up to no good and to keep an eye out for him. Goldberg, with his taxicab ears and shambling walk, would be the easiest of the gang to pick out in a crowd. As a courtesy, NYPD agreed to see if they could find him.

John D. Coughlin had taught his detectives well. The most valued had steel-trap memories equal to his, and the description of Joe Langdon sounded a lot like Shuffles Goldberg, a name they already knew from Baltimore detectives. Although Goldberg hadn't been charged in the Holtzman hijacking after Gilden got off, Herbert O'Conor had stetted a charge against him for the crime. When Baltimore detectives had come to New York in November to stake out 81 Mott Street, they told New York police they were interested in Goldberg too. The mousy drug addict suddenly seemed to be in the middle of everything.

Coughlin's wheels turned, and he sent out three of his best detectives, Walter Sullivan, John Cronin, and Edward Tracey, to make the rounds of Midtown hotels. You didn't have to be a genius to start there. The gangster class liked to be near where the action was.

On March 3, when they described Goldberg to hotel employees at the Empire, a reasonably modest fifteen-story hotel at 44 West Sixty-Third Street, a staff member piped up. A sharply dressed guest with a shuffling gait and big ears had checked in a few days before under the name Martin. He generally got up late and didn't return until dawn. He didn't cause trouble but was sharp with the staff. Police could have picked up Goldberg straightaway, but Coughlin wanted to know where he went and who he knew. He directed his detectives to tail him.

Careful not to tip Goldberg off, they tag-teamed their tails, one man following Goldberg casually for a few blocks, then the other passing and taking over. They kept tabs on Goldberg just as the gang had done with Goudvis and Veerman only weeks earlier.

Most afternoons Goldberg visited Chester Court, then would emerge with a smartly dressed young couple. They'd lunch at the Hotel Astor, joined by a few others, before nightclubbing, always finishing up at the Club Chantee. A little more sleuthing by the police identified the couple as Mr. and Mrs. Horace Q. Waters.

One night at the Chantee, as the man police knew as "Horace Waters"— Richard Whittemore—passed out tips like chewing gum and entertained chorus girls, the plainclothes detectives nursed their overpriced drinks and shuffled through the Rogues' Gallery of mug shots imprinted in their brains. Suddenly, as they eyeballed "Waters" in the company of a much shorter crony, it all clicked. "I think that tall one is Dick Whittemore," one said. "Baltimore wants him."

Whittemore was a big deal, a fugitive wanted for murder, and the murder of a prison guard at that. Although the "Most Wanted List," one of J. Edgar Hoover's many innovations at the FBI, did not yet exist, Whittemore was widely known as one of the most notorious fugitives in the country. Mrs. Waters had to be "Tiger Girl," Whittemore's wife.

Once again, they could have made an arrest, but Coughlin decided to see what they were all up to. How were the Whittemores and Goldberg getting all that dough, and what about the new Cadillac?

Then suddenly, the pattern changed. Over the next few days, the group seemed to scatter, tearing all over the city in a three-Cadillac rotation. One day they would appear in a car with New York plates and the next day in the same car with Ohio plates, switching cars and drivers like tuning in different stations on a radio. Detectives surmised that either the group had spotted the tail or they had something big planned. Most days they managed to give the police the slip, at least for a few hours. And "Mrs. Waters" suddenly disappeared from Chester Court. As it turned out, the change in behavior happened to coincide with two more big gem robberies that took place on back-to-back days in mid-March. Although the gang never took credit for those heists, their fingerprints were all over them.

The first took place on March 13. It was another closing-time job, this time at jeweler William H. Sims and Company at 2486 Grand Concourse in the Bronx, where the Kraemers were buying up a lot of real estate. A few minutes before 8 p.m., two well-dressed young men entered the store. One engaged a clerk in light conversation while the other asked to see some watches.

Then one of the customers whistled; that was the sign. Three more men walked in, and all five drew revolvers. They herded the employees into the back washroom. Although the safe was locked, the five still managed to steal $75,000 worth of jewelry from the open display cases, as well as a wallet containing thirty unmounted diamonds. In less than five minutes, they were out the door and away in a car. The next day, Samuel Kandel, a pawnbroker at 89 Essex Street, was robbed in a job nearly identical in execution to the Prip robbery. When a friend of Kandel's pressed the buzzer to get into his office, three bandits the *New York Times* described as "nattily dressed" followed the friend when Kandel buzzed him in. They produced guns and proceeded to gag and tie up both men while relieving the safe of between $250,000 and $300,000 worth of jewelry and gems before walking out the door. They climbed into a waiting car like they'd just called a cab and disappeared.

Kandel was particularly distraught. He told investigators that, with the recent spate of robberies, he'd been unable to secure an insurance policy to cover his inventory.

Although Goldberg sometimes slipped from the detectives' view, he returned to his hotel after every excursion. One day, while lolling about the front desk, waiting for Goldberg to appear, the detectives saw a message come in over a device known as the telautograph. Originally developed in the 1890s for the banking industry to allow for the remote signing of checks over telegraph lines, the telautograph resembled a sort of primitive fax machine. It allowed the user in one location to handwrite a message onto a scroll of paper using a fixed pen, and the identical handwritten message was then reproduced on the receiving end. Businesses used the device to communicate between offices, as did the better hotels and apartment buildings. It was more secure than a telegraph or phone call because guests could be certain of the sender of a handwritten message.

The note read "Mr. Martin, call Mrs. Black at the Hotel Embassy." One of the detectives managed to eyeball the incoming message and rushed to the Embassy to see if he could ferret out "Mrs. Black."

It was Margaret. After leaving Chester Court, she'd registered as Miss Margaret "Dolly" Collins and secured a suite at the Broadway hotel, where she'd be ready to grab the burglary kit from Penn Station when it was needed. She was now at her post at the Embassy on the other end of the telautograph, back at work serving as the gang's common point of contact. When they needed to meet, they'd contact her, and she would then get in touch with the others, sometimes by phone. But from her time with the phone company, Margaret would have known full well that bored operators sometimes listened in on phone calls and weren't above cashing in on eavesdropped information or whispering what they'd overheard. When the gang needed to speak privately, they used the telautograph to arrange a meeting.

A detective hightailed it to the Embassy, where he spotted "Mrs. Waters," aka Miss Collins, aka Mrs. Black — Margaret Whittemore. He tailed her to the meeting she'd arranged on the telautograph. When he spotted the two men she met, the detective's jaw dropped so hard it almost shattered on the sidewalk.

They were Jake and Leon Kraemer. A short time before, Pinkerton private detectives had told New York police that they'd heard the Kraemers were operating in New York, confirming Coughlin's suspicion. The Pinkertons also claimed to have located an elevator operator on West Forty-Eighth Street who'd identified Whittemore as being in the area shortly before the Goudvis robbery.

The detectives traced the Kraemers to the Hotel Alamac at Seventy-Second Street and Broadway, and Coughlin ordered his men to continue to tail Goldberg in case they all met up. He wanted to know how wide the gang's circle stretched. Following Goldberg to lunch at the Hotel Astor, they watched him take a seat at a table with Richard Whittemore and the Kraemers.

It was all starting to come together. The police knew Whittemore and the Kraemers had served time together, and that the can opener had made the Kraemers legendary among thieves. Although there were no unsolved can opener jobs pending, they also knew that the Kraemers had an appetite for jewelry. That likely explained all the big spending. But they still didn't know precisely what they were up to. They only knew that Goldberg, Whittemore, and the Kraemers were spending a lot of money and time together, and that Anthony Paladino often joined them. The detectives, who knew Paladino as "Tony Palace" through various small-time run-ins with him, learned that he had served time with Whittemore in Elmira and lived at 396 Saint Marks Avenue in Brooklyn.

The group was still hard to track, but every night, almost without fail, Coughlin's men managed to catch up with Whittemore and several of his associates at the Chantee.

It was clear to Coughlin that the gang was still planning something, and he worried that they might strike again soon and immediately skip town. Probably through Tropp, the Kraemers had learned of several other potential jobs, one in the Bronx worth in excess of half a million dollars, and another in Midtown, at M. Rosenthal & Sons, one of the largest jewelry establishments in New York, located at 1637 Broadway. Rosenthal's was apparently due to receive a consignment of diamonds that would make Albert Goudvis look like a fruit peddler. The *Jeweler's Circular* reported that "practically every known precaution against thieves is taken at [Rosenthal's] and two traffic policemen are stationed within a few hundred feet of the place." But that did not seem to concern the crew. If their information was right, they might walk away with $750,000 worth of untraceable diamonds—in a few short minutes, one job could net them all about as much as they had taken in during the past year. The Kraemers were beginning to loop everyone else in.

The detectives didn't know that. They decided to track the gang for one more day, and then arrest Whittemore and whoever he was with.

Late in the afternoon on March 18, Detectives Sullivan and Cronin again tailed Goldberg, who met up for dinner with Whittemore, Paladino, and the Kraemers at the Hotel Astor. After a sumptuous spread, they all piled into a Cadillac and went to the Lincoln Arcade Building on Broadway at Sixty-Sixth Street. The Arcade was the center of New York's bohemian scene; the artists, writers, and actors among its residents in the past decade had included everyone from William Powell and Lionel Barrymore to George Bellows, Marcel Duchamp, and Dadaist Elsa Hildegard, Baroness von Freytag-Loringhoven. The crew stayed less than an hour, probably looking to have a drink in the first-floor saloon, score drugs, or see some girls, or maybe all of the above.

Then the Cadillac headed downtown. Sullivan and Cronin managed to follow them to Mott Street. The detectives parked and kept watch over the entrance of the gang's longtime hangout for several hours, as night bled into morning. They tried to stay alert while the crew indulged inside, probably discussing the upcoming robbery in the Bronx.

Just before 3 a.m., the gang piled into the Cadillac again and headed uptown.

Sullivan and Cronin followed, but lost the Cadillac. Playing a hunch, they went to the Chantee, where they found Whittemore at his favorite table, holding court with the rest of the gang, who were soon joined by Pasquale Chicarelli and Barney Mortillaro. But it was Laura Lee who had Whittemore's full attention. After a while, Goldberg and the Kraemers called it a night. The detectives kept their eyes on Whittemore.

He was drinking heavily and started getting loud. "Wine!" he called out. "I want more wine. *Better* wine." Chicarelli and Mortillaro tried to quiet him and went in a back room to check stock. Whittemore followed and kept up his litany of complaint.

Mortillaro told him, "You've been drinking the best wine in New York . . . There's no better wine in New York than the wine I serve you."

Now Whittemore became belligerent. Laura Lee, concerned, joined the men a few moments later, trying to head off trouble. She saw Whittemore, eyes blazing, holding a gun to Chicarelli's ribs. The waiter called out, "For God's sake, Jack, hold onto yourself!"

Just as quickly, Whittemore, noticing Lee, smiled, gave a big laugh, and put the gun into his pocket. He followed her to his table, drunkenly ordered a steak, and was soon rejoined by Chicarelli and Mortillaro. Then, in his stupor, his mood changed again.

"Listen," he cried, "I have some wine in my hotel room that's got this stuff trimmed a mile. My wine is better than yours. I'm going to prove it to you. You two fellows come with me."

Chicarelli and Mortillaro knew better than to argue.

The three got up to leave, and Whittemore went looking for Lee. He wanted her to ride along as well. But the young dancer was no fool. After seeing the gun, she was afraid. Soon after returning to the table, she had excused herself and was now hiding in the only safe place, the powder room.

Whittemore looked around the club for her, but then, ticked off and impatient, led the two men down the stairs to the street. Lee came out of the ladies' room, looked down the stairs, and saw Whittemore waiting impatiently on the sidewalk. Then, with the impulsive annoyance of a man a drink ahead, he ordered Chicarelli and Mortillaro into the car.

It was 5:10 a.m., and first light was just coming onto the horizon. As the car lurched from the curb into the early morning nightclub traffic, Sullivan and Cronin jumped into their own vehicle to resume their tail.

Whittemore sped up Broadway to Chester Court, pulled the car over, and went inside, leaving the other two men in the car. A few minutes later, he stumbled back out carrying a bottle of his wine, the best in all New York.

The detectives thought about making the arrest right then, but waited, still hoping the three men might lead them to the others. The car careened away again, then stopped at a restaurant at Eighty-Ninth and Broadway. It was almost daylight. The wine and whatever else Whittemore was on were wearing off.

After eating, as New York was blinking awake, the men drove off down Broadway. But as the Cadillac approached Fifty-Seventh Street, daylight betrayed the detectives. Whittemore realized he was being followed and floored it.

Cronin and Sullivan accelerated and gave chase, then took a gamble and guessed that Whittemore, turning onto Fifty-Second, might be headed back uptown. They turned onto Fifty-Third against the traffic and at Seventh Avenue pulled in right behind him. The two cars shot up the street as if their bumpers were locked, cutting between cars and running lights in tandem. After a few blocks, pistol shots rang out from the Cadillac. As Sullivan swerved and turned to avoid the gunshots, Cronin returned fire.

At Fifty-Ninth Street, Whittemore ran out of ammunition and out of luck. The detectives drew alongside the Cadillac, forced it to the curb, and jumped out. Cronin, backed by Sullivan, climbed onto the running board and leveled his gun at those inside, ordering them all out of the car. Now, it was Richard Whittemore on the other end of a gun, shaking in his shoes and being told to put his hands in the air.

The cops patted them all down. As they took a revolver from Whittemore's pocket, the gangster was holding out two $1,000 bills, almost half a year's salary for detectives. The implication was clear: take the money and look the other way.

Sullivan had another idea. He hit Whittemore with a right hook for all his trouble. Whittemore lay on the ground for several minutes, knocked out cold. When the Candy Kid came to, he was wearing a pair of handcuffs.

Eleven

IN A RAKISH WAY

As the sun rose higher and the light filtering into her room grew brighter on Friday, March 19, Margaret grew more frantic. Reports of a shoot-out and an arrest of some people from the Chantee were all over town. Since then no one in the gang had tried to contact her, and when she tried to contact them, phones went unanswered. There were no messages for her on the telautograph in the hotel lobby. Her opulent suite must have started to feel small.

She didn't know what to do. All she had was several trunks of what would later be called a "rich collection of clothing and jewels," a purse that held $3,300 in cash, some of it in the form of another two $1,000 bills, and the burglary kit.

By the early afternoon Margaret began to fear the worst. She sent another telautograph to the front desk at Chester Court addressed to "Mr. Vaughn," hoping it would find its way to her husband.

> Urgent. Call me
> at the Embassy
> Hotel at once.
> Dolly Collins

The minutes dripped away like candle wax. The phone stayed silent.

She swallowed hard and called police headquarters, asking for information on her husband, probably asking about "Horace Waters." The police played dumb: they didn't have anyone with that name in custody. Their operator was able to tell the detectives that the call had come from the Embassy.

Margaret might not have known what to do, but she had to have known not to tell the police a single thing. She waited in her room, hoping she'd hear from one of the other gang members, maybe someone the Kraemers knew, maybe an attorney, maybe someone's girlfriend. She had no idea that the police already knew where she was.

Nor did Margaret know that, after being arrested, her husband and his two companions had been hustled to the West Side police station. Whittemore said he was "John Vaughn" from Cleveland, a traveling salesman, and bragged that he even belonged to the Ohio Automobile Association, as if that proved anything, and said he'd only been carrying so much cash to pay travel expenses. The police told him they knew he was lying. He'd been fingerprinted upon arrival and checked against his Bertillon records.

Coughlin, Commissioner McLaughlin, and Inspector Lahey handled the initial interrogation. It was short. Faced with the fingerprints, Whittemore stiffened and announced, "Yes, you got me." He proudly admitted he was Richard Reese Whittemore, wanted for escape from the Maryland State Penitentiary and for the killing of Robert Holtman.

Whittemore had had a long time to think about this moment. From that minute forward, almost every word, almost every utterance, was not so much a confession as a calculation, one built upon three pillars. The first was that he knew full well the gallows awaited him in the state of Maryland. The second was that the Kraemers had stashed away some $30,000 in a safety deposit box, earmarked to defend the gang, and that they probably had thousands more than that hidden somewhere else. The only way that would be used to help him was to keep the Kraemers happy and not implicate them in any crimes. Lastly, from almost the minute of his arrest, Whittemore had realized that he needed Margaret, and not just for moral support. If she could avoid arrest, she could access any money Whittemore had squirreled away, support him in prison, and serve as a go-between to any cronies who remained free.

Whether he realized it or not, by himself, Richard Whittemore, in spite of his elevated opinion of himself, was just another crook, and a murderer at that. And Margaret, alone, was just another girl dizzied by diamonds and champagne and lured into the fast life of the underworld.

But together they had another identity. As a couple, they were transformed from cardboard cutouts into three-dimensional characters, flesh-and-blood embodiments of a rich and resonant slice of the Jazz Age. Richard wasn't just a gangster, but a husband, a lover, and a sheik, a guy who took what he felt he deserved. And Margaret wasn't just a blond bauble on someone's arm, a svelte figure wrapped in satin, but a devoted partner and a kind of gangster in her own right.

They were like a couple in one of those pulp novels: two separate people who became larger when reflected in the eyes of the other. Other young denizens of the Jazz Age, who may have felt they were being denied the life they'd been promised, would come to look at Richard and Margaret not with disapproval or pity but with envy and admiration.

The press was already poking around—Midtown shoot-outs drew reporters like bad fruit drew flies. The cops had to move fast before word spread. As Whittemore was being quizzed, Cronin and Sullivan went after Goldberg and the Kraemers.

At about 10 a.m., they entered the opulent lobby of the Hotel Alamac, a nineteen-story hotel that had been open less than a year and was one of New York's finest. They spotted Leon Kraemer dressed to go out in a suit and overcoat, standing before the marble front desk and trying to get change for a $1,000 bill. The two detectives identified themselves, ordered him to return to his room, number 333, and took the desk clerk up to unlock the door. At the elevator, they met a bellboy with one of Kraemer's bags. They took Kraemer and the bag back to his room, looked inside, and found a revolver packed with his belongings. More clothes were laid out on his bed. Kraemer had been ready to bolt.

In fact, he'd already called Goldberg to pick up his car and meet him and Jake in the lobby. Goldberg arrived and went up to Leon's room to get him moving. He knocked, entered, and was immediately arrested.

Jake Kraemer turned up about forty-five minutes later. When he didn't find his brother in the lobby, he called his room on the house phone. The detectives ordered Leon to tell him to come up. When Jake knocked on the door, it was opened by Sullivan and Cronin, holding pistols. One of the detectives barked, "We are police. Hands up!"

Jacob Kraemer complied, but after being patted down and told to sit, he turned tough guy and snapped, "What's this all about?"

Sullivan said, "I'll let you know." Then he picked up a shoe from the bed and brought it down hard on Kraemer's head. "Now you know," he said. With that, all three men were taken to the West Side station house.

Goldberg insisted that he was Joe Langdon from Baltimore. He had a gun in his bag and a watch that police hoped to tie to one of the robberies. Leon Kraemer identified himself as Leon Lewis and provided a Brooklyn address, while his brother identified himself as Jacob Kraemer of Philadelphia. In their bags were guns, cash, and jewelry. The guns alone were enough to hold them.

Coughlin already had a plan. He had a pretty good idea that the crew was involved in a whole string of robberies, not just the Goudvis heist. He decided to start by letting them all sweat it out together, seeing what they said, and then taking them out one at a time so none of them would know what the others were saying. He would play each man off against the others.

In the meantime, the cops kept gathering information, quizzing the Alamac's bellhops, desk clerks, and phone operators. They learned that Whittemore had been a frequent visitor to the hotel, that Goldberg and Whittemore often stayed together in the same apartment, and that a man had been trying to reach Whittemore by phone. An operator traced the call to a Brooklyn address belonging to Anthony Paladino.

The police soon realized that Chicarelli and Mortillaro, while crooks themselves, didn't have much to do with the jewel heists, and they would soon release the pair. Goldberg and the Kraemers weren't very cooperative. But there were ways to loosen their lips.

Cops and reporters called it the "third degree," and everyone arrested knew exactly what that meant. Today it would be called police brutality, but in 1926 prisoners' rights were only words in some reformer's speech that no one paid much attention to. The third degree wasn't just a punch in the face upon arrest, but an aggressive extended interrogation, sometimes lasting days, usually accompanied by a beating with a blackjack, rubber hose, or phone book and other kinds of physical intimidation—withholding food, water, cigarettes, dope—whatever it took. Nearly everyone arrested expected to be knocked around. Coughlin and his crew handcuffed the group together in pairs to see what they'd say, hoping one would squawk and push the others onto the subway tracks and spark everyone else to start singing. That worked with a lot of crooks.

Whittemore and the gang, although impeccably dressed, were looking worn. They'd all been awake for most of the last twenty-four hours, and police weren't making them particularly comfortable. Goldberg was already sweating and nervous; he needed a fix. Whittemore's long night of drinking had left him looking haggard.

They asked Whittemore if he was married, already knowing full well he was. Detectives were already on their way to the Hotel Embassy to pick up Margaret.

Whittemore tried to play it tough. At first he said he didn't have a wife. Then he admitted to being married, but said he hadn't seen the missus since escaping from the pen. The cops knew better, but for now, they let it go.

Richard Whittemore's every word was gauged to serve his own interests first. He admitted that he killed the prison guard in Baltimore, claiming it was self-defense and laying the groundwork of a defense if he was extradited. He also copped to the Holtzman hijacking, bragging that he did the job himself and had confessed in that letter he wrote to Gilden's attorney, Harry Nice. It was nothing the detectives didn't already know.

By admitting to that crime, he absolved both Gilden and Kenney of guilt, a useful move if the cops tried to pin their shootings on him. Why would he kill someone over a crime he'd already taken credit for? The admission also absolved Goldberg of the crime, ensuring his continued loyalty.

Then came the big drop. Whittemore admitted to the Goudvis robbery, even copping to being the guy who pistol-whipped the jeweler with the big revolver. He was proud of it. Whittemore realized that the crime was a big deal in New York, and he was already angling for a New York trial, anything to thwart an extradition order to Maryland. He knew that as long as he was useful to New York, they'd keep him around.

But what of the Kraemers? Whittemore played the good soldier and told the cops he hardly knew them.

Coughlin tried to play psychologist. He asked Whittemore why he'd become a gangster, why he risked going back to prison and maybe even being put to death. He was smart, came from a good family. Why did he choose to rob and steal?

Whittemore looked up at him and could hardly suppress a laugh.

"Easy money," he said.

A s afternoon turned to evening, Margaret was still waiting.
       She paced the hotel room till she couldn't stand it for another minute. She fixed her hair and makeup, then put on a fresh blue silk dress before donning her new squirrel coat and several thousand dollars' worth of jewelry.

It was important to look her best. She'd created a fiction at the hotel that she was a stage actress who had given up a career in the theater for a home and a husband, albeit one who was always traveling, a story that earned her good service from the staff. She went to a nearby restaurant and dined alone, trying to decide what to do next. She had to think.

Detectives were waiting for her at the Embassy when she returned an hour or so later, strolling into the lobby, head high, heels clicking smartly on the marble floor, hoping she'd find a message waiting.

The two detectives sandwiched her between them, identified themselves, and told them they knew who she was. Margaret stiffened, and they accompanied her back to her suite.

She feigned outrage, denied everything, and told the police she was "Mrs. John Vaughn, the wife of a Cleveland man, in New York for a bit of business," and demanded to know what this was all about. The police ignored her and started going through her wardrobe trunks, pulling out her clothes, pawing over all her nice, pretty things and tossing them onto the floor, looking for something to tie her to the rest of the gang, as she worried over her dog.

They found plenty. Jewelry worth $10,000 including three gold watches, and $3,300 in cash. Papers for three Cadillacs. And then they found the mother lode, what the *Baltimore News* later described as "instruments not for a society matron." In one bag in a wardrobe drawer were three .38 revolvers, ammunition, flashlights, and, most significantly, two tickets to lockers at Penn Station.

They took Margaret, described as "blonde, rouged, gowned in silks and furs," and the dog from the hotel to the West Side police station and sent a cop to retrieve what was in the lockers. He returned with bags filled with more guns, silk masks, blackjacks, and canvas sacks. In her coat pocket they found a repair ticket from one of the jewelers the gang had previously robbed, dated only a few days before the crime. She'd probably helped case that job. She was no more an innocent pawn than she was a Broadway actress.

Margaret still denied everything. The bags all belonged to her husband, and she didn't have any idea what was inside and couldn't imagine he did either. Then she kept her mouth shut.

The press got busy, filling the press room and roaming the halls, pigeonholing cops, sensing something big was going on. The reporters weren't just the usual suspects from the tabloids who hung around the station all day either, but journalists from more respectable papers like the *Journal American* and the *Times*, correspondents from the Baltimore papers, even reporters from the national wire services. Whittemore's arrest was big news. Lieutenant Cornelius Roche of the Baltimore Police Department was already on his way up.

The New York Police Department needed good press and wanted everyone to know that the Goudvis case was solved. They cultivated the reporters, allowing them to witness portions of the interrogations and even ask a few questions themselves. Cases were won not just in court, but in the public square, and it didn't hurt to start to shape public opinion. That would come in handy when a jury was picked.

They lined everybody up for a photograph to pass out to the press, each of the six men still dressed in a suit and double-breasted coat and a hat, all looking stone-faced and drawn. Chicarelli and Mortillaro looked like they weren't quite sure what they'd gotten themselves into, but Goldberg and the Kraemers looked meek and already a little bored, as though they'd all been through this routine before.

Only one of the six men betrayed any emotion. On the far left end of the lineup stood Richard Whittemore, head tilted, his face a mixture of disgust, disdain, and defiant insouciance, as if ready to spit out a curse word, as if to ask, "*Really?*" He made the others look like sniveling cowards.

The *New York Times* described him as "a rather good-looking fellow in a rakish way," and other press reports went on to describe the fine tailoring of his clothes. When they searched his apartment, the police found "twenty-two bags and three trunks" containing four overcoats, seventeen suits, dozens of shirts, and a half-dozen caps, the kind he wore while robbing, which Baltimore police called "Whittemores."

McLaughlin and Coughlin were confident that after a night or two in jail the gang would fall like dominoes. At an impromptu press conference that afternoon, McLaughlin called the captures "the most important arrests in the history of the New York department." Coughlin bragged that "before nightfall I expect to solve the majority of the big holdups that have occurred recently, not only in New York, but in Baltimore, Philadelphia and Cleveland as well." He ordered detectives in every precinct to round up witnesses for every major robbery of the last two years for a lineup the following day, adding, "We've just begun to open up this thing."

After the photo shoot, as Coughlin preened for the press, he looked at Whittemore and said, "You're at the end of your string, aren't you?" Whittemore only shrugged. All he had left, for now, was his tough guy act.

"What would you rather do," Coughlin asked, "stand trial here for the Fifth Avenue holdup or go back to Baltimore and be tried for murder?"

"Oh, I'll have a lawyer," Whittemore spat back. He was already probing his many ways out.

After grilling Margaret Whittemore for an hour and getting nowhere, Coughlin called to the press room and asked a reporter from the *Baltimore News* to come up and see if he recognized her.

He didn't have to look twice. It was Tiger Girl.

The identification broke her resolve. The reporters from New York peppered their Baltimore counterpart for background information and when they heard the nickname "Tiger Girl," they started to salivate. "Tiger Girl" was a story they could sell, one that now had both a leading man *and* a leading lady.

The police escorted Margaret through the halls to send her for the night to the Jefferson Market Prison on Greenwich Avenue, where female suspects were held. They passed through a gauntlet of reporters, all shouting questions and pointing cameras at Margaret's face like it was opening night for a motion picture. Photographers jostled each other to get the first shots of Tiger Girl for the morning edition.

She turned to the nearest one, and suddenly the Fifteenth Ward burst through her affected Fifth Avenue facade. "You think you're smart," she shouted, "you pug-nosed son of a bitch!" Then she spit in the photographer's face.

There was one more gang member to round up, Anthony Paladino. Detectives staked out his home on Saint Marks Avenue in Brooklyn. When the lights went out at 10 p.m., they went in and rousted him out of bed. Police also found several pistols, ammunition, and fifteen pairs of handcuffs.

Instead of sending him to join his companions, Coughlin kept Paladino separate at headquarters downtown. The rest of the gang spent the night in the prisoners' pen on the West Side, each in his own cell, guarded by two police officers. For the first time in memory, the door from the cellblock to the station house was kept locked, and there were three more guards stationed on the opposite side. They didn't want anyone to try to blast their way in and bust everyone out.

The others hadn't said much of anything the cops didn't already know. Maybe Paladino would.

Coughlin left him to his detectives. At first, Paladino gave the detectives nothing, but as the night dragged on the questioning became more aggressive. As Paladino sat in a chair and gave the same answers to the same questions over and over again, the police punctuated his denials with the slap of a rubber hose. They told him Whittemore had confessed to the Goudvis job. With that, Paladino admitted he was in on it too, but only as a lookout.

He was cracking. He'd accepted their story about Whittemore without question.

The detectives kept at him until dawn, then let him think for a few hours, head pounding, before beginning round two.

Meanwhile, the *Baltimore Post,* an evening paper, broke the news of the gang's arrest in the Whittemores' hometown, pasting photos of the couple from their morgue on the front page. Tiger Girl's photo was the most prominent, a mug shot dating from her Philadelphia arrest. They even managed to get to her mother, Theresa Messler. She told the *Post* she was happy to see her son-in-law arrested, and that she hadn't seen or heard from her daughter since she left Baltimore weeks before. "He always caused trouble," she said of Whittemore, "and my daughter said she was going away to save me any more trouble."

Robert Holtman's widow, Marie, had another reaction. She became hysterical with grief at the news and had to be sedated.

By the morning of Saturday, March 20, as newsboys picked up their morning papers, the name of "the Whittemore Gang" rang out on every corner of the streets of New York and Baltimore. Most stories delivered a brief tick-tock of the arrests and intimated that there would soon be more news to come, that the cops had broken up a ring of jewelry thieves that had been terrorizing New York for months.

Even the *New York Times* was drawn into the story: its page 1 headline blared "Six Men and Woman Held as Thief Gang; Club Is Rendezvous." The *Times* usually gave gangster news short shrift, as if tawdry crimes were beneath their readership, but the Whittemore gang was different.

For one thing, discovering the Club Chantee at the center of the group's activities brought attention to people who didn't want it, namely the rich and powerful and politically well connected, sending shock waves down Fifth Avenue and all the way to City Hall. The *Times* noted that the Chantee had been "lately patronized by persons of prominence and wealth." Whittemore had already started dropping names of people he knew, at least by sight, and some of them were big.

The fact that Whittemore was White and Protestant also got the attention of the *Times*. Stanley Walker, legendary editor of the *New York Herald Tribune*, later wrote that *Times* publisher Adolph Ochs, who was Jewish, "had been puzzled and annoyed by occasional hints that Jews were showing an increasing aptitude" in the gangster underworld. To counter that impression, he "ordered a complete inquiry into the Whittemore gang." In fact, the *Times* would eventually run forty-four stories featuring Whittemore or the gang on the front page in 1926 and a like number on the inside pages. Several of these ran to thousands of words and probed each man's background, as if scrutinizing them for admission to a private club.

The recent arrest of Gerald Chapman, the nation's reigning master criminal, hadn't attracted nearly as much attention. Even Arnold Rothstein, widely acknowledged as the underworld king of New York at the time, would make the front page only eighteen times between 1920 and 1927.

And then there was Tiger Girl. Never before had the American press discovered a pair quite like Richard and Margaret Whittemore, both a married couple and consummate criminals, but also young, quotable, photogenic, and representative of the age. Their story brought all the excesses of the Roaring Twenties to life, sprinkled with a heavy dose of immorality and a dash of danger and romance. Over the next six months, they would become the biggest story in the country, a daily soap opera featuring heroes, villains, antiheroes, worried parents, police brutality, dead bodies, shoot-outs, dope, diamonds, tearful wives, and sneering crooks. It was a real-life gangster film playing out in real time before any gangster films had ever been made. Their story would even eclipse Gertrude Ederle's summer-long attempt to become the first woman to swim the English Channel, the death and funeral of Rudolph Valentino, and a historic hurricane that struck Miami. In recent years, only the 1924 trial of schoolboy killers Nathan Leopold and Richard Loeb, the 1925 Scopes Monkey Trial, and the saga of Floyd Collins, who a little over a year earlier had become trapped in a Kentucky cave for days before succumbing, had received similar sustained national press attention, but none for as long as the Whittemores. Richard and Margaret would soon become America's original gangster crime couple, the templates for later delinquent duos like Bonnie Parker and Clyde Barrow, Charles Starkweather and Caril Ann Fugate.

Yet Margaret, despite her prominence, would only rarely be profiled in any depth in the papers, and then usually only in regard to her feelings toward her husband or her reaction to his incarceration. The embedded chauvinism of American journalism of the era devalued women and their words. What newspapers did value was her photo, and her image. What she actually thought and felt and believed was considered less important than what she was wearing. And unlike Celia Cooney, the "Bob-Haired Bandit" who two years earlier, at her husband's insistence, had sold her story for $1,000 and allowed a ghost-writer to breathlessly invent a persona for her—including a prodigious number of quotes that she herself never uttered—Margaret measured every word and revealed little. One reason for her reticence may have been that Richard had not only a story to tell but one he could sell. The less she said, the more lucrative that story would be.

In another day or two, Richard Whittemore would earn a nickname of his own: the Candy Kid. Precisely who first pinned the name on him is unclear, but it likely came from either the police, who adopted a lot of gangster slang, or reporters seeking a sobriquet that when paired with "Tiger Girl" would roll off the tongue and into hot lead linotype.

The name fit Whittemore. He was a sweet-talking "candy kid" who swiped diamonds (aka "candy") and used drugs (also referred to as "candy") on the streets. However it came to be, only two days after being arrested Richard Whittemore became someone else. Tiger Girl and the Candy Kid were born, a headline writer's dream.

In the same way the name Tiger Girl made Margaret seem both harder and more glamorous, simultaneously sexy and dangerous and sweet, the name Candy Kid gave Richard Whittemore an added dimension, making him seem a bit less threatening and more sympathetic, even romantic. Wrapped in a tabloid headline, Tiger Girl and the Candy Kid bound the two together more tightly than their wedding vows.

Their story had everything: sex and romance, love and diamonds, death and blood, lowbrow lives mixed with highbrow living fueled in equal measure by dreams and desire and greed and fantasy. The couple wrapped up an entire era in one sweet snarling package dropped on the doorstep and sold on the corner every morning for months.

Forget F. Scott Fitzgerald and Zelda, or the fictional Jay Gatsby and Daisy Buchanan. Tiger Girl and the Candy Kid were pure nonfiction, the real deal.

They were about to become *really* famous.

———

Twelve

CANDY KID DARES CHAIR FOR LOVE

When Anthony Paladino came to on Saturday morning, Coughlin's men resumed their rubber-hose interrogation. By this time, armed with enough information to start fitting the puzzle pieces together, they asked Paladino questions littered with enough details to make him believe that everybody else was squealing. Even the Kraemers, they told him, had confessed. Not only that, but they were pinning everything on him. If Paladino knew what was good for him, if he wanted to see his girl again, he'd spill it out. After a few more hours on the end of the rubber hose, he buckled.

In what eventually became a sprawling twenty-two-page confession, Paladino sang like Caruso. All the time thinking he was only telling the police what they already knew, he implicated both Kraemers, Goldberg—as Joseph Langdon—Richard Whittemore, Willie Unkelbach—known to Paladino only as "Willie Rogers"—and Nate Weinzimmer. He provided details of the Stanley robbery, the Ernst robbery, the Prip job, and the Goudvis mugging, explaining how the gang cased the jobs: the Kraemers did all the planning, Whittemore provided the muscle, and Weinzimmer did the driving, while he, Goldberg, and Unkelbach played supporting roles as lookouts, backups, and hired guns. He told the cops how the Kraemers fenced everything, how much they got for the jobs, and how the money was divided. It was hard for the police to keep up.

In the meantime, police contacted witnesses like Folmer Prip and his secretary and Samuel Kandel to ask them to come in and try to identify the prisoners. Prip was certain of their identities, and Kandel said of Whittemore, "I identify him ninety-five percent." They printed photos of the gang to distribute to other witnesses and brought in two hundred cops, masked to disguise their identities, to walk a conga line before the prisoners to try to jog their memories and see if any cops recognized any of the men.

On Saturday, Coughlin brought Margaret into the act and allowed her to see her husband. She'd been allowed to keep her clothes and showed up as if dressed for a date. According to the *Times,* "she wore a small, light tan hat, with a dark tan turned up brim, on the side of which was a light tan pom-pom. Her stockings matched the hat, and her shoes of black patent leather were decorated with suede. She wore a black velvet dress with a small fur collar and she had on a gray squirrel coat." At least this time she didn't cover herself with jewelry.

Richard pretended not to know her at first, uncertain how much the police knew about either her or her involvement with the gang. But she blew that fiction when she walked into the room and tearfully cried out for "her Dickie."

Coughlin needed Whittemore to talk some more and figured that once he knew they had Tiger Girl in a cage of her own, he might be more cooperative. Although he kept Whittemore shackled, he allowed Margaret to get close enough to her husband for them to whisper a few words back and forth, and then he let the press have another look at her.

She'd regained her composure and seemed to have realized that spitting on reporters and photographers hadn't looked good in the papers. She had a story, she was sticking to it, and now she was taking center stage, a martyr for the man she loved above all else.

"He has always been on the level with me," she said about her husband, ignoring his dalliance with Lee, "and my faith in him has not been shaken. I love him and don't believe all the things the police say about him. I will stick by him to the last. If he is sent to Baltimore to go on trial for murder I shall go with him and fight by his side.

"He told me he was a traveling salesman and I always believed him. He has always been kind and gentle to me and now this thing has happened." She spoke about the wonderful life they had lived for the last year, staying in the best hotels, eating in the finest restaurants, and how her husband had provided her with everything she had ever wanted, everything any girl could ever want. She didn't explain how a fugitive wanted for murder had become so successful in such a short time, or what it was he was supposed to be selling to finance such a lifestyle.

"I love my husband and I intend to stand by him," she said. "I don't believe the things the police say about him. He could not treat me as he does and be what the police and press say he is. That is all I care to say, except I love him."

Coughlin still hoped that Margaret might eventually turn on her husband. Although he could have kept her in jail, New York state law also allowed him to send her elsewhere. After spending her first night at the Jefferson Market Prison, he had her remanded to the Florence Crittenton home on West Twenty-First Street, a house maintained by a social service mission designed to support prostitutes, unwed mothers, and other "fallen" women. Coughlin hoped that the mission staff's sympathetic shoulders and wise counsel might cause the tiger to purr.

Coughlin continued to shuffle the deck during the interrogations. His detectives slipped bits of knowledge gained from one prisoner, or from a bellhop or phone operator, to another suspect, leaving the impression that the others were talking. It was slow going, but minute by minute the investigation was gaining traction, even though the Kraemers and Goldberg remained silent.

Then came the master stroke. Coughlin had Paladino taken to the station house, shackled close enough to Whittemore that the two could speak, but not close enough for either to reach the other. Whittemore immediately told Paladino to keep his mouth shut, that no one was talking. Paladino told him he already had, that the cops told him everyone had already talked.

If he hadn't been handcuffed, Whittemore would have throttled Paladino, disgust and anger and dismay throbbing through every vein in his body. Paladino had been played, and now they all would have to pay for it. As the *Daily*

News noted, by "keeping Paladino and Whittemore mutually ignorant of each other," Coughlin had lured each man into "a game of competitive squealing."

Paladino's confessions made him a marked man, not just to the rest of the gang but to any other prisoner. He'd violated the code and turned rat.

That same day, Maryland governor Ritchie prepared a request for Whittemore's extradition to Maryland for New York governor Al Smith's approval. Herbert O'Conor sent a representative of his office to New York to lobby on Maryland's behalf and confer on the case with New York County district attorney Joab Banton. O'Conor announced that if Maryland got ahold of Whittemore, he planned to try Whittemore for Holtman's murder and that he would ask for the death penalty. In Maryland, that meant hanging. New York used the electric chair.

Richard Whittemore started calculating every angle, looking for the triple bank shot that might save his life and maybe even one day set him free. Now he would do anything—and say anything—to avoid extradition and loosen the noose on his neck. That meant it was time to start talking, at least a little, enough to keep New York from sending him to Maryland. Every day in New York might add another day to his life, and each extra minute might provide an opportunity to escape his fate.

For his next grilling, the police again brought Margaret into the station house. They kept her in an adjoining room, where her husband could hear her weeping. The police certainly had a lot of questions, and every couple of hours, as they heard from their colleagues in Baltimore, Cleveland, and elsewhere, they had even more.

Baltimore already suspected Whittemore in the killing of Si Gilden and the shooting of Spike Kenney. In December, Tommy Langrella, the Baltimore bootlegger who gave Whittemore a lift after his escape, had been found dead in New Jersey. Given his connection to Whittemore, they had questions about Langrella too. And then there was the missing private detective, Henry Helwig. Over the past year an awful lot of people who intersected with Whittemore had ended up dead or, in Helwig's case, suspiciously absent.

Hour by hour, police started piecing obscure bits of information together. As they pored over evidence regarding the arrest of Whittemore and the rest of the gang, they realized that a Mott Street address, under his wife's name, had been used to register the car Si Gilden drove to New York. A Mott Street address had also been found on the driver's license Buffalo police found in the Buick used in the Buffalo bank robbery in which the two guards, Yarrington and Clifford, were shot and killed.

By Sunday, deprived of dope for two days and sick with tuberculosis, Shuffles Goldberg was suffering. Still, it took two hours and, presumably, more than a few whacks of the rubber hose before he admitted that the signature on the license was his, tying the gang to the Buffalo murders. When Whittemore was asked about it, he was tight-lipped. He claimed only that he "might know" something about the Buffalo job, playing the tease to keep New York authorities interested. Ever so slowly, the police not only tied up loose ends but with each knot pulled the noose tighter around Whittemore's neck.

New York County authorities passed the information on to Buffalo. Police there immediately made plans to bring witnesses to New York to identify the gang. The number of possible victims of the Whittemore gang was growing.

Over the next few days, authorities in all three cities pondered their next moves. Prosecuting Richard Whittemore would solve a lot of problems for all of them.

Maryland's case was the clearest. O'Conor felt that he had an airtight murder charge. Sending Whittemore to the gallows would be relatively easy, it would justify the end of the reform era in Maryland penology, and it carried the added bonus of boosting O'Conor's own political ambitions. He was already planning his prosecution; he'd even traveled to the penitentiary and instructed guards and other witnesses to reenact Holtman's murder.

Convicting Whittemore in Maryland would also bolster Governor Albert Ritchie's political prospects. The Democrat had run for president in 1924 on an anti-Prohibition platform and was up for gubernatorial reelection at the end of the year. Hanging Whittemore could help set up another run at the presidency and prove that being anti-Prohibition did not equal being soft on crime.

In Buffalo, the hope was that Whittemore's arrest would finally allow Buffalo authorities to clear the Bank of Buffalo robbery. Police had been embarrassed after falsely identifying Harry Harris as the perpetrator. They had been facing withering criticism over the increasing lawlessness of the city. Pinning the crime on Whittemore would silence critics.

In New York County, the situation was a bit more complicated. They'd caught Whittemore, and he'd committed the bulk of his crimes there, including Gilden's murder, if they could develop enough evidence to support the charge. Even without it, Coughlin boasted that he already had enough on Whittemore to send him away for 150 years. District attorney Joab Banton was a Tammany man, as was his number two, ambitious acting district attorney Ferdinand Pecora, who would later spearhead the US Senate investigation into the stock market crash. But while Banton was eager to do his boss's bidding, Pecora was no supplicant. A prosecution could boost his own future prospects.

The result was a messy, sprawling case spread over two states and three jurisdictions with half a dozen suspects and dozens of potential charges among them, from murder to robbery, assault, Sullivan law violations, conspiracy, and a host of other lesser crimes.

The number of charges and suspects kept expanding. After Tiger Girl's arrest, Alice Hahn, the cashier at Ortman's Confectionery, opened up the paper and recognized the now-notorious Margaret Whittemore. Hahn, who had since become Mrs. John Ortman, while expressing fear of retribution, said, "Those pointed features in the picture of Mrs. Whittemore correspond identically with those of the girl who held me up that day. I have never forgotten them. As soon as I saw that picture the resemblance flashed over me." Baltimore police were delighted.

Until this point, New York's hold on Margaret was tenuous, based only on a Sullivan Act charge and maybe a conspiracy charge stemming from the repair slip. But Ortman's identification changed everything, even if the crime had taken place in Maryland. It gave the police in both places more leverage over both Margaret and her husband.

Ultimately, the final prosecution decision in regard to Richard would be up to New York governor Al Smith, a Democrat and supporter of Mayor Walker, whom he'd mentored. A Whittemore prosecution would be a coup. The arrest had already provided Walker with some cover, allowing him to publicly rail against the very cabaret culture he himself enjoyed on an almost nightly basis.

On Monday, Smith chose to sit on the extradition request while police gathered more information. Police were trying to find safety deposit boxes attached to the gang, and they wanted to find Willie Unkelbach.

In preparation for their indictment and eventual arraignment, Richard Whittemore and the others were sent to New York's municipal jail, otherwise known as "the Tombs." The horrible conditions inside the Tombs were as much a deterrent as any sentence — a lot of guys pleaded out just to avoid spending time there. The prison was connected to the Municipal Courts Building by a walkway over the street known as the "Bridge of Sighs," and Whittemore, it was reported, made the crossing from one building to the other "with low hanging head and lagging step." That last night at the Chantee must have seemed a lifetime ago.

As the prisoners were marched into court, the indictments came down fast. The Kraemers were charged with the Prip robbery, Paladino was held on the robbery of Jacques Ross, the two-bit Ernest job was pinned on Whittemore, Goldberg, and Jake Kraemer, and Whittemore, the Kraemers, Goldberg, and Paladino were all charged with the Goudvis robbery. All told, the amount of stolen jewelry in the indictments totaled more than $300,000, with perhaps another $500,000 worth of robberies still under investigation.

After the proceedings, Pecora and DA Joab Banton took over questioning, with help from Detectives Sullivan and Cronin. They bounced the prisoners back and forth between their cells and the interrogation rooms, pulling out a little more information each time. Baltimore detective Cornelius Roche and O'Conor's assistant, Eugene Edgett, took a crack at Whittemore too.

And take a crack they did. As one *Baltimore News* reporter wrote, "Piercing yells could be heard from the inner office . . . What happened was never told, but a good picture can be drawn up in one's mind." Afterwards, one detective bragged, "You can't break this kind of guy by sweet talk . . . Take a wild animal, for instance, if you treat him nice he will bite you, but if you club him he'll behave. That is the only way to make these birds tell the truth."

Whittemore remained defiant, speaking with what Pecora termed "supreme conceit." He continued to insist, against all evidence to the contrary, that he hadn't seen Margaret since escaping from the penitentiary. "You might not believe it, but that's the truth," he said. She was only in New York because he'd written her in Cleveland and asked her to come, but they hadn't even had a chance to meet before his arrest. "She did this, the poor kid," he said, and "the bulls located her and took her into custody thinking she knew something about the charges against me. But she knows nothing."

He also let the authorities know he considered himself a dangerous man. He told Pecora, "I am confident of my ability. When I was free I said I would never be arrested again, and I am above law and order. I like life and intended to keep it at all cost to others. I made up my mind, that to escape capture, I would shoot down anyone who interfered with me, I could have kept that vow, but you overpowered me before I got into action."

If he hadn't been drunk, he continued, he'd never have been caught. "I hardly realized what was happening until they got the handcuffs on me," he said. "Then it was too late. You can bet your bottom dollar they would have never gotten me so easily if it hadn't been for that."

Brave words, and stupid too. Saying that he intended to remain free "at all cost to others" was also a tacit admission that could include killing Si Gilden, Henry Helwig, or Tommy Langrella.

B ack in Maryland, Unkelbach caught wind of the rest of the gang's arrest. He insisted on leaving for New York City, "to see what it was all about." His wife told him not to be an idiot, but Unkelbach responded, "I don't care. I'm gonna drive like hell to get there to see what can be done," as if he intended to bust the gang out by himself. But more than duty drew him to New York: he also needed to score. When he arrived in the city Monday night, he purchased $3,000 worth of morphine.

By then, New York detectives were already on his trail. After learning that someone had tried to book passage to France in Unkelbach's name, they tailed one of his drug-fiend friends to an apartment at 150 Manhattan Avenue. On Tuesday, they made their move.

Three detectives burst into the apartment and found their quarry in bed, reading a newspaper and happily stoned, clippings about the Whittemore gang scattered about the bedspread and a revolver sitting on the nightstand. Unkelbach reached for it in his stupor but quickly realized he was outgunned.

"It's alright," he said to them as he was handcuffed and hauled off, "I was expecting you." Police had a lot of questions, and Unkelbach, whose drug habit made even a few hours without a fix seem like days, gave a deposition almost immediately. The *Daily News* called it an "orgy of confessions." Unkelbach implicated Whittemore in both Gilden's and Langrella's deaths, saying the Candy Kid disposed of both "in his usual ruthless fashion." As Coughlin put it, "If there was any argument that would have resulted in 'peaching' on Whittemore," according to Unkelbach, Whittemore would just "bump them off, . . . he was the boss." He reported that Unkelbach had added, with some regret, that he'd wished he hadn't once missed a chance to pull the trigger on Whittemore himself.

The press was milking the story for all it was worth, making all of the gang members out to be characters from a dime novel. The *Baltimore News* said that Goldberg "snarls and spits out venomous replies to questioners one moment, then turns cringing and meek." Another story analyzed the gang according to their "criminal ears," noting that all of them had ears that were "coarse, large and shapeless" and maintaining that some revealed the "marked peculiarity of degenerates."

Even Margaret didn't escape such crude analysis. The *News* interviewed an "expert graphologist" who had studied Margaret's handwriting and concluded that "half her character is developed. Half of her has pulled away from the copybook pattern of childhood . . . Margaret Whittemore will be a hard person to handle. She is not going to be crushed down as most girls would be . . . she is not a coarse woman, but she could be lured by the promise of money and a high time. She is with the cream of the criminals set, apparently, and this is just what would appeal to her." Readers ate up every overblown word.

At the arraignment at Municipal Court, Margaret drew the most attention. She'd arrived at the arraignment dressed to the nines, wearing a smart tan hat sporting a feather and a full-length fur coat over a one-piece frock. She pleaded not guilty to the robbery charge but was denied bail when the DA's office indicated that they expected to file more charges later.

She broke down in tears. Her attorney, Harry Shulman, refused to allow her to be interviewed by the press, insisting that she was only "an innocent tool in the hands of others." Nonetheless, the *Brooklyn Daily Eagle* noted snidely that "her hair is blond and brittle, as though it had been too long under the curling tongs, and her mouth is of the loose type that finds it impossible to utter a good, firm 'no.'" She was a woman, the article concluded, "who wanted luxury without work."

The arraignment was suspended until later in the week, and Judge Morris Koenig assigned the Volunteer Defenders Committee to provide representation for each man who needed it. Before they were all sent to their cells, the authorities allowed the Candy Kid and Tiger Girl a single furtive kiss. The men then trudged across the Bridge of Sighs, while Margaret was sent to the Jefferson Market Prison. Her soft time at the Crittenton House was over.

When they got back to the Tombs, Buffalo authorities were waiting there. Chief Detective Austin Roche—no relation to the Baltimore detective—had in tow three witnesses to the Bank of Buffalo robbery and killing: Joseph Schabo, who worked in the mechanical department of the *Buffalo Courier*, and two others who were too afraid to reveal their identity. The entire gang, sans Paladino and Unkelbach, who were still segregated from the others, and about a dozen other prisoners took part in a lineup.

It was hardly fair. None of the other men sported finely tailored suits, and the gang's picture had appeared in papers all over the country. Schabo and the other witnesses pointed out Whittemore and Leon Kraemer. Back in Buffalo, four of the twelve John Doe indictments for first-degree murder were amended, the aliases scratched out and replaced with the names Richard R. Whittemore and Leon Kraemer, both charged with two counts of murder.

E arly the following morning a chauffeur noticed smoke pouring from the second-floor windows of the Club Chantee. By the time the fire department squelched the flames, the building was a total loss. The cause of the fire would never be determined. Ever since the arrests, the high-flyers who had given the club its cachet had stayed away, replaced by middle-class gawkers. A place where everybody who was anybody went to be seen became a place where nobody of note dared show their face. Whatever secrets and evidence of the gang's activities could be found there went up in smoke. A lot of well-known people, including those who had happily imbibed with Whittemore during his time as the nightclub king, must have been happy to see it go. They'd never have to answer any questions now.

As each jurisdiction jockeyed for position, the scope and severity of the gang's crimes metastasized. Cleveland police were closing in on the only member of the gang still free, Nate Weinzimmer, and New Jersey was making noise that they wanted Whittemore for the Langrella killing. Rumors of caches of gems and cash were rampant. Pecora said, "We have learned how highly systematized was the crime organization which the gang members formed. The Whittemore band was the most highly organized I ever heard of. They had planned to operate on a national scale with a billion dollars in prospect as loot . . . more harm than you could imagine would be done to the youth of this country if the plan were made public."

Pecora's statement underscored just how effective the gang had been. It wasn't so much that any single thing the gang was doing was so revolutionary —they were hardly the first to time out jobs, or use lookouts, or make arrangements with a fence in advance—but their discipline, consistency, and unbridled ambition were unique. It was the equivalent of assembly-line robbery, repeatable and potentially infinite in scope.

On Thursday, March 26, Rawlings Whittemore, distraught after learning of the arrests, traveled to New York to visit his son. He arrived at Coughlin's office unannounced, and the men chatted for a while. Rawlings Whittemore produced letters of reference attesting to his own fine character, all the while arguing that he and his late wife had always tried their best with their son. Once upon a time, he said, "he was the livest boy in the neighborhood and the brightest. Until he got in with a gang of crooks." After that, "he was always incorrigible, but I didn't think it would come to this . . . sometimes I think if his mother had lived, things would have gone differently." Coughlin was sympathetic and sent the man to the Municipal Courts Building, accompanied by an assistant DA, to see his son.

Richard was in no mood for visitors, telling a guard, "I want to be left alone," before relenting. If nothing else, a visit would provide a brief respite from his fetid cell in the Tombs.

When Whittemore entered, handcuffed to a detective, his father rushed toward him, arms out, "My boy, my son." The Candy Kid acted cool. "Hello, Pop," he said, then meekly offered, not a hug, but a hand.

For the next hour, the father peppered the son with questions, most of which received little more than a one- or two-word response, then silence and a bitter look. Rawlings Whittemore appeared ever more upset. Finally, Richard told his father, "You can't blame yourself for the position I'm in. It was in me and it had to come out."

He said he didn't need an attorney and had no preference where he went to trial. "What's the difference? I don't care what they do," he said. Then Rawlings asked about Margaret. Would she have to stay in jail?

Richard first responded with a flash of anger, then blurted out, "If they turn my wife out on the street, I'll tell the whole works, the whole works, and it will startle New York."

The assistant DA couldn't have been more surprised if Richard Whittemore had pulled a shotgun out of his shorts. To save Tiger Girl, the Candy Kid was promising to tell them everything. As soon as the DA confirmed that Whittemore meant what he said, he raced to tell Banton.

Banton was intrigued, but cautious. He didn't trust the younger Whittemore as far as he could spit. "If Whittemore will tell me things that are true, actually true," he said, "I'll consider his request." For despite Paladino's and Unkelbach's confessions, and the drips and drabs from Whittemore and the others during interrogation, there were still a lot of things the police wanted to know. Where and how much money and jewelry remained stashed away? Who were the fences? What other crimes as yet unknown had Whittemore and the others committed? What of Langrella, Gilden, and Helwig? *And what about Buffalo?*

While her husband let his tongue slip at the municipal jail, Margaret was whiling away the time at Jefferson Market Prison at Ninth Street and Sixth Avenue. The old red jail was a far cry from the Hotel Embassy. Although attractive from the outside, the charms of the Victorian Gothic building stopped at the entrance.

Although better in nearly all ways than the jails that housed men, the cells were dungeonlike, and the sleeping cots only two feet wide. Prisoners were not segregated by either crime or social status and shared accommodations. First-timers were housed with chronic criminals, and prostitutes and drug addicts were incarcerated alongside ladies picked up for shoplifting or larceny and gun molls, like Tiger Girl, who were guilty of marrying the wrong guy for the wrong reasons.

Margaret had fallen hard for her new life with Richard, and now she was being kept in a cage with women below her newfound status. It was like the Fifteenth Ward just wouldn't let them go.

The morning of Friday, March 27, thanks to information provided by Willie Unkelbach, police arrested Joseph Tropp. They found $20,000 worth of gems in his possession when they arrested him, as well as guns and a like amount of cash, but Tropp was hardly concerned. He had built a bank vault of goodwill and knew it would soon be time to make a withdrawal. He got out in less than twenty-four hours, freed on $5,000 bail, which for Tropp was akin to loose change jangling in his pocket.

In Maryland, Elda Unkelbach was also placed under arrest. She freely admitted, to her family's horror, that she and her husband had shared an apartment for a time with the Whittemores in Cleveland, and that she knew all along that he was a fugitive wanted for the murder of Holtman. Asked if he ever talked about it, she said, "No. He never worried about anything."

That same day, before the rescheduled arraignment, the DA's office looped in Margaret's attorney, Harry Shulman, on the deal Richard had inadvertently proposed. Shulman was young, fresh out of Harvard, but wise beyond his years. In 1930, he would clerk for Supreme Court justice Louis Brandeis and later teach at Yale. He knew a good deal when he saw it.

He also realized that the agreement was not so much with Richard Whittemore as with Margaret—her freedom, not her husband's, was at stake. The DA had no choice but to negotiate with Shulman. Since the agreement had a legal impact on Margaret, and not on her husband, there was no real way to tie her release to the contents of her husband's confession, only to the fact of a confession itself. He made certain the deal was legally binding; if Richard talked, regardless of what he said, Margaret walked, provided, as Banton insisted, she had a clean record and was "not wanted on a serious charge in any other city." Maryland hadn't yet decided to charge Margaret in the Ortman robbery, making that moot. If Richard talked, New York could no longer pursue charges against Margaret on either a Sullivan violation or in connection to the Goudvis robbery.

Either Shulman outmaneuvered his more experienced adversary or Banton, in his eagerness to get Whittemore, outmaneuvered himself. That same day Paladino's full confession, all twenty-two pages, appeared in the *New York Times* and several other papers, leaked by either a policeman or someone in the DA's office. Now Whittemore, even if he didn't see a copy of the paper himself, knew the gist of what Paladino had said.

The big news that day was supposed to be the arraignments of Whittemore, the Kraemers, and Goldberg at the Court of General Sessions. Unkelbach and Paladino would be arraigned later, for their own protection.

At the proceeding a few hours later, an armed guard stood behind each man as uniformed police and plainclothes detectives crowded out most spectators, the few allowed in subject to search before gaining entry. This time the men were all appointed counsel: Louis Collings for Whittemore, Leonard Snitkin for Goldberg, and Hyman Bushel for the two Kraemers. Whittemore had claimed to be destitute and unable to afford counsel on his own, saying, "I haven't got a dime. It all went—crap games and playing around in nightclubs." Collings signed off on the confession after Banton agreed that the contents would remain confidential and only be used at trial.

The Kraemer brothers got lucky, or maybe their bank account was already paying dividends, for their attorney, Hyman Bushel, was no backbencher trolling for clients. In recent years, the young Polish NYU grad had cultivated a series of high-profile, well-paying clients, representing such notables as sports promotor Tex Rickard (who built Madison Square Garden), crooner Rudy Vallee, boxer Louis Firpo, and even Babe Ruth. Bushel had already successfully defended the Bambino against a paternity suit and charges that he'd welched on gambling debts, making wise use of the press on each occasion.

Since attorneys had only just been assigned to them, Judge Koenig agreed to another postponement until the following week. As the three suspects all trudged out of the courtroom, Koenig saw fit to single out Whittemore for admonishment. The Candy Kid had put his hat back on his head before exiting the courtroom. The judge told him to stop and take it back off. Whittemore did, but didn't bother to hide his disdain.

• • •

The arraignment may have fallen flat, but by then the talk of the courthouse—and soon the talk of the country—was what had taken place just before. As part of Banton's agreement to release Tiger Girl if the Candy Kid confessed, Banton allowed the two incarcerated lovebirds to meet before the arraignment. But he didn't take any chances. Margaret arrived in the Municipal Courts Building first, while a phalanx of thirty cops delivered the gang from the Tombs.

Surrounded by uniformed officers and detectives, Whittemore stepped out of the Bridge of Sighs and into the building, where he saw Margaret waiting just outside the passageway, eyes already glistening with tears. She and her attorney had just finished meeting with an assistant DA to finalize the deal, crossing all the t's and dotting the i's, and now she stood at the threshold like a bride at the altar. She ran to her husband, flung her arms around his neck, and started kissing him. Whittemore, handcuffed to Detective Sullivan, hugged her back with one arm and did his best to return her passion. The press soaked in the whole scene.

Hand in hand, they were escorted to the DA's office and allowed to sit together in the corner with their detective chaperone. It was an irregular arrangement, but Banton assured both Whittemores that "Sullivan would forget anything he overheard."

The couple snuggled in a corner alongside their escort, whispering, for nearly half an hour. Margaret held her husband's free hand with her own and placed the other on his shoulder, sometimes rubbing his head and brow and shoulder. She occasionally sobbed quietly as the two whispered sweet nothings and significant somethings to one another. The police, members of the DA's office, and the press watched closely. The *New York Daily News* even ran a photograph of the maudlin scene: the Candy Kid in his pinstriped suit, hat perched on his lap, his right arm cuffed to a very uncomfortable-looking Walter Sullivan, while Tiger Girl hangs on his left side, full-length fur coat pulled up to her chin, one bare calf exposed, her half-hidden face pressed against his shoulder.

Allowing the press to witness the meeting would prove to be an error as great as Banton's decision to trade Margaret's freedom for the promise of a confession. Because until that moment, in the minds of most of the public, the

Candy Kid was simply a gangster and a killer, albeit younger, more flamboyant, and more successful than the usual thug, and Tiger Girl was not much more than a garden-variety gun moll, better dressed than most and adorned with more expensive jewelry, but still just a young woman who carried the guns and reaped the benefits of a tide of crime. She was someone Assistant DA Rose Rosenberg referred to as having fallen for "riotous living . . . excitedly awaiting . . . the outcome of a holdup," another victim of the jazz-mad generation addicted to "hectic pleasures" without any consideration of the consequences.

There were a lot of Richard and Margaret Whittemores out there. So far, only the scale of their crimes and desires had set them apart.

Not anymore. Now, as each tear fell from her cheek onto his shoulder, they became more than that. As they embraced in the corner, the spotlight of the press fell on the young couple and the rest of the case faded into the shadows. You could almost hear the harps and violins playing in the background.

Tiger Girl and the Candy Kid were now at the top of the bill, the main attraction, the stars of the show. The deal transformed them both, creating martyrs for love in a sappy tabloid love story. The way the newshounds wrote it up, the Candy Kid had fallen on his sword to save the virtuous Tiger Girl, she of love everlasting.

Young women now looked at Tiger Girl and saw a woman they wanted to be —head over heels in love and full of passionate devotion. They looked at the Candy Kid and saw a dashing, daring sheik who would die for love. Men looked at him and saw a hard guy taking the high road, then looked at Tiger Girl and saw only unbridled desire. Everybody's fantasy was fulfilled. Anyone could fill in the blanks themselves, any way they wanted to. For once, most accounts in the paper the next day didn't focus on Margaret's wardrobe. Neither did they note her husband's crimes. Most, like the *Baltimore News,* seized upon the story by its newly exposed heartstrings: "To see her, dubbed the 'Tiger Girl' . . . lose control and sob on the shoulder of her gangster husband was enough to touch the heart of Detective Sullivan, his captor. A tear could be seen in the eye of the policeman." Meanwhile, the cold mad-dog killer suddenly became a tough guy with a heart. The story continued: "His appreciation could be seen. He dropped the defiant attitude that is characteristic of him . . . As he left the office a faint trace of a smile could be seen on his lips, probably the first since his capture. He had done what he most desired—return the little he now can for his wife's deep affection."

In a few mawkish paragraphs and gauzy photos, the blood was washed from their embrace. The Candy Kid took his place upon the crucifix of love, a previously repellent figure suddenly redeemed by self-sacrifice, a gallant antihero. And Tiger Girl, brave and blinded by love, would accompany him in his slow waltz with the grim reaper.

Hollywood wasn't half as good as this. The story told itself, a tragic romance of the age, all spelled out in garish, oversized type: "CANDY KID DARES CHAIR FOR LOVE."

Thirteen

NOT GONNA BURN ALONE

After the two preening lovers were pried apart, Whittemore met with Banton. With Tiger Girl's freedom in the balance, the district attorney expected him to make good on his promise to confess.

As far as the Candy Kid was concerned, that meant something a little different than it did to the DA. Over the next two days, he'd live up to at least one definition of his nickname. The Candy Kid's silver tongue would work overtime spinning so much yarn he could have knit a sweater for every guy in the Tombs.

Late in the afternoon of March 26, Whittemore started talking and talking and talking. He kept up a steady patter till 11 p.m. that night. Then, after finally being allowed a shave, a shower, and a change of clothes, he was back at the DA's office the following afternoon. As the *Daily News* reported, "The gunman, natty and clean-shaven, might have been mistaken for a dry goods clerk or a drug store sheik, but for the brightly shining chain that linked him to his guard." His appearance triggered another reprieve for Tiger Girl, and they were again allowed to meet and spoon before the press. When she saw him, she called out, "Dick!" and threw herself onto his lap. The two necked ferociously before a crowd of onlookers, her two hands and his free one roaming under a newspaper as if they were two kids on the front porch trying not too hard to control themselves.

When they were finally pulled apart, the Candy Kid picked up where he'd left off, this time also in front of Pecora and a stenographer. Tiger Girl was even allowed to sit next to her husband as he spoke, handcuffed to a chair. She remained silent, but even if she had been allowed to speak, she wouldn't have gotten a word in edgewise. Whittemore rambled on and on and on until 9 p.m., long enough to create a thirty-page document, bettering Paladino's confession by a full eight pages. Pecora hardly had the time, or the need, to ask a question.

The tale Whittemore spun was nearly identical to the one he would later spin in the press. While he had no problem copping to any number of robberies in New York, Whittemore confessed not only to the robberies he was already suspected in, but to a half-dozen more, whether there was any previous evidence he was involved or not. His account of crimes both known and unknown often veered wildly from what the police already knew. In confessing to the crimes the gang was already suspected of, he implicated Paladino and Unkelbach, the two squealers, over and over again, conveniently leaving Goldberg, whom he called the "best friend I have in the world," almost completely out of it. And he still refused to drop anything of value on the Kraemers or to say anything about the disappearance of Helwig or the killings of Gilden, Langrella, and the two guards, Clifford and Yarrington, in Buffalo, except to say he knew nothing about them.

But he went on for hours talking about himself, spinning out the fable that he was a master criminal, the real brains of the whole outfit, responsible not only for the execution of the crimes but also for selecting their targets. He said he lunched every day in a restaurant favored by the denizens of the Diamond District and "soon learned to join in a conversation with them," becoming a trusted equal as he picked up the tips that spurred the gang into action. Take the Ross job. He was the first to hear about the shipment of stones and set the job up himself two days later, "as it did not require any great time to watch the movements of this place." And so what? Dealers like Ross "lost nothing, as he was insured for every dime."

As Whittemore chain-smoked, stubbing one cigarette after another into a great pile in an ashtray, he went on and on about the many good deeds all that dough had allowed him to do. On Thanksgiving, for instance, he claimed he'd taken a group of down-and-outers to a speakeasy, a place they could never go by themselves, bought them drinks, and then treated everybody to a meal of frankfurters and beans in a restaurant. He regularly dropped tens and twenties and fifties on guys in the street, and sent money to "the boys in the penitentiary" and others in Baltimore and elsewhere "who had done me favors." Why, he was a regular Robin Hood, so well thought of around Mott Street that they had masses said in his name and greeted him "as king."

Holtman? The old guard had it in for him, and he'd only got whacked after aiming his gun at Whittemore, who certainly hadn't meant to kill him. He was sorry for the man's wife and children, but the guard's death was an accident, pure self-defense. "It was his life or mine" he said later, "and I thought mine was a lot more important than his." If he was put on trial in Baltimore, he said he was certain he'd beat the charge.

Si Gilden? He'd only known him as a bootlegger, a guy who double-crossed other rumrunners. It was those "dirty tricks that caused his death." Why, he offered, the gang "never fired a shot" on any of their jobs, even as others fired at them.

Margaret? His beloved wife? The demure woman now sitting at his side? She was just a sweet kid who didn't know anything. He said that he told his wife he was a bootlegger, a smuggler who "ran whiskey by boat from the 12-mile limit" marking international waters, and she believed him. He even had friends call her and leave fake orders for whiskey to sell his story. Before every single robbery, "I sent her home, as I did not want her there in case anything did go wrong. And most of all, I did not want her to go through any punishment at the hands of the police." He was a regular Sir Galahad to his loving wife. In fact, he continued to claim, he hadn't seen her for months before his arrest. She'd been in Cleveland the whole time, staying with friends, only arriving in New York the day he was arrested. Poor Margaret didn't know anything, nothing at all. While he talked, she looked on adoringly, occasionally nodding, as her husband put on the best performance of his life.

He laid it on thick, and then the former prison boxing champ let the DAs know he wasn't punched out, not by a long shot. He bragged about his life at the top, and the people he'd met and known and shared a drink or a meal with, entertainers like George Olsen and his crowd. Broadway's Marilyn Miller and Hollywood's Mary Hay had sat at his table, and he'd attended a banquet in honor of Jimmy Walker with a "great number of these police captains and in-spectors . . . officials of high standing . . . he knew some of the biggest people in New York." He'd even met the police commissioner, not McLaughlin, but the guy before him, Enright, dropping name after name to let the DA know he wasn't making everything up. He'd met *a lot* of powerful people, "men in every stage of occupation and life," as well as the women on their arms, their wives and girlfriends. He knew a lot of people, very fine people, some of the same people he'd since seen in the police station wearing a badge, or in court playing prosecutor, or sitting on press row writing lies, people who were now his adversaries and wouldn't look him in the eye because *they knew* that *he knew*.

And now Pecora and Banton knew he knew too. They also knew that he didn't mind talking about it.

The two prosecutors weren't quite sure what to do or how to proceed. Whittemore had talked so much that they were half-dizzy and not quite sure what they had until they were able to fine-tooth the stenographer's transcript and compare it to the facts.

At first, Pecora seemed pleased with the deluge, and that night emerged from the grilling to face the press smiling and rubbing his hands. "I wish to say, gentlemen," said Pecora of Whittemore, "he did not refuse to answer any question we put to him . . . You might say that the district attorney's office will keep any promise it has made."

But Pecora spoke out of turn, and way too soon. Because while Whittemore talked, so did Unkelbach and Paladino, adding to their stories to try to keep Unkelbach's wife and Paladino's girlfriend out of jail. Together, the two men fleshed out more details about the proposed Rosenthal robbery and the fencing of the goods. In return, the two women would never face charges, and Paladi-no's girlfriend was never even publicly identified, to protect her reputation.

The next day, once Banton had sorted through Whittemore's confession and compared it to the deluge of new information, he began to realize just how empty it was. "He tried to kid me," Banton said. "He thought he could out-smart the district attorney's office . . . all his so-called confessions are a tissue of lies." Whittemore had said nothing that implicated anyone but the squealers, Paladino and Unkelbach, providing nothing of real value about anyone else, or about Margaret.

Now expecting to walk, Margaret let down her guard. She came as close as she ever would to admitting that she knew what her husband had been up to, telling a court attendant, "Now at least I will be free to help him. Maybe it isn't much but I will stick with him to the finish. Life holds nothing for me without him, I don't care what people say about him or what he has done, he has always treated me kindly and stuck by me. You can see that or he never would have sent for me. He had murder staring him in the face. How could he go straight? I begged him to drop the game, but it's all over now, too late."

Banton was livid. Whittemore had broken his promise. "I agreed to let his wife go if he told me the whole truth. I, of course, am the sole judge of the truth." Instead of releasing Margaret as promised, he kept her in jail. That may have been just to save face, because after the confession, the New York DA seemed to lose all interest in trying to prosecute either of the Whittemores. Banton suddenly had no objection to releasing Whittemore to Maryland to face the murder charge. Unkelbach and Paladino had given him enough to charge the Kraemers and Goldberg for the Prip robbery, providing his strongest case against the three men. The pair cut their own deal and agreed to plead out in exchange for soft time and other considerations, in particular a promise that neither man would serve time in the same institution as the others.

Now even the Kraemers tried to cut a deal. They offered to talk in exchange for a light sentence, dangling the possibility that they'd reveal where thousands —perhaps hundreds of thousands—of dollars' worth of cash and gems might still be stashed. Banton refused, claiming that he already had enough on Jake Kraemer to send him away for eighty years. He didn't give a damn about Whittemore anymore; a murder conviction in Maryland was good enough for him. And if Erie County wished, they would be free to try Leon Kraemer or any of the others for the Buffalo robbery after the Prip trial.

One factor in Banton's sudden lack of interest in Whittemore was not what the gangster didn't say, but more likely what he did. If he were called to the stand, the Candy Kid had made it clear he intended to name names. The last thing Banton or Pecora or McLaughlin or Coughlin or Mayor Jimmy Walker needed was for Whittemore to testify about people who didn't want to be talked about—all the big shots he'd shared a table with at the Chantee and elsewhere, including a number of detectives, New York pols, and other well-known people

—and who might cause trouble if they were. If he took the stand for any of the New York jewel robberies, there was no telling what he might say, or who he might implicate. Let someone else have him.

Whittemore had outfoxed the prosecutor. Margaret was still in jail, sure, but the agreement to release her was still in place, and they didn't have anything on her. He wasn't going to be extradited to Maryland, and perhaps most importantly, by not squealing on the Kraemers, he'd made sure the brothers owed him. It was in their best interest to provide Whittemore with legal and financial help.

While the Candy Kid had been sweet-talking the two DAs, Buffalo pressed Governor Al Smith to send Whittemore their way. They already had his name on two indictments for murder, and as Erie County DA Guy B. Moore kept explaining, "I will fight Baltimore's claim on Whittemore till the last ditch. Not only was the Buffalo Holdup a more atrocious crime than the killing of a guard, but it aroused more public indignation."

"Public justice demands he be brought back here for trial," Moore claimed, "rather than surrender to some foreign state. We have identified Whittemore positively and I expect to go on trial with him in two weeks' time."

It was also politically expedient. Moore was a Republican, and a trial victory could only boost his future political prospects. He'd already made a run for governor in 1924 and was looking to do so again. There was also a matter of a $15,000 reward that had been offered in the event of a conviction in Buffalo. Spreading the reward among a number of witnesses would earn Moore a lot of goodwill.

So far, Smith had been sitting on the Maryland extradition order. Now that New York County didn't plan to put Whittemore on trial, it was time to weigh in.

Smith, too, had political concerns. He was up for reelection in the fall and was already the odds-on favorite to secure the Democratic nomination for president in 1928. Now that Whittemore wasn't going to be prosecuted in New York County, it wouldn't look good to leave the prosecution of some master criminal to another state. Smith could claim some of the credit by keeping the prosecution in New York.

In the end, a legal issue proved to be the determining factor, or at least provided cover for everyone. Extradition orders applied only to fugitives who committed a crime in one state and then fled to another, as Whittemore had done by committing a murder in Maryland and then fleeing to New York. That gave Maryland grounds to ask for his extradition.

But if Smith allowed the extradition and Whittemore somehow beat the murder rap in Baltimore, New York would have no subsequent claim on him; Whittemore would not have fled New York as a fugitive, and therefore could not be extradited from Maryland back to New York, no matter the crime. Although if he were found innocent in Maryland he would still have to serve out the remaining fourteen and a half years on his sentence for the Holtzman robbery conviction in Maryland, plus added time for the escape, one day Whittemore could end up a free man.

That would not look good at all. The safe bet, the smart play, was to allow Whittemore to be tried in Erie County for the Buffalo murders. Moore claimed he had an airtight case. With a conviction, everybody could claim victory and look smart.

On Wednesday, March 31, Smith informed Governor Ritchie of Maryland that he would not sign the extradition order, pending the outcome of a trial in Erie County. Buffalo detective Austin Roche and two associates raced to New York to take possession of their prize.

They arrived by train the next morning and delivered their warrant to the Tombs. Meanwhile, Whittemore, Goldberg, and the Kraemers were arraigned on ten different indictments covering twenty-one counts of first-degree robbery, then returned to their cells.

Whittemore knew something was up, but didn't realize how fast everything was moving. That afternoon he was told to get dressed and was pulled from his cell with no explanation, and no opportunity to contact his wife. Hauled into court again, flanked by police, he faced Judge Koenig as he read the order: "It is the policy of the District Attorney's office and the court that the most serious charge of murder would be tried first. If the defendant did not commit murder he can be brought back here and be tried for robbery later. The recommendation is approved and the defendant is discharged at his own recognizance."

Whittemore smiled, perhaps realizing that, ever so briefly, he was a free man. But it was April Fools' Day; his momentary freedom was only procedural. He was immediately brought back to the Tombs, where he was placed under arrest by Roche and handcuffed to two other Buffalo detectives.

Now that Whittemore realized exactly what was taking place, he wasn't happy about it. As a photographer moved in for a close-up, Whittemore lashed out at the cameraman and yelled, "I'll kick you all over this station." Five detectives wrestled him into a car waiting outside the courthouse, and they were all driven to Grand Central Terminal.

For the moment, the fight was gone from the Candy Kid, at least most of it, although he snarled at and eyeballed anyone who caught his eye in Grand Central. He was hustled on board the Buffalo train into a private drawing room for the overnight trip, his feet shackled together and one arm cuffed to a detective.

In the Jefferson Market Prison, Margaret had no idea her husband had been sent to Buffalo. When Harry Shulman broke the news, he tried to reassure her that he was still pressing for her release, and he made a public case to try to force Banton's hand. He'd told the press that if Banton reneged and tried to put her on trial now, he'd be "laughed out of court."

So far, Banton was unmoved. He maintained that Richard's confessions "fooled no one. We have decided to hold his wife, the 'Tiger Girl' I believe she is called, in her cage. Detectives working on this case describe her as a 'Hard-Boiled Baby.' She is better off in jail."

The train snaked its way north through the Hudson Valley, past Sing Sing, then west to Buffalo. One detective remained shackled to Whittemore the entire time, while another kept a gun trained on their cargo. "He'll be taken to Buffalo dead or alive," promised Roche. "If he tries anything foolish I'll execute him myself."

Once the train started moving, Whittemore was almost jovial. He had an audience all to himself and enjoyed every second of the trip. He didn't want to talk about the Buffalo job, but he didn't mind talking about everything else. The detectives were all ears. Anything he said was evidence.

All night long, as the captors and the captured played pinochle and the train rumbled upstate past farmers' fields frozen beneath the last of the winter snow, Whittemore regaled his escorts with an underworld version of *True Detective*

Mysteries, casting himself as the hero. He once again pumped up his own role in the gang and bragged that they'd outfitted some of their cars with a concoction of kerosene and sulfur that could be pumped into the carburetor to create a smoke screen. He also ragged on Paladino relentlessly for his cowardice, saying, "What hurts me is that I made that dirty dago $70,000 in record time and now he goes and does this to me." He bragged that he'd bluffed his way past detectives oblivious to his identity dozens of times, that the gang made detailed drawings and diagrams of their targets, and that he, not the Kraemers or anyone else, cased most of the jobs. He claimed the other gang members called him "the Judge," because whatever he said was the law.

Why did he do it? "Money. And plenty of it," was his only explanation. He went on and on, insisting that he'd been caught only because of the screwups and loose talk by everybody else, then tripped over his own tongue.

As dawn broke and the train slowed in its approach to the New York Central train station in Buffalo, Whittemore, knowing that a conviction in Buffalo could end with his body being placed in a casket, looked Roche in the eye and made a promise.

"Believe me, I'm not gonna burn alone for this job," he said, referencing the electric chair. "If I go to the chair some of these other guys are going with me." The old detective didn't react, hoping Whittemore would say more. That ended the rant, but Roche filed it away, knowing that Guy Moore would be interested in those words. In fact, Moore would consider Whittemore's promise an admission of guilt.

Buffalo police weren't taking any chances. When the train jolted to a halt at the platform, it was met by more than a dozen police officers.

They weren't there for show. Although the gang's exploits had been featured in virtually every paper in the country, coverage had been particularly intense in Buffalo, where no fewer than six daily newspapers jockeyed for the same readers. And in a city with such a lawless and wide-open reputation, there was real fear that Whittemore's underworld acquaintances, or even some local thugs hoping to burnish their reputations, might try to spring the prisoner.

They didn't show up at the train station, but everyone else did. It was packed with onlookers, and the police had to create a cordon to get Whittemore through the crowd. The press was there as well, and when a photographer tried to take his picture, shoving a camera under his chin, Whittemore again lashed out.

This time his boot made solid contact, sending the camera flying through the air and leaving the photographer rubbing his chin as the crowd surged and police descended on the prisoner. Some wondered if he was trying to escape, sending a thrill through the crowd. After a moment the police regained control, pressed the crowd back, and ushered Whittemore to the street, where several police cars waited to escort him to police headquarters.

Hundreds of people lined the sidewalk and spilled onto the pavement. Dozens stood on cars and shinnied up street signs and anything else they could climb or stand on to see over the heads of people blocking the way.

They weren't sleepy commuters who had decided, on their way to work, to stop for a moment to catch the show. Nor was the crowd made up of the righteous citizens of Buffalo looking to jeer a murderer and cheer the pending arrival of justice for the killer of two guards, not by a long shot.

No, they were mostly kids like Richard and Margaret—fifteen, twenty, twenty-five years old, single and married and in between, flappers and sheiks and swains, dressed up as wannabe gangsters and gun molls, all enthralled by the excitement, the celebrity, the story of Tiger Girl and Candy Kid. Maybe they longed for a glimpse of the man they considered not all that different from themselves, only one without fear, a gutty, gallant hero taking it on the chin, like a man, to save his girl. To them, the Candy Kid exposed the whole rotten mess their generation had run up against: a world without much of a tomorrow where corrupt politicians filled their own pockets and dirty cops only protected the money, where getting a drink could put you in jail but bootleggers roamed free, where the rich could break the law and everybody else was stuck with their noses pressed up against the glass, gawking at a life they could never hope to lead.

The Candy Kid provided a vision of who some in the crowd probably wished to be themselves—someone who rejected the hand he had been dealt, spat in the face of power, and then grabbed what he wanted, without looking back and without regret, a man's man full of passion and willing to die for it. Tiger Girl, of course, wasn't present in the flesh, but her name was on everyone's lips. It was she who made the Candy Kid, she who provided the counterpoint to the killer. In the eyes of their adoring fans, her blind love appeared to have tamed him and inspired the act of chivalry that promised to set her free.

Some cheered for him and called his name, some roared and clapped, some booed the cops and spat, and everyone strained for a look at the man they had read so much about. The girls swooned and fainted and screamed, as if Valentino had just swooped into town, while their boyfriends stood by, maybe a little more tough-talking, a little coarser, and a lot braver. You didn't often get a chance to call a cop a dirty name or give him an elbow without getting a mouthful of broken teeth in return. But right now, right here, there was nothing the cops could do.

Shoved into the car, flanked by the police, Whittemore was driven to the jail as if he were some foreign dignitary, his police vehicle escorted by several others, all manned by armed police officers, guns drawn and pointed out the window. He ducked in the seat as the car pulled away, pulling his overcoat up over his ears as the sirens roared.

For the rest of the weekend, the Candy Kid cooled his heels in a double-locked cell on the fifth floor, number X-3, awaiting his Monday arraignment. He knew how to do time and spent the hours napping, playing solitaire, writing letters, smoking, and killing time, just as he had done countless times before, his every move watched by a guard. The jailer let him order his own meal. He asked for a steak and got it.

Meanwhile, the Buffalo papers convicted him in a hundred different ways. They reported every possible rumor that pointed to his guilt in attention-grabbing headlines to sway public opinion — "Gangster in Defiant Mood," "Whittemore Conviction Sure, Moore Declares" — while at the same time playing to the worshiping crowd that had shown up at the train station. Reporter after reporter made their way to the jail, where the police allowed them to ask questions through the bars.

Whittemore appeared to enjoy the attention; he could talk all day. He told the reporters he was broke and reiterated his claim that, having given most of the money "to the poor people around Mott Street," he would have to accept a court-appointed attorney. To underscore his poverty he quipped that "any paper that wants to pay me $5000 can have my life story." Otherwise, apart from the guards and his attorneys, he was allowed no visitors other than the jailhouse's resident cat, which slunk in and out between the bars of his cell.

Most reporters painted a romantic picture for readers, making note of his sartorial style and bearing. "He carries himself erect," noted the *Buffalo Courier*. "He has a high forehead, high cheekbones and a pleasing countenance when he smiles. His hair is black, inclined to be wavy and is parted on the left side. His eyes are black and when he talks on subjects distasteful to him they flash in anger and his upper lip curls in a wolfish smile. His speech shows he is of more than average intelligence, although he unconsciously slips into the argot of the underworld. In general, this strange young man is no 'gorilla' gunman." The story went on to note that the Candy Kid "lived well, dressed well, and traveled fast and furiously."

At least the *Courier* also saw fit to give a few lines to Louis Yarrington's widow. She said that although she forgave Whittemore, "I see why it is necessary for him to die. If they give him a prison term he may get out and he would kill some other woman's husband . . . he is not fit to live or die."

On Monday, April 5, Whittemore was delivered to the Supreme Court at County Hall for his arraignment. Over four hundred spectators mobbed the building, most staked out at the end of the corridor that led to the "Tunnel of Tears," the underground passageway between the hall and the jail. Built in 1891, the tunnel had last been used in 1901 to safely transfer the assassin of President William McKinley, Leon Czolgosz, back and forth between the jail and court. Since then it had been walled off, but the authorities reopened the tunnel for Whittemore—the crowd at the train station showed them the need for increased security. After seeing the mob packing County Hall, though, they used the tunnel this day only as a diversion, stationing sheriffs at the threshold to make it appear that Whittemore was coming while he was actually ushered across the street and into an elevator. Still, as the *Courier* noted, "he was accorded the greatest city hall audience" since Czolgosz.

Several hundred more spectators had managed to squeeze into the massive courtroom as Whittemore entered, surrounded by police carrying sawed-off shotguns. After pleading poverty, Whittemore asked the court to assign counsel, and Supreme Court Justice Thomas Noonan appointed J. Bartlett Sumner and Melvin Greene to serve as his attorneys. Whittemore pleaded not guilty to both murder charges and was hustled out of the courtroom and back to the jail.

This time he went by way of the tunnel. As they approached the dank passageway lined with granite, dimly lit by a few bare light bulbs strung along the ceiling, even the police shuddered before entering. "It's like the Bridge of Sighs," said Detective Roche to Whittemore. Glancing around and sniffing the dank air, the prisoner corrected him. "It's like the sewers of Paris," he said.

DA Guy Moore didn't want any delays and aimed to begin jury selection that Friday. Not only would that schedule make it hard for Whittemore's attorneys to mount an effective defense, but he wanted to seat a jury before Whittemore got any more popular than he already was. Women wouldn't be allowed on the jury, but men had daughters and wives, and it could be difficult to seat a jury in Erie County. People simply didn't trust the courts, and many sided with the defendants.

Officially, Sumner and Greene would be paid only a nominal fee by the state to provide Whittemore's defense. Greene was a young attorney working his first big case, but Sumner was a talented and experienced jurist. Moore had hired him for the DA's office a decade earlier, but Sumner had moved into private practice in 1925. It would be his first trial against his former boss, but professionally it made sense for him to take the case. If Sumner got Whittemore off, his services would be in demand, and Buffalo's criminal underworld provided plenty of well-heeled defendants.

Immediately after being appointed, Sumner went to New York to examine evidence, try to drum up an alibi, and confer with attorneys Shulman and Bushel to see if their clients could be of any help. Whittemore himself wasn't much help, but the trip still proved fruitful. By the time Sumner returned for the scheduled start of the trial on April 9, everything had changed.

For one, Bushel came through with cash and contacts courtesy of the Kraemers. Money would be no object for the defense. And Moore soon knew it. He'd ordered that all of Whittemore's mail, incoming and outgoing, go through his office. From those letters Moore learned that Hyman Bushel and the Kraemers had agreed to bankroll Sumner's efforts to mount a defense, figuring that if Whittemore got off, Moore was unlikely to try Leon for murder.

The letters also revealed to Moore that Whittemore had no defense and no way to prove he'd been anywhere but Buffalo, and that he was fishing for an alibi. Whittemore had even written Shuffles Goldberg to see if he had any ideas. That inside knowledge made Moore confident, perhaps too confident, of a conviction.

The trial would reveal the contrast between the two attorneys. As the *Buffalo Times* later noted, "Moore is the more dramatic orator that sweeps the crowd with him as a grain in the wind." He was accustomed to wielding the full authority of his office. Sumner, on the other hand, "is quiet, suave, gentle. His speech will trickle along like a brook. Moore's will be the peal of thunder and the flash of lightening [*sic*]." Sumner knew how his former boss operated and thus far in his legal career had achieved success in trial court by counterpunching. The fact that Moore was rushing to trial didn't seem to faze Sumner.

On Thursday, Greene asked for a continuance. Sumner was still in New York City and claimed to have located alibi witnesses who would prove that Whittemore couldn't have been in Buffalo at the time of the crime. Moore reluctantly agreed. The DA was a publicly elected post and he knew better than to alienate his constituents making goo-goo eyes at the defendant. Justice Noonan concurred and set a new trial date of April 19. That gave Sumner time to get everyone's story straight, while every day Whittemore, in the eyes of the public, became ever more human, his crimes a little more remote.

I n Manhattan, Tiger Girl was on the verge of walking free. All week Shulman had pressed for her release, and his charge that Banton had backed out of the deal was starting to gain traction in the press. He demanded that she either be discharged or immediately be put on trial for robbery. But Banton wanted a win in exchange, a headline he could wrap around the release that claimed victory.

Paladino's girlfriend, whom the police referred to by the pseudonym "Florence Carter" to protect her from the press, had been cooperating and made it clear that she and Margaret were close. She even told the DA that the Whittemores had stayed with her and Paladino over Christmas—she'd cooked them all Christmas dinner. Margaret, however, was still insisting that she didn't know anything and hadn't been in New York until just before her arrest.

On Saturday, Banton had Margaret hauled to Pecora's office. When she arrived, Carter rose from her chair. Chewing and snapping her gum, Carter reached out for a hug and greeted Margaret warmly, saying, "Hello, dear."

Tiger Girl looked right through her and tried to act befuddled. She insisted that there was some mistake, that she'd never seen this woman before in her life.

Shulman asked to see his client in private. Stepping into an adjoining room, he sat her down and explained that he'd cut a deal that would allow Banton to save face and set her free. Banton, he told her, wanted her to agree to testify as a witness in the Kraemer and Goldberg trial if called to do so and admit that she'd been in New York over the winter. If she did, she'd be let go.

Tiger Girl looked at him hard. She had to have been tired of jail, tired of being interrogated, tired of being treated like she was no better than some common streetwalker.

When Shulman brought Margaret back out, she looked at Carter and her eyes softened. Carter leaned in, whispering something, and Margaret whispered something back. The two embraced and started chatting, catching up like the old friends they were. Of course, Margaret now said, she knew Florence, and yes, she'd been in New York for most of the winter. She'd sign the damn agreement.

She met with Pecora and Shulman for the next few hours as they hammered out the paperwork. The binding stipulation was that, if Banton called Margaret to testify against Goldberg or the Kraemers, "she will not contest." He retained the right to prosecute her too, but Shulman knew Banton had no case. Neither her husband nor anyone else had implicated her. In exchange, Tiger Girl would be released on her own recognizance.

The next day Banton got the headlines he'd wanted. Papers in Buffalo, Baltimore, New York, and other cities across the country screamed hysterical references to her so-called confession with headlines like "Tiger Girl Loses Battle of Nerve, Will Confess All." The headlines weren't true—she hadn't really confessed to anything material—but the claim served everyone's purpose.

On Monday morning, April 12, pale but impeccably dressed as always in a full-length fur coat, a platinum and diamond wedding ring sparkling on her finger, Margaret arrived at the Court of General Sessions and, according to the signed stipulation, was discharged from bail and released.

On her way out of the courthouse, she was mobbed by the press and unsheathed a few claws. She'd seen the headlines touting her confession, and now Tiger Girl wanted everyone to know she was no rat.

Appearing alongside Florence Carter afterwards, reporters' notebooks in her face, she stood her ground and laid it on thick, her blue eyes already teary. It was the lengthiest statement she would make to the press.

"How can I squeal," she said, "when I have nothing to squeal about? I knew the Kraemer boys, but only as the Lewis brothers. I never suspected my husband was guilty of any crime of violence and I do not believe it now.

"I think he is innocent of the Buffalo murders. I have never been in Buffalo, though it is hinted I may know something about what happened there."

Then she started really crying, dabbing her eyes with a handkerchief. "I wouldn't exchange my husband's love for a million dollars," she said. "I am going to my husband's assistance. I am going to do what I can to help him. I am deeply in love with my husband. He is the first and only man I have ever loved and if anything happens to him I do not care to live. My love for my husband is undying. I will never desert him. He means everything in this world to me. There is nothing else and nobody else that counts. I cannot understand how any woman can marry a man, loving as she must love him to marry him, and then desert him when he is in trouble." She was careful to make sure her story mirrored what her husband had told Banton and Pecora and the cops on the train. "I thought he made his living bootlegging and by luck in gambling. I believed him absolutely and still do. Several times people called him up and I answered the phone, and the order was like this: 'Tell Mr. Whittemore to send me a case of Scotch or a case of rye.' Well, what was I to do except take the order?

"Last June, July and August we lived at a hotel at Coney Island. We had a little tiff over something and I went home to Baltimore and did not see Richard again until near Christmas. After the Christmas holidays we went to Cleveland and it was there I got so many orders for booze." Then she remembered something.

Margaret Whittemore (R) following her arrest with Marion Davis (L) and other members of the "Whittemore-Schaefer Gang" in Philadelphia, January 1925. The women fed guns to gang members during a shootout with police, earning Margaret the nickname "Tiger Lil," which later became "Tiger Girl." The sable coat she is wearing was later identified as having been stolen during a robbery spearheaded by her husband, Richard Whittemore. *Baltimore Sun Media*

Police mug shot of Richard Reese Whittemore, aka "The Candy Kid," likely taken after his 1925 arrest in Philadelphia. He was returned to Baltimore and on January 29, 1925, was sentenced to a 15-year term for robbery at the Maryland State Penitentiary. Less than a month later, he escaped, killing guard Robert Holtman. *Baltimore Sun Media*

A formal portrait of Margaret Whittemore decked out in the fashionable clothes and expensive jewelry she favored. Although Margaret was not present during the Whittemore Gang's jewelry heists, she helped to case locations, carried weapons in true "gun moll" fashion, and benefitted materially from the crimes. For a time, she and her husband lived the kind of life others of their generation could only dream of.

Baltimore Sun Media

The beating and robbery of Albert Goudvis and Emmanuel Veerman on January 10, 1926, in New York's Diamond District was the Whittemore Gang's most lucrative to date. Although the perpetrators were unknown at the time, Chief Inspector John Coughlin of the New York Police Department eventually tied the gang to the robbery. It made headlines not just in New York, but all over the country, and estimates of the haul were later raised to as much as $500,000.

The Standard Union *(Brooklyn, NY) Mon, Jan 11, 1926*

NOTED GEM DEALER BEATEN AND ROBBED OF $100,000 STONES

Emanuel Veerman, of Amsterdam, Held Up With Broker Goudvis In Hallway Near Fifth Avenue.

HERE FROM HOLLAND WITH UNSET STONES

Forced Into Dark Passage, Is Made Victim of Gun-butts by Thieves.

(L-R) Leon Kraemer, Barney Mortillaro, Milton (Shuffles) Goldberg, Jacob Kraemer, Pasquale Chicarelli, and gang leader Richard Reese Whittemore in a police lineup, after they were implicated in the Goudvis robbery in New York City, February 1926. Chicarelli and Mortillaro, who worked at the Club Chantee, were arrested with Whittemore following a shootout but were not full members of the gang. Within days, gang members Anthony Paladino, Willie Unkelbach, and Margaret Whittemore were also arrested. The gang indulged in an "orgy of confessions" and squealed on one another, leading Richard Whittemore to offer a confession in exchange for the freedom of his wife.

NY Daily News Archive/Getty Images

Margaret Whittemore immediately following her arrest at the Hotel Embassy in New York on March 20, 1926. In a wardrobe trunk, police found guns, cash, and expensive clothes and jewelry.

Bettmann/Getty Images

TIGER GIRL BLOWS KISSES INTO CELL FOR THE CANDY KID

After Margaret Whittemore was arrested and identified as "Tiger Girl," the press could not resist focusing on the romance between her and her husband, Richard Whittemore, "The Candy Kid." Once Richard Whittemore traded a confession for his wife's freedom, young people all over the country swooned at the sacrifice.

The Brooklyn Daily Eagle *(Brooklyn, NY) Sun, Apr 25, 1926*

Margaret Whittemore being set free on her own recognizance by New York authorities as they reluctantly upheld their promise to release "Tiger Girl" if "The Candy Kid," Richard Whittemore, cooperated. His wife would soon travel to Buffalo to be with her husband as he prepared to go on trial for murder. *Bettmann/Getty Images*

The photograph of Richard and Margaret Whittemore separated by a screen in the Erie County Jail while awaiting trial made them sympathetic figures to a generation of young Americans. When Richard Whittemore later went on trial in Baltimore, he and his wife were also kept apart by a screen.

Photography Collection, Harry Ransom Center, University of Texas at Austin

Richard Whittemore meeting with his father, Rawlings Whittemore (C), and attorney Melvin Greene (L), likely during his trial for the murders of Charles Clifford and Louis Yarrington. *Bettmann/Getty Images*

Richard Whittemore mugs for the camera behind the screen in the jailer's office at the Erie County Jail. Although he was only allowed to meet with visitors behind the screen, the press was given ready access to the prisoner. Whittemore played his role to the hilt and enjoyed mostly sympathetic coverage after the judge discharged the deadlocked jury.

International Newsreel c. 1926.
Courtesy of the author's collection.

Margaret Whittemore (C) flanked by an attorney (L) and her father-in-law, Rawlings Whittemore, likely taken in Erie County while Richard Whittemore was on trial for the killing of bank guards Charles Clifford and Louis Yarrington.

Photography Collection, Harry Ransom Center, University of Texas at Austin

Three days before her husband's execution, Margaret Whittemore (L) leaves the Maryland State Penitentiary following a visit with her husband, accompanied by her sister-in law Aisley and brother-in-law Rawlings Whittemore Jr. *International Newsreel c. 1926. Courtesy of the author's collection.*

Supported by her brother-in-law, Margaret leaves the Maryland State Penitentiary after seeing her husband for the last time, with her sister-in-law, trailed by her father-in-law and her mother, Theresa Messler. *Bettmann/Getty Images*

On the evening of August 12, 1926, police control the crowd as thousands packed the streets surrounding the Maryland State Penitentiary in what was described as a "carnival-like" atmosphere, with vendors hawking soda pop and hot dogs. Most of the crowd supported Richard Whittemore. Just after midnight, on Friday, August 13, he was hung for the murder of Robert Holtman. *Acme Newspictures c. 1926. Courtesy of the author's collection.*

After a funeral service at the home of his brother's mother-in-law, Richard Reese Whittemore was laid to rest at Baltimore's Loudon Park Cemetery as hundreds watched. Margaret Whittemore had to be restrained from throwing herself into the grave.

Acme Newspictures c. 1926. Courtesy of the author's collection.

"But I must explain about the revolvers. One half of my husband's wardrobe trunk was always locked. The other half he used for his clothes, hanging all of them on hangers on one side. Then I found out he had only a couple of pairs of shoes, so I slipped a few of my shoes in," trying to explain away how her belongings were found with the weapons. "I never did see what he had on one side," she said.

She was just an innocent dupe. "When I was arrested the police opened the trunk, and to my amazement in the side he always kept locked were revolvers — you could have hit me with a feather and I'd have fallen dead."

That was a funny way to put it. The reporters scratched down every word, even if they didn't believe them.

Then she set her jaw and said, "I have been so pulled and jerked around that I know I'm going to require a doctor's care. I'm awfully sick." She refused to pose for any pictures, blocking half her face with her gray fur cloak when a photographer raised a camera, but then she promised to "pose as many times as you like on Monday, for I'll be feeling better then." Before she left, she asked the Baltimore newspapermen in attendance to deny that she had ever been known as Tiger Girl.

With that, she grabbed Florence Carter by the arm. The two exited the courthouse, climbed into a taxi, and took off. She was free at last, and likely in need of a hot bath and a stiff drink, or something else that would make her feel better about having a husband on trial for murder. For the next few days she would stay out of the spotlight, trying to decide what to do next.

Before the press scattered, Shulman gave the newshounds a little more to chew on. "She was absolutely released on her merits. She was not in any way implicated in any of the crimes for which she was arrested." That wasn't entirely true, but the battle now wasn't so much in the courts as in the papers. To that end, he released another statement as well: "Mrs. Whittemore deeply regrets the references that have been made in the newspapers, saying she has never been known as 'tiger girl.'" Asking that the statement be published, Shulman added that she "deplores the fact that it was applied to her."

Most didn't bother. Why ruin a good story?

• • •

I n the Buffalo jail, mail addressed to the Candy Kid was piling up. There were mash notes from young women, fan mail from boys, cookies and candy from matrons, and ravings from lunatics. The only time he'd ever been this popular before was at the Chantee.

But some of Whittemore's letters raised alarm in Moore's office. Before he was allowed to read them, Moore and his staff examined every package and read every scented card. When they found letters that appeared to be written in a simple alphanumeric code, the DA first dismissed them as the product of cranks who read too many detective stories. But on Wednesday, April 14, they received four identical envelopes postmarked in Buffalo and stuffed with fancy blank stationery, apparently gifts so the Candy Kid could respond in style. Opening the envelopes, they discovered a hacksaw blade sandwiched in the stationery of each one. A note was signed "Rich, fondest regards and best wishes, J., N., and S."

At first Moore didn't take the threat of escape too seriously, since Whittemore was watched over by a guard holding a shotgun twenty-four hours a day. It would be virtually impossible for him to put the hacksaw blades to use. But on closer examination they also found a doubled piece of stationery with a diagram of the tunnel and a coded message that, when translated, read "Judge. I am here. All set surprise." It was signed "Etan," which Moore assumed to be Nate Weinzimmer. He'd been picked up in Cleveland but was free on $50,000 bail. They were trying to extradite him back to New York, but the chauffeur had hired pricey legal help and the state was having a hard time proving his fugitive status.

This was more serious. A later coded message indicated that a plan was in place for ten armed men to overpower the guards as Whittemore entered County Hall from the tunnel as Whittemore escaped through the basement of the building and then up a flight of stairs and into a waiting Ford coupe that would be waiting near the Delaware Avenue entrance.

Moore sensed an opening. Candy Kid was becoming way too popular. The blades and the note provided an opportunity not only to take action to thwart any possibility of escape but to cut him back down to size and counteract what Moore viewed as too much positive propaganda.

Authorities ominously warned that Whittemore was "not without friends," intimating that those friends just might try to storm the jail and spring him, using overwhelming force. At Moore's behest, Erie County sheriff Frank Tyler immediately instituted some new rules. Now, in addition to the guard with the shotgun, other guards and sheriff patrols were added to other parts of the jail, and no one, not even Sumner, would be allowed to visit Whittemore in his cell.

He was a special prisoner and required special arrangements. In a conference room adjoining jailer Charles Lieb's office, they installed a heavy steel-mesh holding pen. If Sumner or anyone else wanted to meet with Whittemore, he would be brought in, locked inside, and they'd have to speak to him through the screen. Whittemore's attorneys screamed, but it did no good. In the end, however, the setup would backfire. Putting Whittemore in a special cage only made him appear more sympathetic—an undeserving victim of a cruel and unjust system of crime and punishment. The photographers couldn't get enough of it.

As the DA and Sumner prepared for trial, Moore was doing everything he could to make Whittemore seem as dangerous as possible and his case appear to be airtight. He touted the vast number of eyewitnesses he planned to call, all of whom were certain of Whittemore's guilt, and he alluded to other mysterious irrefutable evidence. Sumner countered, saying that he had six or eight alibi witnesses ready to testify.

For now, Whittemore wanted to keep Tiger Girl out of it. He wrote her and his father regularly. Addressing Margaret as "Margie," he urged her not to come to Buffalo, at least not yet. Sumner told the press that "she has greatly aided the defense in preparing the case and we believe she could be of no additional assistance if she were in Buffalo. We know where Mrs. Whittemore is living and if she is needed she will come to Buffalo without delay ... we are ready to go to trial. All that I ask is that the public suspend judgement on this particular crime."

He didn't intend to claim that Whittemore was a choir boy, only that he had not been in Buffalo. The entire defense would hinge on that argument ... and on whether Sumner could come up with any proof of it, whether true or not.

Fourteen

THE TUNNEL OF TEARS

Moore's goal of scaring Buffalo out of its wits worked too well, just not in the way he intended. The threat of a daring breakout may have frightened the older set, who still didn't understand jazz, but to the flappers and sheiks the possibility made the Candy Kid saga even more romantic and melodramatic. Maybe he and Tiger Girl would go on the run together. Maybe they'd beat the odds, get away scot-free, thumb their noses at the world, and live like big shots. Maybe their story would become a movie.

The prosecution already enjoyed every advantage. Whittemore had been charged under what was known as a common-law indictment: he was culpable for murder as a participant in a crime resulting in a murder. Whether or not he fired a fatal shot didn't matter. He'd be considered just as guilty if he'd been eating a sandwich instead of wielding a gun.

Before the trial began, Justice Noonan announced that what the *Buffalo Times* called "the morbidly curious" would be barred from the courtroom during voir dire. Only attorneys, jurors, witnesses, the press, the police, and all their attachés would be allowed inside.

On Monday morning, April 18, Whittemore dressed for the occasion. He was allowed to shave, and he donned a smartly tailored pinstriped suit, a gray shirt, and a colorful striped tie. The *Courier* claimed he rivaled "Beau Brummel in the faultlessness of his attire."

He looked more like a well-paid accountant than a criminal. A month in jail, eating three squares a day and going without booze or drugs, had done him good. His previously gaunt face had filled out, making him look a little soft, even boyish.

Whittemore trudged through the Tunnel of Tears, handcuffed on each wrist and escorted by Lieb, Sheriff Tyler, and ten detectives, while dozens of policemen and sheriff's deputies lined the public hallways of the court-house. As the entourage exited the tunnel, it soon became clear why they were needed.

When County Hall opened that morning, a mob on the street was waiting to get inside the massive four-story structure, the 270-foot clock tower looming overhead. They weren't there to pick up a permit or pay a parking ticket either. Although Justice Noonan had banned the public from the courtroom itself, he couldn't shut down County Hall.

They were all there for Whittemore. As 10 a.m. approached, they filled the hallways and vestibules of County Hall, chattering like a crowd in a theater lobby. They only wanted to see him, their hero, in the flesh.

When first the deputies and then Whittemore emerged from the tunnel, the crowd roared as if seeing a prizefighter enter the arena on his way to the ring. "Here he comes!" one squealed. Whittemore couldn't suppress a smile. He was the people's champion, the biggest man in town.

A headline in the *Daily Star and Inquirer* the next day read, "Flappers Storm City Hall for Whittemore." Every day for the duration of the trial the papers reported his every move and word, and photos of Whittemore, his attorneys, and even his adoring fans adorned the front pages. His hundreds of fans — young women all dolled up who had formed a crush on him, older women armed with motherly concern, and jealous but admiring sheiks — turned out in force.

The police, billy clubs in hand, pushed the crowd back as it pressed forward and tried to follow them into the courtroom. Whittemore behaved like the guest of honor and looked clearly pleased with the reception. When a pho-tographer leaned in to take a flash shot, this time Whittemore didn't kick, but paused for a moment and posed, smug and self-assured, before entering the courtroom. Seeing police stationed inside, shotguns at the ready, the defendant chuckled. "Look at the armed dicks," he said. "They must think I'm a tough guy."

The first day was taken up entirely with jury selection. None of the prospective jurors were female. Not until passage of the Civil Rights Act of 1957 would women have the right to serve on a federal jury, and it was 1973 before all fifty states passed similar legislation. In fact, only four women were allowed into the courtroom at all.

One woman swept inside wearing a leopard skin coat, and rumors quickly spread that Tiger Girl had arrived. They were disappointed to learn that she was only a newspaper reporter.

The other three, acquaintances of a judge, attended as a courtesy of the court. They were giddy to be inside. When a reporter asked one, a "dashing blonde in a child's navy and red ensemble," why she had come, she answered, "I came to see what he looked like. I am so excited to see a man like that." The other two were similarly smitten. One told the reporter that seeing the Candy Kid in the flesh was a "thrill," and the other, sighing and starry-eyed, swooned that Whittemore "certainly didn't look like a murderer."

Each attorney asked prospective jurors the same few questions. Moore was primarily interested in whether they believed in the death penalty, whether they had formed an opinion on the case, and whether they understood and agreed with the common-law indictment. Sumner's queries were more probing, designed to root out any hidden prejudices. Whittemore sat at his side, occasionally giving the thumbs-down sign. Earlier, he had warned Sumner, "For God's sake, don't get any bank men on this jury. They'd send me to hell in ten minutes. I know that gang."

He scanned the faces of the prospective jurors and smiled as if welcoming them to a dinner party, giving them a full dose of Candy Kid charm.

By day's end, eight jurors were seated. Few seemed eager to serve. It was obvious from their answers that most didn't want anything to do with the case, and for good reason.

The jurors were not anonymous. In Buffalo anyway, their names, addresses, and other personal information would appear in the newspapers, as would their photos, leaving each potentially exposed to threats of intimidation, to both

themselves and their families, to tampering, and to possible retribution from
the underworld if Whittemore was convicted. For most prospective jurors, being empaneled was like wearing a target on their forehead, and it was the last
thing they wanted.

Witnesses were similarly hesitant to participate. A lot of people who had
seen something happen at the bank back in October suddenly found their recollections becoming cloudy.

The Candy Kid seemed determined to face his charges alone. Earlier that
day, a court attendant had slipped him a wire from Rawlings Whittemore, telling his son he wanted to be with him. After court was adjourned, in a letter
leaked to the press by the jailer, Richard replied, "Don't come to Buffalo. Eight
jurors have been chosen and the trial is going fairly well. But don't come to
Buffalo because you can't do anything to help me." But his father was already
on his way.

Rawlings arrived the following morning and checked into a hotel under an
assumed name. He wanted to be with his son but seemed to realize he had little
to offer. Now that Richard Whittemore was on trial for murder, a measure of
that responsibility, as both a father and a man, now rested on Rawlings's shoulders.

The next morning the Candy Kid prepared for court, brightly telling a
guard, "Well, it looks like a busy day." Before leaving his cell, he consumed a
stack of newspapers, reading every word about the trial, critiquing the photographs, and seemingly thrilled with being the center of so much attention.

After being led through the Tunnel of Tears, Whittemore once again ran
a gauntlet of giddy flappers and sheiks, just as intensely interested as the day
before, on their way to court. He embraced his new role as matinee idol as he
moved through the crowd. According to the *Buffalo Times,* he was "his usual gay
and debonair self," looking almost haughty, as if attention was the unavoidable
burden of his fame, and leaned back in his chair in the prisoner's box awaiting
the judge "apparently without a care in the world."

The remaining four jurors were selected in only a few hours. All told, the
court questioned 117 men before selecting 12 who were both willing to serve
and accepted by both the prosecution and defense. When the final juror was

sworn in at 2:40 p.m., Justice Noonan ordered the trial to proceed at once. He opened the courtroom, and the crowd poured inside, racing for open seats and fighting each other to get the best view of the defendant. As the cavernous three-hundred-seat courtroom filled to overflowing, hundreds more remained in the building, blocking the halls. They made such a racket that the judge ordered the transoms closed so everyone inside could hear the testimony.

Rawlings Whittemore was one of the lucky ones with a reserved seat. Recognized by the press as he approached the courtroom, he was hounded by photographers into posing, while reporters did their best to insinuate themselves into his company. Haggard and drawn, he seemed overwhelmed. He rambled on about his son, wondering aloud whether he and his wife had been right to bail him out of trouble time and time again, casting about for a reason to explain how a Whittemore had come to such an inglorious place. He blamed gambling, booze, his son's friends, even that fall from the window as a child, saying, "Perhaps that has something to do with the kinks in his brain." Then he added, "But he never killed anybody. I know that. Dick would never kill anybody."

Tired and alone, Rawlings started to cry. "O God, pity me," he said. "God pity me and help my poor boy Dick. And right or wrong, he's my boy, my son, and I'll stick to him until the end." He implored the photographers to leave him be. He only wanted to see his son. He took a seat in the last row, alone, nervously cleaning his glasses over and over again, as if he could not believe he was seeing his son on trial for murder. Richard sat at the defense table, oblivious to his father's presence. When a court attendant told him his father was in the courtroom, "he paid no attention to the old man."

In his opening statement, Moore spoke deliberately and forcefully. Whittemore's guilt was beyond question, and the dapper young man was evil in the flesh. Moore claimed to have four rock-solid witnesses, men he referred to time and time again as "reputable businessmen . . . When you have heard them I have no doubt you will declare the defendant guilty of murder in the first degree." Then, in a surprise, he said that Whittemore wasn't just culpable in the murders but had killed one man by his own hand.

"I will prove," he continued, addressing the jury, "that this man, this cringing prisoner, fired the shots that on the morning of October 28 killed Charles W. Clifford. I will prove that he engineered the robbery of the Bank of Buffalo branch of the Marine Trust Company. I will bring witnesses to prove these things."

Pointing his finger at Whittemore, Moore shouted, "I will prove this man is a wanton killer and guilty of murder in the first degree!" Rawlings Whittemore bowed his head into his hands. His son looked at Moore without expression.

It was puzzling. Moore hadn't mentioned any material evidence, even though in the preceding weeks he had referred to such evidence time and again. He had boasted that he could place Whittemore at a hotel in Buffalo, prove that he had been in the city many times, and tie the stolen automobile to the gang.

But now, nothing. The case would apparently be built entirely on eyewitness testimony. It would be up to the jury to decide who to believe.

Moore began by calling a few fact witnesses, such as the medical examiner, to prove that a death had occurred. Even while going over these mundane matters, however, there were still some unexpected early fireworks.

A teller from the Federal Reserve testified that he had been notified the day before the robbery that Yarrington and Clifford would come the next morning to pick up the money that was later stolen, and that he provided them with the cash the following day. On cross-examination, Sumner asked, "Who else besides you knew on the night before the holdup that the bank guard would call for the money?"

Moore jumped to his feet and roared, "You are not insinuating that this witness was a member of the gang that stole the money?" At that, Richard Whittemore shot up from his seat and leaned forward toward Moore, nothing sweet about the Candy Kid's enraged face, giving everyone in the courtroom a start. The deputy who served as Whittemore's chaperone grabbed him by his jacket and pulled him back into his seat. The Candy Kid slumped back like a schoolboy told by the teacher to settle down.

Then, after a pause, he broke out in slow applause, each of the dozen claps of his hands echoing through the courtroom, every eye looking his way. Certain of his audience, he then stopped and said snidely, "Moore is playing for the gallery again; let's applaud!"

Justice Noonan finally swung his gavel and called for order as several policemen made their way toward Whittemore. Point made, he sat up in his chair,
a choir boy smile on his lips, and the trial resumed. A short time later, Moore
requested an adjournment. He had not anticipated that the trial would begin so
late in the day and none of his other witnesses were in court. The judge agreed
to adjourn and admonished the jury, as he would every day, not to discuss the
case with anyone, read the papers, or visit the scene of the crime. They were
not sequestered. In fact, during the trial they would even be allowed to mingle
with the crowd during breaks.

That evening, a trembling Rawlings Whittemore visited his son in jail.
Richard agreed to see him when he learned that his father was carrying a message from Margaret. He was taken from his cell into the mesh cage created
especially for him.

So far, Richard Whittemore had put up a good front in jail, pulling off
the hard guy act. After all, he knew how to do a stretch. He was moved to
a new cell every day, as a precautionary measure, and was on suicide watch,
though he'd shown no signs so far of killing anything but time. He'd suc-
ceeded in befriending the guards, enough to make casual conversation about
such things as baseball and boxing. Apart from visits from his attorney, he
spent most of his cell time playing solitaire, chain-smoking, or staring at the
ceiling.

After a few minutes of halting, awkward conversation, Rawlings not knowing what to say and Richard apparently not caring, Rawlings took the note
from his pocket and handed it to the jailer. The jailer took a perfunctory look
to make certain there was nothing concealed in the small, single folded page,
then passed the note to Richard Whittemore.

O Daddy, my heart is almost broken. O, how I love you. I am worried
to death for fear they may frame you like they did Chapman. All I can
say is just have faith in God because HE is just, if anything should
happen to you I will die I know it, because life don't mean anything
to me without you. If they give you life it won't be too bad because
where there is life there is hope. I am praying and hoping for the best,
so brace up dear. I am sure everything will turn out all right. Don't

believe things you hear. I made no confessions as I have nothing to confess.

All my love to you, dear heart, until we meet again.

xxxx From your true wife to the end.

Margaret was no dummy. She knew that by now he'd likely read all about her "confessions," and she wanted him to hear from her that she had done no such thing and wasn't plotting to turn against him. She likely also didn't want the Kraemers to pull their support, thinking she'd ratted them out.

Whittemore softened as he read the note and remained quiet for a moment before assuming his usual glib and unconcerned demeanor. He was then returned to his cell, and his father went back to the hotel. The next day Margaret's paean to her husband—and the subtle message it contained for the Kraemers—would be repeated verbatim in dozens of newspapers.

When the trial resumed that morning, Moore began by calling some of the "reputable businessmen" he'd introduced the day before—Alfred Guggisberg, Harry Russell, and Leslie Kraft—to make the case that Richard Whittemore was a killer.

Russell and Kraft, both printers, saw the crime from the vantage point of their offices across the street, and both men's testimony placed Whittemore on the running board of the getaway vehicle. But neither was as effective as Moore had hoped. There were inconsistencies in their testimony, and Sumner got Russell to admit on the stand that he had poor eyesight.

Guggisberg was a surprise. His name hadn't been mentioned in the papers. Moore was convinced that his testimony would send Whittemore to the electric chair.

When called to the stand, the man Moore had called a reputable businessman described himself as "just a laborer." A thin, rangy, nervous-looking young man, Guggisberg described encountering Whittemore just a few minutes before the gangster shot John Meyer. "I arrived at the bank just before nine that morning—I came to deposit ten dollars," he said. "I saw a man standing around and I talked to him. We talked about the weather, things like that." Then Moore, pointing to Whittemore, asked if Whittemore was the man. "He is," answered Guggisberg.

Richard Whittemore sneered, and his father, again sitting in the back row, reflexively rose from his feet as if to protest.

But the highlight of the day was the testimony of bank guard John Meyer, who had taken the money from the armored truck and was shot in the arm by Whittemore. He testified that when he approached the bank door, a pistol was thrust in his face and he was ordered to raise his hands.

"I was thunderstruck," said the guard. "But I didn't obey. I made a dash for the bank door and tried to open it, but it was locked. Then a shot was fired, and I was hit in the arm. I dropped the bags."

Moore asked, "And have you since seen the man who held you up?" expecting Meyer to answer in the affirmative.

Meyer could barely speak. "I can't say," he said. "I was too excited. That gun looked too big to me at the time."

The courtroom buzzed. After a few more questions, Sumner began his cross-examination, asking Meyer about his failure to identify Whittemore, but Meyer's answers were slow and halting. He looked as if the witness stand was the last place in the world he wanted to be.

Moore jumped up. "Just a minute," he interjected. "This man is worrying about something, aren't you?"

"Yes" answered Meyer, before Sumner yelled out, "I object! The question tends to create a prejudice!"

Noonan, however, overruled Sumner. Moore asked the question again, and Meyer answered, his voice hushed and barely audible.

"Why yes, yes. I'm afraid." He glanced toward Whittemore, and then looked away.

"What are you afraid of?" asked Moore.

"Why, I don't know. I suppose I got sort of an idea they'll get me."

"Get you?"

"I mean," said the guard, his wounded left arm hanging all but useless, "kill me for testifying."

As if a message from on high, a springtime thunderstorm cut loose outside. Rain pelted the windows of the courtroom, thunder boomed, and lightning flashed in the sky.

Meyer's answer hung in the air.

He had voiced what every other witness feared, and now every member of the jury as well: crossing Richard Whittemore might get you killed. The fear lingered long after the rain stopped.

Moore spent the rest of the day trying to buck up his case, calling several more witnesses, each of whom had seen some part of the crime, but none of whom could state with any confidence that Richard Whittemore was one of the men they saw, or that they saw him clearly enough to be certain, or if they saw him fire a gun.

Moore's case was in trouble, but observers still expected a host of other witnesses and evidence. The next morning he called several doctors to the stand to try to prove that Whittemore was the man who had been running with the loot, took a bullet in the arm, and dropped one bag. They had all examined Whittemore, paying particular attention to a scar measuring one inch by one quarter-inch on his lower left forearm. Whittemore claimed that the scar was six years old, but the physicians testified that the wound came from a bullet and was less than six months old.

It was interesting testimony, but hardly definitive. Moore then called a handful of other witnesses who claimed that the man they saw running was Whittemore, but each time, on cross-examination, Sumner was able, either directly or by inference, to cast doubt on their veracity. The descriptions simply didn't match up; he wasn't wearing a hat, he was wearing a cap, he was wearing a fedora, his coat was brown, it was gray. It was a mess of testimony, a mess of contradictions, and a mess of a prosecution.

Then abruptly, the prosecution rested. That was their case. There had been no material witnesses, and no one testified, as Moore had promised, that Whittemore had shot Clifford.

Without delay, Sumner followed with an opening statement of his own that was quieter and less strident but no less confident. He told the jury that he had no fewer than eight alibi witnesses who would prove that Richard Whittemore could not have committed the crime.

"I shall show you gentlemen," he said, "that this defendant at 6 o'clock on the evening of the day before the crime was committed left New York in company with Jacob Kraemer and Milton Goldberg to attend a birthday party in Philadelphia in the home of a Mrs. Jansen, a lifelong friend of Kraemer and a woman of high standing and good repute.

"I shall show that he left to return to New York about 4 or 5 that morning and that, that afternoon, he was in a reputable high-class tailoring establishment on Broadway in New York." Richard Whittemore, he claimed, was nowhere near Buffalo on October 28.

When Sumner's witnesses took the stand, they didn't exhibit the same fear or uncertainty as those Moore had called. Something, it seems, had caused a few tongues to come loose and a few to stay closed.

Sumner first called two revenue agents to the stand who witnessed the robbery. They testified that the man they saw was much shorter than Whittemore, contradicting Moore's witnesses. Next was the Buffalo chief of police, James Higgins, who admitted that immediately after the crime Buffalo police were certain that Harry Harris, not Richard Whittemore, had been behind the robbery.

Then Sumner moved to the heart of his defense. Ben Kupnick, a tailor, testified that on October 28, at 3 p.m., Whittemore and Paladino had come into the shop where he worked to ask about a suit. He remembered it, he said, because it was the birthday of his nephew, who had been in the store as well.

On cross, Moore went after the tailor and tried to infer that his employer was a friend of Whittemore's and even accompanied the Candy Kid to cabarets. "Naw," replied Kupnick. "He wouldn't go to a cabaret. He's a married man." Even Whittemore laughed.

Sumner next produced witnesses who had attended the Philadelphia birthday party the evening before the robbery in Buffalo as guests of the host, Mrs. Dora Jansen, a longtime friend of the Kraemers. According to these witnesses, they met the Kraemers and Whittemore—who was introduced as "George" —that night for the first time. It wasn't much of a party. The guests testified that they spent the entire evening playing piano, singing, and dancing till 4 a.m., and that not a drop of liquor was consumed.

Mrs. Jansen's husband, a Swedish masseur, testified next. The Jansens were separated, but he claimed to have dropped by that evening to use her phone, and he remembered seeing Whittemore and Goldberg. And come to think of it, he'd even given Kraemer a massage.

Then Dora Jansen took the stand. She was no Tiger Girl, but a nearly middle-aged matron, well dressed, with an air of refinement. She said that she had known the Kraemers for years, and that Jake visited her nearly every weekend. She confirmed Whittemore's presence at her party, adding that she had met him only once before.

That was just the opening Moore needed. When the trial resumed the next day, he went after Jansen, trying to dirty her up. She was not, as Sumner had said, a woman of integrity. Moore got her to admit that not only had she known the Kraemers for nearly a decade, but that she had visited Jake in prison, and that his weekend visits were sleepovers that lasted from Friday evening till Monday morning. She had left her husband for him, and her attorney was also one Hyman Bushel. In addition, when police interviewed her, they had confiscated as stolen property a diamond ring given to her by Jake. Although Jansen insisted that her only interest was in helping Kraemer "as far as I can by means of truth and justice," and that she knew nothing about any criminal activity on the Kraemers' part, Moore's implication was clear: she was a kept woman who would say anything to save her man.

Moore then went in for the kill. "I do not want to do anything that will cause you embarrassment," he said, his voice dripping with sarcasm, "but I want you to tell the jury who is the father of your oldest boy?"

The courtroom gasped. Mrs. Jansen looked aghast. "I refuse to answer," she sputtered.

Moore had her by the throat. Now his tone turned accusatory. "Didn't you tell Officer Malone that Jake Kraemer was the father of your child?" Once again, Mrs. Jansen refused to answer, looking down in shame. Moore had made his point.

Sumner concluded by calling a few more witnesses to show that Buffalo police had all but convicted Harry Harris in the days after the trial, then rested his case. Justice Noonan adjourned the court till Monday morning, when each attorney had the right to cross-examine witnesses called by the other side earlier in the case.

The drama was just beginning. With the case winding down and about to go to the jury, it was time for Tiger Girl to make an appearance. That evening Rawlings Whittemore sent Margaret a telegram in Baltimore: "Richard wants to see you badly. Take night train."

Margaret, who'd been out of jail and out of the spotlight, for nearly a week, didn't hesitate. She took the next train to Buffalo.

When Margaret was first arrested, she may have felt as if her life was over. But now she was in the midst of a different life. For the last year she had lived a lifestyle she could have only dreamed of as a young girl, a life marked by wealth, leisure, and every imaginable pleasure. Now, whether she wished to or not, she would step into the crosshairs of the tabloid press alongside her husband and soon become a celebrity as famous as any woman in America, her picture everywhere.

She tried and failed to sleep as the New York Central Pullman chugged its way to Buffalo, following the same route Richard had traveled a few weeks before. At 8:45 a.m., she arrived at the Exchange Street depot, where she was met by Melvin Greene, her father-in law, and a reporter and photographer from the *Daily Star and Inquirer.*

She was pleased when no one at the station recognized her. She claimed to be too tired for photos and hid her face from the camera, saying only, "I have come to help Dick all I can. He is innocent of this crime." The reporter described her later as "a handsome young woman," with a "quiet and well-modulated voice ... nothing rough or flashy in her appearance ... excepting for beauty and style."

She may have been too tired for the camera, but she allowed the reporter to accompany her to her room. Morning newspapers waited at the threshold of every room, and a headline blaring "Whittemore Trial Nears Close" drew no comment from her. Before excusing herself from the persistent reporter, she asked, "Please don't write any of that Tiger Girl stuff; it is ridiculous." Then she added, "I am sure my husband is innocent. I don't know how any man can get up in court and point out my husband, and I don't believe the jury will believe them."

A few hours later, she accompanied Melvin Greene to the jailhouse to see her husband for the first time since they'd appeared together in court back in Manhattan.

They were not alone. A half-dozen guards and deputies joined another half-dozen reporters and photographers in the jailer's office, including *New York Daily News* star reporter Frank Dolan. His inclusion was no accident. A hard-boiled, old-school tabloid newspaper man, Dolan had spearheaded *News* coverage of the case, just as he had done for every other sensational story during the 1920s. He was one of many so-called jazz journalists who would later write for Hollywood and the stage. Many of the screenplays and dramas they later penned drew upon their experiences covering Tiger Girl and the Candy Kid and other gangsters of the era. The couple's every word and deed would contribute to the template for how the era was soon portrayed in popular culture, particularly when the gangster film emerged as its own genre with the advent of talking motion pictures. Journalists like Dolan and his contemporaries, not only in New York but in Baltimore and Buffalo, knew their job was to give the people what they wanted. And what the people wanted now wasn't Richard and Margaret Whittemore, but Tiger Girl and the Candy Kid, together again.

Margaret strode into the jail dressed smartly, wearing a rose-colored, close-fitting straw turban and black satin ensemble, the cloak adorned with white ring figuring, what the *Daily Star* described as "reeking of class and costliness," highlighted by a sparkling, diamond-studded wristwatch, diamond and platinum wedding band, and pearl necklace.

As she entered the jailer's office, Dolan described her as nervous, tired, and pallid-looking, presenting "a placid mask of resignation." Behind the heavy steel-mesh barrier stood her husband, haughty and in control, dressed, "as for a Broadway party," in blue trousers and a light blue dress shirt.

Seeing him, Tiger Girl paused and said, "I'm here to help you in any way," before rushing forward and placing her hands on the screen. "I know you're innocent," she cooed, "and no matter what the world says, I'll always believe you, sweetheart."

As if on cue, she began to cry, and even the Candy Kid's eyes filled with tears and one rolled down his cheek. "I wanted to be here, to be at your side," she continued, "I knew you needed me, and I knew you knew you only had to call to bring me here." She pressed her hand against the steel mesh, and he mirrored it with his own.

"You're here and I'm satisfied," he said. "I can stand anything as long as I know you're with me. This case is as good as beaten now. They can't possibly convict me." A few more minutes of stilted conversation followed, long lingering looks into each other's eyes interspersed with some sotto voce sweet talk whispered through the steel.

When it was time to leave, they posed for the cameras as if for a movie still, Tiger Girl with her back to the camera, her face demurely turned toward her husband, her hand placed on the screen over her husband's heart. The Candy Kid played his part to a tee, looking straight at the camera in his shirtsleeves as if he had nothing to hide, appearing almost bashful, head cocked to one side, hands at his hips. Together, they gave both male and female worshipers plenty of fodder for whatever fantasy they entertained as the image found its way into papers everywhere. And if a juror happened to glance at a Buffalo newspaper over the weekend and see the same photo, well, all the better.

O n the final day of the trial, both Moore and Sumner intended to throw haymakers, each determined to destroy the credibility of the other's case. Moore had the greater challenge. Sumner had followed through with his initial defense, presenting alibi witnesses who disputed Whittemore's appearance in Buffalo, bolstered by effective cross-examination that exposed Moore's eyewitnesses' lack of credibility. Moore, on the other hand, had presented only half a case, and even that seemed built on sketchy and often contradictory testimony. He'd provided virtually no material evidence and none of the evidence he had promised that would prove that Whittemore had shot Clifford. His theatrics proved to be just that.

The flappers and swains returned on Monday morning, again scrambling for a place in the courtroom. They'd spent the weekend reading about Tiger Girl in all the papers touting her arrival, and it seemed likely they would finally get a real live look at the woman who had won the Candy Kid's heart and whose devotion had earned his sacrifice. Every blonde entering County

Hall got a once-over from the crowd, but word soon leaked out that Tiger Girl had arrived early and they had missed their chance. To see her, you had to get inside the courtroom.

"I didn't sleep a wink last night," Margaret told a reporter, "and I don't think I'll sleep a wink tonight. I spent the night reading the papers over and over, and I even read all the ads." She and her father-in-law had arrived shortly after dawn with Greene, and they were taken inside before the building had been opened to the general public. Now Rawlings took a seat in the first row set aside for spectators near the defense table; he was hard of hearing, and on this day he didn't want to miss a word. Margaret sat in the same row, sandwiched between two newspaper messenger boys, where she had a view of the proceedings and a clear look at her husband, and where the jury could see her. She nervously fingered her pearls until her husband was brought into the courtroom.

There was the now-accustomed rush when the courtroom was opened. When the doors were finally closed, hundreds of rubberneckers remained outside, gathered in knots, their numbers growing by the minute as they peppered messenger boys carrying copy in and out of the courtroom with questions. A longtime court employee shook his head in wonder. Not even the Czolgosz trial had seen crowds like this.

The defense had the first chance at rebuttal, and Sumner called Moore's most important witness, Alfred Guggisberg, to the stand. Since his earlier appearance, the defense team had poked around in Guggisberg's background, and Sumner used what he had learned to lay waste to the witness. This was no reputable businessman. Guggisberg had first come to Buffalo from Dayton during a bitter 1922 transit strike to drive a trolley as a scab, a dirty word in a union town. As if that wasn't bad enough, he'd been a lousy driver. "Tell us," Sumner asked, "about when you ran a man over with your street car?" Moore objected, but the point was made.

There was more. Guggisberg had left his wife and four children and been jailed over his failure to make court-ordered payments, leaving them to live in squalor while he shacked up with another woman. The cad hadn't even met his youngest child, an infant only eight months old.

Then Sumner drew the stiletto. He asked about the $15,000 in reward money at stake, and whether Guggisberg expected to receive any of it. When the man stammered that he did not, Sumner brought up an acquaintance, "a man named Mike," and asked, "Didn't you tell him you expected to get $1500 from this case and would buy a car and go around riding?"

Guggisberg denied it, but then Sumner pushed the dagger in to the hilt. He brought Mike Melandino to the stand to corroborate Guggisberg's statement, then Frank Kirsch, the head bookkeeper of the Bank of Buffalo. Guggisberg had claimed, Sumner reminded the jury, that on the morning of the crime he had gone to the bank to deposit ten dollars, and that was when he also claimed to have chatted about the weather with Whittemore. Kirsch, however, testified that although Guggisberg had at one time had an account at the bank, it had since been closed.

Sumner feigned shock. "He has had no account with your bank since January, 1925?" the attorney asked, his voice rising with incredulity. "No," answered Kirsch.

The jury would now have to decide if Guggisberg was really at the bank to make a deposit into an account that did not exist, or whether he was simply aping earlier reporting in order to collect a reward, willing to lie and send a man to death for enough money to buy a car.

Moore tried to fire back, but he lacked ammunition. He finally produced material evidence in the form of two matchbooks found in the stolen car used in the robbery. Moore called Max Saty, owner of the stolen car, to the stand and asked if the matchbooks, their covers imprinted with the address "no. 841 Broadway," were his.

"No," Saty said, "I don't use matches." Moore then tried to attach the matchbooks to Whittemore. The address was only a few doors away from the tailor shop whose tailor Sumner had used to create Whittemore's alibi the day after the crime. Moore hoped the jury would make the leap.

The prosecutor's final witnesses were Inspector John Coughlin and Detective Walter Sullivan of New York. They had been in attendance for the entire trial, for the dual purposes of serving as witnesses and taking Whittemore into custody in the event he avoided conviction.

Coughlin testified that "previously to leaving New York City, Detective

Sullivan and myself talked to Whittemore. That was just before he was brought to Buffalo. He said if he burned he would not burn alone. He said that 'those other two rats'" would also burn. Coughlin added that Whittemore had been referring to Unkelbach and Paladino, "the 'squealers' of the gang." Asked by Moore what he meant by "burn," Coughlin answered, "Why, to a crook means by that death by electrocution."

That was certainly convenient. That was exactly what Whittemore had said to Roche and the Buffalo detectives on the train as he arrived in Buffalo.

To close the case Moore produced photos of both Whittemore and Harry Harris to make the point that it was easy to confuse the two men. Sumner objected, but Noonan allowed the evidence. With that, the prosecution rested its case.

It was 11:35 a.m. All that remained were the closing arguments. Noonan didn't want to waste any time. "We ought to finish the case today," he said. Lunch could wait. After a moment, Sumner launched his summation.

To no one's surprise, he focused on the eyewitness testimony. Sumner asked the jury, "Are you going to let witnesses swear this man's life away on the most terrible discrepancies and rottenest identifications I have seen in twenty years of experience? When I was first assigned this case I wouldn't have given a nickel for Whittemore's life." Sumner then assailed the testimony of each of the state's witnesses, ending by referring to Guggisberg as "Daffy" and, his voice rising, "a half-baked, half-witted individual who hasn't supported his family and never seen his eight-months old baby!"

He implored the jury to act with decency in regard to Mrs. Jansen. "Jesus Christ said 'let he who is without sin cast the first stone.' Just because Mrs. Jansen had a child with Kraemer—do you believe she is not telling the truth? We're gambling here with a human life—it's up to you to cast the die."

To end, Sumner turned teary-eyed. "It has been a tremendous strain on me," he said, gesturing to the district attorney, his former mentor, "to come up here and fight the man for whom I have the greatest respect and love." He then thanked the jury and sat, exhausted, next to the defendant. Noonan adjourned the court for lunch.

Margaret and Richard had remained composed all morning. Her eyes flitted back and forth between her husband, the attorneys, and the jury, while he mostly watched the witnesses, his foot nervously tapping the floor. The crowd stole furtive glances at Tiger Girl as often as they could, though most could glimpse little more than the back of her head. But then, as the guards escorted the Candy Kid out of the courtroom for lunch, the gallery finally got what they had all come to see.

As Whittemore passed by his wife, he stopped, muttered, "Please . . . please," and paused. Arms shackled, he leaned down to her, she leaned up toward him, and they shared a tender kiss.

Whittemore's father tenderly smiled at them both, then led his daughter-in-law outside, where they were both spirited away for lunch. Most spectators remained inside, transfixed and unwilling to risk losing their seats.

When the crowd outside heard that the closing arguments had begun, that Tiger Girl and the Candy Kid *had kissed*, and that the case was about to go to the jury, they began to mass at the door. The crowd grew so large that it spilled down the stairs and onto the first floor of County Hall, "a seething mass of humanity." When Whittemore returned to the court through the Tunnel of Tears, police had to form a gauntlet around the prisoner.

It took them a full three minutes to push and shove their prisoner through the adoring crowd. Had Whittemore not been shackled to an officer, the crowd would surely have pulled him free. As it was, they had to turn and use the full force of their bodies to close the door behind them.

Justice Noonan had just resumed his place at the bench when the crowd stormed the courthouse door, forcing it open as everyone tried to squeeze inside. The jurist, in a panic, summoned Police Chief Higgins and ordered the door sealed until the situation was under control. The chief called every available cop and deputy in the building to the courtroom to secure the room.

They arrived en masse, one group taking aim at the door full on and another from the flank as the crowd fought against the police and scratched to hold their place, neither side willing to give, every step a battle. Caught in the melee, Sheriff Tyler was manhandled by officers and shoved down the stairs. Even newspapermen were denied entry.

It took police nearly half an hour to take control as the mob fought the full force of the Buffalo Police Department and the Erie County Sheriff's Office to a near-standoff. The billy clubs and badges barely held their own against the determined mob of obsessed fans. Whittemore's father and wife and attorneys reentered the courtroom by way of a rush line, as if trying to score the winning touchdown behind a flying wedge.

As soon as everyone was safely inside, Noonan ordered the door sealed again. Officers inside and out lined up before the doors and even jammed a heavy chair under the door handle as a last line of defense.

For the remainder of the afternoon, no one not already inside would be allowed to get into the courtroom, not even reporters. As a result, Moore's closing arguments took place before the smallest crowd of the entire trial. Still, he struggled to be heard over the cacophony roaring outside.

Never before had County Hall seen such spectacle.

The case, Moore said, boiled down to "whether this defendant was in Buffalo at the time of the murder or Philadelphia." He defended his own witnesses, arguing that the question was not one of their veracity. "Before you say these men are wrong," he said, "you've got to say they've perjured themselves to send this man to the electric chair!"

He then assailed the alibi witnesses, ridiculing Mrs. Jansen's supposedly booze-free party. He said, "The last defense of a guilty man charged with a crime is a fake alibi."

He continued: "They bring in the old family alibi and dust it off . . . Where did this alibi come from?" he asked. "From Hymie Bushel, because the Kraemers are going to be tried here for the same crime." It was likely no accident that he referenced Bushel in a way that underscored his ethnicity to play to any anti-Semites on the jury. Moore went on like this for more than an hour, condemning Whittemore as much through inference as with evidence.

"If you acquit this defendant," he concluded, "then you are making the streets of Buffalo, the home of Buffalo, the open hunting grounds for the criminals of the underworld."

It was over. At 5:45 p.m., Justice Noonan gave final instructions to the jury. Their options were to find Richard Whittemore either not guilty or guilty of murder in the first degree. The law allowed no diminishment of the charge. The judge ordered them to begin deliberations after dinner and to continue until 11 p.m. if necessary.

The crowd outside finally started to thin, everyone exhausted from the battle. The jurors were all taken to the Statler Hotel to deliberate. They would spend the night there if they had to.

Whittemore too was taken from the courtroom, but not before he received another quick kiss and embrace from his wife. Margaret stayed behind with Rawlings, awaiting a verdict that they both knew could arrive at any time.

At 11 p.m., deliberations had ended for the night. By then, much of the crowd had cleared, but County Hall telephone operators were kept busy, taking hundreds of calls from the public asking if there was a verdict. Margaret gave a brief interview on her way to her hotel.

"I'll die if anything happens to Dick," she said. "Oh I know he's innocent. I hope the jury will find him not guilty, I did not sleep a wink Sunday night and do not expect to close my eyes tonight." She wanted to visit her husband, but was told he would be allowed no visitors until the verdict was in. He wasn't as nervous as she was. In his cell he was already snoring.

After breakfast the next day, the jury resumed deliberations at the courthouse while everyone else convened in the courtroom. The largest crowd to date again crammed into every nook and cranny of County Hall. Late that morning, and again at 4:55 p.m., the jury emerged with questions—first to have portions of the eyewitness testimony read, and the second time to have the judge explain reasonable doubt.

Rumors swept the courthouse that the jury was deadlocked nine to three in favor of conviction; others claimed it was seven to five for acquittal. Just before 11 p.m., the judge called the jury back and had Richard Whittemore roused from sleep and brought to the courtroom. Earlier that evening, Whittemore had received a telegram that read:

Congratulations. Best Wishes. Hope for your speedy return.
—The Boys

Maybe they knew something he didn't. Twenty-nine hours had passed since the trial's end, and fifteen hours had been spent in jury deliberations. Neither Sumner nor Moore was present. They'd gone home hours before, expecting a call if a verdict was reached.

Noonan asked foreman Roscoe C. Stacy if the jury had a verdict. He answered, "We have not reached a verdict."

"Is there anything the Court can enlighten you on?" asked Noonan.

"No," replied Stacy, circles under both eyes. "This jury is unquestionably deadlocked."

"In a case like this you should negotiate as long as you can if there is any possibility of coming to a conclusion," said Noonan.

"We have given it every possible consideration. We are just where we would be if we remained out thirty-six or forty-eight hours."

Maybe some believed Sumner and his alibi witnesses. Maybe some didn't believe Moore and his, or didn't like the DA's badgering style. Maybe some were swayed by their wives and daughters and those pictures of Tiger Girl in the paper and the soft kiss at the end of the trial. Maybe some were afraid and had been threatened, and maybe, if that telegram meant anything, some knew all along how they planned to vote and would soon be able buy a new car or take a nice vacation.

The exasperated judge called Melvin Greene and Assistant DA Walter Hofheinz to the bench.

"I don't believe, Mr. Hofheinz, that there is any use keeping the jury out any longer. Under the circumstances then, I think I'll discharge the jury."

What? It took a moment to settle in. Neither the prosecution nor the defense had asked for a mistrial. Noonan, on his own authority and apparently with the cooperation of both the prosecution and defense, simply ended the trial. There would be no verdict.

While not a formal, legal acquittal, Whittemore had not been found guilty.

All that mattered was that the Candy Kid had dodged the electric chair.

The deputies immediately led Whittemore from the courtroom, spiriting him away without allowing the Whittemores to meet or embrace. All they could manage were disbelieving, incredulous smiles at each other. The crowd outside, which had begun to stir as soon as Whittemore was brought back into the courtroom, all turned to look, hundreds of eyes suddenly fixed on the door swinging open. Whittemore delivered the verdict by the smile on his face.

As he stepped out to where he could be seen, flanked by ten deputies and handcuffed to one of them, he was greeted by cheers and a roar that cascaded into a rumbling thunder. Men threw their hats in the air. Newspapers were shredded into confetti that floated down the stairwell. Women and girls screamed and wept and hugged each other.

"The yells and shouts rocked city hall," reported the *Buffalo Times*. "They could be heard for blocks."

Those close enough to Whittemore tried to touch him, to pat his back or clasp a hand. People shouted, "That's the boy, Dick!" Women pressed forward, trying to clasp his neck and plant a kiss. Some even held out their babies and children for him to touch.

"Riot and glee were everywhere," continued the *Buffalo Times*. "Men were knocked down, police officers were buffeted and all the while the din increased. Never had a hero returned from war to the reception Whittemore got."

To the crowd, it had indeed been a war, one between those with power and those without it, a battle between love and something else. Was he guilty? Was he innocent? To Whittemore supporters, nearly all of them young and many of them women, guilt didn't seem to matter as much as the power of his sacrifice.

The bandit himself seemed a little stunned, a little amused, a little thrilled. As the deputies shuffled him out of the courtroom and through the throng, he "lifted his manacled hands," like a boxer after scoring a knockout; neither free nor innocent, but a man who knew he would survive at least a few more weeks or months to fight again. The mob followed his crooked walk through the throng to the Tunnel of Tears, weeping with joy.

Justice Noonan was not amused by the celebration outside the courtroom, which was now spilling into the street. "A fine lot of citizens we have in Buffalo," he sniffed, disgusted. In all the commotion, Tiger Girl and Rawlings were nearly forgotten. She broke down in tears. The discharge, she said, was "practically the same as an acquittal. I don't think they will ever try him again. He is innocent. I knew always that he was innocent. I am so happy that the jury did not find him guilty. I'll die if anything happens to Dickie. I love him so. If they would put me behind bars I would gladly spend the rest of my days there, or just as long as they kept Dickie."

A stout middle-aged woman who had lingered behind rushed over to Margaret, three carnations in hand, and held them out to Tiger Girl, saying, "God bless you. I am praying for you." Margaret refused the flowers, turned to Rawlings, and snapped, "Let's get going. I can't bear to stay here another minute. I want to go someplace where I can have a good cry."

In Baltimore, Herbert O'Conor prepared to try Richard Reese Whittemore for the murder of Robert Holtman.

Fifteen

BEWARE THE VERDICT

The Candy Kid may have not been proven guilty of murder in Erie County, but he was not free. One last time he traveled through the Tunnel of Tears and was escorted into the steel-mesh cage, where he held an impromptu press conference, grinning and making wisecracks.

Lighting a cigarette, he quipped, "I'm sorry I can't offer you boys one, but this confounded screen is in the way."

He managed to pass two pages of penciled scrawl to the jailer to hand out to the press. He'd written out his thoughts, which he now paraphrased. "The worst thing I was hoping for was a disagreement," he said. "I knew they would never convict me, and I thought I would get acquitted, sure as hell.

"Say, boys," he added, "Here's something I would like to have you get in the papers. I'm just as innocent of that job here as the judge and the jury that sat in the trial. I am perfectly innocent. I didn't have a thing to do with it."

Before the press was shooed out and Whittemore taken to his cell, a photographer asked him to pose. "Hold a match near your face and smile," he told him, an old photographer's trick to soften a subject's features so the flash wouldn't make him look startled. Whittemore happily obliged. Image mattered.

The next morning, headlines from Cincinnati to Wilkes-Barre, Louisville to Muncie, Santa Fe to Altoona, Atlanta, and almost every place in between touted the Candy Kid's freedom on the front page, and his picture gazed out from newsstands on both coasts. His body may have been behind bars, but his face was everywhere, his nickname on everyone's lips.

While that thrilled readers and circulation managers, the editorial pages had a different response. They found the public reaction, particularly among the young, absolutely confounding. Even the *Daily News,* which had helped fuel the Candy Kid's skyrocketing popularity, saw fit to back off. An editorial headlined "Soft-Hearted Boobs," began: "That is what Americans seem to be, when you read of the scenes that surrounded The Jury's discharge" of Whittemore. "Had it been May 1, flowers and confetti would doubtless have been thrown and Whittemore crowned the king of May." The editorial bemoaned how easily forgotten were the crimes and the victims and cynically concluded that, "really, we deserve to have crime waves." The *Buffalo Courier* wondered, "Why did the crowd cheer Whittemore . . . Was it sympathy for the underdog? Was it based on reports of evidence which a good many of the cheerers did not hear?" The paper provided no answer but mob psychology, finding it "deplorable for a city to become a byword throughout the country and around the world as a place where they make heroes of criminals."

Even the sob sisters were mystified. Gertrude Price, the city editor for the *Los Angeles Record* who penned a syndicated women's column under the name "Cynthia Grey" that pandered to young women who followed every desire, or at least wanted to, was flummoxed. While recognizing that "the public applauded and wiped its eyes over the brave lover who would save his wife at the cost, perhaps, of his own neck," she warned readers that "a man is not likely to be a thug, a murderer or even a drunkard and still maintain a clean spot in his heart for love." Such men, she warned, were beyond reform.

What none of these editorialists understood was the tenor of the age and the increasingly addictive pull of stardom, an ambition more powerful than wealth or achievement. Tiger Girl and the Candy Kid had leapfrogged their station in life to become celebrities, and that was what their readers wanted for themselves — to be seen and recognized, to seize a small piece of this new American Dream just coming into focus.

Swooning over the Candy Kid provided a vicarious thrill and an opportunity to go along for the ride. Of course he might be awful, morally rotten even, but he didn't pretend to be otherwise. And look! Love had changed him! Coupled with the vast contradictions and disparities in the justice system, many saw little difference between the criminal and his jailer. Gangsters, particularly those younger, attractive and glib, like Whittemore, were victims themselves, more honest and authentic than either the cops or the courts. At least they didn't booze it up and then act all high and mighty and arrest some regular Joe for acting just as they did.

Back in Baltimore, State's Attorney Herbert O'Conor did not share those feelings. His morality was black-and-white. When he looked at the papers, he didn't see the Candy Kid, but Richard Reese Whittemore, a murderer. At 9 a.m. the morning after the discharge, he fired off a telegram to Guy Moore, asking that Erie County waive the right to retry Whittemore and send him to Baltimore. He had an "open and shut case" for a conviction. In fact, Moore had already decided not to attempt a retrial of Whittemore, and not to bring charges against the Kraemers or any other members of the gang either. "When a jury disregards testimony of unimpeachable witnesses produced by the state, there is no use," he said. Without his witnesses, he had nothing, and it was pretty clear his witnesses had all chosen, either because of fear, public opinion, a sudden loss of memory, or Moore's failure to provide any physical evidence, not to go along with a conviction. Moore was cutting his losses.

Meanwhile, in the Manhattan District Attorney's Office, Ferdinand Pecora and Joab Banton wanted Whittemore back. It would look better for them all, McLaughlin, Coughlin, and Jimmy Walker included, if New York County, not Erie County, delivered the prisoner to Maryland.

Moore had no choice but to agree. Whittemore was still under indictment in New York County, and without an extradition order, Moore couldn't send him to Maryland anyway. All interested parties concurred, including Governors Smith and Ritchie. The Maryland governor would refile the extradition order, and then New York State would turn him over. Once again the prisoner would be booted from one institution to another, one jurisdiction to another, as the courts sought a lasting solution to the chronic problem of Richard Reese Whittemore, his crimes having compounded from boyhood hooky all the way to first-degree murder. Now, at last, the answer seemed close at hand.

They all spent the remainder of the day making arrangements. As soon as Margaret and Rawlings learned of that decision, they made plans to leave Buffalo. Margaret asked to see her husband before leaving but was turned down—Erie County authorities were through accommodating Tiger Girl. She boarded a train to New York City, where she needed to pick up both her belongings and her husband's, and Rawlings went home to Baltimore.

The next morning Richard Whittemore was roused from sleep. A guard told him he was "gonna take a little trip."

"Where am I going?" Whittemore asked. "Can't tell you," the man replied.

Erie County was done with being nice. Just before 8 a.m., Whittemore, in manacles, was led from the jail onto the street, now empty of supporters. The *Buffalo Times* reported that he was "literally hurled over the sidewalk" and into a waiting sedan. No one cared if he bumped his head.

He was treated just as roughly at the train station, where he was shoved and pushed and carried to the waiting train, then taken into a private drawing room. On the return trip to New York his escorts, instead of Buffalo police, were Coughlin, Sullivan, and several other New York City cops. The only difference this time was that two of the men had testified against him.

Coughlin and Sullivan had heard it all, but Whittemore still couldn't keep his mouth shut. "I'm glad to shake the dust of this town from my heels. I don't wanna knock your little hotel," he said of Erie County, "but I must say the meals were rotten." This time the only one of his crimes he spoke about was the killing of Holtman. He knew that anything else he said might come up in trial. As he munched on peanuts and smoked, he told Coughlin and the detective that Holtman "was a bad guy. He'd already killed three prisoners before I killed him." He explained the attack by saying, "I wasn't in very good humor." He tested the self-defense case he hoped to mount in Baltimore by insisting that his escape had been a spur-of-the-moment decision made under the duress of an attack, that there was no premeditation, and that the killing was accidental. He had to have known that in Maryland premeditation was a prerequisite for the death penalty.

In fact, Whittemore was confident that in Maryland he might either receive a life term or even beat the charge and then only have to serve out the remaining years of his existing sentence. Both possibilities held out the prospect of parole or, of course, escape. "I can beat any murder case they bring against me," he said. "I'll beat the case and they know it."

"I've robbed," he bragged. "I admit that. But I never killed." Well, except for Holtman. He noted that the only witness against him in that killing was John Bowie, the Black trusty. He didn't think a Baltimore jury would hang a man based on the word of a Black man. "I'll never hang for it because the only witness they have against me is a Negro," he said, "and you know how much the word of a Negro, especially a convict, goes down there." Not only would a jury be unlikely to put much stock in a Black man's testimony, they would be hesitant to send a White man to the gallows under any circumstance. No White man had been executed in Baltimore since 1904. Whittemore didn't think the state had the nerve to add to that number, but he also didn't yet know that O'Conor's case didn't depend on Bowie's word alone.

The state's attorney had followed the proceedings in Erie County closely and was determined not to make the mistakes that he believed had resulted in Whittemore's acquittal. "There will be no repetition of the Buffalo trial," he announced. By allowing the prisoner to meet with his wife and parading them both before the press, feeding the public's voyeuristic appetite, and by allowing Whittemore's attorney to build a defense, Erie County had let the Candy Kid and Tiger Girl run the show.

O'Conor, as was his custom, was determined to move fast. In the meantime, he'd keep Whittemore out of the sight and mind of the public as much as possible.

When Whittemore's train arrived at Grand Central Terminal that evening, he received a hero's welcome. A mob of flappers and their beaus packed the train platform to catch a glimpse of the star prisoner, alongside every Pullman porter in the station. The all-Black employees weren't shy about supporting a man who they felt had been railroaded, just as Blacks were every day of the week. Other passengers were left to carry their own luggage.

Whittemore posed for reporters and cameramen like a debutante in what the *Daily News* noted was "a perfectly pressed dark suit with a white hairline stripe" under "a stylishly cut black overcoat" and a "rakish gray fedora . . . The Candy Kid in every detail of his attire."

The same scene awaited him at the Tombs. Escorted to a cell, the applause and cheers thundered down the cellblock as the incarcerated welcomed home a man who'd beat a murder charge and defeated the screws.

Whittemore did not linger in the Tombs for long. The next morning Governor Smith signed Governor Ritchie's extradition request, and Whittemore was transferred by train to the Baltimore City Jail. There he was placed in confinement unlike that of any other defendant in Baltimore history. His cell was spartan, unfurnished apart from a small table, wooden chair, and cot. Again placed on suicide watch, guards kept an eye on him twenty-four hours a day. The heavy iron cell door was secured by no fewer than five locks and fastened to the wall by one hundred feet of steel chain. Each time he left his cell, even to receive his twice-weekly shave and shower, he was manacled and accompanied by at least five guards, each arm handcuffed to an escort. Unlocking his cell took a full fifteen minutes, as no single guard was capable of releasing the prisoner on his own.

This time the Kraemers didn't underwrite his defense. They were preoccupied with their own upcoming trial in New York for the Prip robbery. They'd helped out in Buffalo knowing that if Whittemore was convicted, they might face the same charges. That wasn't the case anymore.

While Whittemore awaited arraignment, the body of Henry Helwig was pulled from the East River off Pier Thirty-Three. His corpse was identified by a pair of cufflinks bearing his initials. The coroner didn't find a bullet wound, and after two months in the water, the body showed no signs of a beating. Maybe Helwig couldn't swim and had been pushed. Or maybe he knew the gang was gunning for him and took the easy way out. Although police still believed that Whittemore had played a role in his demise, they had no hard evidence. With no other option, his death was ruled a suicide by drowning.

So far, Tiger Girl had yet to be seen in Baltimore. But when a reporter knocked on her mother's door on the morning of Friday, May 5, Margaret answered. The reporter asked if she thought her husband would be acquitted, to which she responded, smiling through a narrow crack in the doorway, "You know what I think without asking." Rawlings Whittemore arrived a bit later and took her to the arraignment.

The crowds waiting at the Baltimore courthouse were just as frenzied as the crowds had been in Buffalo, and Maryland Supreme Court judge Eugene

O'Dunne's courtroom was packed to overflowing for the proceeding. A crowd also massed outside O'Conor's office, chasing a rumor that he was distributing tickets as if the arraignment was some kind of theatrical production.

Judge Eugene O'Dunne was familiar with the Whittemore case. In 1916, he had defended the Kraemer brothers in the trial for the Norwig robbery, which sent them to the penitentiary for nearly a decade. In another era, that might have been enough to bump him from the Whittemore trial. In 1926, it drew no comment.

O'Dunne had drawn ire for both his demeanor and his decisions. In only two months on the bench, he had paroled more than a hundred defendants and had repeatedly imposed harsh sentences only to reduce them a short time later, leading some to wonder if he was compromised. He also acted, as the *Baltimore News* later noted, upon a "fanatical belief in the divine right of judges." He determined the law and then executed it, not the other way around. Even more than O'Conor, he saw the Whittemore case in terms of his own ambitions. A quick conviction would quiet critics, bury any lingering taint from his defense of the Kraemers, and enhance his hold on an office that he intended to run for in the next election.

Whittemore was transferred to O'Dunne's court under the watch of a half-dozen guards as Margaret, dressed in the same ensemble she had worn in Buffalo, sat alongside Rawlings for the proceeding. The local attorney who appeared with Whittemore, Vincent Demarco, asked for a postponement. Whittemore hadn't yet decided if he wanted Demarco to represent him.

O'Dunne insisted that Whittemore decide on counsel by the following Monday. The only allowance made by Baltimore authorities was having O'Conor provide Margaret with a permit that allowed her to visit her husband. She did so later that day and also the next. Unlike in Buffalo, the press was not allowed to witness their meetings.

Instead, the press came to Margaret. On Sunday, May 7, a young female reporter for the *Baltimore News,* Anne Kinsolving, daughter of the minister who had performed Meta Whittemore's wedding, accompanied Margaret to the jail. In journalism circles, Kinsolving, who married well and later became a respected military historian, was a "sob sister"—a reporter tasked with writing tear-jerking profiles with a woman's touch designed to pull on the heartstrings, regardless of any crime or victims involved.

Margaret turned down an interview request, but Kinsolving nevertheless managed to create a sympathetic portrait of the Tiger Girl. She noted that compared to the usual jailhouse visitors, smartly dressed Margaret was a "startling apparition." Although Kinsolving thought Margaret was not classically beautiful, the reporter found her face "absorbingly interesting" and pronounced her "dignified . . . thin and agile."

She concluded that "Mrs. Whittemore is a feminine mixture of Casablanca and Napoleon. Given an army, she could conquer the world. Given a bandit husband it looks fearfully much as if she will stay with the ship until it burns — and then she will burn with it."

Margaret posed for the accompanying photograph, seated modestly on the front steps of her mother's home in a simple housedress, on the verge of tears, one hand reaching out to pet her dog, Bades. Tiger Girl looked about as threatening as a kitten lost in the rain.

On Monday, Demarco appeared at the arraignment on Whittemore's behalf. Accompanied by Rawlings and Richard's brother, Rawlings Jr., he read a simple statement from Richard Whittemore requesting court-appointed counsel. He was still crying poormouth.

Demarco refused to take the case, and neither Rawlings nor Margaret could raise funds to hire anyone else, so a few days later O'Dunne acquiesced to the request and appointed his former boss, Edgar Allen Poe, to serve as Whittemore's attorney. For a sum of $100, Poe agreed.

The namesake of the renowned poet and his second cousin once removed, Poe was no backbench barrister. He'd served as state's attorney, Maryland attorney general, and president of the local bar association. A graduate of Princeton, he quarterbacked the school's undefeated football team in 1889 and left such an impression that, according to some accounts, when a man once asked a Princeton alumnus if Poe was related to "the great Edgar Allen Poe," the response was, "He *is* the great Edgar Allen Poe." Poe shared a visual resemblance to his more famous forebear, with close, dark-set, penetrating eyes and a sharp, beak-shaped nose that commanded attention.

Although Poe's private practice rarely included defense work, he had plenty of experience as a prosecutor and an unblemished legal reputation. The appointment was undoubtedly made to thwart any later charge that Whittemore had been railroaded on a capital case and to ward off any possible appeal in advance.

Now that Poe was on board, O'Conor moved quickly. Although there was some speculation that Poe might offer a guilty plea in exchange for a life sentence, O'Conor wanted nothing to do with it. He had a body, he had witnesses, and Whittemore had repeatedly admitted to the killing. If O'Conor proved premeditation, Whittemore would hang. The trial would begin May 19 and proceed in double sessions, day and night, until its conclusion. Given the risk of escape, there would be no pretrial arraignment.

Unlike the Erie County legal teams, neither the prosecution nor the defense attempted to try the case in the press. With Whittemore locked up and his meetings with Tiger Girl kept private, that avenue was blocked. All Poe would share with reporters in advance of the trial was the comment that "Whittemore is a much sinned against human being. He was wrongfully accused of committing two murders in Buffalo and was acquitted. He is being wrongfully accused here. This is not a case of first degree murder. I will show this at trial."

The absence of public drama did not stifle interest in the case. To manage the spectacle O'Conor announced in advance of the trial that he would, in fact, issue tickets. He eventually received 5,000 requests for the 350 courtroom seats. The state's attorney's only concern was to seat a jury untouched by the public's fawning obsession with the Whittemores.

From the outside, the press, or at least the tabloid press, tried to frame the trial as a battle between the two extreme forces currently doing battle in society. Representing one side was O'Conor, a stalwart defender of morality and reason and all that was right and good in the world. The other side was represented by the Candy Kid, a product of the moral decay of the Jazz Age, the logical end result of the institution of Prohibition and the madness of the modern freewheeling era that had taken hold of America after the war. Some papers even reported that O'Conor and Whittemore had both served as altar boys at the same church and had attended the same grammar school. Both claims were patently false, but they helped create a narrative that appealed to both readers who prayed for Whittemore's conviction and those who were thrilled by the possibility of his innocence.

On Wednesday morning, May 19, Whittemore was transported from the jail to the court, guarded like the Hope diamond. Each of the more than 350 ticketed guests would be subjected to no fewer than four checkpoints before being allowed inside. Those without tickets were kept quiet and under control by police stationed outside. Sitting just behind the defense and prosecution tables, in the first row, were Margaret and Rawlings Whittemore. Only a few feet away sat Robert Holtman's widow, Marie, and one of the dead man's adult daughters.

Just a few minutes before the start, while O'Dunne was still in his chambers, the judge heard the explosion of the powdered flash of a camera as a pressman tried to take a picture of those entering the courtroom. He leapt up and ordered his bailiff to deliver the photographer to his chamber. O'Dunne berated the man and ordered him to "give me the plate"—the glass plate negative. The shaken photographer did as he was told.

At precisely 10 a.m., O'Dunne entered the courtroom and called out, "Silence!" The room fell quiet. O'Dunne berated the press and threatened that anyone who violated his rules, particularly against the use of photography, would be invited for a "stay in the Baltimore City Jail." The court clerk swore in Whittemore, then read the indictment and asked for his plea.

"Not guilty," he answered, asking for a jury trial.

Poe knew his best chance of getting Whittemore off lay with the jury. During the voir dire process, he hoped he might be able to seat a few younger jurors who would be open to Whittemore's claims of self-defense, or if not, jurors who might wobble on the question of premeditation. The defense retained twenty preemptory challenges, the prosecution ten.

As was customary, O'Dunne swore in the panel and asked each juror if he could give the defendant a fair trial, if he knew any of the principals, if he had already formed an opinion, and if he was opposed to capital punishment. O'Conor and Poe, as was customary, could either reject a juror outright or ask additional questions.

After Poe rejected the first juror after asking a few perfunctory questions about age and occupation, O'Dunne interrupted.

O'Dunne, gazing down over his round, black-rimmed glasses, cut Poe short.

"I want to say, Mr. Poe, no questions may be asked a juror which would divulge anything which will cause either side in arriving at a peremptory challenge." In other words, there would be no questioning of jurors.

Poe was stunned. He'd been in court a long time and had never seen this before. He was accustomed to receiving a certain legal deference, but O'Dunne made it clear that he, not Poe, made the rules. Incredulous, Poe protested, asking, "Must we take jurors without knowing anything about them? It is the first time I have ever heard of any such procedure."

"You are right," answered the judge, "it has never been done before in this court. But the law sanctions this procedure," he explained, "and it is frequently practiced in the counties and in England," citing English common law. Case closed. The only way for Poe to dismiss a juror would be through a random peremptory challenge. So much for Poe's hope to seat a sympathetic jury, or a fair one.

The outrageous ruling made the odds on Whittemore's acquittal, already long, suddenly infinitesimal. In theory, once Poe's peremptory challenges were exhausted, unless either O'Dunne or O'Conor objected, the jury could end up consisting of twelve men whose backgrounds were utter mysteries and might be fully compromised. In fact, O'Dunne even accepted a juror who admitted to having known Holtman, which forced Poe to exhaust a valuable peremptory challenge on a juror who never should have been accepted by the court. But O'Dunne held fast to his decision. If Poe didn't like it, he was free to use the issue in any appeal.

With Poe forced to use his challenges almost blindly, the resulting jury clearly leaned toward the prosecution. Nearly every juror was middle-aged or older and comfortably middle-class; they included salesmen and clerks, even a jeweler, and all of them, as was customary, were White and male. None were representatives of the crowds that formed in the courthouse each day or milled about on the streets outside. None shared the Whittemores' background and tastes. In no sense were these jurors peers of the defendant. Until they delivered a verdict, they would be empaneled, housed in a dormitory in the courthouse where there would be no opportunity for outside influence.

O'Conor stepped forward to make his opening statement, utterly untroubled by the process. The young prosecutor was quick and proficient. Where

Moore had made promises he could not keep and seemed to perform for the courtroom, O'Conor was dispassionate and logical. Without flourish or hyperbole, he laid out his whole case, witness by witness, stating that he would not only prove that Whittemore killed Holtman but also offer witnesses who could prove both premeditation and robbery. Either charge, if proven, could raise the murder charges to a death penalty case.

O'Conor's prosecution proceeded with the efficiency of an assembly line. While Whittemore had been in Erie County, O'Conor had spent time preparing his case, and it showed. The witnesses were called in rapid-fire fashion, each laying out a strand that, when wound together, O'Conor hoped would create a hangman's noose.

After calling the shoe shop foreman and Willie Greene, the trusty who escorted Whittemore from the prison shop to the hospital, O'Conor called Olivia Alkire, a prison hospital nurse, to the stand. She described changing the dressing on the burn on Whittemore's arm and recalled that he quipped, "It's the last time I'm going to have it dressed. I'm going to give it the open air treatment." Clearly, O'Conor suggested, the escape was planned, and by implication, the murder was premeditated.

After several doctors' testimonies established that Holtman had died of a fractured skull and the prison dentist reported hearing a voice ringing out, "Holtman's dead!" O'Conor called his most important witness, the trusty janitor John Bowie, to the stand.

Only a few years older than Whittemore, the prisoner taking the stand presented a stark contrast to Whittemore, owing to not only his race but his demeanor. Unlike Whittemore, whom Anne Kinsolving described as looking "the part of the 'smooth guy' of the underworld and the 'rough guy' of the upper," Bowie appeared beaten down. Richard Whittemore had probably spent more money in a single night in a cabaret than Bowie had seen in his entire life. Whittemore took what he wanted from the world, while men like Bowie survived on the scraps left behind. Yet Whittemore's entire fate rested on the next hour of testimony from the prison janitor.

Bowie was serving ten years for larceny. Quiet and deferential to authority, he had worked in the prison hospital as a janitor for two years and was familiar with the defendant from his work as a hospital orderly.

O'Conor patiently walked him through the events of the morning when Holtman died. Bowie testified that he was in the prison dentist's office with Holtman when he heard the guard on the second floor call out "coming down." He described the movements of the two men in the moments before Whittemore's attack.

"The old man had the keys in the door when this fellow hit him," he said, nodding toward Whittemore.

Bowie spilled out the whole sordid scene, the pipe, the gun, the guard bleeding on the floor, and the way Whittemore grabbed Holtman's wallet before forcing Bowie, at gunpoint, to walk with him before slipping out the Madison Street exit.

"The wall gate was open. He walked past me and left me standing on the steps," Bowie said. Then he had yelled, "Holtman's dead," run back to the fallen guard, picked him up, and helped carry him upstairs to the hospital.

"Was there any quarrel or argument between Mr. Holtman and Whittemore?" asked O'Conor.

"No, no fuss of any kind and they didn't have any fight."

Poe tried his best to cast doubt on Bowie's account, asking him about his mental state during imprisonment, questioning why it took him so long to raise an alarm, and why he hadn't run when Whittemore wasn't looking in his direction.

"He didn't have to keep his eyes on me," said Bowie, "when he had that gun pointing straight at me."

Whittemore laughed, and O'Dunne called for order.

Then the judge interjected, "You could have run away when you were on Madison Street, could you not?"

"Yes," Bowie replied, "but the old man treated me good, so that's why I came back, because I knowed the old man was lying on the ground . . . he was good to me, that old man. That's why." As he spoke, tears formed in his eyes. Any prejudice the jury held against a Black witness must have softened.

Poe wisely concluded his cross-examination. O'Dunne adjourned the trial for the day.

The following morning O'Conor called penitentiary inmate Joseph Dietz to the stand. Whittemore and Dietz had been friends and committed robberies together before being arrested in Philadelphia and convicted for the Gaffney job.

Testifying now because his "conscience hurt him," Dietz said that he and Whittemore had been planning to break out ever since he'd returned to prison, and he described several plans they considered. All of them involved busting out through the hospital, including one plan in which they would chloroform the guard. After being unable to find chloroform, Whittemore abandoned this plot that included Dietz and concluded that his only way out was to "slug his way out through Holtman."

There was little Poe could do on cross-examination other than ask if Dietz had been promised a reduced sentence in exchange for his testimony. When he denied it, Poe asked, "So you squealed on your pal so your conscience would not trouble you?"

"If you want to call it squealing," answered Dietz, "you can, I don't care."

Less than an hour into the session, O'Conor called his final witness.

"Mrs. Holtman, please take the stand."

Marie Holtman, thin and frail, rose from her seat in the first row, still dressed in mourning clothes. Her daughter and a court bailiff had to help her to the stand.

The contrast between her and Tiger Girl, sitting only a few feet away, her rouged face made up, and wearing an "expensive" white shirtwaist dress and contrasting beaver fur collar, could not have been more dramatic. The white dress may have been intended to evoke innocence, but Holtman's mourning clothes made it look garish and cheap.

O'Conor paused to allow the jury to take in these impressions. Then, speaking softly, he asked a few simple questions. "Did you see him that day after he left for work?" O'Conor asked.

"Yes," answered Mrs. Holtman.

"Where and when?"

"In the hospital of the penitentiary, about 4 p.m.," she said.

"Was he conscious or unconscious?"

"He was unconscious."

"And later he was taken to another hospital?" added O'Conor.

"Yes," she replied, "the University of Maryland."

"And you remained with him until he died?"

Speaking through a black veil, the features of her lined face softened. "Yes," she said. "He died on the next day about 5 p.m."

O'Conor paused again, letting the image of a woman sitting with her husband on his deathbed linger. Then he turned to Judge O'Dunne and spoke.

"That's our case, Your Honor. The State rests."

The entire time Marie Holtman spoke, weeping could be heard in the courtroom. Richard Whittemore looked down, a faint smile on his lips, twiddling his thumbs. His eyes never met hers.

Poe wisely chose not to cross-examine. After a fifteen-minute recess called by Judge O'Dunne, Poe began his defense of what seemed indefensible.

His opening statement was brief, formal, and to the point. He explained that he intended to prove that Holtman was killed following an altercation with Whittemore, that Holtman had grabbed Whittemore by his injured arm, and that Whittemore had simply reacted, then fled as "any other prisoner would have done . . . he determined to try to escape the consequences." Why, claimed the attorney, he had even carried Holtman back inside before fleeing.

In Buffalo, Whittemore's attorney had not called his client to the stand. This time would be different. Poe, with little chance of placing much doubt on the testimony of either Bowie or Dietz, had no other choice. The only thing between Richard Reese Whittemore and an appointment with the gallows was the silver tongue of the Candy Kid, a young man who had started out in the Fifteenth Ward, robbed and killed and talked his way into a fortune, and then, the consummate bad actor, lived ever so briefly amid the rich and powerful.

Richard Whittemore still looked the part. Smiling confidently where a moment before a widow had tearfully spoken in a broken voice, he strode to the stand cleanly shaven, hair slicked back, his suit perfectly pressed and shoes polished to a bright sheen, the best-dressed man in the room. As Kinsolving reported, he looked "like a successful bootlegger or night club proprietor telling the world 'I don't know a thing.'"

It probably wasn't the smartest getup to wear before the jury. His attire made him look like every other young gangster in Baltimore, like a playboy sheik who lived for kicks and wanted something for nothing, a shining, contemptible representative of the hordes of young men and women who had turned the world on its head.

It didn't help that since the start of the trial, eight of the eleven jurors had received penny postcards that read:

Beware the Verdict
— The Underworld

A n investigation was already under way.
After Whittemore was sworn in, Poe tried to draw a sympathetic portrait of his client, allowing him to recount his many incarcerations, beginning as a boy put away for playing hooky, all the way up to his latest sentence. He then asked, "Up to the time you killed Holtman, have you killed anyone before?"

Whittemore didn't look at Poe — he spoke to the jury. "No, sir," he said.

"Have you ever killed anyone since?"

"No, sir."

Asked about Dietz, Whittemore became more animated, snarling, "He's a liar," the last word uncurling from his mouth as a smear. Whittemore had never taken responsibility for anything and wasn't about to now. When the facts went against his version of reality, he simply dismissed them. He always had.

Then Poe patiently moved on to Whittemore's version of events in the hospital, trying to allow the jury to replace the earlier version with one he hoped they would find at least as plausible. Whittemore claimed that, after receiving treatment for his burn wound in the hospital, he'd stopped to talk to another prisoner on his way down the stairs. As he did, Holtman, at the bottom of the stairs, began bawling him out as they walked to the door leading to the yard. "We got into an argument over this," said Whittemore. After Holtman unlocked the door, he "grabbed me by the arm. It was the arm that had been burned and it hurt me fearfully."

"I swung on him with my left, hard," he said, speaking like a boxer, "and hit him on the nose and he fell down the steps."

"I went down behind him. Holtman started to get up and I grabbed him. He was reaching for his gun. My right hand groped around, and I picked up a piece of pipe I found in the areaway and struck him."

"You did not intend to kill him?" asked Poe.

"No, sir."

"Why did you strike Holtman?"

"I was afraid he was going to shoot me."

Poe then asked why he chose to escape.

"I became frightened and afraid what would happen to me for striking Holtman . . . I realized what had happened, and what would have happened if I went back.

"I would get my head beat off."

That was his story. He attacked Holtman so the guard wouldn't shoot him, and then escaped out of fear. Everyone else had it wrong or was lying. He made Bowie go with him until he made his escape so the trusty wouldn't sound an alarm.

O'Conor then pulled a fast one. He didn't cross-examine Whittemore himself, as if the defendant was not worth his time. He left that to Rowland K. Adams, his assistant. Adams let Whittemore tell the story again, hoping that each time the jury heard the cocksure account they would find it less believable.

After Whittemore stepped down, Poe called only a few more witnesses—a prisoner who contradicted Dietz, and another convict who said he overheard Bowie say he hadn't seen the guard being struck. Then, in something of a surprise, he called a series of New York detectives, including Walter Sullivan and Inspector John Coughlin, to the stand. In turn, each of the men testified that Whittemore had more or less told them the same story, both in New York before the Erie County trial and again during the return trip to New York.

That's all Poe had—Whittemore's words against everyone else's. With that, the defense rested its case. Knowing that O'Dunne was eager to move things along, Poe asked for an adjournment so he could go over evidence before making his closing argument. The trial would resume the next day.

The room, quieter and more subdued than earlier in the trial, soon emptied. The garish hats of Whittemore's female supporters suddenly seemed out of place. It was as if everyone finally realized that this wasn't just pulp entertainment, a thrilling adventure story, but a real trial about real people with real lives at stake, lives other than those of Tiger Girl and the Candy Kid.

When closing arguments began the following morning, the courtroom remained quiet. It was as if Baltimore's starstruck flappers and sheiks knew how the show was destined to end and couldn't bear to watch. O'Conor again deferred to his assistant, and Adams spoke for nearly two hours, restating the case. He concluded simply and directly. "The issue is sharply drawn," he said. "The state's contention is that Richard Whittemore killed Robert H. Holtman in a deliberate, premeditated plot to escape from the penitentiary. The defense says his act was committed in self-defense.

"It is up to you to accept either of these stories in its entirety . . . The state claims this case was one of willful, deliberate murder."

After a brief break, Poe, his face dark and solemn, followed with his summation. He admitted that he found representing his client to be "distasteful and unpleasant," given Whittemore's criminal background. Nevertheless, he said, his client was but a "pawn in the administration of justice." Whittemore, watching attentively, laughed out loud each time Poe mentioned discrepancies in the testimony of the defense witnesses.

Poe discarded Bowie's testimony as "Negro imaginativeness," a phrase that might reinforce any latent prejudice in the jury. The state, he said, "has a theory" about the crime, "a very beautiful theory, and has a darky up there to testify in support of this theory." Yet "Whittemore was justified in protecting himself, because no prison guard has the right to mistreat a prisoner." In closing, Poe claimed, "It is the burden of the State to prove to you, beyond a reasonable doubt, that the accused committed murder. The testimony does not do this, so I ask you to bring in a verdict of not guilty."

In Maryland at the time, the state, not the judge, submitted the final charge to the jury. When Poe finally exhausted his arguments for the defense, O'Conor stepped forward to set out the charge and have the final word. He asked the jury bluntly to "adequately punish this atrocious crime and earn the gratitude of the decent people of Baltimore," inferring that those in the crowd who supported Whittemore were something other than decent. He quoted the commandment "Thou shalt not kill," then amended it with the moral logic that allowed the state to kill, quoting Genesis 9:6: "Whoever shall shed a man's blood by men, shall his blood be shed." At 4:43 p.m., O'Conor asked the jury for an unqualified verdict of first-degree murder that did not include, as was the jury's right, the qualifier "without capital punishment." Sentencing would be at O'Dunne's discretion.

The jury, Whittemore, and the attorneys filed out. But the crowd barely stirred. O'Dunne had indicated that he would keep the court in session until 11 p.m. in the event of a swift verdict, and few in the crowd would risk missing that. Margaret, Rawlings Whittemore, Rawlings Jr., and his young wife all lingered together in the courtroom, as did Marie Holtman, surrounded by all three of her adult daughters.

Those in attendance had just enough time to settle in when there was a loud knock on the door that led to the jury room. After only fifty-six minutes of deliberations, the jury had reached a verdict.

A bailiff informed Judge O'Dunne, O'Conor's office, and Poe.

In his lockup, Richard Whittemore had been smoking one cigarette after another while waiting for his dinner when he heard the news. He stubbed out a final smoke, pulled on his finely tailored suit jacket, and walked out of the cell. Quick verdicts rarely brought good news. He could not have felt confident.

As her husband was escorted into the courtroom, Margaret, fearing the worst, cried quietly, dabbing her eyes with a lace handkerchief and biting her fingernails as she squirmed in her seat. Rawlings Whittemore glared angrily at those who craned their necks and gawked at his weeping daughter-in-law.

All appointed parties were seated when O'Dunne took the bench.

"The jury has arrived at a verdict," he said. "I want no demonstration of approval or disapproval. Anyone who does not live up to this order will go to jail immediately."

The jury filed into place, a few quietly making small talk.

When they were still, O'Dunne asked, "Gentlemen of the jury, have you agreed upon a verdict?" It was 5:58 p.m., one hour and thirteen minutes since deliberations had begun.

Richard Whittemore stared straight ahead, impassive. It wasn't the first time he'd listened to a verdict.

Jury foreman J. Harry Bauer answered, "We have, Your Honor." Whittemore was ordered to stand.

"Mr. Foreman," said the court clerk, "what is your verdict?"

One second, then two, then three ticked by in silence as the jury foreman turned his eyes toward a piece of paper he held in his hands. Richard Whittemore did not move. Margaret Whittemore did not breathe.

The foreman inhaled and then spoke the words, "Guilty of murder in the first degree." Everyone waited to hear if he would add the phrase "without capital punishment." Bauer looked up from the piece of paper and remained silent.

The clerk spoke again, this time addressing the entire jury: "You have heard your foreman. So say you all?" Their reply was unanimous.

Richard Whittemore began to sit. There were a few gasps and murmurs, then one shrill, startling shriek that faded to a long slow moan.

Margaret Whittemore, sitting almost directly behind her husband, slid from her seat, knees touching the floor, and began to topple over in a dead faint, her arms reaching out toward her husband.

Richard turned and, seeing Margaret on the ground, started to reach toward her, but the guards were already on the move, surrounding him on both sides as other guards flooded the court to keep the aisles clear.

Every member of the gallery stood, straining to see the fallen woman. Rawlings Sr. and Rawlings Jr. placed their arms around Margaret and held her upright. Her brother-in-law began fanning her with a folded newspaper, and a matron waved smelling salts before her face. After a few moments, she stirred, then began to sob and wail. O'Dunne ordered her removed from the courtroom. Rawlings, a bailiff, and a policeman helped her to the jury room, supporting her on each side.

As they carried her away, Richard Whittemore did not look at his wife. Instead, he fixed his eyes on the jury, searching for a pair of eyes that would stare back at his and receive their venom.

"The prisoner is remanded to the custody of the Warden," said O'Dunne. "Sentence will not be passed this week."

A detective and two guards knew the routine. They swiftly and expertly pulled Whittemore upright, then each guard cuffed one arm to his own. Whittemore did not resist. They guided him out from behind the defense table toward the aisle that led from the courtroom.

Margaret's muffled screams spilled out from the jury room.

Herbert O'Conor sat stoically at the prosecution table as Whittemore was led away. The prosecutor and the convicted man were two men on opposites sides of the era, on opposite sides of the law.

As Richard Whittemore passed, their eyes locked.

The Candy Kid suddenly lurched across the table and the murderer spat in the prosecutor's face.

Sixteen

A MORAL LESSON

The crowd erupted at the outburst, straining to see, as the spit hung on O'Conor's face. Some even stood on their seats, their eyes glued on Whittemore as he was led away. O'Dunne banged his gavel, called for order, and adjourned the court until Monday morning.

Everyone leapt from their seats at once, and the press and the gallery surged around O'Conor. Some tried to shake his hand and slap his back, others glared in anger, and reporters shouted out questions.

The crowd parted for Marie Holtman and her daughters. When she reached O'Conor, the mob fell silent. "Thank you," she said. "I am so glad ... We, my daughters ..." Then she could speak no more. O'Conor gently assisted her to a chair, and the woman sat, overcome. Poe rushed to O'Conor, apologizing for his client's behavior.

O'Conor only laughed. "That was the greatest compliment he could have paid me," said the prosecutor.

Poe knew the case was not over. There still remained the question of the sentence and appeals.

For a little over two months since his arrest in New York, the Candy Kid and Tiger Girl had been part of a daily drama, one that catapulted both from obscurity into the daily national conversation. Richard Whittemore had twice gone on trial for his life, but now his fate remained uncertain. All one could say with any certainty was that the public's fascination with the couple had yet to wane. If anything, it had only increased.

O'Conor's decision to take control of the process had resulted in a quick conviction. The *Daily News* noted that "Whittemore got no opportunities to win his case from jail beforehand, by methods beloved by sob sisters. No heart-rending family interviews went out from his cell; no life histories of a good man gone wrong because society was all to the bad." The sentence and its execution, however, would be another matter.

Whittemore was remanded to the city jail under heavy guard. Escorted through the crowds and into a waiting car, Whittemore cut loose and promised to take vengeance on the judge and prosecutor. Police protection was extended to both O'Dunne and O'Conor on their return to their homes.

Margaret and Rawlings did not emerge from the jury room until the courtroom was nearly empty, save for reporters eager to hear from Tiger Girl. Distraught and shaken, she had nothing to say. She begged a bailiff for a chance to meet with her husband but was turned down.

The press found her the next morning sitting on the porch of her mother's home, after an almost sleepless night. She wore the same blue dress with the white fur collar she had worn in court the day before, as if she had not bothered with sleep. She looked haggard and thin.

Her support of her husband was unwavering, and her criticism of the trial withering. "If Mr. O'Conor hangs Reese," she said, "I hope he comes back to haunt him for life. And I know he will do it. My husband would not hurt a flea. Nobody knows that better than I do, for I've lived with him for years." She omitted the fact that, since their marriage, the couple had spent barely a year sharing the same bed.

"He didn't get a fair trial, but I am sure we will win in the end," she said. "But sometimes it seems that we haven't got a chance. My husband didn't mean to kill the guard and O'Conor knows it. It was self-defense, but Reese's record was against him.

"What can I do? What can I do?" she cried. "I haven't got a lot of money and I can't hire a lot of lawyers. But O'Conor will live to see the day when the sin of convicting my husband will weigh heavily on his conscience.

"Why can't the jailer be white about it? They wouldn't let me in to see him.

What harm would it do if I went over to jail and tried to cheer him for a few minutes?" she asked. "But they wouldn't even give me that much."

"I don't care for myself. I am thinking of Reese. He was kind and gentle. He was so good to me. Surely they will not hang him, hang my loving husband."

P oe was incensed by O'Dunne's handling of the trial. While Margaret held court on the front stoop, he was already preparing an appeal.

On Saturday, he filed a motion requesting a new trial, arguing that the verdict was not in accordance with the evidence, that premeditation was not proven, and that Whittemore, at worst, should have been convicted only of murder in the second degree. For the moment, filing the motion would preclude O'Dunne's sentencing. In response, O'Conor pushed to have the sentencing hearing scheduled as soon as possible.

On Monday, Margaret finally received permission to visit her husband in jail, but the setting was tightly controlled. She stayed for only thirty minutes, alone, and was not allowed to touch her husband. With few exceptions, from now on their meetings would take place with no reporters listening to their furtive conversations and any plans they made for an uncertain future.

In Buffalo, Richard Whittemore had joked that he'd sell his story to the papers for $5,000. In Baltimore, it was still for sale. What little money he had — or at least what little police had found — had been confiscated. And although there were still rumors that he was receiving some assistance from his contacts in the underworld, the Kraemers no longer had any motivation to help him. Their trial was just starting in New York, where Paladino and Unkelbach were prepared to testify against both the brothers and Shuffles Goldberg in the Prip trial.

Whittemore was on his own. All he and Margaret had of any value was the story of Tiger Girl and the Candy Kid. In fact, he was already writing his life story. Margaret had told the press virtually nothing about their past lives together, and what little she had divulged was often wrong. Her husband had a story he could sell, and there was no sense giving it away.

Gerald Chapman was one of the only criminals of the age who approached Whittemore in notoriety. His execution in early April 1926 had briefly knocked

Whittemore off the front pages of the tabloids. But before he'd died, word was that Chapman had sold his story for a pretty penny. Whittemore now planned to do the same. It may have been simply a way to make some dough and get in a few sucker punches at all those he felt had wronged him, or it may have been a last-ditch effort to sway public opinion and save his life.

The *Baltimore Post* bought his story, although it is unclear precisely how much they finally paid. But Richard Whittemore didn't leave it to someone else to tell his story, like the movie stars who hired ghostwriters. He scratched out his story on his own.

On May 29, Poe appeared before the Supreme Bench, which included O'Dunne, to argue his motion for a new trial, citing insufficient evidence to support the first-degree murder verdict, errors in rulings made by the court, and questions about O'Dunne's use of common law to prevent Poe from questioning the jurors.

He also claimed to have new evidence. To that end he produced an affidavit from Colonel Thomas Sweezey, who had agreed to help to show his opposition to the death penalty, and who probably hoped to extract some revenge over his dismissal in the wake of Whittemore's escape.

Poe had questioned John Bowie about his mental state, and Bowie had denied having any illness. However, Sweezey claimed, "in the early stages of his confinement [Bowie] seemed at times to be mentally deranged and suffering from fits of melancholia ..., during which time it was necessary to confine Bowie in solitary confinement because he would destroy things in his cell." Bowie's testimony could not be trusted, Sweezey claimed. Without that, there could be no first-degree murder charge.

But O'Conor, too, had secured affidavits regarding Bowie's mental health, including one from Arthur Herring, the state commissioner of mental hygiene. Herring had found "no symptoms indicating delusions or hallucinations" and concluded that Bowie "is a reliable witness and mentally competent."

While Poe exhausted his options, Richard Whittemore did what he could to help himself. He spent the next few days furiously scribbling out his tale, which he probably was allowed to pass to Poe, Rawlings, or Margaret, his only allowed visitors, to deliver to the *Daily Post*. On Wednesday, June 2, to no one's surprise, the Supreme Bench denied Poe's motion for a new trial. In another week, O'Dunne would pronounce sentence, and Richard Whittemore would learn whether he would go to the gallows or spend the rest of his life either plotting an escape or doing enough good time to one day earn parole. After all, he was only twenty-four years old, and it was rare at the time for a life sentence to truly mean life. Even if he served another twenty-five years in prison, he'd be out before he turned fifty.

Two days later, on Friday, June 4, the first of ten daily installments of Richard Whittemore's personal appeal appeared in the *Baltimore Daily Post*; it would later be syndicated nationwide. A portion of the story—nearly fifteen thousand words in its entirety—would appear every day but Sunday.

The newspaper touted Whittemore's tale as "one of the most amazing articles ever written" and claimed that "every word of the story was written by the notorious bandit himself while confined in a cell at the city jail. Not even a comma has been changed by the *Post*." It cautioned, however, that "the *Post* does not vouch for the truth of his story. Whittemore claims every word is true. The *Post* offers it for what it is worth, believing it to be the biggest news story of the year." To prove the veracity of the piece, the *Post* even reprinted a facsimile of the first page in the author's own handwriting.

Whittemore's title?

"A Moral Lesson."

"Why," it began, "do I call this history of my life a moral lesson when I am in the shadow of the hangman's noose? Or maybe sentenced to spend the rest of my life in a living hell is perhaps what you will ask?

"I am only naming it after the cause, in the closing argument of the district attorney in asking the jury of 12 of your citizens to bring in a verdict for that cause alone."

The reference was to O'Conor, who Whittemore recalled had asked in his summation for a conviction due to the "moral lesson" it contained. This muddled beginning was proof enough that the story was written in Whittemore's own hand, although, as the *Post* pointed out, Whittemore framed the story as an object lesson to illustrate "that it does not pay to break the law." As Whittemore himself wrote, "If this story shall reach one wayward boy or girl and herd them back to the straight and narrow, I can at least know or say I did one good. And if I should die it shall not be in vain." Perhaps Poe had suggested creating a narrative to place Whittemore and his deeds in the best possible light. Part biography, part diatribe, part bitter reprisal, "A Moral Lesson" would prove to be entirely self-serving. In it, Whittemore took almost no responsibility whatsoever for anything at all.

In regard to the raw facts of his early life and upbringing, the first few installments are reasonably accurate and occasionally insightful. But once Whittemore leaves reform schools and embarks on more serious crimes, nothing is ever his fault. From his point of view, his criminal behaviors were the fault of society and reformers who tried to "break us as they would a horse or some other dumb animal." His arrests while serving in the Navy? Due to the lies of others. The missing hacksaw blades in Elmira that extended his sentence? An accounting error. His inability to find work? Police harassment. His arrests for robbery? The fault of squealers and drug addict companions. Richard committed crimes only when forced by others or by society, and even then he never harmed anyone. His convictions? Frame jobs by crooked cops and prosecutors.

Whittemore was careful only to cop to crimes the police already knew of and to protect the Kraemers, who he claimed "had nothing to do with any of those robberies" and were "only acquaintances," while taking credit himself for masterminding the Goudvis job. The real responsibility, however, lay with society. "You are to blame," he wrote, "for your crime waves, and every day hold-ups or robberies, for it is you who make the laws and help to break them." He cited Prohibition as an example. His own motives were always pure and never about personal gain.

And Margaret? She was "my only and true pal, my wife, one who knows me as none other." And by the way, she never knew anything about anything.

In the end, if executed, he promised to "die as I have lived—defiantly and spectacularly, and thinking what I might have been. My last thought will be with my wife, praying she shall receive a fair break in life, after I am gone."

The story said just enough to titillate readers, for each to find enough there to justify their own opinion of him. For his fans, there was just enough of their own story in his to justify their notion of Whittemore as a tragic, misunderstood romantic. They too had walked the streets looking for work, seeking good times, easy money, romance, and a better life.

They just hadn't been as brave, or as stupid, as Richard Whittemore to do anything about it and commit murder along the way.

Readers were only halfway through the document when Whittemore was called into court on June 9 for sentencing. If the intention of "A Moral Lesson" was to sway O'Dunne, it was a spectacular failure, but if the goal was to rally Tiger Girl and the Candy Kid's rabid followers, it did the trick.

That morning, when Whittemore was delivered from the courtroom lockup, the corridors of the Criminal Courts Building were crammed with perfumed young flappers and men whose attire mimicked the Candy Kid's. The courtroom itself was overflowing, the crowd packed tighter than on any dance floor. Rawlings Whittemore sat at a table with Poe.

Margaret had been allowed to enter through the judge's chambers in order to avoid the crowd, and now she stood at the threshold of the courtroom, with all eyes on her, awaiting her husband's arrival. Suddenly, she turned and raced back inside, slamming the door behind her, and could be heard crying.

A moment later, Whittemore, handcuffed to two guards, entered from a side door and was escorted to the witness stand. "Take the handcuffs off," ordered the judge. To hear his sentence, Whittemore would stand alone. O'Dunne asked if there was anything he wished to say.

He played it cool. "I want to thank the court for appointing Mr. Edgar Allen Poe to defend me," he said. Then, taking a page from his life story, he added, "I want to say that it was not premeditated murder."

O'Dunne stared at him for a full minute. Whittemore looked back passively, his face blank and bored, as if waiting for an order he'd placed with a hot dog vendor to be filled. Finally, O'Dunne spoke.

"Richard Reese Whittemore, you had all the means at your disposal that you are reputed to have had ... You had a fair and impartial trial. The jury heard evidence for three days and they heard an able and eloquent address by Mr. Poe. The jury rendered what I consider the only possible verdict under the evidence and under the law. I am not insensible to the fact that the Legislature vests in the court a discretionary power in passing sentence for first degree murder."

Whittemore's fans looked at each other, women holding hands, some praying. Maybe that meant life.

Then O'Dunne, breaking protocol, stood. Those who hoped to hear him pronounce a life sentence shuddered.

From his desk, he lifted a carefully worded statement typed on court stationery, held it before him, and started to read.

"Now, therefore, Richard Reese Whittemore," said O'Dunne, speaking slowly and solemnly, "I sentence you to be taken to the Maryland Penitentiary, to remain until such a day as the governor shall appoint, to be taken by the sheriff, and hanged by the neck until you are dead."

There were gasps, and a pause. Margaret's cries could no longer be heard. Whittemore was stoic, his face unflinching, his eyes betraying nothing.

O'Dunne finished with the words, "And may God have mercy on your soul." The final syllable echoed in the silent courtroom.

Richard Whittemore slowly raised both hands, the perfect picture of a martyr accepting his fate, and held them out passively. Two deputies handcuffed themselves to each arm and walked Whittemore across the courtroom, then out the side entrance to the lockup. He stared straight ahead.

The show was over, and the crowd raced from the courtroom and spread through the halls, word of the sentence passing from one person to another, as the newspaper messengers raced away with copy, eager to send out a bulletin.

Margaret hadn't been able to stand the wait. She'd left the judge's chambers by a back entrance, paced in a corridor, then found a place to sit, utterly alone, in the probation office. A spectator walked by and, unaware that she was inside, remarked to someone, as if reporting on the weather, "Well, they're gonna hang him."

Margaret shrieked and once again collapsed in a faint. The probation officer, a Mrs. Hickman, hurried to her side and revived her with a glass of water. Then Margaret began weeping again. Reporters, scurrying through the courthouse corridors, found her and gathered around, pressing close, firing questions. She screamed at them, "Please go away, please go away!" Tired now of center stage, she fainted once again. Hickman shooed them from the room.

Rawlings Whittemore found his way to the office and shielded her from prying eyes. The probation officer escorted Margaret to the courthouse lockup, where she was briefly allowed to see her husband.

The room was crowded with reporters and cops. Surrounded by others watching their every move, the couple held each other for fifteen minutes, Tiger Girl mostly weeping, the Candy Kid keeping it cool. When the guards began to usher her away, their embrace broke and she blurted out, "Good-bye, Dick."

They did not kiss and would not place their arms around each other again.

Outside the courthouse, more than three thousand people had congregated, not to see a killer sent off to die, but to see someone else—the Candy Kid. Earlier that morning, they had read the latest installment of his story, where Whittemore had written of leaving the penitentiary the first time: "If there ever was a man or boy who wanted a chance to go straight, it was I." It was then, after finding it impossible to get a job, that "I decided that if society was laying like a snake in the grass for me to become careless so it could strike, I would strike at it in the only way I knew how. I decided I was not going to be broke any longer."

There was a long, sad tradition in Maryland of lynch mobs tearing prisoners from the grasp of the state and extracting their own form of justice, but this crowd was not out for vengeance. Their desire was to see Whittemore go free, and if they had their way, he would have found safe harbor in the home of almost anyone on the street.

Hordes of police moved in, protecting their prisoner and trying to clear the way. Whittemore was stuffed into a police car, part of a motorcade to bring him safely to the penitentiary.

The crowd then broke through and surrounded the vehicles. As they slowly pulled away, inching forward, the mob reluctantly parted. Hands reached out as Whittemore's car passed, while men in blue shoved and pushed with all their might to open a path.

It took two full blocks before the road opened, the way cleared, and Richard Whittemore sped to his final destination.

Moments later, the motorcade pulled up at the Maryland State Penitentiary, but not at the main entrance, where another crowd had gathered. Instead, the cars stopped at the very gate through which Whittemore had made his escape.

He was walked back inside, taking the reverse route by which he had made his escape, and led nearly past the very spot where he had struck down Holtman, then through the yard into the detention room.

Guards stripped him of his silk shirt, finely tailored jacket, tie, and pants, put his clothes inside a paper bag marked with his name, and handed him the standard-issue prison garb. Whittemore was then taken to a part of the penitentiary where he had never spent time. The cell was on the second floor of a building next to the hospital where Whittemore had killed Holtman and alongside the baseball diamond where he once played third base, close enough to hear the call of balls and strikes.

The death tier.

Six cells faced six others, separated by a corridor. On one end was a door, and beyond that door was the gallows.

All the other cells, save one, were empty. In one of the half-dozen window-less cells sat Isaac Benson, a young Black prisoner awaiting hanging for the murder of his common-law wife and her lover. Prison officials placed Whittemore at the end of the tier, nearest to the gallows, with the door leading to his demise visible between the bars.

For the remainder of his life, his world would now be this cell. Again under twenty-four-hour watch, he would not be allowed into the yard or into any other portion of the prison. Here he would eat his meals and smoke, read the papers and the pulps, and mark off the days until his death. From a small window he could see only the wall of a prison workshop and a small patch of grass.

Prison officials were taking no chances. Each time a visitor entered the death tier, guards set up a floor-to-ceiling steel-mesh barricade three feet in front of the bars, the wire lattice so tight that not even a toothpick could pass through. Margaret would now speak to a man she could barely even see through the screen. Two guards made privacy impossible.

The date of Whittemore's execution was not yet set. There was still a slender chance he might not hang, the smallest of threads. Poe planned a final appeal to Maryland State Appellate Court. If that failed, then Governor Albert Ritchie would set the date of the execution. Then, unless Ritchie either commuted his sentence or, even less likely, a higher court found some reason to intervene, Whittemore would soon hang by the neck.

. . .

On June 18, Poe played his last hand and filed a bill of exception, petitioning for a retrial. He argued that O'Dunne's ruling to bar the questioning
of jurors was illegal and Whittemore should be retried.

Poe argued his case on June 28 before the full bench of eight judges. They
were sympathetic, to a point. One jurist, William Atkins, noted that O'Dunne's
jury selection process "looked like a lottery." But his was only one voice of
eight.

The court upheld the verdict on July 9. Margaret learned about the decision
when a newsboy delivered a newspaper to her door. As soon as she read it, she
shrieked once and fainted. Her mother carried her inside, and a reporter interviewed her at her bedside.

"Reese is a man," she said, "a real man and a whole lot better in many ways
than those who are sending him to the gallows." He was framed, she said. Dietz
lied and so did Bowie, but it was more than that. "The whole thing boils down
to the fact that Herbert O'Conor is running for re-election and he guaranteed
a hanging." Her husband was convicted, she said, "merely because he was Richard Reese Whittemore and he had a record . . . My husband's life is as precious
as a guard and he was only defending himself."

Margaret knew she was running out of time, and money. "It has cost $120
so far to take the case to the court of appeals. I am ready to spend anything to
save him. I love him and will stick by him to the end. He is the only thing in
the world that I love." Only a few months before, $120 had meant nothing more
than a few hours of fun. At her visit later that day, Deputy Warden Kennedy,
perhaps feeling a pang of compassion, allowed her to approach Whittemore
around the screen. They kissed through the bars for what was likely the last
time.

After Warden Brady informed Whittemore of the court's decision on his
appeal, Whittemore shrugged. "It is only as I expected." He was growing tired
of the wait and starting to become circumspect. "I'm not going to do any more
about it," he told the warden. "I guess I'm done for. The quicker they hang me
I'll like it. I want to get it over."

Governor Ritchie announced that he would sign Whittemore's death warrant and that the hanging would take place after the customary thirty-day wait. All that remained to keep Richard Whittemore from swinging from the gallows were miracles and prayers cast to the heavens.

T he whole Whittemore gang was going down at once. Back in New York, the Kraemers, after being found guilty, had been sentenced to forty years each in Sing Sing. Shuffles Goldberg was found guilty as well and received two concurrent twenty-year terms. Unkelbach and Paladino, the squealers, would eventually receive shorter sentences.

Margaret, however, continued the fight on all fronts, for the death penalty had suddenly increased the stakes, as well as the number of parties interested in the outcome. In the wake of the Progressive Era, the death penalty itself had come under increased scrutiny. Some were disturbed by the spectacle of the public executions; others noted the cruelty of executions by hanging, as both the electric chair and the gas chamber had been developed as more humane ways for the state to inflict death; and still others objected to the death penalty on a purely moral basis. High-profile cases such as Richard Whittemore's, and particularly death sentences leveled at White criminals, galvanized those opposed to the practice.

Whittemore's cause was taken up by a female candidate for governor, Virginia Peters-Parkhurst, who was Maryland state president of the Susan B. Anthony Society and would later also run for the US Senate. A longtime opponent of the death penalty and advocate for equal rights, Peters-Parkhurst first voiced her opposition to Whittemore's execution at the conclusion of the trial, when she also petitioned on behalf of the other condemned man, Isaac Benson. Margaret then approached her during the appeals process, and Peters-Parkhurst, again voicing her support, began a petition campaign to plead with Ritchie for a commutation. She was joined in her efforts by the Prisoners' Relief Society. Together, they would eventually accumulate over four thousand signatures asking for mercy.

Whittemore's more fanatical supporters were also throwing everything against the wall, hoping something would stick. One of Margaret's neighbors started her own petition campaign, a young man publicly offered to be executed in Whittemore's stead, and one young woman even offered that it was she, not Whittemore, who had killed Holtman. That claim would prove as ineffective as the petitions.

On July 14, after turning down various petitions and pleas for commutation, Governor Ritchie signed Whittemore's death warrant without ceremony and authorized his execution on August 13 between midnight and 1 a.m. It was the earliest time possible, given the mandatory thirty-day wait.

During her visit later that day, Margaret—now allowed only to stand before her husband's cell but not approach it—told him the date had been set. He acted as if he had not heard her, perhaps because the guard was there, and immediately began speaking about something else, as if she hadn't said anything at all.

It was left to Warden Brady to formally inform Whittemore of the warrant the following morning. The two chatted amiably, as if it were just another day. "Can't I have some lettuce and tomatoes with my dinner?" mused Whittemore, "I like 'em."

When Brady told him the purpose of his visit, Whittemore smirked. "It doesn't make any difference. My wife told me about the date the other day and I read it in the papers. I expected this warrant along in a day or two. So you see, you're not giving me any surprise."

Then Brady got to business. He pulled the order from his pocket and read the order aloud. Richard Whittemore would be put to death on August 13, between midnight and 1 a.m.

Friday the thirteenth.

Whittemore, whose composure had led the press to begin referring to him as a "marble man," sat in his cell as Brady spoke and said nothing.

Puzzled by his lack of reaction, Brady stepped away from the cell and then stood some distance away, out of sight of the prisoner. Maybe he wondered if the man might finally break down and cry, pry at the bars in anger, or scream for God's mercy.

He listened to Whittemore rise from the bed, then heard his footsteps on the concrete floor of the cell as he slowly paced, back and forth, back and forth.

Then Brady heard something else. Straining to hear, he realized that the prisoner was humming. The warden even recognized the melody.

"Yes, we have no bananas, we have no bananas today."

He told his staff to make sure Whittemore received lettuce and tomatoes with his next meal. A dead man walking, he could have whatever he wanted from here on. Except life.

Seventeen

———

A GAUDY SHOW

The state of Maryland had decided to kill Richard Whittemore. There was nothing more to be done.

On July 23, Whittemore received a vision of the future that awaited him. That night, the only other resident of the penitentiary's death tier, Isaac Benson, was scheduled to be hung.

There was no great outcry and no herculean effort was made to save Benson from the gallows, apart from the usual protests from reformers and, in Benson's case, the objections of the *Afro-American,* Baltimore's Black newspaper. From Whittemore's cell, he could hear the gallows being tested as the trap door was sprung again and again, and he watched as the prison chaplain and other clergymen made visits to the prisoner. Benson would die in near-anonymity. Only the minimum number of witnesses required by law would attend his death.

Whittemore and Benson were not close. Their cells were not adjacent, and Whittemore retained much of the racial prejudice common among most White Marylanders of the era. But through his various incarcerations, and even from his time in the cabarets, Whittemore had spent more time in the company of Blacks than most Baltimoreans of his generation. He and Benson had talked now and then, calling out blindly to each other from their separate cells, and they shared a unique bond as the only two residents of death row. During Benson's final hours, the two men indulged in gallows humor and could be heard laughing.

That night, as the hour of Benson's hanging approached, Whittemore's guards placed the screen in front of his cell and covered it with cloth, so he would not see Benson pass. But as the young Black man made his walk to the gallows and passed Whittemore's cell, he called out, "Good-by, Candy Kid."

Richard Whittemore made no reply and soon fell asleep.

Margaret refused to give up. It seemed as if she and Richard had known each other forever. For the last five years she had been his wife, and he her husband, and despite all they had gone through, arrests and imprisonments and escapes and robberies and trials, nightlong parties and poverty, weeks in hotels and in hiding, through it *all*, she had always stuck by him. She was not about to give up now. Margaret visited Richard as often as the state of Maryland would allow. She wrote him almost every day, and he wrote back. The words "till death do us part" apparently meant something, at least to her.

Margaret made two final, desperate attempts to save her husband's life. On July 28, Poe visited Ritchie to appeal for clemency, and he was followed into the governor's office by Margaret, carrying her petition now bearing five thousand signatures .

She arrived at Ritchie's Baltimore office in the Union Trust Building in full Tiger Girl regalia: a white silk dress with sable etching, and a picture hat with the same combination. The office stenographers, who had staked out the elevator, swooned when they saw her outfit.

Yet even such a fetching getup couldn't inspire sympathy in the governor. There would be no clemency.

Margaret spoke to the *Baltimore News* the next day, now dressed in a simple gingham dress and cuddling her dog. She was bitter. "Governor Ritchie had his mind made up beforehand. I knew as soon as he shook hands with me in his office yesterday it was all over."

"I am heartbroken," she said. "When the state of Maryland hangs Dick it will be taking two lives. I cannot live without him. He has been the whole world to me."

She continued, "I can't cry. When one is heartbroken tears are so useless." She blamed the justice system, saying, "There are two kinds—one for a rich man, another for the poor. The rich can buy their way to justice." She'd certainly seen evidence of that—and plenty of the paper's readers had too. She went on, "But we didn't have money enough. If we had there might be a different story today. Dick will be hanged on general principles and as a lesson to others." She claimed to be spending an hour in church with her mother, every day, praying. But day after day passed with no answers from on high.

She asked Poe to take the case to the Supreme Court, but he refused, telling her there were no grounds to do so.

The weekend before the scheduled execution, Margaret and Rawlings contacted attorney Ira Pendleton, known for his success in obtaining last-minute writs of habeas corpus and taking on cases few others would. Proceeds from the publication of "A Moral Lesson" likely covered the lawyer's fees.

Pendleton, a reputable lawyer in Baltimore's Black community, was not often approached to represent White clients. But he accepted the case on principle. As he later explained the reasons behind his decision: "One was the convicted man's life: another was the case itself and the other the welfare of my race. I believe colored men should join in any fight where the rights of any human being are at stake."

He prepared a writ of habeas corpus, basing his plea on a discrepancy between the Fourteenth Amendment of the US Constitution and the fifteenth article of the Maryland constitution, which gave the jury the right to judge both the law and the facts, contradicting the authority of the federal constitution.

As soon as the state provided a counterargument, Judge Robert Stanton ruled immediately in the state's favor, saying, "When the people ratified the constitution they showed they were content with this procedure, and it is due process of law in this community." In other words, the state would not stand in the way of the execution. At the same time, Warden Brady removed John Bowie from the Maryland State Penitentiary to the House of Correction. Other prisoners were threatening to take his life for testifying against Whittemore.

As Whittemore's fate came into focus, officials prepared for the hanging. In the gallows, they attached a two-hundred-pound weight to a new length of rope, then dropped it through the gallows door, both to test its strength and to stretch it. Maryland was not willing to risk either the rope breaking or the weight of the body stretching enough so the hanged man would bounce on the floor.

After the hearing, O'Conor's office learned that Pendleton planned a final petition to a justice of the US Supreme Court. Fearing last-minute interference, Baltimore authorities hounded Pendleton to prevent him from leaving the state, having him tailed by three detectives who were prepared to take him into custody. That wouldn't have been legal, but they hardly seemed to care. At this point they would allow nothing to stop the execution. The state had tired of Whittemore and all he represented.

Pendleton still managed to slip away from his home, eluding the detectives during a car chase when the detective's vehicle stalled. The attorney got onto a train to present his appeal to the esteemed associate justice Oliver Wendell Holmes, in Massachusetts.

When Pendleton arrived the next day at Holmes's home in Beverly Farms north of Boston, Holmes agreed to meet the lawyer in his parlor. The jurist listened for nearly an hour as Pendleton argued the case. When he was through, Holmes sat for a moment, palms pressed to his skull, then picked up his pen:

> Writ of error denied on the grounds that alleged errors do not affect jurisdiction of the trial court and therefore were not a ground for habeas corpus, and further, it does not appear Whittemore was deprived of any rights under the Constitution of the United States.

Holmes then signed his name to the document and gave the pen to Pendleton as a souvenir of his audience before a member of the Court.

There was no further recourse. Whittemore would hang on schedule. When word reached Baltimore, an *Evening Sun* reporter rang repeatedly at Margaret's door until she answered, opening the door only partway.

"Well?" she said.

The reporter told her the court had denied the writ. "Have they?" she cried. She tossed her head back, added, "Well, thank you for the news," and slammed the door in the reporter's face.

When her husband learned the news from a guard, he said, "Just as I expected. They made up their minds to railroad me. I'm to be the horrible example."

Margaret now began a long public keening for her husband. She was allowed to visit each day, sometimes with Rawlings and her mother and sometimes with Rawlings Jr. and his wife. Crowds routinely followed her down the street and watched her enter and leave the penitentiary. She appeared alternately buoyed and fearful, sometimes smiling and saying thank-you for her husband, other times acting frantic and panicked. Photographers and reporters continued to stalk her no matter her mood, asking the same questions over and over: *What did he say? Is he scared? Is there news? Can you kiss?*

That's what seemed to bother her most, the prohibition on a final kiss. Her husband was about to die, and yet they wouldn't let her touch him, wouldn't let her put her arm around his neck and touch her lips to his, not even for a second. She cried, "Why can't they let me go behind the screen in front of his cell just once, to put my arms around him and bid him good-by?

"Reese has repented," she said. "If they hang him he will go straight to heaven.

"I'm so sick," she continued. "It will be terrible to see Reese for the last time on earth. But it won't be the last time I see him. He will go to heaven if they hang him and I will see him there.

"I am going to muster up my courage and be as brave as I can."

Warden Brady was unmoved by her words. "I will allow no scenes," he said. The clock kept ticking, and nothing Margaret said now could slow it down.

As darkness fell on the warm humid evening of August 12, heat lightning flashed on the horizon and automobile traffic on the Fallsway and on the streets surrounding the penitentiary swelled. Flivvers and jalopies and fancy sedans spilled into the streets, windows and tops opened to the still summer air, all of them packed full with young men and women, flappers and sheiks, matrons and older men, even children.

Police wouldn't allow the cars to park along the streets bordering the prison walls, so one after another they simply pulled over on the Fallsway, first a dozen cars and then hundreds. As the crowds piled out, the press reported that "the vicinity of the prison took on the atmosphere of a carnival." They all marched toward the penitentiary, a slow trickle becoming a flood. Children skipped and chased after each other, while couples held hands, laughing and shouting and moving as if penitents to some macabre shrine.

As they walked, some sipped from flasks, bottles of beer clanking in pockets. Couples kissing on the corner called each other "Tiger and Kid" and "Margie and Dick." Young Baltimore, giggling and smiling, was on parade, brought together to see what they could of the end of a story they had spent so many pennies on reading about in the papers, all now about to reach a climax, a story that they somehow felt a part of, and that in some way told part of their own.

Some played ukuleles and others sang along in harmony. Opportunistic ice cream and hot dog vendors worked the crowd, shilling their refreshments, calling out "Ice cold pop. Good to the last drop, like the Candy Kid himself." The crowd was not out for blood or retribution, nor to celebrate a man's demise or cheer his death. Instead, "the streets were jammed with people laughing, shouting, singing, dancing," the scene resembling a raucous, oddly joyful wake, everyone coming to see the end of the show and the final curtain come down.

It was also garish and vulgar, tasteless and loud. The *Washington Post* reported that "young women [chewed] gum and [were] free in their use of cosmetics," like the crowd at Carlin's before a dance contest. The streets outside the penitentiary were a place to see and be seen, to say you were there, to show either that you cared or that you didn't—that it didn't matter that a man had been killed and another soon would be.

The crowd only quieted as they fell beneath the shadows of the prison walls, where armed guards holding guns reminded them that a man was about to die. Fifty police roamed Eager and Forrest Streets around the prison, keeping the crowd moving. The residents of the row houses opposite the prison piled onto their stoops to watch the parade.

Bannon's, a beer hall opposite the jail where the booze flowed open and free, was packed to the gills with pressmen. Typewriters lined the bar, and a temporary telegraph station was set up on a long table, with a half-dozen operators at the ready, all tapping out dispatches as fast as the reporters and messengers delivered frantic, breathless copy. *Candy Kid's final meal! Tiger Girl's hat! Last kiss denied!*

At about 11 p.m., members of the press, witnesses, and the privileged few others with tickets squeezed through the revelers like waiters in a crowded bar to get to the prison's main entrance. Their tickets were checked, and they were all ushered into the prison's main lobby, which rapidly became crowded.

There were supposed to be only forty-four witnesses, but more than a hundred managed to acquire the right credential. About a third of them were pressmen, including reporters from all the local papers and most of the national ones—Frank Dolan of the *Daily News;* Gene Fowler, the best-known and highest-paid magazine writer in the country, covering the hanging for a syndicate; and even H. L. Mencken of the *Baltimore Sun*. Mencken actually liked hangings, in particular their resolute finality. He would later write of Whittemore that "the victim is himself a brute, with little more sensitiveness, than a fox." He called Whittemore both a "moron" and a "happy half-wit," adding that "the whole thing, to him, was a gaudy show." As it was for many members of the press and witnesses, including Mencken himself.

At twelve minutes before midnight, a guard rapped on his desk with a ruler, quieting the guests, who then surged toward an open door that led to the yard. The witnesses, wrote Fremont Haldey of the *Baltimore News,* were "old and young, fat and thin, decorously clad and in knickers, but inevitably each smoking . . . just the type one sees at a prizefight. Tonight they are to witness some real bloodletting."

They all walked single file toward the gallows via a circular iron staircase, wide enough for only one man, that wound down and then out to the prison yard, past the foundry and the shoe shop where Whittemore last worked. Dim light leaked from the windows of the silent cell tiers above. After passing the warden's office, everyone stopped short of the baseball diamond, then turned and passed through a door into the death house. They stubbed out their cigarettes on the ground as they entered, removing their hats. In the chamber itself, which in its dimensions resembled a squash court, two guards stood on the gallows balcony, leaning on the rail beneath two harsh arc lamps that cast dramatic shadows on the walls. The hanging rope and noose, its length measured and tested, hung loosely from the ceiling, threaded through an iron hook, then down in an inverted V where the end was wrapped to a large cleat akin to the mounting used to tie a boat to a dock. When the trap door was sprung, Whittemore would drop from the eighteen-foot-high balcony a full fifteen feet, far enough for his 160 pounds of deadweight to break his neck.

Once inside, the crowd pushed forward but pulled up short of the balcony to see the condemned man enter.

That is, all the men but one. Gene Fowler, the magazine writer, who probably earned more in a week than most of the others earned all year, had witnessed an execution before and been profoundly disturbed. He didn't want to be there, and as the minutes ticked by he made a quip to a guard that got him thrown out, but he still had a deadline to hit. A colleague, Edward Doherty of the *New York Mirror,* covered for Fowler and later filed an account of the hanging that began: "A gray ghost went shrieking out of the death chamber in Maryland this morning, a gray ghost shrieking with laughter . . . watched over by a horde of insufferable busy-bodies who thought they were better men," who later "filed out into the morning light to dream horrid fantasies and wonder if civilization is here yet," an over-the-top example of tabloid journalism at its florid worst.

Fowler, who like so many of his contemporaries later found himself in Hollywood writing screenplays, was embarrassed by the resulting story that bore his name and appeared in papers all over the country, but at least he didn't have to watch a man die.

Earlier that morning, Warden Brady had asked Whittemore what he wanted for his last meal. He asked for a first-class Italian feast, telling the warden the best place to get that was from Marconi's on Saratoga Street. He asked for wine too, figuring it was worth a shot. The warden complied with the meal request—salami, ravioli, spaghetti, and honeydew melon—but said no to the wine. He asked to have the food delivered at 2 p.m.

Richard was eating when Margaret and her mother, accompanied by Rawlings Whittemore and Rawlings Jr. and his wife, left North Gilmor Street by trolley for their last visit. Somehow word spread that they were on their way, and by the time the trolley arrived at the final stop a short distance from the prison, hundreds of women and children stood waiting for them. Police outside the prison were dispatched to see them safely inside. After registering for the visit, they were sent back out and told to walk down Madison Street to the entrance by the hospital — one last indignity. Rawlings Whittemore and his son threatened the crowd with their fists to leave the women alone. Margaret held a newspaper over her face.

They arrived at 3 p.m. and were allowed sixty minutes with the condemned man, with the steel bars of his cell and the mesh screen between them. When Margaret asked to see him alone, she was turned down.

Richard Whittemore was more composed than any of his visitors. Margaret could barely speak between her sobs. "Don't take it too hard, honey, it had to be. You stuck with me and you're a good kid. They can never take our love away from us," he told her. "They've got it in for me and they're going through with it. Be brave . . . Don't worry, Chickie, my last thoughts will be of you."

After sixty minutes on the dot, a guard told them all it was time to go. "Dick, Dick, they're taking you away from me," she screamed, crying and beating her fists against the wire screen. "Oh let me in, let me in, they're taking you away forever! I don't want to live without you. Oh I can't, I can't leave you!"

Her brother-in-law and father-in-law led her away, but at the end of the tier she broke away and stood before the guard, pleading, "Won't you let me kiss him goodby? Pleeease! I shall never see him again!" The guard said something about the rules and pried her hand from the screen.

As Rawlings Sr. and Rawlings Jr. led her away, the last Richard Whittemore heard of his wife were her anguished screams. The mob outside played Pied Piper again as the Whittemores walked back down the street to the prison's main entrance. Margaret signed for her husband's belongings: $100 in cash, a blue suit with white pinstripes, and a gray fedora hat. Warden Brady took pity on the family and called them a cab.

• • •

The Candy Kid's last few hours dragged on, and he tried to rush them along, reading adventure stories, smoking, writing, lying on his cot, and politely receiving visits from prison clergymen. Whittemore neither asked nor expected to receive anything from the divine. As one newspaper noted, he was determined to "hold to his own gods till the end."

Sometime after dark, Black prisoners, according to custom, began singing old spirituals, long and slow and mournful. The words, enveloped by the prison's granite walls, did not reach those gathered outside, who grew more still as the night went on. Other prisoners periodically beat on the bars of their cells with tin cups, the cacophony waxing and waning before fading out as midnight approached.

The prison chaplain, Charles Biggs, spent the last few hours near Whittemore's cell. But Whittemore wasn't much interested in talking with him. He seemed resigned, untroubled, as unconcerned by his own death as he'd been by Holtman's.

He spent most of his last minutes chatting with a guard. "I'm gonna go game," Whittemore told him. "The whole world is against me because of my past reputation. They think I'm gonna put up a fight before you fellows wrap that old noose around my neck. But you can take my word for it that I'll go down game. I won't make any trouble for anyone. I'll show them that I'll be the same game guy dying that I was living."

Whittemore seemed determined to play the part of the tough guy until the final curtain. He knew his role, a role he seemed to have known since he was in short pants and a judge warned him he was headed down the wrong path. "Death isn't such a hard proposition after all," he said. "It's harder on my wife than me."

As the crowd of witnesses and newspaper reporters waited in the harsh light of the gallows, Warden Brady, Baltimore County sheriff John Potee, and prison physician Dr. Frank Powers made their way to Whittemore's cell. Guards pulled the chain from the door and unlocked the multiple locks that secured his cell while Whittemore sat on his bed, watching.

When the door swung open, Whittemore emerged and shook each official's hand. He then turned to the guard outside his cell and said, "There isn't much I can give anyone. But I want you to have this Bible as a gift from me." The guard thanked him and asked how much of it he had read.

"I finished 182 pages," said Whittemore. "I wish I had time to read it all, but . . ." and shrugged his shoulders with perfect timing, one last quip from the lips of the Candy Kid. In truth, he probably hadn't read a word. If he had, the meaning apparently escaped him.

No one mentioned Robert Holtman, or Charles Clifford, Louis Yarrington, Si Gilden, Tommy Langrella, Henry Helwig, or any of the men and women Whittemore had terrorized with a gun, struck over the head, or left bound on some floor, or any widow or child left without a parent.

Neither did Richard Whittemore. And he never mentioned Margaret either.

T he guards now prepared Whittemore to die. As was customary before an execution, he'd been given a clean white shirt but wore his usual pants, and his feet were manacled together with a short chain. He held his arms down to his side, and the guard bound his arms and torso with wide leather straps, "like a trussed fowl," as one paper noted. A guard snatched a last cigarette dangling from Whittemore's lips and threw it to the floor. He then pulled a black shroud, with a hole at the top for his head, over his body like a nightdress, the bottom nearly brushing the floor.

Whittemore must have known that the next day the *Baltimore News* would publish a final missive from his stubby lead pencil, presumably in exchange for a check made out to his wife. He'd finished it earlier that day and had it delivered to the paper. Whittemore titled it "Incarcerated Thoughts While Awaiting Murder."

In many ways it would be a much briefer knockoff of "A Moral Lesson." Whittemore again laid the full blame for his crimes on societal forces acting against him. He ended it by writing:

Saying good-by to you, as, when the true meaning of it gets to you, it is
all the best I can wish all, and that all shall meet with success and some
day we shall meet again on a much better battle ground.

END
Thirteenth day, ending with the Thirteenth page

The last line referred to the fact that the writer, as keenly aware that he was being hung on Friday the thirteenth as everyone else, had in fact produced precisely thirteen handwritten pages. "The slayer," noted the *News*, remained "an actor until the end." Chaplain Biggs asked if he had any last words. Whittemore echoed his final missive and then added, "Only to say goodbye, that's the best I can say to anybody."

Whittemore asked if the chaplain wished to speak his final words for him.

"I would rather you would say it," said Biggs.

At three minutes after midnight on Friday, August 13, the door leading from the death house to the execution balcony opened, and Whittemore shuffled through, with a guard on each side. The rustle of the chains on his ankles dragging on the floorboards greeted the one hundred faces down below, all looking up at him. Whittemore gave a quick downward glance but kept his head upright, looking straight ahead.

He was almost ready and stepped forward on his own to stand on the trap door in the balcony floor. One guard held up a long gray hood, but Whittemore raised his head up, and the guard realized he wanted to speak.

"I wish to say goodbye," he said, his voice clear and firm. "That's the best I can wish anyone."

Down below, the reporters glanced at each other. *That's it? What the hell was that supposed to mean?* They'd never really know.

Whittemore's face betrayed a thin smile as one guard quickly pulled the hood over his head and the other placed the noose around his neck, taking care to pull the knot tight behind his right ear. The men then stepped away quickly, as if worried that they too might be sucked down to their death.

Whittemore did not move. He hardly even looked like a man anymore, only a faceless shape, a shrouded phantom. Warden Brady, standing on the platform, waved his hand at a guard to pull the lever that released the trap door on which Whittemore stood.

Nothing happened.

The guard hadn't seen Brady. The warden gestured again. It was 12:08 a.m.

The door dropped open beneath Whittemore's feet, and his body dropped with astonishing speed, straight down. The only sound was the harsh clatter of the swinging hardware and a few quick, reflexive breaths from the crowd.

His feet gave one quick convulsive jerk as the rope halted his fall and his body recoiled slightly as his neck broke, as planned, between the third and fourth vertebrae. Then Richard Reese Whittemore, the Candy Kid, one month shy of his twenty-fifth birthday, hung by the neck, his body slowly twisting and swaying back and forth, each swing a little shorter than the last.

The crowd remained still, no longer looking upward but straight ahead to where he now dangled at the end of a rope, his feet three feet above the stone floor.

One after another, they started putting their hats back on and lighting cigarettes. Three physicians entered, and each, in turn, placed a stethoscope to Whittemore's chest. A guard brought in a stretcher and placed Whittemore's limp body on it, the noose still tight around his neck.

Each doctor again listened, not for a heartbeat but for the silence of death as the men in the room remained still. First one doctor, then a second, heard nothing. At 12:23 p.m., the third doctor concurred and pronounced Richard Reese Whittemore dead.

The guards quickly got to work on the noose so they could free the body from the gallows, but the rope had cut so deep into his flesh that it could not be loosened. One finally cut it from Whittemore's flesh with a pen knife. They pulled the hood from over his head, exposing his face and neck, now marred by a great, deep bruise. Then they lifted the stretcher and carried him from the room.

The crowd left the way they came in and breathed the cool night air.

W hen they removed the shroud from Richard Whittemore's body in the prison hospital, preparing his body to be transported in a hearse for the burial, they found something inside his shirt. Somehow, Whittemore had secreted away a pin. In the Candy Kid's last little act of defiance, a secret known only to himself, he had pinned two scraps of paper, each torn from a newspaper, over his heart inside his shirt.

One was a poem, entitled "Whittemore," that had appeared in the *Baltimore Post* a few weeks earlier, written by a reader identified only as "Mrs. McLane."

Whittemore

Sitting alone in a prison cell.
Another young victim of life,
Only one gleam of comfort—
The love of a faithful wife
The Tiger Woman, they call her.
Tiger Woman, indeed!
Pity that more of us women
Are not of the Tiger Breed
Instead of sleek little tabbies
Who purr o'er a prosperous mate
And at the first sign of danger flee
And leave him to his fate.
May the powers above us
Spare this poor lad's life—
If not for the sake of humanity
For the sake of his poor young wife.

The other scrap of paper was a photograph, torn from the *Post*, that had been taken several months before and was recently reprinted. It showed perhaps the only two beings Richard Whittemore ever loved beyond himself.

It was not the mug shot of Tiger Girl under arrest, or the photo of her walking outside the prison on the way to visit her husband, or posing as she held her hand up to his through a screen. It was the photo of her sitting on the stoop of her mother's home in a plain housedress, her hand reaching out to pet their little dog Bades.

She was Margaret, not Tiger Girl anymore, barely twenty-three years old but already a widow, her eyes looking straight at the camera.

Alone.

Epilogue

———

TRIBUTE OF SORROW

When Richard Whittemore's body was spirited away in a hearse an hour after the moment of his death, more than a thousand people still lined the streets outside the penitentiary, hoping for a final glimpse of the Candy Kid. All they saw was a deadweight covered by a sheet being hustled into the back of a hearse.

During her husband's final hours, Tiger Girl waited for word at her mother's home. Although the house looked empty, reporters went around back and found Margaret, "in a gingham dress, resting her pallid face on the arm on top of the chair, eyes reddened." She already knew.

The next morning she was spotted at the home of Rawlings Whittemore Jr.'s mother-in-law, a Mrs. Wright, at 1318 West North Avenue, just off the corner of Druid Hill Avenue; Rawlings Jr. lived there with his wife. Shortly after dawn, the body was delivered to Mrs. Wright's home. Word had leaked out, and onlookers were already massing on the sidewalk. As the casket was carried inside, they heard "a single piercing scream, 'Oh Reese!'" followed by sobs. Some tried to push their way inside, only to be blocked by Mrs. Wright.

"The man is dead," she barked, "and friend or foe nobody but his family enters while his body is under this roof."

The previous day Margaret had purchased a small widow's hat of black crepe with the customary black veil. Although she complained that the trunks full of her belongings, including most of her clothes, continued to be held by police in New York, she told friends that she still had two black dresses, enough for mourning until she could buy more.

Florists arrived in a steady stream bearing dozens of tributes from all over the country, including a massive bank of gladiolas and maidenhead fern from Kitty Hart, wife of local gangster and fellow inmate Jack Hart. Rawlings Whittemore sent his son a wreath of bleeding hearts, the card inscribed "from a broken-hearted father." Another arrangement showed a clock face made of flowers, the petaled hands frozen at 12:08 a.m., the time of the hanging.

Whittemore's family held his funeral at the Wright home on the morning of August 16, the Monday following his execution. By the time of the service, more than three thousand people crowded North Avenue, but the service itself was closed to all but a few family members. More than twenty policemen formed a line on each side of the street to control the crowd and keep traffic moving as rubberneckers drove slowly past.

By now, Margaret had tired of the attention. Whatever fleeting enjoyment she may once have taken from her temporary fame was now gone, her private grief now all too public. She asked a neighbor, "Why can't the world leave me alone with him now?" There was no answer to that. Not yet.

The service was short and simple, only twenty minutes. Rawlings Jr.'s sister-in-law sang "Peace, Perfect Peace" and "Nearer My God to Thee." If anyone delivered a eulogy, only the family heard it. Still, the crowd pressed as close to the home as they could. When the door opened and the pallbearers appeared, police had to create a passage through the mob so they could reach the hearse. A second hearse was needed just for the flowers, and a half-dozen private cars were reserved for the family.

Hundreds of mourners followed the cortege to Loudon Park Cemetery, hoping to witness the burial, where hundreds more already waited. Again they were held back by police barricades, but they still pressed within only a few yards, close enough to hear any speakers. As usual, the press covered Margaret like the celebrity she had become. They paid particular attention to her attire, noting that she was "not dressed in expensive mourning." Her black patent leather shoes were scuffed, and she wore a plain black Canton crepe silk dress with a circular skirt over black silk stockings. Her face was shrouded behind her mourning veil.

As the family gathered together before the grave, a young man who claimed to have served with Richard in the Coast Guard boldly asked Margaret if he could play "Taps." She refused, saying of her husband, "He would not like any show."

The crowd grew quiet as pallbearers lifted the casket from the hearse and solemnly delivered it to the grave. A moment later, Margaret's mother stepped forward.

"Has anyone an objection if I say a few words?" she asked. Answered with silence, she began to speak.

As if she were speaking for her daughter, Theresa Messler's voice rose in volume with each bitter word. "They have taken his life and I hope they are satisfied. They put a rope around his neck and broke it. But they couldn't break his spirit to the end. Those men who wouldn't let him kiss his wife good-by should know what kind of dogs they were. Their cruelty made the angels weep. I hope that when these men kiss their wives or other women that his spirit will come between them. I am only an old lady and I am not much on making speeches. But this comes from the bottom of my heart."

From the crowd, voices murmured in support, saying, "She's right, she's right." The pallbearers, reportedly old friends of Richard, then solemnly lowered the casket into the grave. Chaplain Biggs provided the standard Methodist funeral ritual. As an opponent of the death penalty, he made a special point to omit the clause "inasmuch as God in His wise providence has seen fit to take the soul of the departed." He found nothing wise in the execution of a human being, later saying, "I left that out because I do not want to blame the Almighty Savior for something that we are fools enough to do."

The undertaker, as was custom, threw the first handful of dirt on the casket. As the earth rained down upon it, Rawlings Whittemore muttered, "My boy, my boy." One of the pallbearers handed Margaret two rosebuds from the funeral blanket.

At that, Margaret became hysterical. She pulled free, lurched toward the rectangular hole in the ground, and tried to throw herself in on top of her husband's casket. Rawlings took her by the arms and led her away before the now-silent crowd.

The *Baltimore News* later noted, "Few citizens of Baltimore have gone to their graves with greater tribute of sorrow." The crowd lingered for a few moments and then dispersed, their role in the spectacle finally at an end.

A s the first few blades of grass began to sprout on the bare earth atop the grave, Richard and Margaret Whittemore, Tiger Girl and the Candy Kid, left the front page and began a slow fade.

But not entirely, and not immediately. Two weeks later, a few sharp-eyed reporters spotted a weeping Margaret Whittemore in New York standing in line with thousands of others outside Campbell's Funeral Church on Broadway and Sixty-Sixth, waiting to view the funeral bier of the fallen screen idol Rudolph Valentino.

She seemed pleased to be recognized. Her visit to Valentino's bier was a spur-of-the-moment decision. She had come to New York, she said, to buy some clothes, "having absolutely nothing to wear."

"He died in his prime just as Dicky did," she said of Valentino, whom she referred to as a friend, conflating the two Jazz Age icons, before adding that her husband was "the victim of social vengeance."

Those words would be Margaret Whittemore's final public statement about her husband, his execution, and his crimes. If she had more to say, it went unreported. Now that Richard Whittemore was dead and the rest of the gang was in prison—except for Nate Weinzimmer, who was still on the run—the tabloids soon turned their attention elsewhere.

Tiger Girl and the Candy Kid appeared destined to take their place in the annals of American criminal history alongside such notorious bandits as the legendary Dalton Gang, Gerald Chapman, and Billy the Kid. Yet Tiger Girl and the Candy Kid stood apart as America's first gangster couple, for which there was almost no precedent. Ever so briefly, and even as it destroyed them, Richard and Margaret Whittemore achieved the kind of life they aspired to.

The good times did not last, and neither did their individual notoriety. Yet over the next few years their story would be woven into popular culture to create archetypes still recognizable today: Richard Whittemore, the prototypical tough guy gangster with a soft candy center, and Margaret Whittemore, the chic gun moll, a true partner in crime who stuck by her beloved till the end.

Only six months after the execution, a sanitized version of the story of Tiger Girl and the Candy Kid made it to Broadway in a play called *Crime: A Melodrama of New York's Underworld,* written by John Hymer and Samuel Shipman. The drama turned characters based on Richard and Margaret, as one reviewer observed, into reluctant criminals who were "entrapped into leading their life." But as this reviewer also noted, the gist of the story, which included a jewelry job described as "astutely planned" and a scene in a fictional Broadway cabaret called "Hellsden," took inspiration directly from the exploits of the Whittemore gang. Three years later, *Crime* was made into a film entitled *The Payoff,* the story now barely recognizable. The characters inspired by Richard and Margaret had been transformed into naive and absolutely blameless bumpkins coerced by an older, urbane, gun-toting jewel thief to do his bidding.

By then, Hollywood had entered a new era, having consigned the silent screen to the scrap heap. The addition of sound allowed filmmakers to add another dimension to their storytelling and soon helped spawn a new genre of American film, the gangster movie.

By the time *The Payoff* hit theaters in 1930, the Roaring Twenties and the Jazz Age had come to a screeching halt, the decade-long party ending with a thud when the stock market crashed in October 1929. In its wake, the gangster film flourished, feeding the public an unending stream of tough-talking and ambitious crooks, mostly working-class criminals wronged by society. Unlike silent crime films, which usually told the story from the perspective of law enforcement as a kind of morality tale, films in this new genre were more often narrated from the criminal's point of view and were often sympathetic to their struggles.

The Payoff, although hardly a classic of the genre, was nevertheless one of the earliest talking pictures in the genre. It would be incorrect to say that characters in any of these subsequent gangster films were directly based on Richard and Margaret Whittemore, but the Whittemores did leave an unmistakable mark on the genre. Richard's shadow hangs over fictional antiheroes like the Tom Powers character played by Jimmy Cagney in *The Public Enemy* and Cagney's portrayal of Eddie Bartlett in *The Roaring Twenties,* based on a Mark

Hellinger short story. Margaret's essential character underlies a host of fictional gun molls, girlfriends, and femmes fatales, almost always tough-talking blondes cut in her mold who, given the gender norms at the time, are usually relegated to secondary status and supporting roles.

These films provided something Tiger Girl and the Candy Kid could not: tabloid journalism come to life. Hot lead type simply could not compete with a black-and-white screen fifty feet high and a soundtrack punctuated by sirens, machines guns, squealing tires, and screaming victims. Over time the Whittemores' fictional progeny became, in a sense, more real than Margaret and Richard had ever been. So did the next generation of real gangsters—Depression Era outlaws like John Dillinger, Bonnie and Clyde, and Pretty Boy Floyd, notorious figures who could be seen *and* heard on screen.

It became easy to forget Tiger Girl and the Candy Kid, the Kraemers and the Whittemore gang, as the headlines once caught in the flash of a still camera were tucked away in the clip files of newspaper morgues. By the time the popular true crime weekly radio serial *G-Men*, later renamed *Gang Busters*, featured an episode titled "The Capture of Richard Whittemore" in 1936, producers had already broadcast twenty-eight episodes highlighting other criminals.

Richard and Margaret Whittemore weren't the only celebrities of the age to be forgotten so quickly. Gertrude Ederle, who was celebrated with the largest ticker tape parade in New York history at the time for becoming the first woman to swim the English Channel, the same month Whittemore was hung, retreated into obscurity. The young women and men who found the celebrity class so compelling during the Jazz Age, revering Tiger Girl and the Candy Kid and all they represented, passed into adulthood with the onset of the Depression, their spirits broken as the cold reality of poverty overwhelmed the collective memory of an era marked by nothing but good times. People didn't much want to revisit the uncomfortable memories of the 1920s in any detail. They seized on a new generation of heroes and a fantasy version of the lives they had once lived as now delivered by Hollywood, leaving behind the more uncomfortable truths of a bygone age.

Reality was too painful.

· · ·

I n the wake of Whittemore's execution, the law enforcement and legal officials he touched on his way to the gallows resumed their careers of public service. John Coughlin, the silk-shirted and incorruptible cop who spearheaded the gang's capture, emerged with his reputation as New York's finest
cop as burnished as his badge. Yet, only three years later, he fell victim to the
harsh world of New York politics, forced to retire after his department failed
to solve the 1928 murder of Arnold Rothstein (a crime still officially unsolved).
Coughlin became an inspector for the Johns-Manville Corporation, a manufacturer of construction products, until his death in 1951.

Whittemore's defense attorney, Edgar Allen Poe, found his political career
stalled after the Whittemore trial. He remained in private practice until his
death in 1961.

After his failed prosecution of Whittemore, Buffalo DA Guy B. Moore's political career also stalled. He was voted out of office in 1931 and went into private practice. His counterpart, J. Bartlett Sumner, who had earned an acquittal
for Whittemore, went on to a long career as a defense attorney.

Of all the principals, only Herbert O'Conor's star grew brighter in the wake
of his successful prosecution of the Candy Kid. Immensely popular in Maryland, in 1938 he was elected governor, the first Roman Catholic to hold the
office. He was elected to the US Senate in 1946, but chose not to run for re-
election in 1952 after his popularity waned. O'Conor died in 1960. By then, his
prosecution of Richard Whittemore was little more than a footnote in his life
story.

So too for Judge Eugene O'Dunne, who after the Whittemore trial remained
on the Supreme Bench until forced by age to retire in 1945. By then, he had
become a legend in Baltimore legal circles, his defense of the Kraemer brothers, bizarre and now unconstitutional intrusion on the voir dire process, and
jailing of newspaper editors for photographs taken during Whittemore's trial
either forgotten or looked on fondly as examples of his mercurial personality.
Lauded as "the most courageous and fearless individual in Baltimore this century," someone who ran "a court of justice, not a court of law," he was praised
both for his attacks on segregation and for his tough sentencing of criminals.
He died in 1959.

Apart from O'Conor and O'Dunne, the only other person directly connected to the Whittemores who reached the kind of success Richard and Margaret had dreamed of was Laura Lee, the young chorus girl Whittemore courted at the Club Chantee. By 1928, she had escaped the clutches of Harry Thaw and graduated from the cabarets to Broadway, where she earned positive reviews for her dancing, comic skills, and beauty. Noted one reporter, "of blondes that gentlemen prefer, Laura Lee has been called an ideal type." In 1930, Lee went to Hollywood, where she appeared in three films with comedian Joe E. Brown and looked to be on her way to becoming a star. But she married a wealthy furrier and broker and retired from acting before her name became a star in the Hollywood firmament. Yet she still managed to leave a legacy. During World War II, she helped create what would later become the United Service Organizations, which entertained American soldiers deployed abroad, earning her the title of honorary brigadier general. She reportedly passed away in 1971.

Richard Whittemore's execution left the proud Whittemore name in ruins and Rawlings Whittemore a broken man. After Richard's funeral, he withdrew and slipped into anonymity. He lived alone, only a step away from poverty, with one son dead and the other following the same fast track downhill.

Just over two months after the death of his son, on the evening of November 3, 1926, Rawlings Whittemore walked in front of a car at the intersection of Pennsylvania Avenue and Sanford Place in Baltimore. The collision left him with a fractured skull, not unlike Robert Holtman's. He died the next day. The driver was not charged. For the second time in less than three months, a Whittemore funeral was held in the home that Rawlings Jr. shared with his wife and mother-in-law.

Rawlings Whittemore Jr. seemed determined to one-up his famous brother and followed his path into the criminal underworld. After being paroled for a minor larceny charge, he later claimed that he tried to go straight, but then, like his brother, blamed others—namely his nagging mother-in-law—for his failure to do so. A year later he was arrested for a bank robbery in Westminster and sentenced to twenty-one years in the Maryland State Penitentiary. His wife Asley passed away shortly thereafter. Three weeks later, with nothing to lose,

Rawlings Jr. tried to break out of prison, just as his brother had done. He shot a guard after disarming him, but this time the guard would survive. Rawlings Whittemore Jr. would spend the next twenty-five years of his adult life in the Maryland State Penitentiary before earning parole. He eventually remarried and passed away in 1974, the last of Richard Whittemore's siblings. Sister Meta had died in a drowning accident decades before.

T he remainder of the Whittemore gang hardly fared better than their fallen leader. Their rapid demise foreshadowed that all the good times of the Jazz Age were destined to end, and for most, not end very well.

Nate Weinzimmer, the gang's driver, went underground as soon as the gang was first rounded up. Having made a killing running liquor during Prohibition, he hired the best available attorneys and, on February 25, 1927, turned himself in. The state of New York immediately began extradition proceedings, and Weinzimmer's lawyers arranged for him to be freed on $50,000 bail. He paid the money in cash.

For the next eight months, Weinzimmer accumulated another $25,000 in legal fees as his attorneys fought the extradition order, but without success: in mid-November 1927, Ohio governor Victor Donahey ordered that Weinzimmer be returned to New York. That hadn't been part of the plan. He jumped bail and fled, forfeiting $50,000. On December 12, he was captured in St. Louis and sent back to New York to go on trial for his role in the Goudvis robbery. With his arrest, every member of the gang, save for Richard and Margaret, was now in custody.

Weinzimmer was sentenced to a term of twenty years in Sing Sing in 1928. The key piece of evidence against him was the handwriting on his registration card at the Hotel Embassy, which destroyed his alibi. Paroled in 1938, Weinzimmer returned to his wife in Cleveland, where he was later arrested for the illegal sale of liquors and operated a lowbrow hotel. He died in 1961.

Although Anthony Paladino was promised soft time for squealing on the rest of the gang, in the end he got double-crossed. Kept in West Side Prison for his own safekeeping while giving testimony and awaiting trial, in 1929 Paladino was finally given an indeterminate sentence not exceeding three years for his role in the Goudvis robbery. As soon as he was free he was arrested by the US Department of Labor and issued a deportation order to return to Italy, the country of his birth. Paladino fought the order, but the court disagreed, and he was apparently sent to Italy. He might have made his way back to the United States under another name. If he did, his final fate is unknown.

After turning squealer, Willie Unkelbach, who, like Paladino, agreed to testify against the Kraemers, sat in the Tombs, likely on his way to easy time for his role in the Goudvis robbery. Then, perhaps feeling the need to make up for ratting out the others, Unkelbach and two other prisoners attacked a guard, beating him unconscious with a blackjack and his set of cell door keys. They then tried to fight their way out, breaking the jaw and fracturing the skull of a second guard and beating a third before being stopped by a fourth guard with a gun as they tried to commandeer a prison van. Unkelbach received a ten-year sentence for the attack and another ten to twenty years for his role in the Goudvis robbery with the Whittemore gang.

Unkelbach was paroled in 1936 but quickly landed back in prison for parole violations. Freed again a few years later, he became a notorious alcoholic and was in and out of jail the rest of his life for crimes ranging from dodging the draft to public drunkenness. He ended up homeless and a hopeless alcoholic. In 1950, the gangster who had fancied himself a ladies' man was found dead, dressed in rags, in a hobo jungle at the foot of Dukeland Street in Baltimore.

While Whittemore was on trial in Baltimore, the Kraemers went on trial in New York for the robbery of Folmer Prip. After a contentious trial and a spirited alibi defense by Hyman Bushel that centered on a real estate transaction the brothers were allegedly completing in Philadelphia during the time of the crime—which initially led to a deadlocked jury—the three men were eventually convicted. During deliberations, one of the jurors, a real estate man, pointed out discrepancies in the paperwork, convincing his fellow jurors of the Kraemers' guilt.

On June 11, the brothers were sentenced to forty years each, a sentence that, as repeat offenders, was more severe than a second-degree murder conviction would have brought them. They would serve a minimum of sixteen years before becoming eligible for parole.

The Kraemers did not serve their time quietly. Determined to reap the benefits of their still substantial financial holdings, the brothers made repeated attempts to escape. One attempt sparked a multiday riot in Dannemora in 1929; involving more than 1,200 prisoners, the riot left three inmates dead. Later, when another inmate ratted out Leon's plan to escape, Leon stabbed him. The man earned parole, was rearrested, and then, rather than go "back to prison where Kraemer is," hung himself.

Jake Kraemer, meanwhile, made it out of prison. He would die of tuberculosis in July 1932. One month later, Leon escaped from New York's Great Meadow Prison by wiring himself to the undercarriage of the warden's car.

He made his way back to New York City, where he resumed living the high life. But Leon Kraemer had revenge on his mind. According to one report, when the Kraemers were arrested for the Goudvis robbery, Joseph Tropp still owed the gang some $35,000 in cash for stolen gems. But the fence was able to use his connections to stay free. He'd have been better off, perhaps, in jail. On May 29, 1933, Kraemer tracked down Tropp and forced him at gunpoint to cough up somewhere between $35,000 and $50,000, allegedly telling him he "intended to give it to Whittemore's widow."

Tropp complied, then was kidnapped and beaten by Kraemer and some cohorts. They pushed Tropp out of a car onto the street at the corner of Allen and Rivington Streets on the Lower East Side, "his jaw broken and his head a bloody mess." While scores of onlookers watched, Tropp, from his knees, begged for his life. Once Kraemer made sure everyone was looking, he allegedly cut down Tropp by machine-gun fire. To no one's surprise, there's no evidence that the money taken from Tropp ever made its way to Margaret.

Although he was never charged with Tropp's killing, Leon was recaptured a few weeks later, after being shot himself, and returned to Dannemora. He was finally released from prison in 1949. Like Whittemore, he held fast to his innocence. "I was just a bootlegger," he claimed. "I happened to know the Candy Kid.

"All I want is a break. I've paid, paid for a crime I never committed. I'd like to go where I'm not known . . . Somewhere there must be work for a little fellow like me." The trail ends there, as Kraemer—or Miller, or Lis, or whatever name he chose to use subsequent to release—dropped out of sight.

And Shuffles Goldberg? Rumors of his imminent demise proved premature.

Shortly after the Kraemers were convicted, he had pled guilty to the charge of robbery and was sentenced to twenty-five years. His attorney, citing Goldberg's tuberculosis, had called that a "death sentence," but the little man with the big ears and distinctive gait cheated death. He remained imprisoned until earning parole in 1941. He reportedly did not die until 1949.

While the rest of the Whittemore gang rotted in prison, and with her husband dead in the ground, Margaret Whittemore found herself at first living back in the Fifteenth Ward with her mother. Whatever personal fortune she retained rapidly dwindled, and any evidence of her previous status was confined mostly to a closet full of clothes appropriate for places she no longer visited—the cabarets in Baltimore weren't quite like the Club Chantee.

Margaret appears to have turned away from the criminal underworld following her husband's death. She spoke out publicly only once, in a letter to Ruth Snyder, who, along with a lover, murdered her husband, earning them both death sentences. In April 1927, Margaret wrote Snyder, "I am opposed to capital punishment but feel you and your lover should get life imprisonment." She added, "A woman, after taking those marriage vows, should at least be fair to her husband. I loved my husband better than any man on earth, and he will never leave my memory." She finished as if she realized she now had to explain who she was: "I suppose you have heard of me. I am Mrs. Margaret Whittemore, widow of Richard Reese Whittemore, hanged in Baltimore last August."

Margaret did not lack company in those years. A series of men tried to win her favor, curious strangers and old friends alike offering sympathy. There was still occasional public speculation that she might have access somewhere, perhaps in a safety deposit box or another hiding place, to some of the proceeds from Whittemore gang crimes that had escaped the reach of law enforcement. In fact, it was for this reason that the New York Police Department kept tabs on her comings and goings for some time. But there was no evidence of this in the ensuing years, no reports of wild spending sprees or exotic travel. If there was any hidden treasure, it apparently stayed hidden, or at least out of Margaret's reach.

Still, the press speculated that suitors were more likely interested in the whereabouts of the missing fortune than in the widow's charms. One story asked of her lover, "Is it a man she met during her old 'mob' days of 'stick-up' and 'getaway?' Is it a respectable private citizen? Or—boldest and most thrilling conjecture of all—is it a police agent who has insinuated himself into her good graces, in the hope that love will loosen her lips as to the whereabouts of the $500,000 swag?" Other suitors were probably attracted to her infamy, some reports suggested, and openly wondered whether she could overcome the ignominy of what one observer called being "a second-hand wife."

In April 1927, the press reported that Margaret planned to marry a "60-year-old fruit broker" from California, a man of wealth and prominence who could give her legally a semblance of the life Richard Whittemore had provided through illegal means. Richard, she told a reporter, had told her she should marry again and "wished she would do so." But the June wedding date came and went without a wedding ring appearing on her finger.

Margaret then receded further from public view, now apparently content to live a quieter, more anonymous life and determined, as the *Daily News* reported, "to try to live down all that happened." In January 1929, she married a man described as "an old friend of the family and [a] neighbor." Twelve years her senior, he was no dashing sheik but a "tinner," a metal fabricator, for the Baltimore and Ohio Railroad. Tiger Girl made one final brief appearance in New York during their brief honeymoon there. According to the *Daily News*, after being spotted by a photographer, Margaret "showed her fangs and clawed a photographer," and her new husband "socked a reporter." They moved into a small two-story house near the railroad's Mount Clare shop, a working-class neighborhood about a mile south of where Margaret grew up. It was a far cry from Chester Court.

In a sense, Margaret never left home again. She resumed life much as it had been when she was growing up in the old Fifteenth Ward. After two years of marriage, she gave birth to her only child, a daughter, and the couple scuffled along on her husband's modest salary. Like the Bob-Haired Bandit, after her time in the spotlight Margaret Whittemore appears to have done exactly what she said she would do and spent the ensuing years trying to live down all that happened.

As Margaret grew old, Tiger Girl was utterly camouflaged by the passage of time and her wish to be left alone was finally fulfilled. Other criminals captured the attention of the press. From 1931 to 1934, bank robbers Bonnie and Clyde filled the space that Tiger Girl and the Candy Kid had created and once had all to themselves.

By 1939, Margaret's husband was out of work, and their modest home had lost nearly half its value: it was now worth only a few thousand dollars. Once upon a time, the Candy Kid had thrown that much around the Club Chantee in a single night on bottles of wine, steak dinners, and tips for cigarette girls. After her husband's death in 1959, Margaret lived the rest of her life in a house on South Howard Street. An old woman with an untold story and a secret, she shared her home with her daughter until Margaret passed away on April 13, 1993, at age ninety. Her death notice in the *Baltimore Sun* made no mention of her early life, or of Tiger Girl, and did not bother even to spell her name correctly.

Today nothing identifies Richard Reese Whittemore's burial place at the Loudon Park Cemetery. The Candy Kid, a man who once had the attention of the nation, whose exploits commanded the front page of the *New York Times,* who drew crowds of supporters to courthouses from Buffalo to Baltimore, who killed at least one man and perhaps a half-dozen more, who "lived well, dressed well, and traveled fast and furiously," and who died as he promised, "defiantly and spectacularly," is today utterly anonymous. His grave is unmarked, a simple patch of grass unadorned by flowers.

Eight miles away, in a leafy Baltimore suburb, is the grave that holds Margaret Whittemore. The simple, flat memorial stone, flush to the ground, is covered by a modest bronze plaque bordered by flowers and a small bronze vase. The name, of course, does not read "Tiger Girl," but simply "Margaret," followed by her middle initial, "T.", for Theresa, then the surname of her second husband, her daughter's father, and the dates of her birth and death: March 2, 1903, and April 13, 1993.

The remaining inscription consists of a single word:

MOTHER

ACKNOWLEDGMENTS

I first wish to thank and acknowledge the vast number of journalists whose work, now long forgotten and rarely read, made this book possible. The depth of their reporting made it possible to re-create a story nearly one hundred years old from reels of microfilm, many of which have now been digitized. I only hope that writers in the future find it possible to do the same from the journalism produced today. I also thank the librarians whose efforts at preserving that record and providing access to it are so essential. In particular I'd like to thank the staff of the Enoch Pratt Library in Baltimore, Maryland, and in particular Dr. Vincent Fitzpatrick, for their kindness and assistance; the staff of the University of Maryland libraries; the staffs of the Boston Public Library and the New York Public Library; the staff of the Harry Ransom Center at the University of Texas; the staff of the National Archives; and the staff of the Erie County Clerk's Office. Researchers Barrett Gordon, Lee Cyphers, Max Marcovitch, and Kurt Stand were of great help doing targeted research I was unable to undertake in person. Paul McCardell of the *Baltimore Sun*, Michael Gilmore of the Harry Ransom Center at the University of Texas, and Mary Velasco and Eric Simon of Getty Images all went above and beyond to provide assistance in locating photographs. Thanks as well to investigative journalist and friend Stephanie Kuzydym for her help in filing Freedom of Information requests. They proved fruitless, but sometimes it is as important to know what is not available as to know what is.

Every writer needs people they can trust. Kim Cross, Brin-Jonathan Butler, and John Julius Reel all read an early version of this manuscript, provided valuable feedback, and indulged me in long conversations about this project, as did Howard Bryant, Alex Belth, Richard Johnson, and Luke Cyphers. Thanks as well to Jacqui Banaszynski and Rachel Monroe for their valuable feedback when I approached them for their perspective on several key questions. Thanks as well to the many friends and family who, beginning in 2007, shared my enthusiasm for this project, convinced me of its value, and encouraged me to continue to pursue its publication.

Thanks to my agents, John Taylor "Ike" Williams and Katherine Flynn of the Kneerim & Williams Agency, and the staff of Houghton Mifflin Harcourt: editorial associate Ivy Givens, art director Mark Robinson, book designer Lucia Bernard, copyeditor Cynthia Buck, and production editor Beth Burleigh Fuller. Special thanks to my editor Susan Canavan for believing in this book in the first place.

Very special thanks to my brother, Gary Stout, who was enthusiastic about this project from the start, put up with hours of discussion, contributed key genealogical and historical research into the background of all the principal characters, and read portions of the manuscript. As always, my wife Siobhan and daughter Saorla are tasked not just with living with me but with my book projects. I don't know how they do it, but I'm awfully glad they do.

AUTHOR'S NOTE

The vast majority of detailed official records of Richard Whittemore's criminal history—trial records and transcripts, police files, and other documents—simply no longer exist, having been discarded long ago. Freedom of Information requests to the FBI on the Whittemores, the Kraemers, and other principals turned up nothing. That in itself might explain why their story has never been told in any detail previous to this book.

Fortunately, daily newspaper reporting filled many of those informational gaps. During the first two or three decades of the last century, most major metropolitan areas supported not just one or two daily newspapers but several. Serving as the primary resource material for this book were newspapers from Baltimore (the *Evening Sun, Sun, Daily Post, Afro-American,* and *News*), Buffalo (the *Daily Star and Inquirer, Morning Express, Buffalo Courier, Buffalo Times,* and *Buffalo Evening News*), New York City (the *New York Times, Daily News, Mirror, Journal American,* and *Sun*), and Brooklyn (the *Citizen, Daily Eagle,* and *Standard Times Union*); syndicated accounts from the Associated Press, International News Service, United Press, and Universal Service that appeared in various newspapers around the country; and occasional original reporting and useful commentary. Accounts that I found particularly useful and thorough are de-

scribed in the end notes and identified by title. All direct quotations are real
and sourced in the end notes.

Due to his notoriety and long criminal history, more period printed information is available about Richard Whittemore than about his wife. He was
placed on trial twice, and he wrote and published more than fifteen thousand
words telling his own story (albeit in self-serving fashion). His crimes were
covered—sometimes extensively—even before he was known to be involved
in them. During most of the time he spent incarcerated following his 1925 escape from the Maryland State Penitentiary, the press was allowed access to him
in jail and before and after his time in court. Similarly, police and legal authorities often commented extensively and at length about his interrogations, his
behavior while in custody, and other conversations and interactions he had. Yet
apart from accounts written during the period when the Whittemore gang was
active and Richard Whittemore was alive and in the few years immediately
thereafter, little else has been written about the Whittemores, the Whittemore
gang, or their crimes. No previous book covers their activities or tells their
story in any detail. I used the book titles listed in the bibliography primarily
for background and historical and cultural context.

Creating a full portrait of Margaret Whittemore provided a greater challenge, as she had no interaction with the law before her association with Whittemore. Details of her family and background, even after her arrest in 1926, are
nearly invisible in the press. Only after her husband's escape from prison did
she first come under real scrutiny, both from the press and from law enforcement. She was understandably closemouthed and did not appear in the press
on a regular basis until after both were arrested in March 1926. Unlike her
husband, Margaret spent barely six months in public view. During this time,
she gave no extensive interviews, and when she did speak she spoke primarily
of her husband and on his behalf. Readers should keep in mind that journalism
of the era did not produce the kind of penetrating, in-depth feature profiles of
news figures that are so common today. Jazz Age reporters did not probe family
backgrounds and upbringing or provide voluminous and insightful quotations
and self-reflection by their subjects.

But there is more to it than that. The embedded chauvinism of the press
of the era tended to dismiss most women almost entirely. Those they did not

dismiss—movie stars, other celebrities, well-to-do society matrons, those in-volved in scandal—were often either caricatured or covered in the society pages. In this way, many women, particularly working-class women of Marga-ret's generation, were effectively silenced and rendered almost invisible. Per-haps this explains why there are so few accounts of female gangsters of this era.

I first encountered this story in 2007 while researching my biography of another woman of the Jazz Age, Trudy Ederle, *Young Woman and the Sea* (2008). As I scrolled through reel after reel of microfilm, I kept encountering headlines that mentioned "Tiger Girl" and "Candy Kid." I was admittedly intrigued, at first, by the nicknames themselves, which seemed both rich and evocative of an age. Curiosity led me to start reading those stories, and I soon went from intrigued to enthralled. I was stunned to see how much had been written about the Whittemores at the time, and I was doubly surprised to learn how obscure they have since become. These were the questions that drove me: *Who were Ti-ger Girl and the Candy Kid? What did they do and what happened to them? Why were they forgotten?* And perhaps most importantly: *What does their story tell us today, about both their time and ours?*

I hope readers find those answers in this book.

NOTES

Prologue: Particular People

page

1 *They stayed out late and awoke even later:* The most complete accounting of the Whittemores' lifestyle during their time in New York in early 1926 appears in *New York Daily
News,* June 25, 1928; Mark Hellinger, *Moon over Broadway* (New York: William Faro, 1931),
pp. 140–42; and Morris Markey, "A Reporter at Large: Baa, Baa, Blacksheep," *New Yorker,*
April 3, 1926. For the most comprehensive accounting of the gang's activities during this
time period, see "Last of Gang Seized; Says Whittemore Killed His Own Pal," *New York
Times,* March 24, 1926. Although some details are incorrect—the report misstates both
the ages of Richard and Margaret Whittemore and the length of time they had been
married, for instance—its general description of their lives and activities, their style of
dress, and the lifestyle of the Whittemore gang is otherwise accurate and in accordance
with many other newspaper and other print reports. See also "Whittemore Mob Got
Plenty in Its Jobs," *Buffalo Courier,* April 4, 1926; "City's Bandits Rub Elbows with Elite
at Night Clubs," *Brooklyn Times Union,* March 28, 1926 (which places the gang's lifestyle
in context with the behavior of other gangsters of the era); and *New York Daily Mirror,*
March 27, 1926.

2 *"High Class Apartments for Particular People":* Chester Court, "Historic Documents," http://
www.chestercourt.com/historic-documents.
Richard favored adventure stories: Binghamton Press and Sun-Bulletin, August 12, 1926.
Throughout his incarceration, newspaper reports note, Richard had an appetite for adventure stories and newspapers.
Margaret liked the movies: Philadelphia Inquirer, January 15, 1925. Good discussions of the
role and influence of such magazines on young women of the era appear in Joshua Zeitz's

Flapper: A Madcap Story of Sex, Style, Celebrity, and the Women Who Made America Modern (New York: Broadway Books, 2006); and Frederick Lewis Allen's *Only Yesterday: An Informal History of the 1920's* (1931; New York: Harper Perennial Modern Classics, 2010). Apart from attending cabarets with her husband, Margaret's only other consistent leisure activity seemed to be attending movies.

She'd had one before, a poodle: Baltimore News, July 28, 1926. The back story of the gift of the dog, its name and breed, and the fact that it shared the apartment with the couple, appeared in this interview with Margaret. The admission contradicted her long-standing claim, and her husband's, that she had not been in New York at the time of the Goudvis robbery. The poodle's loss was noted in *Philadelphia Inquirer,* January 15, 1925.

3   *lingered just below the knee: New York Times,* March 24, 1926, notes Margaret's general style of dress and describes her clothes as "fine feathers." All subsequent press coverage often described her various styles of dress, almost always in terms of their stylishness and cost, and noted her wearing of stockings.

her nails perfectly manicured: New York Times, March 24, 1926.

there would be even more coming: Betty Miller, "Tiger Girl Loyal to the Man She Loves," Universal Service, undated clipping from the morgue of the *New York Journal,* held at the Harry Ransom Center, University of Texas. A quote from Margaret about her husband's promise of good times and clothing appears in this article.

and then drew a straight razor: Baltimore Sun, May 5, 1926. Newspaper articles often made reference to Whittemore's fastidious appearance.

4   *"travesty of music":* Associated Press, January 11, 1926.

Cadillac Imperial Suburban Sedan: Morning Call (Allentown, PA), April 12, 1925, provides details of this model of Cadillac.

In a few days he would have one: Buffalo Courier, April 4, 1926. Although the story misstates the Whittemores' street address, it notes that after receiving their cut from the Goudvis job, the first thing he and Margaret did was buy the coat and the Cadillac. Afterward, the press often made note of that coat.

"strongly built": "Last of Gang Seized; Says Whittemore Killed His Own Pal," *New York Times,* March 24, 1926.

"smartly cut" overcoat: "Last of Gang Seized."

5   *he was Horace Waters: New York Daily Mirror,* March 27, 1926. Whittemore's aliases are documented in many accounts. The *Brooklyn Daily Times,* March 25, 1926, mentions his use of the alias Johnny Gario, and the *Brooklyn Standard Union,* March 22, 1926, the alias John Vaughn.

7   *She had her eye:* "Last of Gang Seized; Says Whittemore Killed His Own Pal," *New York Times,* March 24, 1926, makes note of the purchase of the coat after the crime.

1. Till Death

9   *On a cool, gray morning: Baltimore Sun,* October 6, 1921. The modest wedding is also briefly described in *Baltimore Sun,* May 25, 1926; *Buffalo Courier,* April 11, 1926; and *Baltimore Daily Post,* June 8, 1926. The Caernarvon Methodist Episcopal Church South was not a wedding venue that often earned a mention on the society page; only a handful of weddings that took place at the church ever garnered a mention in the *Baltimore Sun.*

10   *"Everywhere":* Malcolm Cowley, *Exile's Return* (New York: Penguin, 1994), p. 279.

11 *"a good girl"*: *New York Daily Mirror,* March 25, 1926.

12 *"frivolous, scantily-clad, jazzing"*: *New York Times,* February 5, 1920, quoting Dr. R. Murray-Leslie.
"You've met her often": *Baltimore Sun,* May 23, 1920, advertisement.
a "woman of experience": *The Flapper,* directed by Alan Crosland (Hollywood, CA: Selznick Pictures, 1920), all quotations from title cards. Although hardly a classic by itself, the film is notable for the way it not only parallels Margaret's life but also established an entire genre of "flapper" films, most of which followed the same basic template.
Like Ginger: Zeitz, *Flapper,* pp. 232–33. The influence of *The Flapper* in particular and other related films on young women is discussed in this seminal work on flappers.
"Two bare knees": *Ithaca (NY) Journal,* February 14, 1928.

13 *A small-town girl:* For background information on Olive Thomas, see IMDb, "Olive Thomas: Biography," https://www.imdb.com/name/nm0859310/bio; and Tim Lussier, "The Mysterious Death of Olive Thomas," 2001, http://www.silentsaregolden.com/articles/lpolivethomasdeath.html.
"much more interested in playing": Ethan Mordden, *Ziegfeld: The Man Who Invented Show Business* (New York: St. Martin's Press, 2008), p. 168.

14 *now wore their stockings rolled down:* For a discussion of the development of flapper fashions, see Zeitz, *Flapper,* chap. 15, "Let Go the Waistline."
"mixed strain": *Buffalo Evening Express,* April 19, 1926.
"a broken heart": *Baltimore Sun,* May 25, 1926.

15 *He'd tried working:* Whittemore discusses his checkered work history in "A Moral Lesson," *Baltimore Daily Post,* June 7 and 8, 1926. Part biography and part apologia, "A Moral Lesson," Whittemore's self-penned autobiography, originally appeared in ten installments in the *Baltimore News,* June 4–14, 1926. It was later distributed to other papers around the United States, often truncated, by the Scripps Howard News Service.
His father would always bail him out: "Says Whittemore Cast Shadow on Repute of Respected Family," *Baltimore Sun,* May 25, 1926. Both this source and the *Buffalo Courier,* April 11, 1926, provide a detailed rendering of Richard Whittemore's upbringing and financial dependence on his father.
"I'm wondering": *New York American,* April 21, 1926.
A few weeks before the wedding: Buffalo Courier, April 11, 1926. The same basic information also appeared in the *Buffalo Evening News,* April 3, 1926.
For two bucks: Baltimore Sun, March 31, 1920, notes the cost.

16 *1200 West Fayette Street: Baltimore Sun,* October 17, 1921. On the wedding license dated a week before, Whittemore listed the Bentalou address, but when he was arrested a week later he provided the West Fayette Street address, a location noted in the *Baltimore Sun* on March 21, 1923, to be inhabited by drug addicts. Residential addresses for both the Messler and Whittemore families are cited in *Baltimore City Directories,* which are held in digitized form by the University of Maryland and can be found at https://lib.guides .umd.edu/c.php?g=327119&p=2197762. The US Censuses of 1900 and 1910 were also consulted.
If Margaret did all the housework: Buffalo Evening Express, April 11, 1926.
But she made only about $20 a week: Stephen H. Norwood, *Labor's Flaming Youth: Telephone Operators and Worker Militancy, 1878–1923* (Urbana: University of Illinois Press, 1990),

pp. 180–93; and "Mary Miley's Roaring Twenties," April 27, 2015, https://marymiley
.wordpress.com/tag/telephone-operators-in-1920s/. Both sources discuss the wages of
telephone operators during the 1920s — generally $20 per week, depending on location,
probably even less in smaller towns. According to the IRS, the average annual wage for
men in 1920 was $3,269. See Nicole Vulcan, "The Average Salary in 1920," December 30,
2018, https://careertrend.com/facts-7426286-average-salary-1920.html.

17   *"pretty well ruined this world":* John Carter, "These Wild Young People," *Atlantic Monthly,*
September 1920, pp. 301–4.

In thirty hours: For basic historical background on Baltimore, see Matthew A. Crenson,
Baltimore: A Political History (Baltimore: John Hopkins University Press, 2017). On the
1904 fire, see pp. 332–33.

"a blessing": Baltimore Sun, February 7, 1906.

18   *"be subject to arrest for disorderly conduct":* Baltimore Sun, July 2, 1908.

For them, Armistice Day: Novelist James M. Cain authored a fabulous story about the last
man known to be killed in combat in World War I, a young Baltimorean, a story that
fully symbolizes the futility of the conflict. Only one minute before the 11 a.m. ceasefire
on November 11, 1918, a son of German immigrants, Private Henry Gunther of "Baltimore's Own," the 313th Regiment, fell at Ville-devant-Chaumont in France. Soon after
arriving in France as a supply sergeant in July 1918, he detailed the "miserable conditions" in a letter to a friend back home and urged his pal to do whatever it took to avoid
service. After Army censors intercepted the letter, Gunther was demoted to private and
sent to the front lines.

Cain, later a successful novelist of hard-boiled fiction such as *The Postman Always
Rings Twice* and *Mildred Pierce,* spent the war trying to stay alive and writing occasional
bleak dispatches for the paper. As he later wrote in the *Baltimore Sun* on March 16, 1919,
"Gunther brooded a great deal over his reduction in rank, and became obsessed with a
determination to make good before his officers and fellow soldiers. Particularly he was
worried because he thought himself suspected of being a German sympathizer. The regiment went into action a few days after he was reduced and from the start he displayed
the most unusual willingness to expose himself to all sorts of risks," such as volunteering
to serve as a messenger, a role he continued even after taking a bullet through the wrist.

On the war's final day, with the Armistice signed and scheduled to go into effect at
11 a.m. on November 11, Allied commanders continued to send their troops into battle.
"Gunther," wrote Cain, "still must have been fired by a desire to demonstrate, even at
the last minute that he was courageous and all-American." Or maybe he knew more
about the world that awaited him back home, because his next act was suicidal. Pinned
down with his unit by sporadic fire, according to Cain, "at a few minutes before 11
Gunther announced he was going to take out that machine gun nest, and although his
companions told him that in a few minutes 'the war would be over' he started out, armed
with a Browning automatic rifle. When the Germans saw him coming they waved at
him and called out, in such broken English as they could, to go back, that the war was
over. He paid no heed to them, however, and kept on firing . . . After several vain efforts
to make him turn back, the Germans turned their machine gun on him, and at one
minute of 11 o'clock Gunther fell dead," killed by the war's last gasp, a pointless death
in a pointless war where neither side gained anything much at all beyond misery. The

Germans placed Gunther on a stretcher and carried him across the lines, and as blood pooled on the canvas, soldiers from the two sides then shook hands as if they'd just finished a tennis match.

19 *The Nineteenth Amendment:* Lynn Dumenil, "The New Woman," chap. 3 in *The Modern Temper: American Culture and Society in the 1920s* (New York: Hill and Wang, 1995), provides a good discussion of the new American woman during this time period.

20 *enrollment in American high schools:* Betty G. Farrell, *Family: The Making of an Idea, an Institution, and a Controversy in American Culture* (New York: Routledge, 2019), p. 77.
"splendid character": Baltimore Sun, May 25, 1926.

21 *Such institutions were inspired by reform efforts:* Houses of refuge were inspired by the efforts of the Society for the Reformation of Juvenile Delinquents (SRJD), whose goal was to take youth who had "become subject to the notice of our police, either as vagrants, or homeless, or charged with petty crimes . . . judiciously classed according to their degree of depravity or innocence," and reform them by having them "put to work at such employments as will tend to encourage industry and ingenuity, taught reading, writing, and arithmetic, and most carefully instructed in the nature of their moral and religious obligations while at the same time, they are subjected to a course of treatment, that will afford a prompt and energetic corrective of their vicious propensities, and hold out every possible inducement to reformation and good conduct."

Before then, juvenile criminals had been housed with adult criminals, with predictable results. Troubled kids usually came out of penal institutions far worse than when they went in, if they came out at all. Although the upper-class supporters of the SRJD were well-meaning, they didn't get their hands dirty either. They left that to someone else, motivated as much by their fear of immigrant children and the poor running wild or begging on the streets as they were by moral concerns.
One uncle served as a dentist: Buffalo Courier, April 11, 1926.
Meta was born in 1900: Baltimore Sun, May 25, 1926.

22 *where either would be the minority:* Crenson, *Baltimore,* pp. 340–44. Edgar Allen Poe, who would later defend Richard Whittemore, defended the measure while serving as Baltimore city solicitor.
"Fearsville": Baltimore Sun, January 4, 1928. The term was used to describe the neighborhood "in the vicinity of Clifton and Monroe Street," precisely the neighborhood inhabited by the Whittemore and Messler families.
"plotting my escape": Larry Adler, *Me and My Big Mouth* (London: Blake Publishing, 1994), pp. 18–19.

23 *"extended wedding trip North":* Evening Sun, June 15, 1921. The *Baltimore Sun* and the *Evening Sun,* while under the same corporate control, were separate publications. The former began publishing in 1837. The *Evening Sun* was established in 1910 under the reporter, editor, and columnist H. L. Mencken.
Maryland was the only state in the union: Michael T. Walsh, *Baltimore Prohibition: Wet and Dry in the Free State* (Charleston, SC: History Press/American Palate, 2017), p. 11, discusses in detail Maryland's unique response to Prohibition.
Many were on the take themselves: Henry Raynor, "Baltimore Crime," *Boston Globe,* October 8, 1926, details the widespread corrupt practices of the Baltimore Police Department and judiciary in the early 1920s. The story was apparently too hot to appear in Baltimore.

24   *"politics is my business":* Baltimore Sun, October 15, 1922.

 "They're all desperadoes": Warner Fabian, *Flaming Youth* (New York: Macaulay Co., 1923),
 p. 13. Warner Fabian was the pen name of Samuel Hopkins Adams, who authored several risqué best-selling novels that cashed in on America's growing interest in flapper
 culture.

 "butter-and-egg men: Irving Lewis, *The City in Slang: New York Life and Popular Speech* (New
 York: Oxford University Press, 1993), p. 77. The phrase initially referred to wealthy people who came to the big cities and threw their money around in cabarets, although over
 time it came to mean any big spender.

25   *"I wanted a good time":* Miller, "Tiger Girl Loyal to the Man She Loves." The clip file at
 the Harry Ransom Center contains clippings from not only the *Journal* but also other
 New York papers. Although the clip is undated and unidentified as to the source, accompanying graphics suggest that it comes from an interview shortly after Margaret and
 Richard's arrest in March 1925. In subsequent interviews, she was more circumspect and
 cautious, so this unvarnished response is particularly valuable for the insight it provides
 into her motivations. Apart from meeting her emotional needs, her relationship with
 Richard Whittemore was a calculation based on her desire for material goods and access
 to a lifestyle focused on pleasure.

2. A Very Accurate Prediction

26   *"disgusted with everything":* Richard Whittemore, "A Moral Lesson," *Baltimore News,* June 8,
 1926. "A Moral Lesson" is in many instances self-serving and deceiving, particularly in
 regard to his life as a criminal, but the stories of his early life appear accurate.

27   *Whittemore and his partner sidled:* Details of the robbery, their method of entry, and their
 capture appear in *Baltimore Sun,* October 17, 1921, and *Evening Sun,* October 17, 1921.
 Robbery was becoming commonplace: "Baltimore Crime," *Boston Globe,* October 8, 1926.

28   *"I was a bad kid":* Babe Ruth, as told to Bob Considine, *The Babe Ruth Story* (1948; New
 York: Signet, 1992), p. 1.

 When Richard was a young boy: "Develops as Criminal in Prison," *Buffalo Courier,* April 11,
 1926. This story, credited to "one who served time with Whittemore and is connected
 to the Prisoner's Aid association of Maryland," without question was written by former
 penitentiary inmate Henry Raynor, who worked as a journalist before being imprisoned for larceny. The story provides perhaps the most detailed and accurate objective
 account of Whittemore's early life through his time in the Coast Guard and the beginning of his adult criminal career, including his early run-ins with the law, his interaction with his parents, and so on. In most instances, events described here align with
 Whittemore's accounts of this time period in "A Moral Lesson," without Whittemore's
 self-serving shading of events. Many subsequent accounts of Whittemore's early life
 appear to have been created from this source, occasionally embellished with additional
 detail.

 "In the other studies": Whittemore, "A Moral Lesson," *Baltimore Daily Post,* June 4, 1926.

 At least once, Margaret's family moved: Buffalo Courier, April 11, 1926. The surrounding neighborhood was later the site of the notorious 2015 arrest of Freddie Gray, and it was also
 the setting for the popular series *The Wire.* By then, the border of Sandtown had expanded.

29 *Before sending him on his way:* Whittemore, "A Moral Lesson," *Baltimore Daily Post,* June 4, 1926.

"a very accurate prediction": Whittemore, "A Moral Lesson," *Baltimore Daily Post,* June 4, 1926.

"What! A boy his age report to you?": Buffalo Courier, April 11, 1926.

taught music and directed the band: Baltimore Sun, May 25, 1926. The history and background of Maryland's houses of refuge and related institutions can be found at Maryland Department of Juvenile Services, "History of Juvenile Justice in Maryland," https://djs .maryland.gov/Pages/about-us/History.aspx.

"minor without proper care": Annotated Code of the Public General Laws of Maryland, edited by George P. Bagby, vol. 4 (Baltimore: King Brothers, 1918), chap. 674, sect. 1, p. 188. The phrase was a formal court charge used to take children from their parents' care for a variety of reasons ranging from abject neglect to simple poverty.

30 *knocked to the ground and kicked half senseless: Baltimore Sun,* April 30, 1908.

got his sentence reduced, or was released: In "A Moral Lesson," *Baltimore Daily Post,* June 7, 1926, Whittemore discusses the impact of the "silent system" and general daily life at the school, which is now known as the Charles H. Hickey Jr. School. See Maryland Department of Juvenile Services, "Charles H. Hickey, Jr. School," https://djs.maryland .gov/Pages/facilities/Charles-H-Hickey-Jr-School.aspx.

31 *Even those committed by their parents: Baltimore Sun,* July 31, 1912, recounts the experience of Harry Howard, a student at the school and later an inmate at the Maryland State Penitentiary with Whittemore. Howard was sent to the school after the death of his mother. When his father tried to retrieve him after he had made arrangements for his son's care, his release was denied, despite his father's pleas, because by that point Howard had committed violations at the school. Howard told a judge about his beating, to no avail. His experience was similar to that of Richard Whittemore, who was first institutionalized as a truant, then reincarcerated for repeated institutional violations.

Whittemore was kept in a cell: Whittemore, "A Moral Lesson," *Baltimore Daily Post,* June 4–5, 1926. Details of the escape also appear in *Buffalo Courier,* April 11, 1926.

"brutalized, criminalized and hardened": Whittemore, "A Moral Lesson," *Baltimore Daily Post,* June 4, 1926.

"I was always hungry": New York Daily News, October 14, 2018.

Whittemore showed his father his bruises: Whittemore, "A Moral Lesson," *Baltimore Daily Post,* June 5, 1926.

32 *"a wild, uncontrollable hot-tempered young whelp": Buffalo Courier,* April 11, 1926. Raynor is a fascinating character. Both during his incarceration and after his release, he wrote a number of exposés on the Maryland State Penitentiary, providing a rare inside look at the institution. His accounts provide much detail on prison life. He knew Whittemore and the Kraemers, and after Whittemore's escape, Raynor wrote both anonymous and unbylined accounts about Whittemore and his life inside the prison. After being paroled, Raynor went to work for the Prisoners' Aid Society, only to be arrested and jailed once again for stealing funds from the group.

"had she not snatched it away": Buffalo Courier, April 11, 1926. Raynor makes note of Whittemore's work in a silk mill following his escape, one of many instances in which Raynor's account confirms Whittemore's in "A Moral Lesson." Raynor adds some aspects absent in Whittemore's account, and Whittemore includes details and explanations missing

from Raynor's, but basic biographical details—the wheres and whens—are consistent in both.

When a former classmate, out on parole: Whittemore, "A Moral Lesson," *Baltimore Daily Post,* June 5, 1926. Raynor also recounts the details of this escape.

33   *"help him to get released": Buffalo Courier,* April 11, 1926.

Edna's uncle, Richard Grady: In "A Moral Lesson," *Baltimore Daily Post,* June 7, 1926, Whittemore notes his uncle's attempt to intercede in his life.

When fewer than 100,000 men: For a thorough discussion of underage warriors, see Allan C. Stover, *Underage and Under Fire* (Jefferson, NC: MacFarland & Co., 2014), pp. 24–25. Stover notes that some Americans as young as twelve managed to join the service during World War I.

34   *"palpitation of the heart":* Whittemore, "A Moral Lesson," *Baltimore Daily Post,* June 5, 1926.

enlisted in the Coast Guard: Whittemore's experience in the Coast Guard was gleaned primarily from "A Moral Lesson" and the *Buffalo Courier,* April 11, 1926. The information from these sources aligns with that contained in letters and documents supplied in response to a query to the US National Archives at St. Louis, which maintains Official Military Personnel Files (OMPFs), Official Personnel Folders, and other American military records. At the time, the Coast Guard operated under the control of the US Navy. Without providing much specific detail, these documents verify the charges against Whittemore and the punishment he received while committing petty crimes during his stint in the military, including his two escapes. The documents consulted were: Captain Commandant to the Secretary of the Navy, Washington, DC, July 6, 1918; Judge Advocate General to US Commandant, Navy Yard, New York, July 6, 1918; Judge Advocate General to Captain Sidney W. Brewster, July 5, 1918; Department of the Navy to Captain Sidney W. Brewster, July 5, 1918; untitled document, Judge Advocate General, reference CG 879, August 8, 1918; untitled document, reference CG 879; Department of the Navy, reference CG 11136, August 8, 1918.

Facing another court-martial: Whittemore, "A Moral Lesson," *Baltimore Daily Post,* June 7, 1926. Whittemore's legal issues in the Navy are detailed in the letters cited in the previous note. His account of his Coast Guard experience and subsequent arrest appears in "A Moral Lesson," *Baltimore Daily Post,* June 7, 1926.

35   *The so-called Pennsylvania System:* Edwin H. Sutherland, Donald R. Cressey, and David F. Luckenbill, *Principles of Criminology,* 11th ed. (Lanham, MD: AltaMira Press, 1992), p. 469.

"the vilest forms of sexual perversions": New York Sun, December 11, 1894.

36   *The director himself:* New York Times, October 8, 1893.

"school of crime": Whittemore, "A Moral Lesson," *Baltimore Daily Post,* June 7, 1926.

A tough-talking Italian thug: Case on Appeal: Supreme Court, Appellate Division, First Judicial Department: The People of the State of New York, Respondent, against Jacob Kramer [sic] and Leon Miller, Defendants-Appellants, May 26, 1926, pp. 49–54. Information on Paladino's background comes primarily from his testimony. The entire document is available at: https://www.google.com/books/edition/New_York_Supreme_Court_807/_L976Jky-GwC?hl=en&gbpv=1&dq=%22jacob+Kramer%22+%22leon+Miller%22&pg=RA4-PA28&printsec=frontcover#spf=1598189673647. Although the publication of the appeal is undated, the original judgment was made on June 11, 1926, and the notice of appeal was filed on June 17. It contains what appears to be the full (with the exception of voir dire examination) recorded trial testimony of the original trial of Jacob "Kramer (*sic*)" and Leon Miller aka Leon "Kramer (*sic*)," which began on May 21, 1926, to its conclusion and their conviction on June 11. Paladino was the only gang member to testify for the prosecution; the Kraemers testified on their own behalf, and Milton Goldberg testified for the defendants. It is interesting to note that this trial of the Kraemers on charges of robbery in the first degree was far lengthier than either murder trial of Richard Whittemore.

37   *Charged with burglary:* For the case background and disposition, see *Baltimore Sun,* November 7, 1921.

38   *"to cause the coppers":* Whittemore, "A Moral Lesson," *Baltimore Daily Post,* June 8, 1926.

3. Easy Meat

39   *"a monument to its humanity and wisdom":* For additional background details on the Maryland State Penitentiary and the history of the penal system in Maryland, see Wallace Shugg, *A Monument to Good Intentions: The Story of the Maryland Penitentiary 1804–1995* (Baltimore: Maryland Historical Society, 2000). See also a general history of the facility that appeared in the *Baltimore Sun,* October 15, 1911. Accounts of daily life in the penitentiary are detailed in several stories by Henry Raynor that appeared as "The Other Side of the Penitentiary Walls," *Baltimore Sun,* April 20 and 27, 1924.

40   *Nearly eight hundred men:* State Board of Prison Control, *Warden's Report, Maryland Penitentiary,* October 20, 1921. Of 772 male prisoners, 424 were Black.
Whittemore was a "hopper": *Baltimore Sun,* April 20, 1924. Raynor also notes that Harry Howard served as the prison barber.
"Keep your underwear and shoes": *Baltimore Sun,* April 20, 1924.
systematic, sadistic pleasure in beating inmates: Shugg, *A Monument to Good Intentions,* chap. 5 (on Sweezey's tenure).
introduced a new set of rules: Shugg, *A Monument to Good Intentions,* pp. 126–27.
"not be a place of punishment": *Baltimore Sun,* March 10, 1925.
"dealing" with the men: *Baltimore Sun,* November 8, 1920.
"I'm going to give you fellows": *Baltimore Sun,* November 26, 1920. For a further description of Sweezey's reforms, see Shugg, *A Monument to Good Intentions,* chap. 5.

41   *"imbued with the belief":* *Baltimore Sun,* April 20, 1924.
"To elect a man to the Sweezey Club": H. L. Mencken, "Crime and Punishment," *Evening Sun,* January 28, 1924.
many guards still did things the old way: *Baltimore Sun,* April 20 and 27, 1924. In this extraordinary series, Henry Raynor describes day-to-day life in the Maryland State Penitentiary in precise detail, including cell and living conditions, sanitary conditions, guard-prisoner relations, the food, and so on. Unless otherwise noted, the following details of prison life come from this source.

42   *Most imprisoned men worked:* For details and background on the contract system, see Ryan S. Marion, "Prisoners for Sale: Making the Thirteenth Amendment Case against State Private Prison Contracts," *William & Mary Bill of Rights Journal* 18, no. 1 (October 2009): 213–47. Although contract labor is allowed under the Thirteenth Amendment, a number of laws—the Hawes-Cooper Act of 1929, the Ashurst-Sumners Act of 1935, and

the Walsh-Healey Public Contracts Act of 1936—restricted the use of prison labor by private companies. In 1979, Congress passed a law establishing the Prison Industry Enhancement Certification Program, which relaxed those restrictions.

The system was a good deal for the contractors, who enjoyed an advantage over their competitors, and the practice was eventually restricted. That explains why most prison work today is confined to items needed by the state, such as license plates, road signs, school lockers and furniture, and printing, although technological advances have made even those practices increasingly rare. Still, the contract system provided prisoners with something to do and made it possible to leave prison with money in the bank.

little better than slave labor: Baltimore Sun, April 20, 1924. Raynor details the many ways in which contractors abused prisoners both through overwork and abject neglect of their safety.

"Where's the guy who handles the piece goods?": "Whittemore, Arch Criminal, Got Finishing Touches from Crafty Kraemer in Prison," *Brooklyn Daily Eagle,* May 30, 1926. Under the byline "Fellow Convict" (undoubtedly Henry Raynor), this account provides an inside, detailed look at the growing relationship between the Kraemers and Whittemore during the time they were incarcerated together, as well as a full explication of the brothers' uniquely close relationship.

43   *Together, the brothers were a formidable pair:* "Whittemore, Arch Criminal, Got Finishing Touches from Crafty Kraemer in Prison," *Brooklyn Daily Eagle,* May 30, 1926. Raynor specifically mentions the brothers' dependence on each other.

"bull-headed, self-opinionated": Brooklyn Daily Eagle, May 30, 1926.

44   *"He was easy meat for the older crook": Brooklyn Daily Eagle,* May 30, 1926.

"Whittemore was just the man": Brooklyn Daily Eagle, May 30, 1926.

Natives of Kielce: Buffalo Evening Times, March 25, 1926, provides a good general background on the brothers' activities prior to coming to the United States. Their background is also detailed in a variety of other sources written or related at various times and in varying detail over the course of their criminal careers. For specific biographical detail, I depended primarily on the account of both brothers that appears in *Case on Appeal ... The People of the State of New York, Respondent, against Jacob Kramer [sic] and Leon Miller, Defendants-Appellants,* May 26, 1926, pp. 1, 126–59, 191–99.

As they cased the neighborhood: Buffalo Evening Times, March 25, 1926.

45   *The Kraemers devised their own method:* A good description of the various period safecracking methods, including the can opener, can be found in the *Star Press* (Muncie, IN), March 2, 1913.

46   *deported as "undesirables": Buffalo Evening Times,* March 25, 1926, notes the circumstances of the Kraemers' deportation from England.

"fashionable residence district": Detroit Free Press, February 29, 1916.

"dozens of suits of every description": Detroit Free Press, February 29, 1916.

Developed in 1879 by Alphonse Bertillon: Raymond D. Fosdick, "Passing of the Bertillon System of Identification," *Journal of Criminal Law and Criminology* 6, no. 3 (1915): 363–69. This source provides a good period overview of the Bertillon system.

47   *On the evening of Saturday, September 23:* This composite description of the Steman & Norwig robbery is taken from *Baltimore Sun,* September 25, 1916, October 2 and October 13, 1926; and *Evening Sun,* September 25, 1916. The investigation, capture, and sentencing of

the Kraemers is detailed in *Baltimore Sun*, October 20 and November 1, 10, and 29, 1916, and *Evening Sun*, October 28 and November 2, 11, and 28, 1916.

They then jimmied the door: Baltimore Sun, September 25, 1916. Also notes the tacking up of the rug and numerous other details of the robbery.

48   *"the back of the safe a big wreck": Baltimore Sun*, September 25, 1916.
      it was one of the best-planned "jobs": Baltimore Sun, September 25, 1916.

49   *Inside the trunks: Baltimore Sun*, October 29, 1916.
      "When he is good": H. H. Walker Lewis, "Baltimore's Judicial Bombshell—Eugene O'Dunne," *American Bar Association Journal* 56, no. 7 (July 1970): 650–55.
      A former state's attorney: Evening Sun, August 30, 1935.
      the judge upbraided the brothers: Baltimore Sun, November 29, 1916.

50   *A few days later, the Pennsylvania Board of Censors: The Broad Ax* (Salt Lake City, UT), December 23, 1916.
      After a 1920 petition for a pardon: Baltimore Sun, August 23, 1920. See also *Buffalo Evening Times*, March 25, 1926, and *Brooklyn Daily Eagle*, May 30, 1926, for details on the brothers' approach and behavior in prison, as well as their failure to secure quick parole.

4. Unusual Sacrifices

52   *When pants went missing and were discovered for sale: Brooklyn Daily Eagle*, May 30, 1926. This story goes into extensive detail on the activities of Whittemore and the Kraemers, the dynamics of their relationship, and the ways in which the Kraemers essentially groomed younger prisoners. It also notes that the Kraemers were believed to be behind the illicit sale of pants outside the prison.
      Every night the Kraemers kibitzed: Brooklyn Daily Eagle, May 30, 1926.
      "sly whispered accounts": Brooklyn Daily Eagle, May 30, 1926.
      "they were pikers": Brooklyn Daily Eagle, May 30, 1926.
      the brothers came under Whittemore's spell too: Brooklyn Daily Eagle, May 30, 1926.
      for the very first time in his life of incarceration: Whittemore, "A Moral Lesson," *Baltimore Daily Post*, June 8, 1926. Whittemore mentions his own good behavior and notes that he respected and enjoyed "many a great talk" with the Kraemers.
      "snappy" third base: Brooklyn Daily Eagle, May 30, 1926.
      "prone to hitting below the belt": Brooklyn Daily Eagle, May 30, 1926.

53   *she'd be waiting:* There may have been even more to her devotion to her husband than the fact of their marriage. Although she would later deny it, on several occasions later Richard Whittemore claimed that he'd had a son, a boy killed in a car accident somewhere in New York while still a toddler. Although I could locate no such records, if true, that meant that either Margaret was pregnant when they got married or became pregnant soon afterwards, or that Whittemore had a child with another woman. If the child was Margaret's, at this point she would have been raising the infant on her own, with only her mother's help. Either way, the prospect of being a father may have given Richard Whittemore an extra measure of motivation to get out of jail as quickly as possible, or at least as quickly as possible without going over the wall. I have not included this in the main text because of Margaret's denials and the fact that I could find no documented evidence of the birth of the child, the accident, or the child's death.

Warden Sweezey might set him free: In "A Moral Lesson," *Baltimore Daily Post,* June 8, 1926, Whittemore recounts his strategy to win release from the New York charge.

the Kraemers' plans came into sharper focus: Brooklyn Daily Eagle, May 30, 1926.

"That Polack": Brooklyn Daily Eagle, May 30, 1926.

54 *Prohibition was treated as a minor nuisance:* Walsh, *Baltimore Prohibition.*

J. Edgar Hoover took over as director in 1924: Bryan Burrough, in *Public Enemies: America's Greatest Crime Wave and the Birth of the FBI, 1933–34* (New York: Penguin, 2004), especially pp. 518–19, describes the rise of the FBI and Hoover's courting of the American media to change the image of law enforcement and secure funding.

55 *Justice was something bought and paid for:* See Harry Wynne Irwin, *The Inevitable Success: A Biography of Herbert R. O'Conor* (Westminster, MD: New Man Press, 1962), especially chaps. 4 and 5, which describe the many ways justice could be thwarted in Maryland during this period when crime flourished, indirectly leading to the election of Herbert O'Conor as state's attorney as a reformer who promised to clean up Baltimore's justice system and lower crime rates.

"organized along the lines of a huge corporation": Brooklyn Daily Eagle, April 8, 1926.

56 *"because she liked lively companions": Baltimore Sun,* May 25, 1926.

57 *"wine, women and song": Evening Sun,* May 11, 1918.

cost anywhere from $25 to $100: For a good general overview of clothing costs during this period, see "What Clothing Cost in the 1920s for Women," Vintage Dancer, https://vintagedancer.com/1920s-style-guide/what-clothing-cost/. The figures cited there align with advertisements in the newspapers of the day.

a practice widely known as "treating": Treating was widely practiced and discussed openly during the era. A particularly good description of the practice appears in Elizabeth Alice Clement, *Love for Sale: Courting, Treating, and Prostitution in New York City, 1900–1945* (Chapel Hill: University of North Carolina Press, 2006), pp. 212–19.

Promotor John Carlin bragged: Baltimore Sun, May 20, 1917, discusses the opening of the Pavilion, its size, and the number of couples it could accommodate. Over the next decade, Carlin placed hundreds of advertisements in Baltimore papers, most of them promoting dance nights at the pavilion.

58 *"keyed up like a lot of tightened 'E' strings": Baltimore Sun,* May 17, 1923.

"competing in the contest": Brooklyn Times Union, August 26, 1926. Margaret made specific mention of "competing in the contest." Pictures of the contestants appeared in the *Baltimore Sun* on May 17, 1926. Although the photograph is not captioned, a woman who looks remarkably similar to Margaret, and one of the few contestants with lighter hair, appears in the upper left corner. Unlike the others, who are looking at the camera, this figure is looking at everyone else.

"There's King Tut!": Baltimore Sun, May 17, 1923.

"his caravan left Carlin's Park dancing pavilion": Baltimore Sun, May 17, 1923.

"helped show him about Baltimore": New York Daily News, August 26, 1926.

59 *everybody involved got a little of what they wanted:* A good discussion and accompanying data detailing the impact of new mores on young women of Margaret's generation appear in Zeitz, *Flapper,* chaps. 2 and 3 (pp. 21–38); Dumenil, *The Modern Temper,* chap. 3; and Allen, *Only Yesterday,* chap. 5.

"unusual sacrifices": New York Times, March 24, 1926.

60   *"The Man she loved":* *New York Times,* March 24, 1926.
     his way to a job in the hospital ward: In "A Moral Lesson," *Baltimore Daily Post,* June 8, 1926,
     Whittemore discusses his behavior that led to the hospital job.
61   *Six prisoners had recently slipped away: Baltimore Sun,* April 2, 1922, provides details on the
     escape.
     prying the bars apart on a window: Baltimore Sun, January 24, 1924. After Whittemore, Hart
     was Baltimore's most notorious criminal during this period.
     "suave, courteous manner": *New York Times,* March 24, 1926. Whittemore was adept at pass-
     ing as a thoroughly polite young man when he chose to do so.

5. Tiger Girl

62   *Evelyn Turner, a dancer: Baltimore News,* April 26, 1926.
     The excesses of the era: For a complete accounting and history of "jazz journalism" during
     the tabloid era, see Simon Michael Bessie, *Jazz Journalism: The Story of the Tabloid News-*
     papers (New York: E. P. Dutton, 1938).
63   *"90 percent entertainment":* Bessie, *Jazz Journalism,* p. 139.
     "Porno-Graphic": Bessie, *Jazz Journalism,* p. 184. The *Graphic,* with a circulation base of
     more than one million, was a newspaper nearly everyone read and few ever admitted to.
     Despite its popularity, not a single library preserved the paper, and today only a scant
     few issues remain, a tremendous loss for historians. One can only imagine how the paper
     covered the exploits of the Candy Kid and his gang. Many other tabloids, such as the
     Mirror, are poorly preserved on ancient microfilm, at best, and are unavailable online.
     See Bessie, *Jazz Journalism,* pp. 184–207, for a history of the newspaper.
     "Oh, print us views": Bessie, *Jazz Journalism,* p. 18.
     "national sport": H. L. Mencken, *A Mencken Chrestomathy: His Own Selection of His Choicest*
     Writings (New York: Vintage), 1972, p. 412.
64   *A number of writers who covered Richard Whittemore:* Mark Hellinger, Frank Dolan, Edward
     Doherty, and Gene Fowler were the four most prominent journalists to cover Whitte-
     more, and all four eventually made their way to Hollywood, part of an early wave of
     journalists to parlay their journalism experiences into work as screenwriters. Several
     other had a tangential relationship. Although he grew up in Chicago, John Bright, who
     wrote the screenplay for *Public Enemy,* was born in Baltimore and was probably familiar
     with Whittemore's story.
     there were no gangster films yet: See Drew Todd, "The History of Crime Films," in *Shots in*
     the Mirror: Crime Films and Society, edited by Nicole Rafter (New York: Oxford University
     Press, 2006). Todd provides a basic historical overview of the gangster film and notes
     that with the advent of talking pictures, crime films flourished. Before this time, most
     crime films were told almost exclusively from the standpoint of law enforcement, but
     "gangster films turned criminals into heroes."
65   *Richard moved in with Margaret and her mother:* Whittemore, "A Moral Lesson," *Baltimore*
     Daily Post, June 8, 1926.
     He'd earned a stint of his own at St. Mary's: Baltimore Sun, May 16, 1918, notes Rawlings Jr.'s
     arrest for the shooting.
     "demand on our association": Baltimore Sun, August 13, 1924.

"was harder for me to get than money": Whittemore, "A Moral Lesson," *Baltimore Daily Post,* June 9, 1926.

66　*the so-called "Bob-Haired Bandit":* See Stephen Duncombe and Andrew Mattson, *The Bob-Haired Bandit: A True Story of Crime and Celebrity in 1920s New York* (New York: New York University Press, 2006). Notably, this book is the only other volume that gives any voice to a female criminal during this time period. Celia Cooney of Brooklyn was eventually identified as the "Bob-Haired Bandit" and would serve, along with her husband-accomplice, seven years in prison for the crime. Apart from her haircut, she looked nothing like Margaret Whittemore—Cooney was a brunette and much shorter. After leaving prison, Cooney and her husband lived a quiet middle-class life. Her own children knew nothing of their mother's past until after her death in 1992.

　　precise date of his parole uncertain: Associated Press, June 10, 1926. There is disagreement among various sources as to the precise date of Whittemore's parole. Although I find it likely that the Ortman robbery was done at his behest, and likely with his direct involvement, in an abundance of caution I have chosen not to make that assertion.

　　staked out Ortman's Confectionery: Baltimore Sun, April 12, 1924; *Baltimore Daily Post,* April 12, 1924; and *Baltimore News,* April 12, 1924. The *Sun* gave the crime the most play, writing up the story as a morality tale to criticize wanton youth. A photo appeared in the *Sun* that showed the register and the placement of the doorway.

67　*"excellent taste": Baltimore Sun,* April 12, 1925.

　　she would "know her again": Baltimore Sun, April 12, 1925.

68　*"Not a word out of you": Baltimore Sun,* April 12, 1925.

　　"everything in sight": Baltimore Sun, April 12, 1925.

　　"pronounced suavity": Baltimore Sun, April 12, 1925.

69　*"that I was not going to be broke any longer":* Whittemore, "A Moral Lesson," *Baltimore News,* June 9, 1926.

　　"frequented tough cabarets and wild dives": Brooklyn Daily Eagle, May 30, 1926.

70　*could set you back four or five bucks:* For an idea of drink prices during the era, see the menu from a Chicago speakeasy c. 1926, Calumet 412, https://calumet412.com/post/17114315378/prohibition-era-speakeasy-menu-c1926-chicago.

　　"all used drugs": H. J. Anslinger and William F. Tomkins, *The Traffic in Narcotics* (New York: Funk & Wagnalls, 1953), p. 270. Drug use by the Whittemore gang was mentioned not only in period reporting but also in Winifred Black, *Dope: The Story of the Living Dead* (New York: Star Co., 1926), p. 28. Although the entire gang is implicated, drug use by the Kraemers and Margaret Whittemore is never mentioned directly. I suspect that they used drugs recreationally and intermittently. Goldberg and Unkelbach were full-blown addicts, while Richard Whittemore and Paladino were regular users and may have been addicts at certain times in their lives.

　　they started rousting bootleggers and saloonkeepers: Brooklyn Times Union, August 13, 1926, references these crimes.

71　*Step by step: Baltimore News,* March 25, 1926. After the Ortman robbery, police referred to Margaret as a "cover-up moll," meaning her role was to carry the guns and provide "cover" for the criminal activities of her husband and the rest of the gang. She was never definitively placed at the scene of any other of the gang's crimes while they were being committed. She did, however, take an occasional role in casing jobs and carrying weapons, in true "gun moll" fashion. That phrase first came into widespread use around 1908 to refer to female criminals, and eventually the definition came to include the female companions of criminals.

robbed two gas station attendants: Baltimore Sun, November 18, 1924. Although what became known as "the Whittemore-Schaefer" gang was not identified at the time as perpetrators of this spate of crimes, they were later implicated.

72 *found only $3.65 inside: Baltimore Sun,* November 18, 1924. Again, Whittemore and Schaefer and their gang were not identified at the time as the perpetrators, but were later implicated.

"quiet, well-mannered, and somewhat reserved": Evening Sun, February 6, 1926.

As she bent over from the pummeling: Evening Sun, February 6, 1926. The entire encounter with Kassel is described in detail, credited to her police report.

He and a few others were off-loading the beer: Baltimore Sun, December 12, 1924, and *Evening Sun,* December 13, 1924, provide details of the B&O heist.

73 *Richard gave him a case:* Whittemore, "A Moral Lesson," *Baltimore Daily Post,* June 9, 1926.

"good stuff": Whittemore, "A Moral Lesson," *Baltimore Daily Post,* June 9, 1926.

Whittemore dressed: Whittemore, "A Moral Lesson," *Baltimore Daily Post,* June 9, 1926.

decided to relocate to Philadelphia: Whittemore, "A Moral Lesson," *Baltimore Daily Post,* June 9, 1926. According to Whittemore, the band moved to Philadelphia after "the robbery of the saloonkeeper near the racetrack."

the gang pulled one last job in Baltimore: Sources for the Gaffney crime include *Baltimore Sun,* January 5, 15, and 18, 1925; *Evening Sun,* January 6 and 15, 1925; *Buffalo Courier,* April 11, 1926; and Whittemore, "A Moral Lesson," *Baltimore Daily Post,* June 9, 1926.

74 *"Line up there": Baltimore News,* January 6, 1926.

"Stay right there": Baltimore News, January 6, 1926.

moved into an apartment on Green Street: Baltimore News, January 16, 1925.

"having a good time": Whittemore, "A Moral Lesson," *Baltimore Daily Post,* June 9, 1926.

Dietz and Whittemore burst in: Baltimore News, February 21, 1925. This interesting interaction shows the ease with which law enforcement overlooked Prohibition.

75 *"Whittemore-Schaefer gang": Evening Sun,* January 29, 1925.

gems from a prominent Philadelphia jewelry dealer: Philadelphia Inquirer, January 15, 1925. Like their counterparts later in New York, Philadelphia police suspected a gang was operating in their midst but had not yet tied the crimes to Whittemore.

76 *"I believe I was the victim": Philadelphia Inquirer,* October 25, 1924, also details the circumstances of the robbery.

The Baltimore detectives guarded the front door: Evening Sun, January 29, 1925.

the two Philadelphia cops made their way upstairs: Circumstances and details of the arrest are from *Philadelphia Inquirer,* January 15, 1925, and *Baltimore Sun,* January 15, 1925.

"Tom [Philips] is in jail": Baltimore Sun, January 15, 1925.

77 *Hearing a noise behind the door in an adjacent room: Philadelphia Inquirer,* January 15, 1925. Some subsequent reports appear to conflate the actions of the two women, some indicating that Margaret was the more aggressive. In this regard, I find the reporting done at the time more credible, as later reports tended to be more sensationalistic to fit the emerging persona of Margaret as the "Tiger Girl" character.

five-foot-three and 109 pounds: Baltimore News, March 23, 1926. A facsimile of the card was reproduced after she was identified in the Ortman robbery.

"I think it's terrible": Philadelphia Inquirer, January 15, 1925. Although the speaker is not identified, Margaret was later known to keep a dog.

Dietz and the Whittemores gave their real names; Baltimore News, January 16, 1925.

78 *"married life was too monotonous": Baltimore News,* January 16, 1925.

"cheerful and unconcerned about their fate": Baltimore News, January 16, 1925.

"pathfinders": Philadelphia Inquirer, January 15, 1925.

"Tiger Lil": Baltimore Sun, January 15, 1925.

entitled The Lily and the Rose: *Baltimore Sun,* May 9, 1920. For background on the film, see IMDb, "The Lily and the Rose (1915)," https://www.imdb.com/title/tt0005621/plotsummary?ref_=tt_ov_pl.

79 *"the best novelty song number": Variety,* July 1919.

A newspaperman called her a "tiger girl": The Bulletin (Pomona, CA), October 25, 1922.

"jazz mad": New York Daily News, January 18, 1925.

"Oh, You Candy Kid": Music by John L. Golden, lyrics by Bob Adams, 1910.

"candy" was also a slang word. For a discussion of the various slang definitions of "candy," see Vincent Joseph Monteleone, *Criminal Slang: The Vernacular of the Underworld Lingo* (Boston: Christopher Publishing House, 1949), p. 43.

80 *"That's a lie!": Philadelphia Inquirer,* January 15, 1925.

Then, as now, the Sixth Amendment right: See National Popular Government League, *To the American People: Report upon the Illegal Practices of the United States Department of Justice* (Washington, DC: 1920). This document provides many examples of the rights of criminal suspects being routinely abused in the United States during this period.

In November 1923: For a thorough and detailed biography of O'Conor, see Harry Wynne Kerwin and Herbert R. O'Conor, *The Inevitable Success: A Biography of Herbert R. O'Conor* (Westminster, MD: New Man Press, 1962). See also O'Conor's obituary in the *Baltimore Sun,* March 3, 1960.

81 *"Take him, boys!": Baltimore Sun,* January 24, 1923. For an account of these events, see also Kerwin and O'Conor, *The Inevitable Success,* pp. 54–62.

the number of registered cars: See Kerwin and O'Conor, *The Inevitable Success,* p. 83; and *Baltimore Sun,* March 23, 1923.

82 *They had learned:* See Kerwin and O'Conor, *The Inevitable Success,* p. 144.

the "accused [to] enjoy": Cornell Law School, Legal Information Institute, "Sixth Amendment," https://www.law.cornell.edu/constitution/sixth_amendment.

a man was arrested for larceny: Kerwin and O'Conor, *The Inevitable Success,* p. 109.

83 *But after Dietz balked and pleaded not guilty: Baltimore Sun,* March 23, 1923.

"Mr. Squealer": See Kerwin and O'Conor, *The Inevitable Success,* p. 144.

"the ends of the State": Kerwin and O'Conor, *The Inevitable Success,* p. 151.

They were released from custody on February 9: Baltimore Sun, February 10, 1925.

"You may send me over there": Baltimore Sun, February 21, 1925. After Whittemore's escape, the *Sun* published a lengthy story detailing his earlier return to the penitentiary and his interaction with Sweezey.

84 *"Well, Whittemore": Baltimore Sun,* February 21, 1925.

"It will be a little harder to get out of here": Baltimore Sun, February 21, 1925.

three more took place in 1924: The record of escapes during Sweezey's tenure is discussed in Shugg, *A Monument to Good Intentions,* pp. 126–29.

"You boys, I suppose": *Baltimore Sun,* February 21, 1925.

"I certainly do know how to get around in here": *Baltimore Sun,* February 21, 1925.

85   *He even bragged to Dietz: Daily Mail* (Hagerstown, MD), May 20, 1926. Dietz reported this claim of Whittemore's during the trial.

in Jack Hart's escape: Hart escaped with another prisoner. Shugg, pp. 126–129, notes Hart's escape and the "rash of prison escapes" during Sweezey's tenure.

"watch Whittemore": *Baltimore Sun,* February 21, 1925.

a nasty burn on his arm: Whittemore, "A Moral Lesson," *Baltimore Daily Post,* June 9, 1926.

he had burned himself on purpose: Baltimore News, February 21, 1925. The *Sun* also published a map of the prison grounds that detailed the location of the shop, the hospital, and Whittemore's escape route.

86   *For sixty-year-old Robert H. Holtman:* Holtman's background is discussed in *Baltimore Sun,* February 22 and 23, 1925.

Holtman had taken a particular shine to Whittemore: Brooklyn Daily Eagle, May 30, 1926, describes the relationship between Holtman and Whittemore, noting that the guard sometimes shared his food with him.

would soon call a "whitewashing": Baltimore News, February 21, 1925.

"we find the system in vogue": Baltimore News, February 21, 1925.

"The methods": Baltimore News, February 21, 1925.

87   *"Coming down": New York Daily News,* May 26, 1926. The re-creation of Whittemore's escape and the immediate aftermath is a composite based primarily on the following sources, which include contemporary reporting and trial testimony produced at a later time: *Baltimore American, Baltimore Daily Post, Baltimore News, Baltimore Sun,* and *Evening Sun,* February 21–24, 1925; and *Baltimore Daily Post, Baltimore News, Baltimore Sun, Evening Sun, Buffalo Courier, Buffalo Evening Express, Buffalo Times, New York Daily News,* and *New York Times,* May 20–26, 1926. All direct quotes are sourced individually. Although none of these accounts are identical in every detail, through a careful examination and comparison I have produced a consensus in regard to what took place that day. In particular I have given somewhat more weight to reported trial testimony than to newspaper accounts written within a day or two of the event itself, many of which appear to have been based on incomplete reporting.

88   *"give it the open air treatment": Baltimore Sun,* May 20, 1926.

Guards on each floor yelled out, "Coming down": Baltimore Sun, May 21, 1926.

"a sneer from him": Whittemore, "A Moral Lesson," *Baltimore Daily Post,* June 9, 1926.

A few years earlier, while guarding a road crew: Baltimore Sun, July 29, 1919.

"You had better keep your mouth shut": Baltimore Sun, February 21, 1925.

6. Before Heaven

90   *"Holtman's dead, Holtman's dead!": New York Times,* May 20, 1926.

The man let out a whoop: Baltimore American, February 21, 1925, provides the best account of Whittemore's first few moments of freedom.

91   *"a blue cap": Baltimore Sun,* February 21, 1925.

Margaret wasn't home: All details of Margaret's activities and interactions with the police on the day of the escape were detailed in *Baltimore News,* February 21, 1925.

"a wrecker of men's hearts and happiness": *Baltimore Sun,* February 23, 1925.

92   *on the corner of Baltimore and Gilmor Streets: Baltimore News,* February 21, 1925, details Margaret's encounter with the policemen in the drugstore, her reaction, and her eventual return to her home.

The police officer carried her: Baltimore News, February 21, 1925.

a handful of detectives were waiting in a knot outside: Baltimore News, February 21, 1925.

"Before Heaven": Baltimore News, February 21, 1925.

"I haven't the faintest idea": Baltimore News, February 21, 1925.

93   *flung open the curtain, and looked outside: Baltimore News,* February 21, 1925. Margaret appeared to be unaware that the home was being watched from the rear before spotting the police officer staring back at her.

"told all within hearing": Baltimore News, February 21, 1925. See also *Baltimore Daily Post,* February 2, 1925.

At 5 a.m., he reeled and staggered: Whittemore's brother's activities and behavior the night of the escape are described in *Baltimore Daily Post,* February 21 and 22, 1925.

94   *After sobering up and paying a fine of $6.45: Baltimore Daily Post,* February 21 and 22, 1925.

Holtman sometimes gave a small nod: The description of the scene at Holtman's deathbed comes from *Baltimore Sun,* February 21, 22, and 23, 1925.

"most pathetic" sights he had ever witnessed: Baltimore News, February 23, 1925. O'Conor's attempt to take a deathbed statement was reported in *Evening Sun,* February 23, 1925.

95   *those attitudes began to turn:* Burrough, *Public Enemies,* pp. 518–19.

Whittemore had "no friends": Evening Sun, February 23, 1925.

"no good": Baltimore News, February 23, 1925.

96   *recently caught another recent escapee: Baltimore News,* February 23, 1925. It is interesting to note the lengths to which the police would go to return an escaped prisoner to custody.

Robert Holtman died: Baltimore Sun, February 22, 1925.

The Bureau of Public Welfare offered a $500 reward: Evening Sun, February 23, 1925.

"one of my former friends": Whittemore, "A Moral Lesson," *Baltimore Daily Post,* June 9 and 10, 1925.

97   *speakeasy featuring a still: Baltimore Sun,* July 29, 1926. Langrella was well known in Baltimore. It is not known how he came to be known as "Chicago Tommy."

or that they both went to Chicago: Whittemore told so many stories about Tommy Langrella at different times, many conflicting with his account in "A Moral Lesson," that it is impossible to determine the truth with any confidence, such as whether their meeting was accidental or preplanned, and the full degree to which Langrella provided assistance to Whittemore after his escape. Of course, it was in Whittemore's interest to show a continuing positive relationship with Langrella, as police soon suspected that he was responsible for Langrella's death in January 1926 after he was found full of bullet holes in New Jersey. The motivation behind the killing was never revealed. Police inferred that there was some kind of personal dispute between the two and speculated that Whittemore killed Langrella either after being double-crossed by him or because he was afraid Langrella would turn him in.

"watchful waiting": Baltimore Daily Post, February 23, 1925.

Penitentiary guards served as pallbearers: Evening Sun, February 24, 1925.

"I have been doing all I could possibly do": Baltimore Sun, February 21, 1925.

"the time has come": Baltimore Sun, February 21, 1925.

98   *"Hotel de Sweezey":* Undated *Baltimore Daily Post* clipping contemporaneous to the controversy surrounding Sweezey.

7. A Movie Thriller

100   *They learned nothing useful:* The Baltimore press certainly helped in this regard: in the weeks following the escape, the papers printed every rumor and accepted every police statement without question. They were beginning to realize that any news about Richard Whittemore spiked readership. Some Baltimoreans undoubtedly detested Whittemore and all he represented, but others, usually younger and often female, were increasingly enthralled. Either way, continuing coverage of Whittemore by the press, often on the front page and accompanied by lurid and occasionally misleading headlines, exploited the continued and growing interest in the Whittemores among their readership.

an opportunity too good to ignore: The account of the Holtzman robbery is a composite account taken primarily from the *Baltimore News, Baltimore Daily Post, Baltimore Sun,* and *Evening Sun,* March 16–31, 1925; *Baltimore News, Baltimore Daily Post, Baltimore Sun,* and *Evening Sun,* April 21–28, 1925; and Whittemore's own account in "A Moral Lesson," *Baltimore Daily Post,* June 10, 1926.

It was time to put his newfound expertise to work: Philadelphia Inquirer, January 15, 1939. According to this article, Whittemore used the knowledge he had gained from the Kraemers to put together the gang, telling them, "I've been learning things."

He dyed his hair blond: Whittemore describes the lead-up to the crime in "A Moral Lesson," *Baltimore Daily Post,* June 10, 1926.

101   *laughed and, showing a gun:* The best account of the crime appeared in the *Baltimore Daily Post,* March 17, 1925, which, unless otherwise noted, is the source for the details in this account.

"I didn't want to be killed": Evening Sun, March 16, 1925.

bought him a ticket to Philadelphia: Whittemore, "A Moral Lesson," *Baltimore Daily Post,* June 10, 1926.

There was just one problem: Evening Sun, March 20, 1925, details the identification of the robbers.

102   *their trial scheduled to begin on April 22: Baltimore News,* March 22, 1925.

treat himself to a new wardrobe: Whittemore, "A Moral Lesson," *Baltimore Daily Post,* June 10, 1926.

the Kraemer brothers were finally paroled: See *Baltimore Sun,* April 15, 1925, and *Evening Sun,* April 14, 1925, for details of the release of the Kraemers and the aftermath.

put them on board the next train to New York: Baltimore Sun, April 15, 1925; *Evening Sun,* April 14, 1925.

103   *"Reese Whittemore": Baltimore Sun,* April 21, 1925. See the same source for trial details.

pure "propaganda": Baltimore Sun, April 21, 1925.

104   *he asked Si Gilden to serve as a go-between:* Whittemore mentions sending money to Gilden to be forwarded to his father and Margaret in "A Moral Lesson," *Baltimore Daily Post,* June 11, 1926.

105 *Goldberg had been implicated but not charged:* Baltimore Sun, March 29, 1924. For more background on Goldberg, see *New York Times,* March 24, 1926; *Case on Appeal . . . The People of the State of New York, Respondent, against Jacob Kramer [sic] and Leon Miller, Defendants-Appellants,* May 26, 1926, pp. 160–72; U.S. Census 1900, 1910, 1920, 1930, 1940.

To all outward appearances: For background on William Unkelbach, see *Baltimore Sun,* October 24, 1931, November 13, 1942, and March 8, 1950; *Evening Sun,* December 18, 1944; and *New York Times,* March 24, 1926.

in his old Brooklyn neighborhood: For background on Anthony Paladino, see *Case on Appeal . . . The People of the State of New York, Respondent, against Jacob Kramer [sic] and Leon Miller, Defendants-Appellants,* May 26, 1926, pp. 46–67; *New York Times,* March 24, 1926.

106 *New York's traditional Diamond District:* The history of New York's Diamond District and its slow migration from Lower Manhattan to Midtown is well documented. For a basic overview, see *The Encyclopedia of New York,* edited by Kenneth Jackson (New Haven, CT: Yale University Press, 1995), pp. 332–33; and Barak Richman, "How Manhattan's Diamond District Continues to Operate Like an Old World Bazaar," *Smithsonian Magazine,* January 16, 2020.

The setup on Grand Street: Details of the Grand Street robbery are taken from *New York Times,* May 10, 1925.

107 *New York newspapers even regularly compiled lists:* For one of many examples of the stunning amount of lost jewelry, see *New York Times,* December 30, 1926, p. 20. The majority of "lost and found" classified ads were either looking for lost jewelry or offering rewards for its return.

"gem speculator": New York Daily News, March 27, 1926.

Tropp, after serving time in jail: The Jeweler's Circular, March 31, 1926, discusses Tropp's early life and background as a pickpocket. For more background on Joseph Tropp (aka Trop), see *New York Times,* March 27–30 and June 2, 1926.

belonged to more than fifty fraternal organizations: Jeweler's Circular, March 31, 1926. Mrs. Harry Sitamore, "Secrets of the Great Jewel Robberies, Part II," *Pittsburgh Sun-Telegraph,* October 7, 1934, also mentions Tropp's many fraternal connections and charitable contributions, which helped keep him out of jail.

his business to know who wanted what: Sitamore, "Secrets of the Great Jewel Robberies, Part II," is particularly useful in noting the ways in which Tropp was allowed to openly operate for so many years. Mrs. Sitamore's husband, Harry Sitamore, was a jewel thief who operated in Florida and New York and had earned the nickname "Prince of Thieves." She told her story about her husband and others in a multipart syndicated series.

The Kraemers would go to Tropp a few days before: Brooklyn Times Union, March 27, 1926, notes the unique method of ascertaining identity.

"Disposing of stolen jewelry": Whittemore, "A Moral Lesson," *Baltimore Daily Post,* June 11, 1926.

108 *On the morning of May 9:* Details of the Ross crime are taken from *Brooklyn Standard Union,* May 9 and 10, 1925; and *Brooklyn Daily Eagle,* May 9 and 10, 1925.

The three gang members all produced guns: Brooklyn Daily Eagle, May 9, 1925.

109 *he'd already been arrested nearly two dozen times:* Cleveland Plain Dealer, August 17, 1942. For additional background on Weinzimmer, see *New York Daily News,* July 22, 1928; and "Last of Whittemore Gang May Get 40 Years for Part in Sensational Robberies," undated clipping (c. 1928) from the morgue of the *New York Journal American.*

no fewer than three thousand speakeasies: Leslie Basalla and Peter Chakerian, *Cleveland Beer: History and Revival in the Rust Belt* (Charleston, SC: History Press/American Palate, 2015), chap. 6.

"we would go into a business": Whittemore, "A Moral Lesson, *Baltimore Daily Post,* June 11, 1926.

110   *Willie Rogers or "Baltimore Willie":* "Text of Anthony Paladino's Confession," *New York Times,* March 26, 1926. In some instances, gang members did not even know each other by their real names. New York authorities have a hard time getting the names straight, and even after the Kraemers were convicted, Leon Kraemer entered the New York penal system under the name "Leon Miller."

This time they targeted Stanley's: For details of the robbery, see *Brooklyn Daily Eagle,* July 16, 1925; *New York Daily News,* July 17, 1925; *New York Times,* July 17, 1925; and *New York Daily News,* July 17, 1925.

"Stick 'em up": *New York Daily News,* July 17, 1925. Although the phrase "stick 'em up" was in common usage, much of the language used by both the Whittemore gang and other gangsters of this era had yet to appear widely in popular culture outside of the tabloid press. They could not have been imitating the language of movie gangsters, as there was little dialogue in the movies of the silent era, there was no specific genre of gangster films, and most crime films were told from the perspective of the authorities rather than that of the criminals (which would later be an earmark of the gangster film drama). Serials of crime stories were not yet in vogue in the newly emerging medium of radio, and "hard-boiled" detective novels were not yet a popular literary genre. The Whittemore gang and others of the era were the real thing, the first of their kind to be documented by the press. It was their language and behaviors that were later embraced by popular culture and used to create the gangster template. Gangster films began to flourish after 1930, and Depression-era gangsters, inspired by the portrayal of 1920s gangsters in popular culture, aped both their language and style.

"each of the two bandits": *New York Daily News,* July 17, 1925. Oddly, although gloves were later found in the gang's robbery kit, this was the only time the press made mention of their use of silk gloves in reporting on a heist.

111   *"gave it up when I nearly got caught":* Whittemore, "A Moral Lesson," *Baltimore Post,* June 11, 1926.

"an exclusive car for exclusive people": *Brooklyn Standard Union,* January 12, 1923.

When Margaret walked out: In "A Moral Lesson," *Baltimore Daily Post,* June 11, 1926, Whittemore states bluntly, "We kidnapped her."

far more exclusive than garish Coney Island: For background on Long Beach during Prohibition, see Jonathan Olly, "Long Island During Prohibition, 1920–1933," *Long Island History Journal,* 26, no. 1 (2017). Precisely how long Richard and Margaret remained in Long Beach is uncertain. The pattern of Whittemore and the gang's activities suggests that they stayed only a few weeks, but some later reports indicated that they may have been there for much of the summer, perhaps even moving back and forth between Long Beach and New York City several times.

112   *The Sullivan Act made unlicensed possession of guns:* *New York Post,* January 16, 2012; see also Peter Duffy, "100 Years Ago, the Shot That Spurred New York's Gun-Control Law," *New York Times,* January 23, 2011, https://cityroom.blogs.nytimes.com/2011/01/23/100 -years-ago-the-shot-that-spurred-new-yorks-gun-control-law.

For now, Margaret returned: Whittemore, "A Moral Lesson," *Baltimore Daily Post,* June 11, 1926. Whittemore didn't want to risk another excursion into Baltimore, where it was more likely that he'd be recognized.

113   *a crime Peck managed to keep out of the papers:* The Peck robbery was only credited to the gang after their capture, yet I found no mention of the robbery in any of the New York newspapers. In keeping it out of the papers, Peck was probably either embarrassed by the heist or concerned for his future security.

diamond dealer John Linherr's shop: Details of the Linherr robbery are taken from *New York Daily News,* October 6, 1925.

a "closing time" job: New York Times, March 26, 1926. Unless the crime was taking place on the street, as in the upcoming Goudvis robbery, the Whittemore gang generally struck just as a store opened for business or just as it was closing, the two times when safes were open for either the distribution or return of stock.

"Life is short!": New York Daily News, October 6, 1925.

and struck on the morning of October 19: The crime details are primarily from *New York Times,* October 20, 1925. The crime was also covered in *Brooklyn Daily Eagle,* October 20, 1925; and *Brooklyn Times Union,* October 20, 1925.

114   *"a big sedan of an expensive make": New York Times,* October 20, 1925.

"Let's walk over now": New York Times, March 26, 1926. Some crime details were not revealed until they appeared in Anthony Paladino's confession.

"shoot him full of holes": New York Times, October 20, 1925.

"scores of persons": New York Times, October 20, 1925.

115   *"watches, cufflinks, and penknives": New York Times,* March 26, 1926.

he bought her a Cadillac: Whittemore, "A Moral Lesson," *Baltimore Daily Post,* June 11, 1926.

116   *the city of 700,000 was awash with money: Buffalo Times,* November 1, 1925. This boosterish account provides evidence of the city's economic vitality.

to purchase a fully armored car: Buffalo Times, October 4, 1925. The purchase of the armored car was a newsworthy event.

"a city where thieves can colonize": Buffalo Times, November 1, 1925.

117   *"has been the custom": Buffalo Times,* October 30, 1925.

they stole a Buick sedan: Buffalo Morning Express, March 23, 1926.

parked the Buick overnight: Buffalo Morning Express, April 2, 1926. *Buffalo Courier,* March 30, 1926, also notes that the car was retrieved from the garage.

118   *"Good morning": Buffalo Courier,* October 31, 1925. The bank robbery was covered extensively in every Buffalo newspaper of the time, as was the later trial. However, reportage in the day or two following the crime was wildly inconsistent, and few reports were in agreement. I have attempted to base this account on a consensus arrived at not only from the contemporaneous reporting but also from the reports on the subsequent trial.

"Stick 'em up!": Buffalo Courier, October 31, 1925.

"My God I've been shot!": Buffalo Times, October 29, 1925.

119   *"in second gear": Buffalo Morning Express,* April 24, 1926.

"We're being held up!": Buffalo Courier, October 30, 1925.

like a "movie thriller": Buffalo Morning Express, October 29, 1925.

120   *They dumped the two big guns: Buffalo Evening News,* November 2, 1925. The "freak gun" was included in a photograph of the weapons.

121   *"shoot to kill": Buffalo Courier,* October 30, 1925.

"guerilla gunmen": Buffalo Times, November 1, 1925.

"the most intensive manhunt": Buffalo Courier, October 30, 1925.

"They're dogs": Buffalo Courier, October 31, 1925.

122   *"Eye-Witnesses Drink Deep": Buffalo Courier,* October 30, 1925.

buried on page 22: Rochester Democrat and Chronicle, November 3, 1925.

Dutch Anderson was killed in a police shoot-out: Buffalo Courier, November 3, 1925. After Anderson's death, it became obvious that he had not been in Buffalo.

claiming crime was down: Buffalo Courier, November 1, 1925.

Some weeks later, the police admitted: Buffalo Evening Express, November 24, 1925.

the Erie County court had authorized twelve indictments: Buffalo Times, October 30, 1925.

The defendants named on the indictments: Twelve indictments, each for one count of murder in the first degree, were first filed in October 1925 and apparently are the only remaining records of the case. I obtained copies from the Erie County Clerk's Office.

8. A Great Many Good Times

123   *He never gave Rawlings Whittemore:* Whittemore, "A Moral Lesson," *Baltimore Daily Post,* June 11, 1926.

"bleach-bottle blondes": Baltimore News, March 30, 1926.

124   *"I don't like those sort of wise cracks": Daily Times* (Salisbury, MD), May 3, 1926.

He waited outside: This account of the Kenney shooting is taken primarily from *Baltimore Sun* and *Evening Sun,* November 2, 1925.

"volley of shots": Evening Sun, November 2, 1925.

"They ain't got me yet": Baltimore Daily Post, November 3, 1925.

125   *"You had better get off that case": Baltimore Daily Post,* November 6, 1925. Margaret's experience as a phone operator, which may have been in play here, points to her involvement. Had the call been a long-distance call placed from outside of Baltimore, it would have been possible for police to trace the call through interviews with telephone operators, as such calls were still rare and costly and had to be manually patched through by telephone operators. It would have been much less difficult to place a call from in or around Baltimore, which would have carried no extra charge and would arouse little suspicion from an operator. A long-distance call not only might be remembered but was more likely to have a curious operator listening in.

he first rented an apartment at 110 West Eightieth Street: For a building description and photo, see StreetEasy, https://streeteasy.com/building/110-west-80-street-new_york.

had lived just a few doors down: Kevin C. Fitzpatrick, *The Algonquin Round Table New York: A Historical Guide* (Guilford, CT: Rowman & Littlefield/Lyons Press, 2014). Kaufman lived at 150 West Eightieth St.

126   *"day and night" service:* For a reproduction of the flyer given to prospective renters that described the building, floor plans, lobby, and amenities in detail, see Chester Court, "Historic Documents," http://www.chestercourt.com/historic-documents.

presented himself as Horace Q. Waters: "The Inside Story of Whittemore's Capture," *Brooklyn Daily Times Union,* March 25, 1926.

"taking her away": Whittemore, "A Moral Lesson," *Baltimore Daily Post,* June 11, 1926, details the second kidnapping of Margaret.

Si Gilden hadn't given her a Cadillac: Whittemore, "A Moral Lesson," *Baltimore Daily Post,* June 11, 1926.

127 *they robbed jewelry dealer R. M. Ernest: New York Daily News,* December 3, 1925; *New York Times,* December 3, 1925; and "Text of Anthony Paladino's Confession," *New York Times,* March 26, 1926.

a small jewelry manufacturing business: The robbery of Folmer Prip was the only jewelry robbery perpetrated by the gang that ever went to trial, and subsequently accounts of its execution are also the most detailed. For a thorough retelling, see *Case on Appeal . . . The People of the State of New York, Respondent, against Jacob Kramer [sic] and Leon Miller, Defendants-Appellants,* May 26, 1926. Goldberg, the Kraemers, Unkelbach, and Paladino were all charged with robbery, although Unkelbach and Paladino testified for the prosecution in exchange for the promise of lighter sentences. Richard Whittemore, although known to be involved, was never tried and was not called on to testify. The Kraemers appealed their conviction, and it is the published transcripts of that appeal that create the most detailed and authoritative account of any crime the gang committed, as well as providing detailed background information on various gang members and on the behavior of the police and their interrogation tactics, as well as the tactics of the New York County district attorney's office after the gang was arrested following the Goudvis robbery. Although the Prip jewelry business robbery was not the most lucrative of the gang's many crimes, Prip and his employees were able to provide detailed eyewitness testimony and positive identification of gang members that made a conviction more likely than had they been tried for any other crimes. Other sources consulted include *New York Daily News,* December 24, 1925; *New York Times,* December 24, 1925; and "Text of Anthony Paladino's Confession," *New York Times,* March 26, 1926, but in virtually every instance trial testimony was the primary source. For details on the Armeny Building, see Daytonian in Manhattan, "The 1888 Armeny Building—No. 90 Nassau Street," September 21, 2012, http://daytoninmanhattan.blogspot.com/2012/09/the-1888-armeny-building-no-90-nassau.html.

"FLEXIBLE PLATINUM BRACELETS": The painted sign on the outside of the building was still legible in a 1986 photo taken by Walter Grutchfield and reprinted at: https://www.waltergrutchfield.net/prip.htm.

128 *and that a "Mr. Siegel": Case on Appeal, . . . The People of the State of New York, Respondent, against Jacob Kramer [sic] and Leon Miller, Defendants-Appellants,* May 26, 1926, p. 24.

"something fancy": Case on Appeal, . . . The People of the State of New York, Respondent, against Jacob Kramer [sic] and Leon Miller, Defendants-Appellants, May 26, 1926.

"out with the stock": Case on Appeal, . . . The People of the State of New York, Respondent, against Jacob Kramer [sic] and Leon Miller, Defendants-Appellants, May 26, 1926.

129 *"come back later": Case on Appeal, . . . The People of the State of New York, Respondent, against Jacob Kramer [sic] and Leon Miller, Defendants-Appellants,* May 26, 1926.

"I felt there was something coming off": Case on Appeal, . . . The People of the State of New York, Respondent, against Jacob Kramer [sic] and Leon Miller, Defendants-Appellants, May 26, 1926.

130 *"There ain't no use":* "Text of Anthony Paladino's Confession," *New York Times,* March 26, 1926. In the confession, Paladino describes the circumstances that caused the gang to abort the job and their actions.

Gilden was in hiding: The circumstances surrounding Gilden's trip to New York and sub-

sequent death are detailed in *Baltimore Sun,* December 24, 26, and 30, 1925; *Evening Sun,* December 24, 26, 28, and 29, 1925; *New York Times,* April 1 and 13, 1926.
she'd better "shut up": *Baltimore Daily Post,* December 25, 1925.
Baltimore detectives had received a tip: Baltimore Sun, December 23, 1925, and March 28, 1926, details the stakeout in New York.

131   *Gilden was next seen two days later: Evening Sun,* December 23, 1925, provides details of Gilden's death.

132   *he'd learn he had tuberculosis:* Unless otherwise noted, the following account of the Prip robbery is taken from *Case on Appeal . . . The People of the State of New York, Respondent, against Jacob Kramer [*sic*] and Leon Miller, Defendants-Appellants,* May 26, 1926. Goldberg's illness is directly referenced in the trial testimony.
*"How are you, Mr. Prip?": Case on Appeal . . . The People of the State of New York, Respondent, against Jacob Kramer [*sic*] and Leon Miller, Defendants-Appellants,* May 26, 1926, p. 25.

133   *young and rich and ready for fun:* New York's cabaret nightlife and accompanying lifestyle during the mid-1920s is well documented in a number of sources. Details here have been gleaned from Paul Sann, *The Lawless Decade* (New York: Crown, 1961); Hellinger, *Moon over Broadway; The Flapper* (1920 film); Lois Long's period reporting in her column under the pseudonym "Lipstick" in her regular column "Tables for Two" from *The New Yorker* in 1925 and 1926; and Whittemore's own boasting accounts in "A Moral Lesson." Mark Hellinger wrote an entire "Behind the News" column on the Whittemores' behavior and lifestyle during this period that was published in *New York Daily News,* June 25, 1928.

134   *were regulars at their favorite haunts:* The general scene at the Chantee is described in Lois Long's "Tables for Two" column in *The New Yorker,* January 16 and 30, 1926; Morris Markey, "Baa Baa Blacksheep," *The New Yorker,* April 3, 1926; and Willard Keefe, "City's Bandits Rub Elbows with Elite at Night Clubs," *Brooklyn Times,* March 28, 1926. Long notes the presence of Miller, while Keefe mentions Miller, Swanson, and others.
"very fine people": Whittemore, "A Moral Lesson," *Baltimore Daily Post,* June 11, 1926.

135   *Guinan's 300 Club: Brooklyn Times Union,* March 25, 1926, details the gang's travels to each of the clubs mentioned and their usual nightly routine during this period.
"Hello, Sucker": Sann, *The Lawless Decade,* p. 183. Tex Guinan was one of New York's best-known and more colorful characters of the Jazz Age, and the subject of the biography by Glenn Shirley, *Hello, Sucker! The Story of Texas Guinan* (Austin, TX: Eakin Press, 1989). She was the inspiration for the character "Panama Smith" played by actress Gladys George in the seminal gangster film *The Roaring Twenties,* which was based on a vignette written by Mark Hellinger. Jimmy Cagney's character was roughly based on Guinan's partner, gangster Larry Fey, although elements of his story, his language, and his behavior seem lifted from the story of Richard Whittemore as earlier outlined by Hellinger.
"as beautiful a night club": *New York Daily News,* January 31, 1926.
"nearly naked cuties": Lloyd R. Morris, *Incredible New York: High Life and Low Life from 1850 to 1950* (Syracuse, NY: Syracuse University Press, 1996), p. 331.
a brief movie career: New York Times, November 4, 1972, p. 35.
"mix where the Rockefellers": "Puttin' on the Ritz," words and music by Irving Berlin, 1930; for lyrics, see https://genius.com/Harry-richman-puttin-on-the-ritz-lyrics.

136   *earned write-ups in* The New Yorker: General background on the Club Chantee can be found in the "Tables for Two" column in *The New Yorker,* January 16 and 30, 1926.
"nicely decorated and softly lit": The New Yorker, January 30, 1926.

Whittemore also was tight: Brooklyn Times Union, March 28, 1926, notes Whittemore's relationship with Chicarelli and Mortillaro. There were rumors that Whittemore himself may have owned a piece of the club.

they knew enough to act one way: New York Daily Mirror, March 27, 1926. Laura Lee, a dancer at the club, mentioned the change in Whittemore's behavior when Margaret was present.

most popular club band of the era: See "George Olsen, 78, Bandleader of the 20's and 30's, Is Dead," *New York Times,* March 19, 1971.

"Who means my happiness": SongLyrics, "George Olsen—Who? Lyrics," http://www.songlyrics.com/george-olsen/who-lyrics/.

137 *"We lived very nicely":* Whittemore, "A Moral Lesson," *Baltimore Daily Post,* June 11, 1926. For more details on their nightly excursions, see *Brooklyn Times Union,* March 25, 1926.

9. The Usual Route

138 *Tropp was one of the best-known fences:* Tropp is compared to Rothstein in Sitamore, "Secrets of the Great Jewel Robberies, Part II."

In late December 1925: The account of the planning and execution of the Goudvis Brothers robbery is a composite taken from a number of newspaper accounts. Those contemporaneous to the event best describe the attack itself, while reports, in particular the confession of Anthony Paladino, supply details of the planning of the crime and the aftermath. See primarily *Brooklyn Standard Union,* January 11, 1926; *Brooklyn Times Union,* January 11, 1926; *New York Times,* January 12, 1926; "Text of Anthony Paladino's Confession," *New York Times,* March 26, 1926; *New York Daily News,* January 12, 1926; and *Philadelphia Inquirer,* January 12, 1926.

A year later, the firm would acquire: For the history of the Kazanjian Red Diamond, see *New York Daily News,* January 10, 2009.

139 *The area was heavily policed:* "New Deadline Guards Midtown Wealth," *New York Times,* November 16, 1924, provides an account of the evolution and activities of this special unit.

140 *"tailed it up":* "Text of Anthony Paladino's Confession," *New York Times,* March 26, 1926. Paladino provides quite a detailed account of the planning of the crime and a detailed, step-by-step accounting of the gang's actions before, during, and after the robbery.

141 *The vestibule was narrow: Brooklyn Standard Union,* January 11, 1926, provides the best description of the vestibule of the building, which the paper described as a "hallway."

142 *tore a dollar bill in half: Salt Lake Tribune,* June 28, 1936.

the gang met one last time: "Text of Anthony Paladino's Confession," *New York Times,* March 26, 1926.

143 *she retrieved a bag: Baltimore News,* March 20, 1926. The precise contents of the gang's robbery kit are known from Margaret's later arrest.

144 *he thought the guy was "a bull": New York Daily News,* May 4, 1926.

Henry Helwig had retired: New York Daily News, May 4, 1926.

146 *Helwig emptied his revolver: New York Daily News,* January 12, 1926, describes the actions of Helwig and the police and details Weinzimmer's driving route.

147 *His work over:* "Text of Anthony Paladino's Confession," *New York Times,* March 26, 1926.

148 *Goudvis needed eight stitches: New York Times,* January 12, 1926.

10. King of This Empty Domain

150 *someone did memorize the plate number: Brooklyn Times Union,* March 26, 1926. The car bearing plate number 6N-19-58 was found the next day.

McLaughlin was a money guy: See his obituary, *New York Times,* December 8, 1967.

"We want to know where the police were": New York Times, January 12, 1926.

151 *"just one of those things":* New York Times, January 12, 1926.

"The estimate of $100,000": New York Times, January 12, 1926.

estimated to be as much as $500,000: "Crime Plans to Net Billion Revealed in Confession," *New York Journal-American,* undated clipping from the Whittemore clipping file that appears to date from late March 1926. The true value of any jewelry robbery committed by the Whittemore gang is nearly impossible to pin down with certainty. Newspaper accounts were often based on an estimate before a full accounting had taken place, and since only the Prip robbery went to trial, figures were not always updated or verified. In some instances, jewelers and dealers may have inflated amounts for insurance purposes or deflated those amounts in the information provided to the public, owing to embarrassment or to security concerns related to keeping other potential thieves from knowing precisely how much stock they kept on hand. Value may also have been provided according to either wholesale or retail value, which could vary wildly. In general, however, reported value, particularly in regard to the Goudvis heist, tended to inflate over time. I've done my best to compare accounts and provide a consensus in terms of value.

each man's take came to $11,000: "Text of Anthony Paladino's Confession," *New York Times,* March 26, 1926.

152 *Richard got his new Cadillac:* For the Whittemores' spending spree after the robbery, see *Baltimore Sun,* April 4, 1926.

"Madame asked for a fur coat": Buffalo Courier, April 4, 1926.

"an exclusive store": Baltimore Sun, April 4, 1926.

if they could hold on to any of it: Baltimore Sun, April 4, 1926. More on the profligate spending habits of the Whittemore gang, particularly in the wake of the Goudvis job, is recounted in *Brooklyn Daily Times Union,* March 25, 1926; *Brooklyn Times Union,* December 29, 1927; Mark Hellinger's vignette on Whittemore at the Chantee in *New York Daily News,* June 25, 1928; and *New York Times,* April 4, 1926.

$52,000 a year in 1926: For Ruth's annual salary, see Baseball Reference, "Babe Ruth," https://www.baseball-reference.com/players/r/ruthba01.shtml.

not quite as much as F. Scott Fitzgerald: F. Scott Fitzgerald, "How to Live on $36,000 a Year," *Saturday Evening Post,* April 5, 1924. If anything, when the gang was flush during the first few months of 1926, they spent money even more extravagantly than Fitzgerald.

the idea of opening their own cabaret: Whittemore, "A Moral Lesson," *Baltimore Daily Post,* June 11, 1926. Whittemore claimed that they were ripped off for $11,000 during this process of setting up the cabaret business, which may have increased the gang's need for money.

153 *already had a couple of close calls:* Whittemore, "A Moral Lesson," *Baltimore Daily Post,* June 11, 1926.

He was fifty-two-year-old John D. Coughlin: Background on Coughlin appears in an extensive profile by Niven Busch and A. Barr Gray, "The Cop in the Silk Shirt," *The New Yorker,* September 25, 1926.

154   *"race track or watering resorts":* Busch and Gray, "The Cop in the Silk Shirt," *The New Yorker,* September 25, 1926.

"Crooks are caught by information": Busch and Gray, "The Cop in the Silk Shirt," *The New Yorker,* September 25, 1926.

155   *with his Sunday column "About Town":* For more background on Hellinger, see Jim Bishop, *The Mark Hellinger Story: A Biography of Broadway and Hollywood* (New York: Appleton-Century-Crofts, 1952).

"Dick was always welcomed there": Hellinger, *Moon over Broadway,* p. 140. One entire chapter of *Moon over Broadway,* "The Better Wine," is about Richard Whittemore, his lifestyle and the larger gang's lifestyle in the week immediately preceding their capture, and the capture itself.

named Laura Lee: "Dancer Friend of Thief Says She Saw Him Use Gun," *New York Daily Mirror,* March 27, 1926. The *Mirror* was apparently the only newspaper to speak with Lee about Whittemore. She described her relationship with him in some detail, as well as Whittemore's activities on the night of his capture.

156   *covered for a lot of sins:* "Girls and Harry Thaw," *The Times* (Shreveport, LA), May 2, 1926. This syndicated story from International Feature Service mentions Lee's involvement with Thaw during this period, which overlapped with her relationship with Whittemore, and it also provides evidence of just how successfully Whittemore had penetrated a different social stratum. The story of Thaw and the White murder has been the subject of numerous books and films, including E. L. Doctorow's *Ragtime* and the 1955 film starring Ray Milland, *The Girl in the Red Velvet Swing.*

"me taking that down whole": New York Daily Mirror, March 27, 1926.

"He spent money like a millionaire": New York Daily Mirror, March 27, 1926.

He called her "Miss Lee": New York Daily Mirror, March 27, 1926.

157   *at the famed Belasco Theater:* Internet Broadway Database (www.ibdb.com) is the standard source for such data. The play was the first stage success for MacArthur, who turned to writing during the Great War and became a member of the famed Algonquin Round Table, New York's legendary literary salon. He dated Dorothy Parker before eventually marrying actress Helen Hayes in 1928 and going on to write the stage classic *The Front Page* and finding success in Hollywood as a screenwriter. It's interesting to note that *The Front Page* was later made into the film *His Girl Friday,* starring Rosalind Russell and Cary Grant. The film, which centers on the reaction in the tabloid press to a scheduled hanging, contains some unmistakable echoes of Whittemore's story.

"was thrilled": New York Daily Mirror, March 27, 1926.

158   *everyone was back in New York:* Willard Keefe, "Inside Story of Whittemore's Capture," *Brooklyn Times Union,* March 25, 1926. As recounted in the story, when police began tailing Goldberg in early March, they were led to the others in a matter of a few days. On March 21, 1926, the *New York Daily News* reported that the six gang members had been tailed for "seventeen days" before their arrest.

known as a "fly tip": Keefe, "Inside Story of Whittemore's Capture," *Brooklyn Times Union,* March 25, 1926. This report also provides the most detailed account of the gang's roundup and activities in the day before Whittemore's capture.

159   *and didn't return until dawn:* Keefe, "Inside Story of Whittemore's Capture," *Brooklyn Times Union,* March 25, 1926.
      "I think that tall one": Morris Markey, "A Reporter at Large: Baa, Baa, Blacksheep," *The New Yorker,* April 3, 1926.
      see what they were all up to: Brooklyn Times Union, March 25, 1926. This detailed story notes Coughlin's decision to continue having the gang tailed, traces their nightlife excursions, and notes the changes in their pattern the week before their arrest.

160   *It was another closing-time job:* All details of the Sims robbery are taken from *New York Daily News,* March 15, 1926.
      was robbed in a job nearly identical: All details of the Kandel robbery are taken from *Brooklyn Citizen,* March 15, 1926. Most New York papers failed to report on the crime.
      "nattily dressed": New York Times, March 15, 1926.

161   *a device known as the telautograph:* See Nathan Brewer, "Your Engineering Heritage: The Telautograph: Handwriting at a Distance," February 1, 2018, https://insight.ieeeusa .org/articles/history-telautograph/. The teleautograph was still commonly used into the 1960s.
      "call Mrs. Black at the Hotel Embassy": New York Daily News, July 22, 1928.
      registered as Miss Margaret "Dolly" Collins: Baltimore News, March 20, 1926.

162   *his associates at the Chantee: Brooklyn Times Union,* March 25, 1926.
      "practically every known precaution": Jeweler's Circular, March 31, 1926, p. 95. *Jeweler's Circular* was an industry publication known to virtually every jeweler and dealer, and it provided a good overview of the gang's activities and investigations into those activities.

163   *the artists, writers, and actors:* Elsa Hildegard, Baroness von Freytag-Loringhoven's life in the Arcade building is detailed in Irene Gammel, *Baroness Elsa: Gender, Dada, and Everyday Modernity* (Cambridge, MA: MIT Press, 2003). Other notable residents are discussed in Peter Salwen, *Upper West Side Story: A History and Guide* (New York: Abbeville Press, 1989).
      Just before 3 a.m.: The following is a composite account of the capture of Whittemore and the remainder of the gang based on weeks of reporting that began on March 19, 1926, in the *New York Times, New York Daily News, New York Mirror, Brooklyn Times Union, Brooklyn Daily Eagle, Buffalo Evening News, Baltimore Sun, Baltimore Daily Post,* and *Baltimore News.* No two reports of the capture of Whittemore and the others paint precisely the same portrait. In Whittemore's "A Moral Lesson," he claims to have been arrested just out-side the Chantee — another instance of Whittemore twisting his story to make himself appear more agreeable. Other sources disagree. Also, Whittemore makes no mention of the shoot-out in "A Moral Lesson." However, the consensus among all these reports is that the gang was arrested after a shoot-out with the detectives who had tailed them throughout the night and into the next morning. See also Markey, "A Reporter at Large: Baa, Baa, Blacksheep," *The New Yorker,* April 3, 1926, and Hellinger, *Moon over Broadway.* Details of Whittemore's relationship with Laura Lee and their activities that night were reported in the *New York Mirror,* March 27, 1926. Specific details of the circumstances of the arrest stem primarily from "Six Men and Woman Held as Thief Gang," *New York Times,* March 20, 1926; "Fugitive Slayer Held with Two Companions," *Washington Post,* March 20, 1926; "Mrs. Whittemore Arrested," *Baltimore Sun,* March 20, 1926; "Inside Story of Whittemore's Capture," *Brooklyn Times Union,* March 25, 1926; and "Captor of Bandit King Describes Chase," *Baltimore News,* March 22, 1926.
      "Wine!" he called out: Hellinger, *Moon over Broadway,* p. 140.

"You've been drinking": Hellinger, *Moon over Broadway,* p. 141.

"For God's sake, Jack": New York Daily Mirror, March 27, 1926.

164   *"You two fellows come with me":* New York Daily Mirror, March 27, 1926.

165   *the gangster was holding out two $1,000 bills:* Whittemore, "A Moral Lesson," *Baltimore Daily Post,* June 10, 1926. Whittemore claimed that he offered the police two $1,000 bills for his freedom, although again, his account conveniently leaves out the car chase through the streets and subsequent gunplay.

He hit Whittemore with a right hook: Baltimore News, March 20, 1926. *Baltimore Sun,* March 21, 1926, notes that "a few blows were passed."

11. In a Rakish Way

166   *"rich collection of clothing and jewels":* Brooklyn Times Union, March 21, 1926. Bills larger than $500, including $1,000, $5,000, $10,000, and even $100,000 bills, were printed until 1946 and not withdrawn from general circulation until 1969, when President Richard Nixon, believing that bills in such large denominations made it easy to launder money, ordered them recalled.

"Urgent": Baltimore News, March 20, 1926. The newspaper included a facsimile of the note, presumably a true copy.

167   *Their operator was able to tell the detectives:* Baltimore News, March 21, 1926. Calls were traced at the time through interviews with operators, who manually had to put calls through exchanges. It was easier to trace calls from hotels than from other locations because all calls had to go through the hotel's phone service. Many hotels also logged all calls and charged guests for each call.

"John Vaughn" from Cleveland: Philadelphia Inquirer, January 15, 1939.

belonged to the Ohio Automobile Association: Baltimore Sun, March 21, 1926.

"Yes, you got me": Baltimore News, March 21, 1926.

168   *went after Goldberg and the Kraemers:* Details of the arrest of Goldberg and the Kraemers are recounted in *Case on Appeal . . . The People of the State of New York, Respondent, against Jacob Kramer [sic] and Leon Miller, Defendants-Appellants,* May 26, 1926, pp. 129–39.

170   *Whittemore tried to play it tough:* Brooklyn Daily Eagle, March 21, 1926.

171   *"Easy money":* New York Times, March 24, 1926.

As afternoon turned to evening: Margaret's arrest and her actions beforehand are detailed best in "Tiger Girl Betrayed by Bandit Luggage," *Baltimore News,* March 21, 1926. Subsequent reports indicate that she may have also been returning from dinner to walk her dog.

She'd created a fiction: Baltimore News, March 21, 1926.

she was "Mrs. John Vaughn": Baltimore News, March 21, 1926.

172   *"instruments not for a society matron":* Baltimore News, March 21, 1926.

"blonde, rouged": Baltimore News, March 20, 1926.

They lined everybody up for a photograph: The photograph of the gang, minus Margaret but including Chicarelli and Mortillaro, would be widely reprinted in subsequent months.

173   *"a rather good-looking fellow":* New York Times, March 20, 1926.

"twenty-two bags": Buffalo Courier, April 3, 1926.

"the most important arrests": Baltimore Sun, March 21, 1926.

"before nightfall I expect to solve": Baltimore News, March 21, 1926.

"We've just begun": Baltimore Daily Post, March 20, 1926.

"You're at the end of your string": Baltimore Sun, March 21, 1926.

174   *"You think you're smart": Baltimore News,* March 20, 1926.

fifteen pairs of handcuffs: New York Times, March 21, 1926.

the questioning became more aggressive: Paladino testified openly during the Kraemer trial about being beaten by police. See *Case on Appeal ... The People of the State of New York, Respondent, against Jacob Kramer [sic] and Leon Miller, Defendants-Appellants,* May 26, 1926, pp. 58–59.

175   *"He always caused trouble": Baltimore Daily Post,* March 19, 1926.

She became hysterical: Baltimore Daily Post, March 19, 1926, notes Marie Holtman's reaction.

"Club Is Rendezvous": New York Times, March 20, 1926.

"lately patronized": New York Times, March 20, 1926.

"had been puzzled": Stanley Walker, *City Editor* (New York: F. A. Stokes, 1934), p. 32. Walker was probably referring to the rising prominence of gangster Arnold Rothstein.

12. Candy Kid Dares Chair for Love

178   *Coughlin's men resumed: Case on Appeal ... The People of the State of New York, Respondent, against Jacob Kramer [sic] and Leon Miller, Defendants-Appellants,* May 26, 1926, pp. 58–59.

only as "Willie Rogers": "Text of Anthony Paladino's Confession," *New York Times,* March 26, 1926.

179   *"I identify him ninety-five percent": Buffalo Evening Express,* March 22, 1926.

brought in two hundred cops: Brooklyn Daily Eagle, March 21, 1926. It is interesting to note that at the time victims were not kept anonymous during lineups. As noted in the story, the victim identified suspects by standing behind them.

"she wore a small, light tan hat": Evening Sun, March 21, 1926.

cried out for "her Dickie": New York Daily News, March 21, 1926.

"He has always been on the level with me": Buffalo Times, March 21, 1926.

180   *"I love my husband": Evening Sun,* March 21, 1926.

he had her remanded to the Florence Crittenton home: New York Daily News, March 23, 1926.

181   *"keeping Paladino and Whittemore":* Jack O'Brien, "Candy Kid Confesses Jail Killing," *New York Daily News,* March 21, 1926.

her husband could hear her weeping: O'Brien, "Candy Kid Confesses Jail Killing," *New York Daily News,* March 21, 1926.

182   *A Mott Street address: Buffalo Times,* March 22, 1926.

claimed only that he "might know": Buffalo Times, March 22, 1926.

boosting O'Conor's own political ambitions: O'Conor's biography is appropriately entitled *Inevitable Success.* Although O'Conor was a dedicated public servant, at every step of his political career he was also keenly aware of the impact of his every decision not only on his own political aspirations but on those of everyone he interacted with. His genius was ensuring that the public never really viewed him as calculating. For discussion of the Whittemore case, including all the various political machinations and calculations by all parties, see Kerwin and O'Conor, *The Inevitable Success,* pp. 107–23.

183   *In New York County:* Criminal prosecution in New York City proceeded by borough, along county lines. Manhattan is New York County.

ambitious acting district attorney Ferdinand Pecora: For more on Pecora, see Michael Perino,

The Hellhound of Wall Street: How Ferdinand Pecora's Investigation of the Great Crash Forever Changed American Finance (New York: Penguin Press, 2010).

"Those pointed features": Baltimore News, March 22, 1926. Margaret Whittemore was never charged in the Ortman robbery. After her husband made his decision to confess, Maryland and New York officials both agreed not to prosecute her for any crime, although Baltimore police were certain of her involvement in the confectionery holdup.

Baltimore police were delighted: Baltimore News, March 22, 1926.

The arrest had already provided: New York Times, June 8, 1926. Subsequent to Whittemore's arrest, Walker supported a law to roll back the hours that cabarets were legally allowed to operate, a move widely seen as politically expedient and made in reaction to the Whittemore arrest. See also Peter Levins, "Close Broadway! Fight On," New York Daily News, June 27, 1926.

184   "with low hanging head": New York Daily News, March 23, 1926.
      "Piercing yells could be heard": Baltimore News, March 23, 1926.
      "supreme conceit": Baltimore Sun, March 23, 1926.

185   "I am confident of my ability": Baltimore News, March 24, 1926.
      "I hardly realized": Baltimore News, March 24, 1926.
      "I don't care": Philadelphia Inquirer, March 27, 1926.
      he also needed to score: Baltimore News, March 25, 1926. This source and the Baltimore Sun of the same day detail the circumstances of Unkelbach's arrest.
      "It's alright": New York Daily Mirror, March 24, 1926. The newspapers strewn on Unkelbach's bed, detailing their crimes, were yet more evidence of how enthralled he and the rest of the gang were by their own notoriety.

186   "orgy of confessions": New York Daily News, March 24, 1926.
      "in his usual ruthless fashion": Baltimore News, March 25, 1926.
      "If there was any argument": Baltimore Sun, March 24, 1926.
      pull the trigger on Whittemore himself: Baltimore News, March 25, 1926.
      "snarls and spits": Buffalo Times, March 25, 1926.
      "criminal ears": Baltimore News, March 25, 1926.
      "half her character": Baltimore News, March 27, 1926.
      "an innocent tool": Brooklyn Daily Eagle, March 24, 1926.
      "her hair is blond and brittle": Brooklyn Daily Eagle, March 24, 1926.

187   the authorities allowed: Baltimore News, March 25, 1926. The press seemed rarely to allow a kiss between the two to go unnoted.
      took part in a lineup: Brooklyn Standard Union, March 24, 1926.
      the building was a total loss: Brooklyn Times Union, March 25, 1926. See also New York Times, March 25, 1926.

188   Rumors of caches of gems and cash: See, for instance, Post Star (Glens Falls, NY), March 22, 1926, one of many stories that mentioned the supposed cache of cash and stolen gems. Such speculation continued for years.
      "We have learned how highly systemized": Associated Press, March 25, 1926.
      "he was the livest boy": Baltimore Daily Post, March 25, 1926.
      "I want to be left alone": Baltimore Daily Post, March 25, 1926, is the source of this account of Rawlings's visit with Richard.

189   "If they turn my wife out on the street": Baltimore Daily Post, March 25, 1926. See also Buffalo Evening News, March 26, 1926.

"If Whittemore will tell me things": New York Daily News, March 26, 1926.

190 *The morning of Friday, March 27: Brooklyn Daily Times,* March 27, 1926, details the circumstances of Tropp's arrest. This report and some others spell his name "Trop." Similarly, Tommy Langrella is referred to in some accounts as "Langella," and some reports spell Unkelbach's name "Unkelback." In all such cases of spelling discrepancies, unless I have found definitive information in regard to the proper spelling, I have chosen to use the most common form of the name then used.

He got out in less than twenty-four hours: New York Daily News, March 28, 1926. After making bail, Tropp, true to form, would skate on most of the charges and continue to operate with impunity.

"He never worried about anything": Baltimore Sun, March 27, 1926.

would clerk for Supreme Court justice Louis Brandeis: For background on Shulman, see his obituary, *New York Times,* March 21, 1955.

"not wanted on a serious charge": New York Daily News, March 28, 1926.

191 *At the proceeding a few hours later:* This is a composite account of the March 28 hearing, with details drawn primarily from the *Brooklyn Daily Eagle, Brooklyn Standard Union, New York Daily News,* and *New York Times,* March 28 and 29, 1926.

"I haven't got a dime": New York Daily News, March 27, 1926.

Bushel had already successfully defended: New York Daily News, March 14, 1923. For Bushel's background, see *New York Times,* March 10, 1969.

stop and take it back off: New York Times, March 27, 1926.

192 *Margaret arrived in the Municipal Courts Building first:* This composite account of the meeting between Richard and Margaret is taken primarily from *Buffalo Courier, Brooklyn Citizen, Brooklyn Times Union,* and *New York Daily News,* March 28, 1926.

"Sullivan would forget": New York Daily News, March 27, 1926.

ran a photograph of the maudlin scene: New York Daily News, March 26, 1926, p. 3. Researchers should be aware that the scanned version of the *New York Daily News* available online includes multiple editions of the newspaper published on the same day. A story or photo that appears in one edition may not appear in another, or it may appear on a different page or in a different form. This is the case for the photo of Richard and Margaret, which does not appear in some editions and appears on a different page in others.

193 *fallen for "riotous living": New York Daily News,* March 27, 1926.

"To see her": Baltimore News, March 27, 1926.

194 *"CANDY KID DARES CHAIR FOR LOVE": New York Daily News,* March 27, 1926.

13. Not Gonna Burn Alone

195 *"The gunman, natty and clean-shaven": New York Daily News,* March 28, 1926.

she called out, "Dick!": New York Daily News, March 28, 1926.

196 *Whittemore rambled on: Brooklyn Times Union,* March 27, 1926, notes the length of the confession. Some later sources claimed it was only twenty-five pages.

"best friend I have in the world": Baltimore Daily Post, March 29, 1926.

"soon learned to join in a conversation": Whittemore, "A Moral Lesson," *Baltimore Post,* June 11, 1926. Although a transcript of Whittemore's confession was never publicly released, from a comparison of reports both at the time and later, it is clear that in tone and content Whittemore's confession was nearly identical to the contents of "A Moral Lesson."

From the time he began confessing until the moment of his death, with only a few variations, Whittemore was remarkably consistent in the version he told of his own story.
"as it did not require any great time": Whittemore, "A Moral Lesson," *Baltimore Post,* June 11, 1926.

197 *"the boys in the penitentiary":* Whittemore, "A Moral Lesson," *Baltimore Post,* June 11, 1926.
"It was his life or mine": Whittemore, "A Moral Lesson," *Baltimore Daily Post,* June 9, 1926.
"dirty tricks that caused his death": Whittemore, "A Moral Lesson," *Baltimore Daily Post,* June 11, 1926.
"never fired a shot": Whittemore, "A Moral Lesson," *Baltimore Daily Post,* June 12, 1926.
"ran whiskey by boat": Whittemore, "A Moral Lesson," *Baltimore Daily Post,* June 11, 1926.
"I sent her home": Whittemore, "A Moral Lesson," *Baltimore Daily Post,* June 11, 1926.

198 *"great number of these police captains":* Buffalo Courier, April 23, 1926.
"men in every stage of occupation": Buffalo Courier, April 23, 1926.
"I wish to say, gentlemen": New York Daily News, March 28, 1926.
"He tried to kid me": Baltimore Daily Post, March 31, 1926.

199 *"Now at least I will be free":* Baltimore News, March 31, 1926.
I agreed to let his wife go": New York Times, March 30, 1926.

200 *"I will fight Baltimore's claim":* Evening Sun, March 30, 1926.

201 *Whittemore could end up a free man:* Buffalo Courier, March 30, 1926.
Austin Roche and two associates raced to New York: Buffalo Courier, March 30, 1926.
"It is the policy": Baltimore Sun, April 2, 1926.

202 *"I'll kick you":* Evening Sun, April 2, 1926.
"laughed out of court": New York Times, April 1, 1926.
"fooled no one": Baltimore Daily Post, March 31, 1926.
"He'll be taken to Buffalo": New York Daily News, April 2, 1926.

203 *a concoction of kerosene and sulfur:* Buffalo Morning Express, April 3, 1926.
"And plenty of it": Buffalo Morning Express, April 3, 1926.
"Believe me, I'm not gonna burn alone": Buffalo Times, April 2, 1926.
no fewer than six daily newspapers: Buffalo daily newspapers included the *Buffalo Evening News, Daily Star and Inquirer, Buffalo Times, Buffalo Courier, Buffalo Morning Express,* and *Buffalo Evening Express.*

204 *Hundreds of people lined the sidewalk:* Buffalo Times, April 2, 1926. The scene surrounding Whittemore's arrival, including his lashing out, was also described in some detail by several other Buffalo newspapers.

205 *He asked for a steak:* Buffalo Courier, April 6, 1926, describes in detail the conditions of Richard Whittemore's incarceration.
"Gangster in Defiant Mood": Buffalo Morning Express, April 3, 1926.
"Whittemore Conviction Sure": Buffalo Daily Star, April 3, 1926.
"to the poor people": Buffalo Times, April 3, 1926.

206 *"any paper that wants to pay me":* Buffalo Times, April 3, 1926.
he was allowed no visitors: New York Journal American, May 1, 1926.
"He carries himself erect": Buffalo Courier, April 3, 1926.
"I see why it is necessary": Buffalo Courier, April 3, 1926.
the tunnel had last been used: Buffalo Morning Express, April 4, 1926.
"he was accorded the greatest city hall audience": Buffalo Courier, April 6, 1926. Except where the sources of specific quotes are cited, this is a composite account of Whittemore's Buffalo

trial, gleaned from the Buffalo newspapers—the *Buffalo Courier, Buffalo News, Daily Star,* and *Buffalo Evening News*—and the Baltimore and New York papers that covered the trial: the *Baltimore Sun, Baltimore Daily Post,* and *Baltimore News;* and the *Evening News, New York Daily News,* and *New York Times.* A transcript was produced of the court proceedings at the time, as the prosecution and defense both expected an appeal if Whittemore was convicted. My inquiries to the Erie County Clerk's Office and the New York State Archives, however, indicate that these transcripts apparently no longer exist. Fortunately, newspaper and wire service reporting later reproduced significant portions of the spoken record of the trial. Although individual reports might differ slightly in regard to specific wordings, they are generally consistent. Readers should be aware that, depending on the newspaper and the edition, some stories appeared in the paper on the day of the event or the day following, and that some reporting appeared in subsequent stories at a later time.

207   *"It's like the Bridge of Sighs":* Buffalo Courier, April 6, 1926.
  Moore had hired him: For Sumner's background, see *Buffalo Evening News,* December 30, 1916; and *Buffalo Courier,* February 19, 1925.
  From those letters Moore learned: Buffalo Evening News, June 2, 1928. These letters explaining how Whittemore was able to finance a defense received no mention during the trial.
208   *"Moore is the more dramatic orator":* Buffalo Times, April 25, 1925.
209   *"Hello, dear":* New York Daily News, April 11, 1926, fully describes their interaction.
  "she will not contest": Brooklyn Standard Union, April 12, 1926.
  "Tiger Girl Loses Battle of Nerve, Will Confess All": New York Daily News, April 12, 1926.
210   *"How can I squeal":* Baltimore Daily Post, April 12, 1926.
  "My love for my husband": Brooklyn Daily Eagle, April 12, 1926.
  "I thought he made his living": Baltimore Daily Post, April 12, 1926, is the source of quotes from Margaret Whittemore's statement to the press upon leaving the courthouse that day.
211   *"pose as many times as you like":* Baltimore Sun, April 11, 1926.
  "She was absolutely released": Baltimore Sun, April 11, 1926.
  "Mrs. Whittemore deeply regrets": Baltimore Sun, April 11, 1926.
212   *When they found letters: Buffalo Evening News,* June 2, 1928.
  "Rich, fondest regards": Buffalo Courier, April 15, 1926.
  "Judge. I am here": Buffalo Evening News, June 2, 1928, also describes subsequent letters.
  "not without friends": Buffalo Times, April 15, 1926.
213   *Putting Whittemore in a special cage: Buffalo Times,* April 24, 1926. The impact on the public of placing Whittemore in a special cage would be underscored once pictures of Margaret visiting Whittemore while he was caged began to appear in the press.
  he urged her not to come: Buffalo Courier, April 21, 1926, pp. 1 and 10.
  "she has greatly aided": Buffalo Times, April 16, 1926.

14. The Tunnel of Tears

214   *"the morbidly curious":* Buffalo Times, April 18, 1926.
  "Beau Brummel": Buffalo Courier, April 21, 1926.
215   *"Flappers Storm City Hall for Whittemore":* Buffalo Daily Star, April 19, 1926.
  His hundreds of fans: Buffalo Daily Star, April 19, 1926.
216   *"Look at the armed dicks":* Baltimore Post, April 19, 1926.

a "dashing blonde": Buffalo Courier, April 20, 1926.
"For God's sake": New York Daily News, April 20, 1926.

217 *"Don't come to Buffalo": Buffalo Courier,* April 21, 1926.
"it looks like a busy day": Buffalo Times, April 21, 1926.
"his usual gay and debonair self": Buffalo Times, April 21, 1926.

218 *"Perhaps that has something to do": New York Daily News,* April 21, 1926.
"O God, pity me": New York Daily News, April 21, 1926.
"he paid no attention to the old man": Buffalo Times, April 21, 1926, notes Richard's lack of reaction to being told his father was present.
"reputable businessmen": New York Daily News, April 21, 1926.
"I will prove": New York Daily News, April 21, 1926.

219 *"Who else besides you": New York Daily News,* April 21, 1926.
"You are not insinuating": New York Daily News, April 21, 1926.
"Moore is playing": Buffalo Courier, April 21, 1926.

220 *would even be allowed to mingle: New York Journal American,* April 21, 1926.
handed it to the jailer: New York Daily News, April 22, 1926.
"O Daddy": Buffalo Daily Star and Inquirer, April 22, 1926.

221 *"just a laborer": New York Times,* April 22, 1926.
"I arrived at the bank": New York Times, April 22, 1926.

222 *"I was thunderstruck": Baltimore News,* April 21, 1926, recounts this entire exchange, including the description of the weather.

223 *Whittemore claimed that the scar: Buffalo Times,* April 22, 1926.
"I shall show you gentlemen": Baltimore News, April 21, 1926.

224 *"Naw": New York Times,* April 23, 1926.

225 *She was no Tiger Girl:* Jansen's demeanor during the testimony is best described in *Buffalo Courier,* April 23, 1926, from which this account of her testimony is taken.

226 *"Richard wants to see you badly": Baltimore Sun,* April 25, 1926.
where she was met by Melvin Greene: Buffalo Daily Star and Inquirer, April 24, 1926. Given its access, the newspaper was probably tipped off to her arrival.
"I have come to help Dick": Buffalo Daily Star and Inquirer, April 24, 1926.
"a handsome young woman": Buffalo Daily Star and Inquirer, April 24, 1926.
"Whittemore Trial Nears Close": Buffalo Courier, April 24, 1925.
"Please don't write": Buffalo Daily Star and Inquirer, April 24, 1926.

227 *"reeking of class and costliness": Buffalo Daily Star and Inquirer,* April 24, 1926.
"a placid mask of resignation": New York Daily News, April 25, 1926, is the source of this account of the meeting between Richard and Margaret.

228 *they posed for the cameras:* The photo described, one of only a few that showed the couple together, was widely reprinted, both during the trial and after, and was also one of the most abused photos of the pair, making its provenance uncertain. When Whittemore went on trial later in Maryland and was incarcerated in a cell behind a similar screen, the Buffalo photograph was often used to represent the circumstances of his incarceration in Maryland. Newspaper editors found the image of Margaret, her hand placed on the screen over her husband's heart, irresistible.

229 *"I didn't sleep a wink": Buffalo Courier,* April 27, 1926.
She nervously fingered her pearls: Buffalo Courier, April 27, 1926, notes that she "fingered her pocketbook and the string of pearls around her neck."

"Tell us": Buffalo Times, April 26, 1926. This newspaper report is the source of the following account of the questioning on the stand of Guggisberg, Saty, Coughlin, and Sullivan.

231   *"We ought to finish the case today": Baltimore News,* April 26, 1926.

"Are you going to let witnesses": Buffalo Courier, April 27, 1926, reports on Sumner's summation.

"It has been a tremendous strain": New York Times, April 27, 1926.

232   *"Please . . . please": New York Times,* April 27, 1926.

"a seething mass of humanity": "Milling Mob Storms Court," *Buffalo Courier,* April 27, p. 1. This article also provides a detailed description of the scene throughout the courthouse from adjournment through the resumption of the trial after lunch.

233   *even jammed a heavy chair: Buffalo Morning Express,* April 27, 1926.

"whether this defendant": Buffalo Courier, April 27, 1926.

"Before you say these men are wrong": New York Times, April 27, 1926.

"The last defense of a guilty man": New York Times, April 27, 1926.

"They bring in the old family alibi": Buffalo Courier, April 27, 1926.

"If you acquit this defendant": Buffalo Evening Express, April 27, 1926.

234   *"I'll die if anything happens to Dick": Buffalo Times,* April 27, 1926.

he was already snoring: Brooklyn Standard Union, April 27, 1926, notes that Whittemore fell asleep in his cell almost immediately.

the jury emerged: New York Daily News, April 28, 1927, reports on the size of the crowd, the time line in court that day, and the rumors about the jury vote. *Buffalo Times,* April 28, 1926, estimates the size of the crowd as more than 1,000.

it was seven to five: Buffalo Evening Express, April 28, 1926.

"Congratulations": Buffalo Times, April 28, 1926. The telegram certainly points to the possibility of jury tampering. It was later reported that Whittemore told people he could secure a "not guilty" verdict in Maryland at the cost of $200,000.

235   *"We have not reached a verdict": Buffalo Courier,* April 28, 1926, is the source of this discussion between the judge and the foreman.

"I don't believe": New York Times, April 28, 1926.

236   *"The yells and shouts": Buffalo Times,* April 28, 1926. This report includes a detailed account of the courthouse reaction to the verdict.

"That's the boy, Dick!": Buffalo Times, April 28, 1926.

"Riot and glee were everywhere": Buffalo Times, April 28, 1926.

"lifted his manacled hands": Buffalo Morning Express, April 28, 1926.

The mob followed: Buffalo Courier, April 28, 1926, notes Whittemore's reaction immediately following the verdict. Newspaper reports are remarkably consistent in their descriptions of the emotional reaction of the crowds.

"A fine lot of citizens": Buffalo Times, April 28, 1926.

"practically the same": Buffalo Times, April 28, 1926.

"God bless you": Buffalo Morning Express, April 28, 1926.

237   *"Let's get going": Buffalo Times,* April 28, 1926.

15. Beware the Verdict

238   *"I'm sorry I can't offer you boys one": Buffalo Times,* April 28, 1926.

"The worst thing": Buffalo Times, April 28, 1926.

"Say, boys": *Buffalo Times*, April 28, 1926.

"Hold a match": *Buffalo Times*, April 28, 1926.

headlines from Cincinnati to Wilkes-Barre: According to a search on Newspapers.com, Whittemore was front-page news in newspapers not only in these cities but in every region of the country.

239   *"Soft-Hearted Boobs"*: *New York Daily News*, April 30, 1926.

"Why did the crowd": *Buffalo Courier*, April 28, 1926.

"deplorable for a city": *Buffalo Courier*, April 29, 1926.

"the public applauded": *Buffalo Times*, April 29, 1926.

240   *"open and shut case"*: *Baltimore Sun*, April 29, 1926.

"When a jury disregards testimony": *Baltimore Daily Post*, April 29, 1926.

241   *"gonna take a little trip"*: *Buffalo Times*, April 29, 1926.

"literally hurled over the sidewalk": *Buffalo Times*, April 29, 1926.

"I'm glad to shake the dust": *New York Daily News*, April 30, 1926.

"was a bad guy": *Baltimore News*, May 1, 1926.

"I wasn't in very good humor": *Baltimore News*, May 1, 1926.

242   *I can beat any murder case"*: *Washington Post*, May 2, 1926.

"I've robbed": *New York Daily News*, April 30, 1926.

"I'll never hang": *Baltimore Post*, April 30, 1926.

No White man: *Baltimore News*, May 22, 1926. In the previous thirty years, forty-eight men had been executed in the state of Maryland, but only four had been White.

"There will be no repetition": *New York Times*, May 1, 1926.

The all-Black employees: *New York Daily News*, April 30, 1926, notes Whittemore's popularity among the Redcaps.

"a perfectly pressed dark suit": *New York Daily News*, April 30, 1926.

243   *There he was placed in confinement*: Specific details of Whittemore's incarceration in Maryland are best described in "Say He Asks for New Lawyer," *Buffalo Courier*, May 24, 1926, p. 18; and "15 Minutes Required to Open Door of Whittemore Cell," *New York Daily News*, May 24, 1926.

a suicide by drowning: *New York Daily News*, May 5, 1926.

"You know what I think": *Baltimore News*, May 5, 1926.

244   *"fanatical belief"*: *Baltimore News*, May 5, 1926.

"sob sister": Phyllis Leslie Abramson, *Sob Sister Journalism* (Westport, CT: Greenwood Press, 1990), provides a complete discussion of the journalistic style.

245   *"startling apparition"*: *Baltimore News*, May 7, 1926.

"absorbingly interesting": *Baltimore News*, May 7, 1926.

"Mrs. Whittemore is a feminine mixture": *Baltimore News*, May 7, 1926.

"the great Edgar Allen Poe": Mark F. Bernstein, *Princeton Football* (Charleston, SC: Arcadia Publishing, 2009), p. 17.

246   *"much sinned against human being"*: *New York Daily News*, May 19, 1926.

The absence of public drama: Except where specific quotes are cited, this composite account of Whittemore's Baltimore trial is gleaned primarily from the *Baltimore News*, *Baltimore Daily Post*, *Baltimore Sun*, *Evening Sun*, and other papers that covered the trial, including the *New York Daily News*, *New York Times*, *Brooklyn Times Union*, *Buffalo Courier*, and *Buffalo Times*, from May 19, 1926, through the end of the trial. As with the Buffalo trial, the transcript of the proceedings produced at the time—because both the prosecution and the defense expected an appeal if Whittemore was convicted—apparently, after inquiries to the Baltimore County Archives and the Maryland State Archives, no longer exist. Fortunately, as in Buffalo, newspaper and wire service reporting later reproduced significant portions of the spoken record of the trial. Although these reports may differ slightly in the specific wordings of exchanges, they are generally consistent. Readers should be aware that stories appeared in the paper either on the day of the event or the day following, depending on the newspaper and edition, and that some stories were reported later. Both the Buffalo and Baltimore trials, both for capital crimes, proceeded with a speed that seems appalling today: each lasted only a few days.

the same grammar school: New York Daily News, May 23, 1926.

247   *"give me the plate": Baltimore News,* May 20, 1926.

"Silence!": Baltimore News, May 20, 1926.

"stay in the Baltimore City Jail": Baltimore News, May 20, 1926. After Whittemore's trial, O'Dunne did have charges pressed against several *Baltimore News* editors in regard to the photography incident, and several men were briefly jailed.

"Not guilty": Baltimore News, May 20, 1926.

248   *"I want to say": Baltimore News,* May 20, 1926.

"Must we take jurors": Baltimore News, May 20, 1926.

"You are right": Baltimore News, May 20, 1926. O'Dunne's ruling is still cited in voir dire case law today.

249   *"It's the last time": Baltimore Sun,* May 20, 1926.

"Holtman's dead!": New York Times, May 20, 1926.

"the part of the 'smooth guy'": Baltimore News, May 20, 1926.

Bowie was serving ten years for larceny: Baltimore Sun, January 10, 1923.

250   *call out "coming down": Baltimore Sun,* May 20, 1926, is the source of this account of Bowie's testimony.

251   *"conscience hurt him":* Associated Press, May 20, 1926.

"slug his way out": Baltimore News, May 20, 1926.

"So you squealed": Baltimore News, May 20, 1926.

"If you want to call it squealing": Baltimore News, May 20, 1926.

"Mrs. Holtman, please take the stand": Baltimore News, May 20, 1926.

her rouged face made up: New York Daily News, May 22, 1926, mentions Margaret's rouge.

"expensive" white shirtwaist dress: Baltimore News, May 20, 1922.

"Did you see him": Baltimore News, May 20, 1922, is the source of this account of Marie Holtman's testimony.

252   *"That's our case": Baltimore News,* May 20, 1922.

Richard Whittemore looked down: New York Daily News, May 21, 1926.

"any other prisoner": Baltimore News, May 20, 1926.

"like a successful bootlegger": Baltimore News, May 20, 1926.

253   *"Beware the Verdict": Baltimore News,* May 24, 1926.

"Up to the time you killed Holtman": Baltimore News, May 20, 1926, is the source of this part of Whittemore's response to Poe's questioning.

254   *"I went down behind him":* Details on the remainder of Poe's questioning of Whittemore are taken from *Baltimore News,* May 20, 1926.

255   *"The issue is sharply drawn": Baltimore News,* May 21, 1926.

"*distasteful and unpleasant*": *New York Times,* May 22, 1926, is the source of this account of Poe's closing statement.

"*adequately punish*": *New York Times,* May 22, 1926.

"*Thou shalt not kill*": *Baltimore Sun,* May 22, 1926.

"*Whoever shall shed*": *Baltimore Sun,* May 22, 1926.

256   *the qualifier "without capital punishment*": *Washington Evening Star,* May 22, 1926.

fearing the worst, cried quietly: New York Daily News, May 22, 1926, fully describes Margaret's actions and demeanor and the reactions of others in the courtroom as the verdict was delivered.

"*The jury has arrived*": *Baltimore News,* May 22, 1926, is the source of details on the reading of the verdict.

257   *Richard Whittemore began to sit: New York Daily News,* May 22, 1926, also describes in detail the reactions of significant parties in the immediate aftermath of the verdict.

"*The prisoner is remanded*": *New York Daily News,* May 22, 1926.

16. A Moral Lesson

259   "*Thank you,*" *she said: Baltimore Sun,* May 22, 1926. Accounts of the immediate aftermath of the reading of the verdict in the *New York Daily News, Baltimore Sun,* and *Baltimore News* are remarkably consistent.

"*That was the greatest compliment*": *Baltimore Sun,* May 22, 1926.

260   "*Whittemore got no opportunities*": *New York Daily News,* May 24, 1926.

"*If Mr. O'Conor hangs Reese*": *Baltimore News,* May 22, 1926.

"*He didn't get a fair trial*": *Baltimore News,* May 22, 1926.

261   *a motion requesting a new trial: Buffalo Courier,* May 30, 1926.

What little money he had: New York Times, June 11, 1926, indicates that Whittemore likely received between $500 and $1,000 for his life story, worth perhaps as much as $20,000 in today's currency.

Their trial was just starting in New York: New York Daily News, May 23, 1926. The Kraemers were found guilty on May 30, 1926.

he was already writing his life story: The *Baltimore Daily Post* began promoting Whittemore's story on June 3, 1926, which may explain Margaret's relative silence after the trial ended.

262   *He also claimed to have new evidence: New York Daily News,* May 30, 1926.

"*in the early stages*": *Baltimore Sun,* May 29, 1926.

"*no symptoms indicating delusions*": *Baltimore Sun,* May 29, 1926.

263   "*one of the most amazing articles*": *Baltimore Daily Post,* June 4, 1926.

"*A Moral Lesson*": Whittemore, "A Moral Lesson," *Baltimore Daily Post,* June 4–14, 1926.

"*Why,*" *it began:* Whittemore, "A Moral Lesson," *Baltimore Daily Post,* June 4, 1926.

The reference was to O'Conor: Whittemore may have misheard the phrase "moral lesson," or the press may simply have not reprinted it in their accounts of the summation, as it appears in no source that I could uncover.

"*that it does not pay*": Whittemore, "A Moral Lesson," *Baltimore Daily Post,* June 4, 1926.

"*If this story*": Whittemore, "A Moral Lesson," *Baltimore Daily Post,* June 4, 1926.

264   "*break us as they would a horse*": Whittemore, "A Moral Lesson," *Baltimore Daily Post,* June 6, 1926.

"had nothing to do": Whittemore, "A Moral Lesson," *Baltimore Daily Post,* June 10, 1926.

"You are to blame": Whittemore, "A Moral Lesson," *Baltimore Daily Post,* June 14, 1926.

"my only and true pal": Whittemore, "A Moral Lesson," *Baltimore Daily Post,* June 14, 1926.

"die as I have lived": Whittemore, "A Moral Lesson," *Baltimore Daily Post,* June 14, 1926.

265   *sat at a table with Poe: Baltimore Sun,* June 10, 1926, details the scene in court.

Suddenly, she turned: Evening Sun, June 10, 1926.

"Take the handcuffs off": *Baltimore Post,* June 10, 1926.

"I want to thank": *Baltimore Sun,* June 10, 1926.

"Richard Reese Whittemore": *Baltimore Post,* June 10, 1926.

266   *"Now therefore"*: *Baltimore Post,* June 10, 1926.

"And may God": *Baltimore Post,* June 10, 1926.

"they're gonna hang him": *Baltimore Post,* June 10, 1926.

"Please go away": Associated Press, *The News* (Frederick, MD), June 10, 1926. This Associated Press report detailing her reaction was distributed nationwide.

267   *she was briefly allowed: Baltimore News,* June 10, 1926.

"Good-bye, Dick": *Baltimore News,* June 10, 1926.

"If there ever was a man or boy": Whittemore, "A Moral Lesson," *Baltimore Daily Post,* June 9, 1926.

268   *He was walked back inside: Baltimore Sun,* June 11, 1926, describes the route taken by the guards bringing Whittemore back inside the prison.

placed Whittemore at the end of the tier: Baltimore Sun, June 11, 1926, also describes the layout of the death tier.

she could barely even see through the screen: Baltimore News, June 11, 1926, notes the number and rotation of the guards and the process to unlock Whittemore from his cell. Although the use of the mesh screen was mentioned in the press many times, no photographs of it exist. Precisely how it was used was not described until the execution of Isaac Benson and during Margaret's final few visits, when a representative of the press was presumably allowed in the death tier.

269   *He argued that O'Dunne's ruling:* The report on Poe's appeal in *Evening Sun,* June 21, 1926, also explains the bill of exception.

"looked like a lottery": *Daily Times* (Salisbury, MD), June 28, 1926.

Margaret learned: Baltimore News, July 9, 1926.

Her mother carried her inside: Baltimore News, July 9, 1926.

"Reese is a man": *Baltimore News,* July 9, 1926.

"It has cost $120": *Baltimore News,* July 9, 1926.

They kissed through the bars: Baltimore News, July 10, 1926. There are no reports of later physical contact of this nature.

"It is only as I expected": *Baltimore News,* July 10, 1926.

270   *the Kraemers, after being found guilty: Baltimore News,* June 11, 1926.

Whittemore's cause was taken up: Baltimore Sun, July 20, 1926, describes Parkhurst's full involvement and the petition.

One of Margaret's neighbors: Baltimore News, June 19, 1926.

271   *It was the earliest time possible: Baltimore Sun,* July 14, 1926.

"Can't I have some lettuce and tomatoes": *Baltimore News,* July 15, 1926.

"It doesn't make any difference": *Daily Mail* (Hagerstown, MD), July 16, 1926.

a "marble man": *New York Daily News,* July 16, 1926.

272 *"Yes, we have no bananas": New York Daily News,* July 16, 1926, fully describes Whittemore's and the warden's reactions.

17. A Gaudy Show

273 *During Benson's final hours: New York Daily Mirror,* July 23, 1926, describes the interaction between the two prisoners.

274 *"Good-by, Candy Kid": New York Daily Mirror,* July 23, 1926.

soon fell asleep: New York Daily News, July 24, 1926, notes that Whittemore was soon asleep. *The office stenographers: Baltimore News,* July 28, 1926.

"Governor Ritchie had his mind made up": Baltimore News, July 28, 1926, carries Margaret's remarks after her visit to the governor.

275 *"One was the convicted man's life": Baltimore Afro-American,* undated clipping from August 1926.

"When the people": Baltimore Post, August 11, 1926.

Warden Brady removed: Baltimore Daily Post, August 6, 1926.

officials prepared for the hanging: New York Daily News, August 12, 1926, mentions the stretching of the rope as part of the preparation for the hanging, as does *Daily Mirror,* August 11, 1926. Other details of the preparations for the hanging are discussed in *Baltimore News,* August 12, 1926.

276 *Baltimore authorities hounded Pendleton:* "Geo Pendleton in Fight for Whittemore," *Baltimore Afro-American,* undated clipping from August 1926.

"Writ of error denied": Evening Sun, August 12, 1926.

gave the pen to Pendleton as a souvenir: Baltimore Afro-American, undated clipping, c. August 15, 1926. Pendleton accepted the pen as a "family heirloom." Their meeting took place on August 12, 1926.

"Well?" she said: Evening Sun, August 12, 1926.

277 *"Just as I expected": Chicago Tribune,* August 13, 1926.

continued to stalk her: Baltimore Sun, August 13, 1926, notes that Margaret and other visitors were pursued by crowds outside the prison during their final visits. There is also photographic evidence of this in the papers.

"Why can't they let me go": New York Daily News, August 12, 1926.

"Reese has repented": Baltimore News, August 12, 1926. A very similar conversation is recounted in the *New York Daily News* of the same date.

"I will allow no scenes": Baltimore News, August 12, 1926.

278 *all of them packed full: Boston Daily Globe,* August 13, 1926, makes special note not only of the entire scene but of the jarring presence of so many children in the crowd. Except where specific quotes are credited, this account of Whittemore's hanging and the scenes at the penitentiary earlier that day and immediately afterward is taken from contemporaneous accounts from newspapers that covered the execution, primarily the *Baltimore News, Baltimore Daily Post, Baltimore Sun, Evening Sun, New York Daily News, New York Times, Brooklyn Times Union, Buffalo Courier,* and *Buffalo Times,* as well as wire reports from Associated Press, International News Service, United Press, and United Service.

"the vicinity of the prison": Chicago Tribune, August 13, 1926.

"Ice cold pop": Edward Doherty, *Gall and Honey: The Story of a Newspaperman* (New York: Sheed & Ward, 1941), p. 230.

"the streets were jammed": Doherty, *Gall and Honey*, p. 230.

Washington Post *reported that "young women"*: *Washington Post*, August 13, 1926.

279   *Typewriters lined the bar*: *Baltimore News*, August 13, 1926, printed a photograph of the makeshift telegraph office.

"the victim is himself a brute": Mencken, *A Mencken Chrestomathy*, p. 123.

"old and young": *Baltimore News*, August 13, 1926.

280   *"A gray ghost"*: *Cincinnati Enquirer*, August 13, 1926. The same story, under Fowler's byline, appeared in papers nationwide. Doherty recounts the circumstances of Fowler's departure and describes ghostwriting a story in Fowler's name in his autobiography *Gall and Honey*, pp. 229–30.

He asked for a first-class Italian feast: *Baltimore Post*, August 12, 1926. The *New York Daily News*, August 13, 1926, provides a slightly different account of the menu.

281   *"Don't take it too hard"*: *New York Daily News*, August 13, 1926.

"Don't worry, Chickie": Evelyn Lee Boone, *Saint Petersburg Times*, August 13, 1926. This Universal Service report appeared in many papers nationwide.

"Dick, Dick": *New York Daily News*, August 13, 1926.

"Won't you let me": *Buffalo Evening Express*, August 13, 1926.

Margaret signed for her husband's belongings: *Baltimore News*, August 13, 1926.

282   *"hold to his own gods"*: *New York Daily News*, August 13, 1926.

Other prisoners periodically beat: *New York Daily News*, August 13, 1926.

the cacophony waxing and waning: *Washington Post*, August 13, 1926.

"I'm gonna go game": *New York Daily News*, August 13, 1926.

"Death isn't such a hard proposition": *Buffalo Evening Express*, August 13, 1926. Biggs's visit is also noted in this report.

283   *"There isn't much I can give anyone"*: *New York Times*, August 14, 1926.

"I finished 182 pages": *New York Times*, August 14, 1926.

"like a trussed fowl": *Baltimore News*, August 9, 1926, provides details on how Whittemore would be dressed for the hanging.

"Incarcerated Thoughts While Awaiting Murder": *Baltimore Daily Post*, August 13, 1926.

"Saying good-by to you": *Baltimore Daily Post*, August 13, 1926.

284   *"The slayer"*: *Baltimore News*, August 12, 1926.

"Only to say goodbye": Associated Press, *The News* (Frederick, MD), August 13, 1926. This Associated Press report was distributed nationally and was the account most Americans read detailing Whittemore's last moments. Many other accounts of Whittemore's final moments and interactions are consistent enough to appear to have been written off this one, suggesting that the AP reporter was the only member of the press allowed to accompany Whittemore from his cell to the gallows and witness his final moments before the hanging.

"I would rather you would say it": Associated Press, *The News* (Frederick, MD), August 13, 1926.

"I wish to say goodbye": Associated Press, *The News* (Frederick, MD), August 13, 1926.

Whittemore's face betrayed a thin smile: *New York Daily News*, August 13, 1926, describes the placement of the hood and Whittemore's final movements.

285   *they found something inside his shirt*: *Baltimore Sun*, August 13, 1926. Some reports indicate that the photograph was on a cord around his neck.

286   *"Sitting alone in a prison cell"*: *Baltimore Post*, August 13, 1926.

It was the photo of her sitting on the stoop: The photograph described was originally taken to accompany a story by Anne Kinsolving on Margaret, and first appeared in the *Baltimore Daily Post* on May 5, 1926. How Whittemore managed to save a copy is unknown.

Epilogue: Tribute of Sorrow

287   *"in a gingham dress":* Baltimore Daily Post, August 13, 1926.
      "a single piercing scream": New York Daily News, August 14, 1926.
      "The man is dead": New York Daily News, August 14, 1926.
288   *she told friends:* Baltimore Daily Post, August 13, 1926, notes both Margaret's purchase of the veil and the fact that she still had two black dresses in her possession. The *New York Daily News* also reported on her purchase of a veil on August 13. Unless otherwise noted, all details of the funeral and burial are taken from the detailed reporting in the *Baltimore Post.*
      "from a broken-hearted father": Baltimore Sun, August 16, 1926.
      12:08 a.m., the time of the hanging: Baltimore Sun, August 16, 1926.
      "Why can't the world": Baltimore Post, August 16, 1926. This report is the source of the following account of Whittemore's funeral.
289   *"I left that out":* New York Times, August 17, 1926.
      "My boy, my boy": Baltimore Post, August 17, 1926.
290   *"Few citizens of Baltimore":* Baltimore News, August 17, 1926.
      "having absolutely nothing to wear": Baltimore News, August 17, 1926; *New York Daily News,* August 25, 1926.
291   *"entrapped into leading their life":* Baltimore Sun, March 13, 1927.
      Crime *was made into a film: The Payoff* is rarely broadcast but is available online — for anyone who can bear watching it, considering the questionable logic of the story line. The character loosely based on Jacob Kraemer is presented as an urbane sophisticate, albeit a criminal.
      the gangster film flourished: Todd, "The History of Crime Films," in Rafter, *Shots in the Mirror.*
292   *later renamed* Gang Busters: For a list of *Gangbuster* episodes and broadcast dates, see http://www.otrr.org/FILES/Logs_txt/Gang%20Busters.txt. Although some episodes are commercially available, the Whittemore episode apparently no longer exists.
293   *Coughlin became an inspector:* See Coughlin's obituary, *New York Times,* October 1, 1951.
      He remained in private practice: See Poe's obituary, *Evening Sun,* November 30, 1961.
      By then, his prosecution: See Irwin, *The Inevitable Success,* especially pp. 114–23. See also O'Conor's obituary, *Baltimore Sun,* March 3, 1980.
      "the most courageous and fearless individual": Baltimore Sun, July 8, 1981.
      He died in 1959: Baltimore Sun, July 8, 1981.
294   *"of blondes that gentlemen prefer":* Brooklyn Times Union, January 22, 1928. For more on Lee, see *New York Daily News,* July 17 and 21, 1929.
      He died the next day: Brooklyn Standard Union, November 4, 1926.
      sentenced to twenty-one years: Evening Sun, May 9, 1928.
      His wife Asley: Morning Herald (Hagerstown, MD), August 20, 1930.
295   *He eventually remarried:* Baltimore Sun, September 16, 1974.
      Sister Meta had died in a drowning accident: Philadelphia Inquirer, September 6, 1931.

he was captured in St. Louis: New York Daily News, December 12, 1927.

The key piece of evidence: Cleveland Plain Dealer, June 20, 1928; *Brooklyn Daily Eagle,* June 1, 1928; and *New York Daily News,* June 20, 1928.

Paroled in 1938, Weinzimmer returned: Cleveland Plain Dealer, August 17, 1942.

He died in 1961: Social Security Death Index.

given an indeterminate sentence: Brooklyn Daily Eagle, June 25, 1929.

296   *As soon as he was free: United States v. Commissioner of Immigration,* 43 F.2d 821 (2d Cir. 1930), US Court of Appeals for the Second Circuit, July 21, 1930, details Paladino's fight against his deportation.

Unkelbach and two other prisoners attacked a guard: New York Daily News, June 15, 1927.

He ended up homeless: Baltimore Sun, March 8, 1950.

After a contentious trial: New York Daily News, May 30, 1926.

a minimum of sixteen years: Brooklyn Daily Eagle, June 11, 1926.

297   *One attempt sparked: New York Daily News,* July 24, 1929.

"back to prison where Kraemer is": New York Daily News, August 14, 1949.

He would die of tuberculosis: Baltimore Sun, September 15, 1932.

One month later, Leon escaped: Baltimore Sun, September 15, 1932.

"intended to give it": Sitamore, "Secrets of the Great Jewel Robberies, Part II."

"his jaw broken": Sitamore, "Secrets of the Great Jewel Robberies, Part II."

"I was just a bootlegger": New York Daily News, September 15, 1949.

298   *was sentenced to twenty-five years: New York Daily News,* June 26, 1926.

"death sentence": Brooklyn Daily Eagle, June 25, 1926; *New York Daily News,* June 26, 1926.

He reportedly did not die until 1949: New York Daily News, August 13, 1949. Goldberg appeared in prison records at Sing Sing as late as 1940. The *Daily News* article of August 13 notes that he died earlier in 1949, but I found no further confirmation of that.

"I am opposed to capital punishment": Brooklyn Times Union, April 21, 1927.

299   *"Is it a man she met": Pittsburgh Press,* July 24, 1927.

"a second-hand wife": Tennessean, January 16, 1927.

"60-year-old fruit broker": Miami Herald, April 20, 1927.

"wished she would do so": Miami Herald, April 20, 1927.

"to try to live down": New York Daily News, October 19, 1930.

"an old friend of the family": New York Daily News, October 19, 1930.

"showed her fangs": New York Daily News, February 1, 1929.

300   *Her death notice: Baltimore Sun,* April 15, 1993. I have chosen not to provide any further details in regard to the identity of Margaret Whittemore's now-elderly daughter. I did not wish to cause any disruption in the life of a person who may or may not have any knowledge of her mother's former life, and whose physical or emotional condition is unknown to me. I did make contact with a distant relative, as she had no siblings or children of her own. I explained my project and the purpose of my inquiry and left it to this relative to decide whether or not Margaret's daughter should be informed. He was kind enough to approach her and let her know she was welcome to make any kind of contribution she wished, either in person or by some other method. Very politely, she chose not to. Her response speaks for itself. It is my wish that readers will also choose to respect her privacy.

"defiantly and spectacularly": Whittemore, "A Moral Lesson," *Baltimore Daily News,* June 14, 1926.

SELECTED BIBLIOGRAPHY

The vast majority of the source material for this book, as mentioned in the Author's Note, is contained in newspaper coverage of the era. The following book titles were particularly useful in providing background and cultural history.

Adler, Larry. *Me and My Big Mouth*. London: Blake Publishing, 1994.

Bessie, Simon Michael. *Jazz Journalism: The Story of the Tabloid Newspapers*. New York: E. P. Dutton, 1938.

Burrough, Bryan. *Public Enemies: America's Greatest Crime Wave and the Birth of the FBI, 1933–34*. New York: Penguin, 2004.

Crenson, Matthew A. *Baltimore: A Political History*. Baltimore: Johns Hopkins University Press, 2017.

Downey, Patrick. *Bad Seeds in the Big Apple: Bandits, Killers, and Chaos in New York City, 1920–1940*. Nashville: Cumberland House, 2008.

Downey, Patrick. *Gangster City: The History of the New York Underworld 1900–1935*. Fort Lee, NJ: Barricade Books, 2004.

Dumenil, Lynn. *The Modern Temper: American Culture and Society in the 1920s*. New York: Hill and Wang, 1995.

Duncombe, Stephen, and Andrew Mattson. *The Bob-Haired Bandit: A True Story of Crime and Celebrity in 1920s New York*. New York: New York University Press, 2006.

Fabian, Warner. *Flaming Youth*. New York: Macaulay Co. 1923.

Fass, Paula S. *The Damned and the Beautiful: American Youth in the 1920s*. New York: Oxford University Press, 1977.

Goldberg, David J. *Discontented America: The United States in the 1920s*. Baltimore: Johns Hopkins University Press, 1999.

Hellinger, Mark. *Moon over Broadway.* New York: William Faro, 1931.

Irwin, Harry W. *The Inevitable Success: A Biography of Herbert R. O'Conor.* Westminster, MD: New Man Press, 1962.

Mencken, H. L. *A Mencken Chrestomathy: His Own Selection of His Choicest Writings.* New York: Vintage, 1972.

Rafter, Nicole, ed. *Shots in the Mirror: Crime Films and Society.* New York: Oxford University Press, 2006.

Rizzo, Michael. *Gangsters and Organized Crime in Buffalo: Histories, Hits, and Headquarters.* Charleston, SC: History Press, 2012.

Sann, Paul. *The Lawless Decade.* New York: Crown, 1961.

Shugg, Wallace. *A Monument to Good Intentions: The Story of the Maryland Penitentiary 1804–1995.* Baltimore: Maryland Historical Society, 2000.

Sklar, Robert. *Movie-Made America: A Cultural History of American Movies.* New York: Random House, 1975.

Walker, Stanley. *City Editor.* New York: F. A. Stokes, 1934.

Walsh, Michael T. *Baltimore Prohibition: Wet and Dry in the Free State.* Charleston, SC: History Press/American Palate, 2017.

Zeitz, Joshua. *Flapper: A Madcap Story of Sex, Style, Celebrity, and the Women Who Made American Modern.* New York: Broadway Books, 2006.

INDEX

Unless otherwise indicated, "Whittemore" is Richard Whittemore.